CADOGAN CHESS BOOKS

Fianchetto Grünfeld

T0170575

CADOGAN CHESS BOOKS

Chief Advisor: Garry Kasparov
Editor: Murray Chandler
Russian Series Editor: Ken Neat

Other chess titles from Cadogan include:

Accelerated Dragons
John Donaldson & Jeremy Silman

Caro-Kann Advance
Byron Jacobs

Caro-Kann: Smyslov System 4...Nd7
Eduard Gufeld & Oleg Stetsko

Easy Guide to the Nimzo-Indian
John Emms

Easy Guide to the Réti Opening
Angus Dunnington

**English Opening:
Classical & Indian**
Vladimir Bagirov

English Opening: Symmetrical
Vladimir Bagirov

The French Advance
Tony Kosten

**King's Indian Defence:
Averbakh Variation**
Margeir Petursson

The Modern French Tarrasch
Eduard Gufeld

Play the Evans Gambit
Harding & Cafferty

Queen's Gambit Accepted
Iakov Neishtadt

The Queen's Gambit Declined: 5 Bf4!
Colin Crouch

Queen's Indian Defence
Bogdan Lalic

The Semi-Slav
Matthew Sadler

The Trompowsky
Joe Gallagher

For a complete catalogue of CADOGAN CHESS books (which includes the
Pergamon Chess and Maxwell Macmillan Chess lists) please write to:

Cadogan Books plc, 27-29 Berwick St, London W1V 3RF
Tel: (0171) 287 6555
Fax: (0171) 734 1733

Fianchetto Grünfeld

by

Alexander Belyavsky & Adrian Mikhalchishin

Translated and Edited by Ken Neat

CADOGAN CHESS
LONDON, NEW YORK

English Translation Copyright © 1998 Ken Neat

First published 1998 by Cadogan Books plc, 27-29 Berwick Street,
London W1V 3RF

Distributed in North America by The Globe Pequot Press, 6 Business Park
Rd, P.O. Box 833, Old Saybrook, Connecticut 06475-0833

British Library Cataloguing in Publication Data
A CIP catalogue record for this book is available from the British Library

ISBN 1 85744 402 0

Typeset by Ken Neat, Durham

Printed in Great Britain by BPC Wheatons Ltd, Exeter

Contents

Introduction

White has many interesting continuations against the Grünfeld Defence, but the most reliable is undoubtedly the set-up with the fianchetto of his king's bishop. In this way he strengthens his castled position, and the bishop creates pressure on d5, the main point in his opponent's position.

It is interesting that one of the first to choose such a set-up against the Grünfeld was the great Akiba Rubinstein, which in itself serves as a stamp of quality. Moreover, White can continue in a great variety of ways – he can play an early e2-e4, strengthen his centre with e2-e3, or allow ...dxc4, which also leads to a quite distinctive type of centre. Black too has a very wide choice of plans for counterplay. He has ...c7-c5 in various modifications, and ...e7-e5, which has the slight disadvantage of restricting his dark-square bishop. Finally, there is Black's quietest plan with ...c7-c6, whereby he lends maximum support to his centre. White can then continue the pressure on the centre in various ways – he can try to advance e2-e4, force Black to concede the centre after ♕b3, or else set up a solid position by ♘e5 and f2-f4. As can be seen, the choice of possible continuations is very broad for both sides, and there is enormous scope for every player to choose something to his taste.

We have examined many sources on the Grünfeld Defence, such as the classic Russian work by Botvinnik and Estrin, and the *Encyclopaedia of Chess Openings* (*ECO*). To our surprise, during the ten years since the publication of *ECO*, practically all the evaluations of variations in this fundamental work have changed – the flow of information in the Grünfeld Defence is exceptionally high. We have tried to create a kind of encyclopaedia-cum-textbook on the g3 Variation of the Grünfeld Defence. Whether or not we have succeeded, it is up to the readers to judge, but when playing these variations, irrespective or whether with White or Black, every player can find a line to his taste.

One further exceptionally important feature of these variations should be mentioned, which is that many variations can arise by different move orders. White sometimes begins 1 ♘f3, 1 c4 or even 1 g3, but in every case the game can then smoothly transpose into the variation of the Grünfeld Defence in question.

1 Exchange Variation with 6 e4

Everyone knows that the great Akiba Rubinstein opened only with 1 d4! and that he discovered numerous paths for White in the Closed Games. We were always interested to know what Rubinstein had thought up against the Grünfeld Defence – in *ECO* there was no reply to this question, and it was only by accident that we found the game Rubinstein-Réti (Semmering 1926), which began with the following moves:

1	d4	♘f6
2	c4	g6
3	g3	♗g7
4	♗g2	d5
5	exd5	♘xd5
6	e4!	

This is where the idea of this variation came from! White's main idea is to gain as much space as possible with the help of a protected outpost pawn at d5. An enormous contribution to the development of this variation was made by GM Vladimir Antoshin, who recently died, after which the variation was revived at high level by the Armenian GMs Vaganian, Akopian and Arshak Petrosian. An interesting gambit variation was devised by Oleg Romanishin, and several interesting ideas have been introduced by Alexander Goldin. In general, the variation has progressed and in recent times it has occupied a prominent place in the praxis of the Grünfeld Defence.

In the diagram position Black has two critical continuations: **6...♘b4 (1.1)** and **6...♘b6 (1.2)**.

1.1 (1 d4 ♘f6 2 c4 g6 3 g3 ♗g7 4 ♗g2 d5 5 exd5 ♘xd5 6 e4)

6	...	♘b4

A sharp and tactical continuation. With piece pressure Black wants to weaken White's centre as much as possible, by forcing the d4-d5 advance immediately. Its drawback is that White gains too much freedom, and also there is no strong pressure on the centre by Black.

Here White has these possibilities: 7 ♘f3 (1.11), 7 a3 (1.12) and 7 d5 (1.13).

1.11 (1 d4 ♘f6 2 c4 g6 3 g3 ♗g7 4 ♗g2 d5 5 exd5 ♘xd5 6 e4 ♘b4)

7 ♘f3

An original pawn sacrifice, introduced by Romanishin. White forces Black to accept the offer, otherwise after a2-a3 it is not clear where the black knight can go.

The similar idea 7 ♘e2 is weaker: 7...♗xd4 8 0–0 ♗g7 9 ♕a4+ ♘4c6 10 ♖d1 ♗d7 11 ♘bc3 0–0 12 ♗e3 ♕c8 13 ♕c2 ♗h3 14 ♗h1 ♘e5 15 ♘d5 ♘bc6 16 ♘d4 ♖e8, and White has insufficient compensation for the sacrificed pawn (Deak-Zezulkin, Kobanya 1992).

7 ... ♗xd4
8 0–0 ♘8c6!

Black need not begrudge giving up this bishop. He played less strongly in Romanishin-Gavrikov (Lviv 1987): 8...♗g7 9 ♕a4+ ♘4c6 10 ♖d1 ♗d7 (after 10...♘d7 11 ♘c3 0–0 12 ♗f4 White has the initiative) 11 ♘c3 0–0 12 ♕a3! ♕c8 (12...a5!?, Gavrikov) 13 ♗g5 f6 (or 13...♖e8 14 ♘d5 with an attack) 14 ♗e3 ♗g4 15 h3! ♗xf3 16 ♗xf3 ♘d7 17 b4! e6, and here 18 ♗e2 intending 19 f4 would have given White serious compensation for the pawn.

9 ♘xd4

After **9 a3 ♘d3!** 10 ♘xd4 ♕xd4 11 ♗e3 ♕xb2 12 ♕xd3 ♕xa1 13 ♘c3 ♕xa3 White has no compensation.

9 ... ♕xd4

Dangerous is **9...♘xd4** 10 ♕a4+ ♘bc6 11 ♗h6 and Black has problems.

10 ♘c3 ♗e6
11 ♘d5

11 ♗e3 is rather better, gaining some compensation for the pawn.

11 ... ♕xd1
12 ♖xd1 0–0–0
13 a3

In the game Romanishin-A.Mikhalchishin (Dortmund 1991) after **13 ♗f4?** ♖d7 14 ♘xc7 ♖xc7 15 a3 ♗b3! 16 axb4 ♗xd1 17 ♗xc7 ♔xc7 18 b5 ♘d4 19 ♖xd1 ♖d8! White had a bad ending.

13 ... ♘c2
14 ♖b1

Worse is **14 ♖a2** f5! 15 b4 fxe4 16 ♗xe4 ♘2d4 with advantage to Black.

14 ... ♖d7
15 b4 ♖hd8

As 16 ♗b2 can be met by 16...f5!, it is doubtful whether White has serious compensation for the pawn, although he does have some threats.

1.12 (1 d4 ♘f6 2 c4 g6 3 g3 ♗g7 4 ♗g2 d5 5 exd5 ♘xd5 6 e4 ♘b4)

7 a3

The original move played in the source game, forcing the black knight to leap all over the board.

7 ... ♘4c6
8 d5 ♘d4

Here White has 9 ♘e2 (1.121) or 9 ♘c3 (1.122).

There is also the interesting alternative 9 ♘f3!? ♘xf3+ (nevertheless 9...♗g4 is better) 10 ♕xf3 0–0 11 0–0 e6 12 ♕b3 exd5 13 exd5 ♘d7 14 ♗e3

♘e5 15 ♘c3, when he has the advantage (Sekulic-Janjgava, Belgrade 1988).

> **1.121 (1 d4 ♘f6 2 c4 g6 3 g3 ♗g7 4 ♗g2 d5 5 exd5 ♘xd5 6 e4 ♘b4 7 a3 ♘4c6 8 d5 ♘d4)**

9   ♘e2   c5

Or 9...♗g4 10 ♘bc3, and now:

(a) 10...e5 11 0-0 ♕f6 12 f3! ♗d7 13 ♗e3 c5 14 dxc6 (14 f4 is also good) 14...♘bxc6 15 ♘d5 ♕d6 16 ♘xd4 ♘xd4 17 f4 0-0 18 ♗xd4 exd4 19 e5 with advantage to White (Rubinstein-Réti, Semmering 1926);

(b) 10...♘f3+ 11 ♔f1 ♘d4 12 h3 ♘xe2 13 ♘xe2 ♗c8 14 ♕b3 c6 15 ♗e3 0-0 16 ♔g1 b6 17 ♔h2 ♗b7 18 ♖hd1 with advantage to White (Akopian-Svidler, Haifa 1995);

(c) 10...c6!? (more interesting) 11 0-0 ♘xe2+ (less good is 11...♘f3+ 12 ♔h1 h5 13 h3 ♘d7 14 ♘g1 ♘h2 15 f3 ♘xf1 16 ♗xf1 with a material advantage, Zaichik-Fernandez, Eskadi-Georgia 1991) 12 ♘xe2 cxd5 13 exd5 ♕d7 and Black does not stand badly (A.Petrosian-A.Mikhalchishin, Ptuj 1997).

10   0-0   0-0
11   ♘xd4

11 ♘bc3 or 11 ♗e3 is also possible,

delaying the capture on d4. However, the weakness of the d4 pawn is quite appreciable.

11   ...   cxd4
12   ♘d2   ♘a6

Less good is 12...e5 13 f4 ♘a6 14 ♘c4 f6 15 a4! b6 16 b3 ♘c5 17 b4, when White has the advantage (Steckner-Steiger, Germany 1992).

13   b4   ♘c7
14   ♗b2   ♘b5
15   ♘b3   ♕b6

White also stands better after 15...e5 16 f4 f5 17 fxe5 ♗xe5 18 exf5 ♗xf5 19 ♕e2 ♕e8 20 ♖ae1 ♗g7 21 ♕c4 (A.Petrosian-Aronian, Yerevan 1991).

Shirov-Gavrikov (Klaipeda 1988) now continued 16 ♖c1 e6 17 ♖e1 e5 18 ♘c5 ♗h6 19 ♖c2 with a slight advantage to White – he has more space.

> **1.122 (1 d4 ♘f6 2 c4 g6 3 g3 ♗g7 4 ♗g2 d5 5 exd5 ♘xd5 6 e4 ♘b4 7 a3 ♘4c6 8 d5 ♘d4)**

9   ♘c3   0-0

9...c5 leads to the same positions.

10   ♘ge2   c5
11   0-0   e5

Black can consider 11...♘a6 12 ♖b1 e5 13 b4 b6 14 f4 ♘xe2+ 15 ♘xe2 ♕d6 with a complicated game (Deak-A.Mikhalchishin, Budapest 1991).

Now a recommendation by Antoshin is interesting: **12 dxe6** ♗xe6 13 ♘xd4 cxd4 14 ♘d5 with slightly the better position for White.

12 ♗e3   a5

Black tries in the first instance to secure himself against b2-b4, but 12...**b6** is also satisfactory, or else 12...♘a6!? 13 ♘c1 f5 14 f4 fxe4 15 ♗xe4 ♗f5 with excellent chances (Donner-Keres, Beverwijk 1964).

13   h3

Interesting is **13 f4** b6 or **13 a4** b6 14 ♘b5 ♗a6 15 ♘ec3 (Epishin), in both cases with a complicated game.

Epishin-Babula (Brno 1994) continued 13...b6 14 f4 ♗a6 15 ♖f2 ♘d7 16 f5 ♕e7 17 a4 ♖ab8 with a complicated game. White has pressure on the f-file, but no particular threats at present.

> **1.13 (1 d4 ♘f6 2 c4 g6 3 g3 ♗g7 4 ♗g2 d5 5 exd5 ♘xd5 6 e4 ♘b4)**

7   d5

The critical continuation – White is now threatening to drive the black knight to a6. Black has two methods of counterplay: the sharp **7...c6 (1.131)** and the quiet **7...0-0 (1.132)**.

7...c5?! is very risky: 8 a3 ♘4a6 9 ♘c3 0-0 10 ♘ge2 ♘d7 11 0-0 c4 12 ♗e3 ♘ac5 13 ♕c2 ♘b3 14 ♖ad1 ♘e5 15 h3 ♘d3 16 ♘f4 with a clear advantage to White (Gregor-M.Pribyl, Prague 1990).

> **1.131 (1 d4 ♘f6 2 c4 g6 3 g3 ♗g7 4 ♗g2 d5 5 exd5 ♘xd5 6 e4 ♘b4 7 d5)**

7 ...   c6

Now we consider: **8 ♘e2 (1.1311)** and **8 a3 (1.1312)**.

Weaker is **8 ♘c3** cxd5 9 exd5 ♗f5 10 ♔f1!? 0-0 11 g4 ♗c2 12 ♕d2 ♗d3+ 13 ♘ge2 ♗c4 14 ♗e4 ♘d7 15 a3 ♘a6 16 ♗d3 ♘e5, when Black has no problems (Azmaiparashvili-Dvoiris, Moscow 1995).

> **1.1311 (1 d4 ♘f6 2 c4 g6 3 g3 ♗g7 4 ♗g2 d5 5 exd5 ♘xd5 6 e4 ♘b4 7 d5 c6)**

8   ♘e2   cxd5

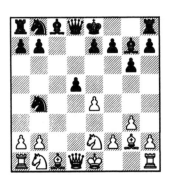

If **8...e6** 9 a3 ♘4a6 10 ♘bc3 0-0 11 0-0 ♘c7 12 ♘f4 exd5 13 exd5 ♘xd5 14 ♘fxd5 cxd5 15 ♘xd5 ♘c6 16 ♗f4 ♗f5 17 ♕d2 ♕d7 18 ♗h6 f6!? 19 ♖fe1 with a minimal advantage for White (Averbakh-Ilivitsky, 22nd USSR Ch 1955), or **8...0-0** 9 ♘bc3 e6 10 ♗e3 ♖e8 11 a3 ♘4a6 12 0-0 e5 13 ♕b3 c5 14 ♘b5 b6 15 ♘ec3 ♘c7 16 ♘xc7 ♕xc7 17 ♖fd1 with a clear advantage to White (Hoelzl-Groszpeter, Haifa 1989).

9   exd5

9 a3 is the alternative:

(a) 9...♘4c6 10 exd5 ♘e5 11 0-0 0-0 12 ♘bc3 ♗g4 13 h3 ♗f3 14 ♗xf3 ♘xf3+ 15 ♔g2 ♘e5 16 ♕b3 ♕c8 17 ♗g5 ♖e8 18 ♖fd1 ♘a6 and Black held the position (Illescas-J.Polgar, Dos Hermanas 1996);

(b) 9...♘4a6 10 exd5 0–0 11 ♘bc3, and now:

(b1) 11...♘c7 12 0–0 ♘e8 13 ♗e3 ♘d6 14 ♗d4 ♗xd4 15 ♘xd4 ♘d7 16 g4! ♘f6 17 h3 ♗d7 18 ♖e1 with a slight advantage to White (Dorfman-Semeniuk, Saratov 1981);

(b2) 11...♘d7 12 0–0 ♘e5 is the more classical approach:

(b21) 13 ♗f4 ♘c5 14 b4!? ♘cd3 15 ♗e3 ♘b2 16 ♕b3 ♘bc4 17 ♗f4 ♘d6 with equality (Euwe-Barcza, Venice 1949);

(b22) 13 ♘e4 ♗g4 14 h3 ♗f3 15 ♗xf3 ♘xf3+ 16 ♔g2 ♘e5 with an equal game according to Osnos, although after 17 ♘2c3 ♕d7 18 ♕e2 ♖fc8 19 ♖d1 ♘c4 the position probably favours Black;

(b23) 13 h3 ♘c4 14 b3 ♘d6 15 ♗e3 ♗d7 16 ♗d4 ♗xd4 17 ♕xd4 ♘f5 18 ♕d2 ♕b6 with equal chances (Goldin-Krasenkov, USSR 1987);

(c) 9...♕a5 is sharper: 10 0–0 dxe4 11 ♗d2 ♘8c6 (dubious is 11...♘8a6 12 ♕e1 f5 13 ♗xb4 ♘xb4 14 ♕xb4 ♕xb4 15 axb4 ♗xb2 16 ♖a2 followed by f2-f3, when Black's compensation for the piece is inadequate, R.Byrne-Benko,

USA Ch 1962/3) 12 ♗xe4 ♕a6 13 ♘bc3 (the alternative is 13 ♗c3 0–0 14 ♗xg7 ♔xg7 15 ♘bc3 ♖d8 16 axb4 ♖xd1 17 ♖xa6 ♖xf1+ 18 ♔xf1 ♗h3+, when Lepyoshkin considers the position unclear, although it seems to us that after 19 ♔e1 bxa6 20 ♗xc6 White has an obvious advantage) 13...♘d3 14 ♘d5 (interesting is 14 ♕c2 ♘de5 15 b4 with positional compensation for the pawn) 14...0–0 15 ♘c7 ♕c4 16 ♗xd3 ♕xd3 17 ♘f4 ♕e4 (less good is 17...♕d6?! 18 ♘xa8 ♕b8 19 ♗c3 e5 20 ♘d5 ♕xa8 21 ♗b4!? ♖d8 22 ♘e7+ ♔h8 23 ♘xc6 ♖xd1 24 ♖fxd1 ♗f6 25 ♘xe5 with advantage to White, Osnos-Baikov, USSR 1978) 18 ♖e1 ♕f5 19 ♘xa8 g5 20 ♘g2 ♘d4 21 ♖e3 ♗d7 22 ♘c7 ♗c6, and Black has some compensation for the sacrificed material (Osnos-Vaiser, USSR 1977).

    9 ...   **♗f5**

    10 0–0

10 ♕a4+ ♘8c6 is clearly worse:

(a) 11 0–0 ♗c2 12 ♕a3 ♘xd5 13 ♕c5 ♗xb1 14 ♖xb1 (or 14 ♗xd5 ♗f5 15 ♗xc6+ bxc6 16 ♕xc6+ ♗d7 with the better chances for Black, Szabo-F.Olafsson, Dallas 1957) 14...e6 15 ♘c3 ♕b6 and Black seizes the initiative (Porath-Barcza, Moscow 1956);

(b) 11 ♘bc3 ♘c2+ 12 ♔f1 0–0 13 dxc6 (if 13 ♖b1 b5 with the better game for Black) 13...b5 14 c7 ♕xc7 15 ♗f4 e5 16 ♘xb5 ♕d8 17 g4 ♘xa1 with advantage to Black (Zlatichanin-B.Nikolic, corr. 1974).

    10 ...   **0–0**

At the given moment, and as is usual in such situations, **10...♘c2** is bad because of 11 g4.

    11 ♘bc3

Rather less good is **11 ♘ec3** ♘8a6 12 a3 ♘c2 13 ♖a2 ♘d4 14 b4 ♕d7 15

♗e3 ♗xb1 16 ♘xb1 ♘f5 17 ♗f4 ♘c7 18 ♖e1 a5!, when Black held the position (Euwe-Van der Vliet, Holland 1974).

11 ...   ♘8a6

Worse is **11...♘d7** 12 a3 ♘d3? 13 g4!, when 13...♘xc1 is not possible because of 14 ♘xc1 (P.Nikolic-Hellers, Biel 1993), or **11...♘d3** 12 ♗g5 h6 13 ♗e3 ♘e5 14 ♗d4 with the better game for White.

12 ♗g5

Alternatives:

12 ♗f4 ♘d3 13 d6 ♘xf4 14 ♘xf4 ♘c5 15 dxe7 ♕xe7 with equality (Pachman-Stahlberg, Prague 1954).

12 ♘f4 ♘c5 13 ♗e3 ♘cd3 (13...♖c8!?) 14 ♘xd3 ♗xd3 15 ♖e1 ♗a6 and now in Panno-Sajtar (Amsterdam 1954) 16 ♕b3 ♘d3 17 ♖ed1 ♘e5 would have led to equality.

12 h3 ♘c5 13 ♗e3 ♖c8 14 g4 ♗d3 15 a3 ♗xe2 16 ♕xe2 ♘bd3 17 ♖ad1 ♘e5 18 d6!? exd6 19 ♘b5 with a complicated game (Teske–Mohr, Bern 1996).

P.Nikolic-I.Horvath (Europa Cup 1993) now continued 12...h6 13 ♗f4 ♘d3 14 ♗e3 ♘xb2 15 ♕c1 ♘d3 16 ♕d2 g5 17 h4! gxh4 18 g4 ♗h7 19 ♗xh6 ♘ac5 with a very complicated game, but Black should not have any problems.

1.1312 (1 d4 ♘f6 2 c4 g6 3 g3 ♗g7 4 ♗g2 d5 5 exd5 ♘xd5 6 e4 ♘b4 7 d5 c6)

---

8 a3   ♕a5

One of the sharpest variations in the entire g2-g3 system. The more modest **8...♘4a6** gives Black a solid but somewhat inferior position after 9 ♘c3 cxd5 10 exd5 ♘d7 11 ♘f3 (11 ♘ge2 ♘e5 12

0–0 0–0 13 h3 ♘c4 14 b3 ♘d6 15 ♗e3 ♗d7 16 ♗d4 ♗xd4 17 ♕xd4 ♘f5 18 ♕d2 ♕b6 leads to equality, as already examined in the previous variation, Goldin-Krasenkov, USSR 1987) 11...♘b6 12 0–0 0–0 13 ♗f4 ♘c7 14 d6 exd6 15 ♕xd6 ♘e6 16 ♖ad1 (Goldin-Malisauskas, Vilnius 1988).

9 ♘c3   cxd5
10 ♗e3

The strongest used to be considered **10 ♗f4** ♘4c6 11 exd5 ♘d4 (11...♗xc3+? 12 bxc3 ♕xc3+ 13 ♔f1 ♗f5 14 ♘e2 ♗d3 15 ♖c1 ♕xa3 16 dxc6 and wins, De Folis-Lamon, USA Open Ch 1990) 12 ♘f3 ♗g4 (12...♘b5 is worse because of 13 0–0 ♘xc3 14 bxc3 0–0 15 c4! ♗xa1 16 ♕xa1 ♖e8 17 ♖e1 ♘d7 18 ♗h6 f6 19 ♘g5! ♘b6 20 c5! with a strong attack, Ornstein-Wiedenkeller, Stockholm 1987) 13 0–0 0–0 14 ♖e1 ♖e8 15 ♗e5 ♗xe5 (15...♘xf3+ 16 ♗xf3 ♗xe5 17 ♖xe5 ♘d7 18 ♖e3 ♗xf3 19 ♕xf3 with the better chances) 16 ♖xe5 ♘b5 (16...♗f5 17 ♖e4 ♗xf3 18 ♕xf3 ♘d7 19 ♖b4 with advantage to White, Dvoiris-Ornstein, New York 1987) 17 ♘xb5 ♕xb5 18 ♖e4 ♗xf3 19 ♕xf3 ♘d7 20 ♖b4 ♕a6 21 ♖d1 with some advantage (Djuric-Smejkal, New York 1986).

10 ... d4

The alternatives are clearly weaker:

10...♘4a6 11 exd5 0–0 (11...♗xc3+ 12 bxc3 ♕xc3+ 13 ♗d2 ♕e5+ 14 ♘e2) 12 ♘ge2 ♘d7 13 0–0 ♘e5 14 b4! ♕d8 15 ♕b3 ♘g4 16 ♗d2 ♘c7 17 ♖ad1 with advantage to White (Loktev-Borodenko, corr. 1974);

10...♘4c6 11 exd5 ♘e5 12 ♘ge2 0–0 13 b4 ♕d8 14 0–0 ♘bd7 15 ♗d4 with the better game for White (Mozny-Schmidt, Prague 1988);

10...♘c2+ 11 ♕xc2 d4, and now:

(a) 12 b4 ♕c7 13 ♗xd4 ♗xd4 14 ♘ge2 ♗xc3+ 15 ♕xc3 ♕xc3+ 16 ♘xc3 ♘c6 17 f4 e5 18 0–0 0–0 19 b5 ♘d4 20 fxe5 ♗e6 and White retained some advantage (Bareev-Krasenkov, Elista 1995), although 20...♗g4! 21 ♘d5 ♗e2 was stronger, with an unclear game;

(b) 12 ♗xd4 ♗xd4 13 ♘ge2 ♘c6 14 0–0 0–0 15 ♘d5 ♕d8 16 ♘xd4 (16 ♖ad1!?) 16...♘xd4 17 ♕c4 e5 18 f4 ♗e6 19 fxe5 ♘c6 20 ♕b5 ♖b8 (Makarov-Novik, Leningrad 1989), and here 21 ♖ad1 would have given White a serious advantage.

11 axb4 ♕d8

12 e5!?

12 ♗xd4 is the old-fashioned move:

(a) 12...♗xd4 13 ♘ge2 ♗b6 (worse is 13...♗xc3+ 14 bxc3 ♕xd1+ 15 ♖xd1 with a slight advantage to White, or 14 ♘xc3 ♕xd1+ 15 ♖xd1 ♗g4 16 ♖c1 ♘a6 17 ♘d5 with a clearly better ending for White, Lehmann-Nei, Beverwijk 1966) 14 ♘d5 (after 14 0–0 0–0 15 ♕xd8 ♗xd8 16 ♖fc1 ♘c6 17 b5 ♘b4 18 ♘f4 e6 the game is equal, Evans-Pachman, Helsinki 1952) 14...0–0 15 0–0 ♗e6 16 ♘xb6 ♕xb6 17 ♕d4 ♘a6 18 ♕xb6 axb6 19 b5 ♘c5 with an equal game (Donner-Smejkal, Wijk aan Zee 1975);

(b) 12...♕xd4 is more modern – after 13 ♕xd4 ♗xd4 14 ♘d5 ♘a6 15 b5 e6 16 bxa6 exd5 17 ♘e2 ♗b6 18 axb7 ♗xb7 19 exd5 0–0–0 Black successfully holds the position (Hort-Fernandez, Debrecen 1992).

12 ... dxc3

Weaker is **12...dxe3** 13 ♕xd8+ ♔xd8 14 f4 ♘c6 15 0–0–0+ ♔c7 16 ♘d5+ ♔b8 17 b5 ♘a5 18 ♘xe3 with the unpleasant threat of b2-b4.

13 ♕xd8+ ♔xd8
14 bxc3 ♗xe5
15 ♘e2 a5!

In the ending White has a lead in development and unpleasant threats, so it is simplest for Black to return the material.

15...♘d7 is less good because of 16 0–0 a6 17 ♖fd1 ♔c7 18 ♘f4 ♗xf4 19 ♗xf4+ e5 20 ♗e3 f5 21 ♖a5! with advantage (Goldin-Banas, Trnava 1989), but possible is **15...♔c7** 16 ♖a5 ♗d6 17 ♘d4 ♘c6 18 ♘b5+ ♔d7 19 ♘xd6 exd6 20 ♖d5 ♔c7 21 ♗f4 ♖e8+ 22 ♔d2 ♘e5 with a complicated game (Howell-A.Ledger, British Ch 1989).

Now after 16 ♗b6+ ♔c7 17 ♗xa5 ♗xa5 18 ♖xa5 ♖xa5 19 bxa5 ♔c7 20 ♘d4 ♗d7 21 f4 ♗c6 Black holds on (Jasnikowski-Novak, Poland 1990).

1.132 (1 d4 ♘f6 2 c4 g6 3 g3 ♗g7 4 ♗g2 d5 5 cxd5 ♘xd5 6 e4 ♘b4 7 d5)

	7	...	0–0
	8	a3	

8 ♘e2 c6 9 ♘bc3 is possible, transposing into the Hoelzl-Groszpeter game (section 1.1311).

	8	...	♘4a6
	9	♘e2	

There is also **9 ♘f3** c6 10 0–0 cxd5 11 exd5 ♘d7 12 ♘c3 ♘b6 13 ♖e1 ♘c7 14 ♘e5 ♘e8 15 ♗f4 ♗d6 16 ♕e2 ♖e8 17 ♖ad1 with some advantage to White (Fedorowicz-Kudrin, USA 1989), but in principle the knight stands better at e2.

9 ...   c6
Dubious is **9...c5** 10 0–0 ♘d7 11 ♘bc3 (less good is 11 a4 ♘b4 12 ♘a3 b6 13 ♘c2 ♗a6 14 ♘xb4 cxb4 15 ♘d4!? with chances for both sides, Buslaev-Bokuchava, Tbilisi 1966) 11...c4 12 ♕a4 ♘b6 13 ♕a5 ♗d7 14 ♗e3 and White has the advantage.

10 0–0   e6
10...♘d7 is possibly no worse: 11 ♘bc3 ♘b6 12 dxc6 (12 ♗g5!? should be tried) 12...bxc6 13 ♗g5 ♗e6 14 ♕xd8 ♖fxd8 15 ♗xe7 ♖d2 with compensation for the pawn (Smyslov-Bronstein, Moscow 1952).

	11	♘bc3	cxd5
	12	exd5	exd5
	13	♘xd5	

White achieved nothing with **13 ♕xd5** ♘c6 14 ♗g5 ♕xd5 15 ♗xd5 ♘c7 16 ♗e4 ♗e6 with equality (Bjun-Filip, Helsinki 1952), but 14 ♕xd8 ♖xd8 15 ♗g5 ♖e8 16 ♗e3 ♘a5 17 b4 ♘c4 18 ♗d4 ♘c7 19 ♖fc1 ♘e5 20 f4 nevertheless gave him slightly the better game in Bareev-Lputian (Lviv 1987).

	13	...	♘c7

Or **13...♘c6** 14 ♘ec3 ♘c7 15 ♘xc7 ♕xc7 16 ♘d5 ♕d8 17 h4! h6 18 ♗f4 ♗f5 19 ♖c1! g5 20 hxg5 hxg5 21 ♕h5 with advantage to White (Averbakh-

Ilivitsky, 21st USSR Ch 1954), which, however, in fact transposes into the main line.

Antoshin-Tseitlin (Riga 1970) now continued 14 ♘ec3 ♘xd5 15 ♘xd5 ♘c6 16 h4 h6 17 ♗e3!? (17 ♗f4 is also good, as played by Averbakh) 17...♗e6 18 ♕d2 ♔h7 19 ♖ad1 ♖c8 20 h5, when White's pieces occupy more active positions and his initiative is rather unpleasant, despite the symmetric structure.

> **1.2 (1 d4 ♘f6 2 c4 g6 3 g3 ♗g7 4 ♗g2 d5 5 exd5 ♘xd5 6 e4)**

6 ...   ♘b6

A quieter continuation – Black defers the attack on the white centre, but retains a wide choice of subsequent plans.

7   ♘e2

Now Black has three fundamentally different approaches to the position: an attack with pieces by 7... ♘c6 (1.21) or 7...♗g4 (1.22), the pawn attack 7...c5 (1.23), and the pawn attack ...e7-e5 after the preparatory 7...0–0 (1.24).

Dorfman-Molnar (Nice 1996) saw the surprise innovation 7...h5!? 8 h3 ♘c6 9 d5 ♘e5 10 ♘bc3 c6 11 f4 ♘ec4 12 dxc6 (12 b3! ♘a5 13 ♗e3 would have given White the advantage) 12...♕xd1+ 13 ♔xd1 bxc6 14 b3 ♘a5 15 ♗e3 ♗a6 16 ♖c1 ♖d8+ 17 ♔e1 ♖d3 18 ♔f2 h4! 19 g4 e5! and Black gained counterplay.

> **1.21 (1 d4 ♘f6 2 c4 g6 3 g3 ♗g7 4 ♗g2 d5 5 exd5 ♘xd5 6 e4 ♘b6 7 ♘e2)**

7   ...   ♘c6
8   d5   ♘a5

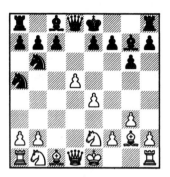

This piece attack resembles a position from the main variation with ♘f3, but in principle the knight stands better at e2 here, as after ...c7-c6 the diagonal of the bishop at g2 is opened, and also after b2-b3 the knight at a5 remains out of play.

8...♘b8 is possible, but rather passive: 9 0–0 0–0 10 ♘bc3 (or 10 ♘ec3 c6 11 a4 cxd5 12 exd5 ♘c4 13 ♖e1 ♖e8 14 ♘a3 ♘d6 15 ♘ab5 with advantage, Donner-Klein, England 1951) 10...c6 (10...e6 is poor: 11 a4 exd5 12 exd5 ♖e8 13 ♕b3 c6 14 ♗e3 ♘xd5 15 ♘xd5 cxd5 16 ♗xd5 with a big advantage to White, Donner-Larsen, Santa Monica 1966) 11 ♕b3 cxd5 (Black should not be in a hurry to open the file; after 11...♘8d7 12 dxc6 bxc6 13 ♗e3 ♗a6 the game is unclear) 12 exd5 ♘8d7 (weak is 12...e6 13 ♖d1, when White is better prepared for the opening of the centre) 13 a4! (13 ♗e3 is also good) 13...♘e5 14 a5 ♘bd7 15 ♗e3 ♘f6 16 ♖fd1 ♗g4 17 h3 ♗f3 18 ♗xf3 ♘xf3+ 19 ♔g2, and White has a great advantage (Flohr-Lilienthal, 17th USSR Ch 1949) – cf. *Game 1*.

9   0–0

After **9 a4 c5!** 10 0–0 0–0 11 ♘bc3 c4 12 ♗e3 e6 13 h3 exd5 14 exd5 ♗f5

15 ♖e1 (P.Nikolic-Kozul, Belgrade 1989) 15...♘d7! 16 g4 ♗d3 17 ♘f4 ♘e5 would have given Black an excellent game.

9 ...   c6

The centre must be attacked immediately. After **9...0–0** there follows 10 ♕c2 c6 11 ♗d2! ♘ac4 12 ♗c3 cxd5 13 ♖d1 ♗h6 14 a4! ♗g4 15 a5 ♘d7 16 ♖xd5 ♕c7 17 ♗b4 ♖fe8 18 ♘bc3 with advantage to White (Simkin-A.Mikhalchishin, Lviv 1984).

10 ♘bc3   cxd5

After **10...0–0** the 'severing' move 11 b3 is very unpleasant: 11...cxd5 12 exd5 ♗g4 13 f3 ♗d7 14 ♗a3 ♖e8 15 ♖c1 e6 16 d6 ♗c6 (Obukhov-Kotsur, Kurgan 1994), and here 17 ♔h1! ♘d5 18 ♘xd5 exd5 19 ♘d4 would have given White the advantage.

11 exd5   ♘ac4

After **11...0–0**:

(a) 12 b3 ♗g4 (12...e6 is not in the spirit of the chosen system: after 13 ♗a3 ♖e8 14 d6 ♗d7 15 ♖c1 ♗c6 16 ♘d4 the d6 pawn severs Black's position in two, Antoshin-Smejkal, Polanica Zdroj 1970) 13 ♗d2?! e6! 14 dxe6 ♘c6! 15 ♕e1 ♘e5! and Black has a good game (Ruban-Kozul, Sibenik 1988) – cf. *Game 2*, but 13 f3 is correct, transposing into the Obukhov-Kotsur game;

(b) 12 ♖e1 e6 13 ♘f4 e5 14 ♘d3 ♘ac4 15 b3 e4 16 ♘xe4! ♗xa1 17 bxc4 ♗g7 18 ♕b3, and White has a powerful position for the exchange (Akopian-Shmuter, St Petersburg 1993).

12 b3   ♘d6
13 a4   a5

Now White's plan is to eliminate the blockading knight at d6, after which the d5 pawn will be able to advance further. Matanovic's recommendation of **13...a6**

is also dubious because of 14 ♗e3 ♘f5 15 ♗c5 with advantage.

Now after 14 ♗a3 ♗g4 15 ♖c1 0–0 16 h3 ♗xe2 17 ♕xe2 ♖c8 18 ♘b5! White has a clear advantage (Hübner-Gheorghiu, Skopje 1972).

1.22 (1 d4 ♘f6 2 c4 g6 3 g3 ♗g7 4 ♗g2 d5 5 exd5 ♘xd5 6 e4 ♘b6 7 ♘e2)

7 ...   ♗g4

A dubious plan – White has several ways of gaining an advantage.

8 f3

Also quite possible are:

8 ♘bc3 ♘c6 9 d5 ♘d4 10 h3 (or 10 0–0 c5 11 h3 ♗d7 12 f4 e6, Donner-Uhlmann, Halle 1963, when 13 e5! consolidates White's advantage) 10...♗f3 11 ♗xf3 ♘xf3+ 12 ♔f1 c6 13 ♔g2 ♘e5 14 f4 ♘ed7 15 dxc6 bxc6 (Donner-Korchnoi, Wijk aan Zee 1971) 16 e5 with the better game.

8 d5 c6 9 0–0 0–0 10 ♘bc3 cxd5 11 exd5 ♘a6 12 h3 ♗d7, and here not 13 ♗g5 h6 14 ♗e3 ♘c4 15 ♗d4 ♘xb2 16 ♕b3 ♗xd4 17 ♘xd4 ♘d3 with complications (Geller-Boleslavsky, 17th USSR Ch 1949) but simply 13 ♔h2, again with the better game.

8 ...   ♗e6

After 8...♗c8 9 ♘bc3 ♘c6 10 d5 ♘b8 11 ♗e3 0–0 12 ♕b3 e6 13 0–0 White has the freer position (Najdorf-Boleslavsky, Budapest 1950).

In A.Petrosian-Hachian (Yerevan 1991) Black managed to equalise after 8...♗d7 9 0–0 0–0 10 ♘bc3 e5 11 dxe5 ♗xe5 12 ♗h6 ♗g7 13 ♕c1 ♘c6 14 ♗xg7 ♔xg7 15 f4 f6 16 ♖d1 ♕e7 17 h3 ♖ad8, but stronger was 13 ♗xg7 ♔xg7 14 ♕d4+ f6 15 ♖ad1 ♘c6 16 ♕f2 ♕e7 17 ♘f4, when Black has not yet overcome all his difficulties.

9 ♘bc3

The obvious 9 d5 is rather worse, since later after ...c7-c6 White may have problems with his d5 pawn, and his bishop at g2 is blocked in by the f-pawn.

9 ...   0–0
10 0–0   ♗c4
11 f4

11 ♗e3 followed by b2-b3 is also interesting.

Timoshchenko-Lanka (USSR 1982) now continued 11...e6 12 b3 ♗xe2 13 ♘xe2 ♘c6 14 ♗e3 ♕d6 15 ♕d2 ♖fd8 16 ♖fd1 a5 17 a3 a4 18 b4 ♘c4 19 ♕c1 ♘xe3 20 e5 with a serious spatial advantage for White.

1.23 (1 d4 ♘f6 2 c4 g6 3 g3 ♗g7 4 ♗g2 d5 5 exd5 ♘xd5 6 e4 ♘b6 7 ♘e2)

7 ...   c5

If Black wants to play this variation, he should play this immediately.

8 d5

Less good is 8 dxc5 ♕xd1+ 9 ♔xd1 ♘a4 10 ♘bc3 ♘xc5 11 ♗e3 ♘ba6 followed by ...♗e6 and ...0–0–0 (Stohl).

8 ...   e6

8...f5 is very suspect: 9 exf5 ♗xf5 10 ♘bc3 0–0 11 0–0 ♘a6 12 ♘f4 ♘c7 13 ♗e3 ♕d6 14 g4 ♗c8 15 ♘e4 with clearly the better position (Korchnoi-Katalymov, USSR 1958), since Black has many weaknesses.

9 0–0

Tempting, but risky, is 9 d6 ♘c6 10 f4 e5 11 ♘bc3 0–0 12 ♗e3 ♘d4 13 fxe5 ♗xe5 14 ♘xd4 cxd4 15 ♗xd4 ♕xd6, when Black has excellent play (Kaidanov-Baikov, Roslavl 1989).

9 ...   0–0
10 ♘ec3

Here the question also arises: why this knight, and not the other? At e2 the knight has no future, although 10 ♘bc3 is quite often played. Here are some examples:

(a) 10...exd5 11 exd5 ♘a6, and now:

(a1) 12 b3 ♗f5 13 ♗b2 ♕d7 14 ♘f4 ♘b4 15 ♕d2 ♖fe8 16 ♖ac1 ♗h6! with counterplay (Gauglitz-Lehmann, Budapest 1990);

(a2) 12 ♘f4 ♘c4 13 ♖e1 ♘d6 14 ♘e4 ♗f5 15 ♘xd6 ♕xd6 16 g4 ♗d7 17 ♘d3 ♖ae8 18 ♗f4 ♖xe1+ 19 ♕xe1 ♕b6 with a good game (Goldin-Karasev, St Petersburg 1993);

(a3) 12 h3 ♖e8 13 g4 ♘c4 14 ♘e4 ♘xb2 15 ♕b3 c4 16 ♕f3 ♖xe4 17 ♕xe4 f5 18 ♕f3 ♘d3 with interesting counterplay for the exchange (Sekulic-Ilincic, Kladovo 1992);

(b) 10...♘a6 (Black avoids exchanging immediately on d5) 11 ♘f4 e5 12 ♘fe2 ♘c4 13 ♘b5 ♘c7 14 ♘ec3 a6 with equality (Bolbochan-Flores, Dubrovnik, 1950), but stronger is 12 ♘d3 ♘c4 13 ♖e2 ♘d6 14 f4 f6 15 fxe5 fxe5 16 ♖xf8+ ♕xf8 17 ♗e3 b6 18 ♖f1 ♕e8 19 ♖d1 with advantage (A.Petrosian-Lin, Shanghai 1992).

10   ...   exd5

Black probably does better to delay this exchange in favour of the immediate 10...♘a6 11 a4 exd5 12 exd5 ♗f5 (12...♘c4 13 ♘d2!? ♘xd2 14 ♗xd2 ♗f5 15 ♗e3 gives White a slight advantage, Stohl, but 12...♘b4 13 ♗e3 ♗d4 is satisfactory) 13 ♘a3 (interesting is 13 g4!? ♗xb1 14 ♖xb1 ♘c4 15 ♘e4 ♘d6 16 ♗g5 f6 17 ♗f4 ♘xe4 18 ♗xe4 f5 with a slight advantage to White, Vaganian, but 13...♗d7! 14 ♘a3 ♗xc3 15 bxc3 ♗xa4 is better with an unclear game, or 14...♕h4 with counterplay, Stohl) 13...♘b4 (weaker is 13...♕d7?! 14 a5 ♘c8 15 ♕b3 ♘d6 16 ♗f4 with advantage, Ilincic-Popovic, Novi Sad 1995 – *Game 3*) 14 ♗e3 ♖c8, and now:

(a) 15 ♕d2 a5 (less good is 15...♗d3 16 ♖fe1 c4 17 a5 ♘6xd5 18 ♘xd5 ♘xd5 19 ♗xa7 b5 with chances for both sides, Ftacnik) 16 ♗h6 (16 ♖fd1 ♗d3 17 b3, Vaganian-Ftacnik, Naestved 1985, 17...c4! 18 bxc4 ♗xc4 with an unclear game) 16...♗d3 17 ♖fe1 ♗xh6 18 ♕xh6 ♘4xd5 19 ♘xd5 ♘xd5 20 ♖ad1 ♘b4 (20...c4 21 b3!) 21 ♗xb7 ♖c7 22 ♗g2 ♗d7 23 ♕c1 ♗f5 with a good game for Black (Hellers-Ftacnik, Biel 1993);

(b) 15 d6 ♗d3 16 a5!? (the rehabilitation of this variation, which used to be considered bad because of 16 ♗xb7 ♖b8 with advantage to Black, Euwe-Smyslov, Zurich 1953) 16...♘d7 17 ♗xb7 ♖b8 18 a6 ♕b6 (Stohl-Ftacnik, Germany 1994; accepting the exchange sacrifice 18...♗xf1 19 ♕xf1 ♖e8 20 ♖d1 allows White a strong initiative), and here correct was 19 ♘d5!? ♘xd5 20 ♕xd3 ♘xe3 21 ♕xe3 ♕xd6 22 ♖ad1 ♗d4! 23 ♘b5 ♕b6 24 ♘xd4 cxd4 25 ♖xd4 ♘c5 26 ♖h4 h5 27 ♗d5 with advantage (Stohl).

11   exd5

11 ♘xd5 is an interesting new try: 11...♘c6 12 ♘bc3 ♗e6 13 ♗f4 ♕d7 (worse is 13...♗xd5 14 exd5 ♘e5 15 d6 ♘bc4 16 ♘e4 ♘xb2 17 ♕d5 ♘ed3 18 ♗g5 ♕d7 19 ♘xc5! with a strong initiative, Nikolaev-Lagunov, Blagoveshchensk 1988) 14 ♗h6 f6 15 ♗xg7 ♔xg7 16 ♕d2 and White is better.

11   ...   ♘a6
12   ♘d2

The other knight route is also possible: 12 ♘a3 ♗f5 13 ♗e3 c4 14 ♗d4 ♗d3 15 ♗xg7 ♔xg7 16 ♖e1 with a slight advantage to White (Fedorowicz-Gutman, Paris 1989).

12   ...   ♗f5

Taking the pawn is highly dangerous: 12...♗xc3 13 bxc3 ♘xd5 14 ♘e4 with numerous threats.

A.Petrosian-Fogarasi (Siofok 1990) continued 13 ♘de4 h6 14 ♗f4 ♘c4 15 ♕b3! (Black's problem is that he is unable to blockade the d5 pawn) 15...e5 16 ♕xb7 ♕a5 17 ♘d6 ♗d3 18 ♖fe1 ♖ab8 19 ♕e7 with advantage to White in this sharp position.

1.24 (1 d4 ♘f6 2 c4 g6 3 g3 ♗g7 4 ♗g2 d5 5 exd5 ♘xd5 6 e4 ♘b6 7 ♘e2)

7	...	0–0
8	0–0	

White sometimes plays 8 ♘bc3, but the game always transposes.

Now Black has several possibilities: **8...e5 (1.241)**, **8...c5 (1.242)**, **8...e6**

(1.243) and **8...c6 (1.244)**.

8...♘c6 is considered earlier (section 1.21). There is also Gutman's favourite idea **8...a5!?**, but after 9 ♘bc3 a4 10 h3 e6 11 ♗f4 ♕e7 12 ♕c2 ♘c6 13 ♖ad1 e5 14 dxe5 ♘xe5 15 ♗e3 ♘ec4 16 ♗d4 White gained the advantage (Djuric-Gutman, Hastings 1979).

1.241 (1 d4 ♘f6 2 c4 g6 3 g3 ♗g7 4 ♗g2 d5 5 exd5 ♘xd5 6 e4 ♘b6 7 ♘e2 0–0 8 0–0)

8	...	e5
9	d5	♘c4!?

Black wants immediately to transfer his knight to the blockading square. **9...c6** is considered in section 1.244.

10	b3	♘d6
11	♗b2	♖e8
12	♘d2	♘a6
13	f4	♗d7
14	♖c1	

After 14 ♗xe5 ♗xe5 15 fxe5 ♖xe5 16 ♘c3 ♕e7! (Donner-Hort, Wijk aan Zee 1973) Black holds the position, since if 17 ♘f3 ♖xe4 18 ♘xe4 ♕xe4 with compensation for the exchange.

14	...	♗b5

If 14...♘b4 15 fxe5 ♗xe5 16 ♗xe5 ♖xe5 17 a3 with advantage to White.

15 a4   ♗xe2
16 ♕xe2

White has a spatial advantage, and after ♗a3 he will begin threatening to exchange the blockading knight at d6 (analysis).

1.242 (1 d4 ♘f6 2 c4 g6 3 g3 ♗g7 4 ♗g2 d5 5 exd5 ♘xd5 6 e4 ♘b6 7 ♘e2 0–0 8 0–0)

---

8 ...   c5?

This should be played a move earlier, as in the ending the black knights are unable to find squares for themselves.

9 dxc5!   ♕xd1

If 9...♘6d7 10 ♕c2 ♘a6 (bad is 10...♘c6 11 ♗e3 ♘de5 12 ♘bc3 ♕d3 13 ♕xd3 ♘xd3 14 b3 with advantage, Hort-Gutman, Dortmund 1985) 11 c6 bxc6 12 ♕xc6 ♖b8 13 ♘bc3 with a slight advantage (Hort).

10 ♖xd1   ♘a4
11 ♘bc3   ♘xc5
12 ♗e3   ♘ca6
13 a3   ♘c6

14 b4!

The black knights are restricted, and in addition all White's pieces are more actively placed. After 14...♘c7 15 ♖ac1 e5 16 b5 ♘a5 17 ♗xa7! ♖xa7 18

b6 White has the advantage (Kengis-Levchenkov, Riga 1987).

1.243 (1 d4 ♘f6 2 c4 g6 3 g3 ♗g7 4 ♗g2 d5 5 exd5 ♘xd5 6 e4 ♘b6 7 ♘e2 0–0 8 0–0)

---

8 ...   e6
9 ♘bc3

Other moves are less logical:
9 a4 a5 10 ♘a3?! (10 ♘bc3) 10...♕e7 11 ♗f4 ♖d8 12 ♕c1 ♘a6 13 ♘c4 ♘xc4 14 ♕xc4 e5 and Black's chances are not worse (Donner-Smyslov, Havana 1967).

9 ♘d2 ♗xd4 (9...a5 10 ♘f3 a4 11 h4 ♘c6, Osnos-Gutman, USSR 1972, and here 12 ♗g5 ♕d6 13 ♖c1 would have given White an appreciable advantage, Osnos) 10 ♘xd4 ♕xd4 11 ♕e2 ♘c6, and it is unclear whether White has enough compensation for the pawn.

9 ...   ♘c6

Or 9...♕e7 10 e5! ♖d8 11 ♘e4 h6 12 ♗e3 ♘d5 13 ♕c1 ♔h7 14 h4 with a solid advantage for White (Vaganian-Gutman, Biel 1985).

10 e5!   f6

Black does best to attack the centre immediately – if 10...♘b4 11 ♘e4 h6 12 ♘f6+ ♗xf6 13 exf6 ♕xf6 14 ♗xh6

and the weakness of the dark squares gives White the advantage.

11   exf6

If **11 f4** ♘e7 12 ♘e4 f5 13 ♘c5 ♘bd5 14 ♘d3 b6 with equality (Mahacek-Smejkal, Gavirzhov 1970).

11   ...   ♕xf6

11...♗xf6 is no better because of 12 ♗e3 ♘d5 13 ♕d2, 14 ♖ac1 and 15 ♘e4 with unpleasant pressure on the dark squares.

Now after 12 ♗e3 ♘d5 13 ♖c1 White has a serious advantage.

1.244 (1 d4 ♘f6 2 c4 g6 3 g3 ♗g7 4 ♗g2 d5 5 exd5 ♘xd5 6 e4 ♘b6 7 ♘e2 0–0 8 0–0)

---

8   ...   c6

9   ♘bc3

Sometimes White solves the problem of his e2 knight by ♘ec3, but only when Black chooses the move order **8...e5** 9 d5 c6 10 ♘ec3 cxd5 11 exd5 ♘a6 12 a4!? ♗f5 13 ♘a3 (13 g4!?) 13...♘b4 14 ♗e3 a5 15 ♕d2 ♖e8 16 d6 (16 ♖fd1!? with the idea of 17 ♗f1 is interesting) 16...♗d3 17 ♖fd1 e4 18 ♖ac1 f5 19 ♘cb5 ♘6d5 20 ♘c4 ♖a6 with a very sharp game (Svidler-Birnboim, Beer Sheva 1987).

9   ...   e5
10   d5

Weaker is **10 dxe5** (as always in the g2-g3 variations, this exchange does not favour White) 10...♗xe5 11 ♕c2 ♘a6 12 ♗h6 ♗g7 13 ♗xg7 ♔xg7 14 ♖fd1 ♕e7 15 b3 ♗e6 16 ♘d4 ♖ad8 with equality (Priehoda-Banas, Trnava 1986).

10   ...   cxd5
11   exd5   ♘a6

The alternatives also do not promise Black an easy life:

11...♘c4 12 ♘e4 (perhaps even better is 12 b3 ♘d6 13 a4! ♖e8 14 ♗a3 ♗f5 15 ♗xd6 ♕xd6 16 ♘b5 with advantage, Manor-Liss, Israel 1994) 12...♗f5 13 ♘2c3 ♗xe4 14 ♘xe4 ♘d6 15 ♗g5 f6 16 ♘xd6 ♕xd6 17 ♗e3 with a slight advantage (Stahlberg-Smyslov, Budapest 1950).

11...♗g4 12 h3 ♗d7 13 b3 ♘a6 (Stolz-Banas, Stary Smokovec 1986) and here 14 ♗a3 ♖e8 15 d6 ♗c6 16 ♗xc6 bxc6 17 ♕d3 ♖b8 18 ♖ac1 would have given White a slight advantage (Stolz).

11...♗f5, and now:

(a) 12 ♘e4 ♗xe4! 13 ♗xe4 ♘c4 14 ♕b3 ♘d6 15 ♗g2 ♘d7 (Romanishin-Anand, New York 1994), and here 16 ♗e3 ♕a5 17 ♖fd1 ♖fc8 would have led to a complicated game;

(b) 12 b3!? is an interesting and logical recommendation by Boleslavsky, after which Black's knight is restricted and he must seek energetic counterplay:

(b1) 12...♕d7 13 a4 (White also has the advantage after 13 ♗a3! ♖d8 14 ♖e1 ♘a6 15 ♕d2 ♖ac8 16 ♖ad1 ♘c5 17 ♕e3 ♗f8 18 d6!, Morovic-Miles, Linares 1994) 13...♘a6 14 ♗a3 ♖fd8 15 d6 ♗h3 16 ♗xh3 ♕xh3 17 ♘b5 ♘d7 18 ♘ec3 with a serious advantage (Fedorowicz-Kudrin, New York 1989);

(b2) 12...♘c8 is somewhat stronger: 13 ♗a3 ♘d6 14 h3 h5 15 ♕d2 ♘a6 16 ♘d1 ♖e8 17 ♘e3 ♗h6!? and Black has excellent counterplay (Stolz-Doncevic, Germany 1993);

(c) 12 h3 h5!? 13 b3 ♕d7 14 ♔h2 ♘c8 15 ♗e3 (weaker is 15 ♗a3?! ♖e8 16 ♕c1?! [16 ♖c1!?] 16...♘a6 17 ♕e3 b5! 18 ♗b2 ♘b4 19 ♖ad1 ♘d6 with advantage to Black (Goldin-Terentiev, USSR 1984) 15...♘a6 16 ♕d2 ♘d6 17 ♖ac1 with a slight advantage to White.

12 d6!?

An interesting and risky continuation. The advanced pawn restricts Black, but at the same time it draws the attention of all the black pieces.

However, the modest **12 b3** does not look any weaker:

(a) 12...f5 (too risky) 13 ♗a3 ♖e8 14 ♕d2 ♗d7 15 ♖ad1 ♕f6 16 d6 ♖ab8 17 ♘d5 and White has a clear advantage (Anderton-Ostenstad, Gausdal 1992);

(b) 12...♖e8 13 ♗a3 (the bishop is more useful here than 13 ♗e3 ♗g4 14 f3 ♗d7 15 ♕d2 ♘c8 16 ♖ac1 ♘d6, when White has only a slight advantage, Antoshin-Tukmakov, USSR 1972) 13...♗f5 14 d6 (less dangerous is 14 ♘b5 ♕d7 15 ♘d6 ♖ed8 16 ♘xf5 ♕xf5 17 ♘c3 ♖ac8 with a good game for Black, Shehn-Roze, Germany 1992) 14...♕d7 15 ♘d5 ♘c8 16 ♘e7+ ♘xe7 17 dxe7 ♖xe7! 18 ♗xe7 ♕xe7 19 ♕d5 ♘b4 20 ♕xb7 ♕xb7 21 ♗xb7 ♖b8 22 ♗g2 ♗d3 and in Timoshchenko-A.Mikhalchishin (Frunze 1981) Black gained excellent play for the exchange, but only because White missed 16 ♘e3! with an obvious advantage;

(c) 12...♘c7 (best) 13 a4 ♗g4 14 a5 ♘c8 15 ♗a3 ♖e8 16 ♖a2 ♘d6 17 h3 ♗xe2 18 ♖xe2 ♘cb5 with equal chances (Akopian-Hachian, Yerevan 1995).

12 ... ♕d7

12...♘c4 does not work because of 13 b3! ♘xd6 14 ♗a3, while if **12...♘c5** 13 ♗e3 ♘e6 14 b3 ♘d4 15 ♘xd4 exd4 16 ♗xd4 ♕xd6 17 ♗xg7 ♕xd1 18 ♖fxd1 ♔xg7 19 ♘b5 with advantage to White (Stohl).

13 b3 ♖d8
14 ♗a3 ♗f8!

Weaker is 14...f5? 15 ♖c1 ♕f7 16 ♘d5 ♘xd5 17 ♕xd5 (or 17 ♖xc8!? with advantage, Stohl) 17...e4 18 ♕xf7+ ♔xf7 19 f3! and White has the better position (Stohl-Banas, Trnava 1987).

15 ♘e4! ♕e6 16 ♕d2 h6 17 ♖fd1 ♗d7 18 ♖ac1 ♗c6 with a very complicated game, where Black tries to surround the d6 pawn.

Game 1
Flohr-Lilienthal
17th USSR Championship
Moscow 1949

---

1 d4 ♘f6 2 c4 g6 3 g3 d5 4 ♗g2 ♗g7 5 cxd5 ♘xd5 6 e4 ♘b6 7 ♘e2 0–0

7...♗g4 is sometimes played. Here is one example: 8 ♘bc3 ♘c6 9 d5 ♘d4 10 h3 ♗f3 11 ♗xf3 ♘xf3+ 12 ♔f1 c6 13 ♔g2 ♘e5 14 f4 ♘ed7 15 dxc6 bxc6 16 ♕c2 0–0 17 ♗e3 ♕c7 18 ♖ad1 ♕b7 and in Donner-Korchnoi (Beverwijk 1971) Black obtained the better game. The weakness of the c6 pawn is not felt, and the pressure on the b-file after ...c6-c5-c4 will be unpleasant for White. However, after the correct 16 e5! White would have stood better.

8 0–0 ♘c6

White's centre must somehow be forced to advance, but an interesting alternative is 8...e6!? 9 a4 (this move, with the idea of a4-a5, is very strong with the black knight at a6, but here it simply weakens the b4 square) 9...a5 10 ♘a3 ♕e7 11 ♗f4 ♖d8 12 ♕c1 ♘a6 with excellent play against the centre (Donner-Smyslov, Havana 1967).

9 d5 ♘b8 10 ♘bc3 c6

Flohr thought that it was better to play 10...e6, opening the e-file rather than the c-file, but modern experience has not confirmed this – cf. the analysis.

11 ♕b3

11...cxd5

Black should not be in a hurry to open the file – simpler is 11...♘8d7 12 dxc6 (12 a4 ♘c5 13 ♕b4 ♘d3) 12...bxc6 13 ♗e3 ♗a6 with a complicated game.

12 exd5 ♘8d7

Weak is 12...e6 13 ♖d1, opening the

centre with White strongly centralised.

13 a4!

Now this is strong – ...♘e5-c4-d6 was threatened, and 13...a5 is met by 14 ♗e3, when it is hard to disentangle the knights.

13...♘e5 14 a5 ♘bd7

Not 14...♘bc4 15 f4!

15 ♗e3 ♘f6 16 ♖fd1

After 16 a6 bxa6 17 d6 ♗e6 18 ♕a3 exd6 19 ♗xa8 ♕xa8 Black has excellent play for the exchange.

16...♗g4

The typical 16...♘e8 is met by 17 ♘b5! a6 18 ♗b6 with advantage.

17 h3

Clearly not 17 ♕xb7? because of 17...♖b8 and 18...♖xb2, activating the rook.

17...♗f3 18 ♗xf3 ♘xf3+ 19 ♔g2 ♘e5 20 ♕xb7

But now the pawn sacrifice can be accepted, since without the light-square bishops ...♖b8xb2 is not dangerous for White.

20...♘c4 21 ♗c5 ♘d7 22 b4 a6 23 d6 ♘xc5 24 bxc5 exd6

25 ♕b4?

After the centralising 25 ♕d5! ♘e5 26 cxd6 White would have easily converted his advantage.

25...♘e5 26 ♖xd6 ♕c8 27 ♖ad1 ♖e8 28 ♘d4 ♗f8 29 ♘d5

And here 29 ♘e4 would have been somewhat simpler.

29...♗xd6 30 cxd6 ♖b8 31 ♕a3?

Better 31 ♘f6+ ♔h8 32 ♕d2, threatening ♕h6.

31...♕b7 32 ♘f3 ♘d7?

After 32...♘xf3 33 ♕xf3 ♖e6 34 ♘e7+ ♔f8 Black would have easily held on.

33 ♕c3 f6 34 ♕c7 ♔g7

Now the pin is very unpleasant – 34...♔f8 was simpler.

35 ♘b6 ♖ed8 36 ♖e1 ♔f8 37 g4 ♘e5 38 ♖e3 ♘xf3 39 ♖xf3 ♔g8 40 ♔g3 ♕e4 41 ♖e3

The last move in time trouble, and as usual, not the best. 41 ♘d7 was simpler, regaining the exchange and exploiting the passed d6 pawn.

41...♕d4 42 d7 ♖f8 43 ♕c3!

The correct decision – had White played 43 ♘c8 ♖b1 44 ♘e7+ ♔h8 45 ♘c6 ♕d5 46 ♖f3 ♖h1 47 d8♕, then after 47...♖xh3+! Black would have had perpetual check.

43...♕xc3 44 ♖xc3 ♔f7 45 ♖c6 ♔e7 46 ♔f4 ♖fd8 47 ♔e4 ♖b7 48 h4 f5+ 49 gxf5 gxf5+ 50 ♔e5 ♖dxd7 51 ♘xd7 ♔xd7 52 ♖xa6 ♖b5+ 53 ♔f4 h6 54 ♖a8 ♔c7 55 h5 1–0

Game 2
Ruban-Kozul
Sibenik 1988
---

1 d4 ♘f6 2 c4 g6 3 g3 ♗g7 4 ♗g2 d5 5 cxd5 ♘xd5 6 e4 ♘b6 7 ♘e2 0–0 8 ♘bc3 ♘c6

Black refrains from pawn pressure on the centre (...e7-e5 or ...c7-c5) and tries, after forcing an advance of the white d-pawn, to begin an attack on the white centre, and also to exploit the weakness of the light squares. Besides, in contrast to other variations, the d5 pawn is not a strong passed pawn.

9 d5 ♘a5 10 0–0

Risky is 10 a4 c5! 11 0–0 c4 12 ♗e3 e6!? (12...♘b3 is not at all bad) 13 h3 exd5 14 exd5 ♗f5 15 ♖e1 (P.Nikolic-Kozul, Belgrade 1989), and now 15...♘d7! 16 g4 ♗d3 17 ♘f4 ♘e5 18 ♗d4 ♕g5 19 ♗xe5 ♗xe5 20 ♘xd3 cxd3 21 ♕xd3 ♕f4 would have given Black a reasonable initiative.

10...c6 11 b3!

In such positions it is very important to deprive the black knights of c4, in order to forestall an attack on b2 or their manoeuvre to the blockading square d6.

11...cxd5 12 exd5 ♗g4

12...e6 does not look in the spirit of the chosen system: 13 ♗a3 ♖e8 14 d6 ♗d7 15 ♖c1 ♗c6 16 ♘d4 with advantage to White, since the d6 pawn cleaves Black's position in two.

13 ♗d2

If 13 ♗b2? Black had prepared 13...♘ac4!, a typical blow in such positions. However, 13 f3 looks better.

13...e6!

It is essential to free the knight at a5, by exchanging the d5 pawn.

14 dxe6 ♘c6!

Kozul values the initiative higher than a pawn. If now 15 exf7+, then after 15...♖xf7 the highly unpleasant 16...♖d7 is threatened.

15 ♕e1

After the exchange sacrifice 15 ♗e3 ♕xd1 16 ♖axd1 ♗c3 17 ♘xc3 ♗xd1 18 exf7+ ♔xf7 19 ♖xd1 ♖fd8 Black has the advantage.

15...♘e5

15...♘b4 is weaker on account of 16 ♘f4 ♘c2 17 e7.

16 ♘f4 fxe6 17 h3

Not 17 ♗xb7? ♘d5!, while 17 f3 is strongly met by 17...♗f5 18 g4 ♘d3 19 ♘xd3 ♗xd3 20 ♕xe6+ ♔h8 21 ♖fe1 ♗c4! 22 bxc4 ♕xd2, when White's dark squares are very weak.

17...♘f3+ 18 ♗xf3 ♗xf3 19 ♘xe6

Somewhat stronger was 19 ♕xe6+ ♔h8 20 ♕e3 ♗c6 when Black has the initiative on the light squares.

19...♕d7 20 ♕e3

After 20 ♘xf8 ♖xf8 21 ♔h2 ♖e8 22 ♗e3 ♖e5! the threat of ...♖h5! works even after 23 g4.

20...♖f6! 21 ♖ae1 ♖e8 22 ♘c5 ♕xh3! 23 ♕xf3

There is nothing else – 23 ♕xe8+ ♗f8 is clearly hopeless.

23...♖xe1! 24 ♕g2 ♖xf1+ 25 ♕xf1 ♕xf1+ 26 ♔xf1 ♖f7 27 ♘3e4 ♗d4 28 ♘e6 ♖e7! 29 ♘xd4 ♖xe4 30 ♘b5 a6 31 ♘c3 ♖e6 32 ♗e3 ♖c6 33 ♗d4 ♘d7

Black gradually improves the placing of his pieces – White's position is hopeless.

34 ♔e2 ♔f7 35 ♔e3 ♘f6 36 ♔d3 g5 37 ♘a4 h5 38 ♘c5 b5 39 b4 h4 40 gxh4 gxh4 41 ♔e2 ♘d5 0–1

Game 3
Ilincic-Popovic
Novi Sad 1995

1 d4 ♘f6 2 c4 g6 3 g3 ♗g7 4 ♗g2 d5 5 cxd5 ♘xd5 6 e4 ♘b6 7 ♘e2 c5

Some players prefer a different way of opposing White's centre. This, for example, is what Anand played against Romanishin: 7...e5 8 d5 0–0 9 0–0 c6 10 ♘bc3 cxd5 11 exd5 ♗f5 12 ♘e4? (better 12 b3! with advantage to White) 12...♗xe4! 13 ♗xe4 ♘c4 14 ♕b3 ♘d6 15 ♗g2 ♘d7 with a good game for Black (7th match game 1994).

8 d5 e6 9 0–0 0–0 10 ♘ec3 ♘a6 11 a4!

A manoeuvre typical of the given variation – by the advance of his a-pawn White wants to disrupt the coordination of the black pieces. He can exploit the d5 pawn, his main trump (but also sometimes a weakness), only after fully completing his development.

11...exd5 12 exd5 ♗f5

A very serious alternative is 12...♘b4 13 ♗e3 ♗d4 14 a5, which *ECO* considers unclear. But what is unclear about it? – after 14...♘6xd5 15 ♘xd5 ♘xd5 16 ♗xd4 cxd4 17 ♕xd4 or 14...♘d7 15 ♗xd4 cxd4 16 ♕a4 dxc3 17 ♕xb4 cxb2 18 ♕xb2 White has an obvious advantage.

13 ♘a3

Vaganian's recommendation of 13 g4!? is interesting: 13...♗xb1 14 ♖xb1 ♘c4 15 ♘e4 ♘d6 16 ♗g5 f6 17 ♗f4 with a slight advantage to White. The knight at a3 prevents the manoeuvre ...♘c4-d6, although the knight can also reach d6 via c8.

13...♕d7?!

An innovation of dubious value. Better is 13...♘b4 14 ♗e3 ♖c8 15 ♕d2 (if 15 d6 ♗d3 16 ♗xb7 ♖b8 17 ♗g2 ♗xf1 with advantage to Black, Euwe-Smyslov, Zurich 1953, although later this variation was rehabilitated in Ftacnik-Stohl, Germany 1994: 16 a5! ♘d7 17 ♗xb7 ♖b8 18 a6 with a complicated game) 15...a5 (15...♗d3!? 16 ♖fe1 c4 or 16...a5 with a complicated game) 16 ♖fd1 ♗d3 17 b3! c4! with very interesting play (Vaganian-Ftacnik, Naestved 1985).

14 a5 ♘c8 15 ♕b3

15 ♘ab5 ♘b4 16 ♗e3!? is also possible.

15...♘d6 16 ♗f4 ♘b4

There is no other defence against ♗xd6 – if 16...♖ab8 17 ♗xd6 ♕xd6 18 ♘ab5 and 19 ♘xa7.

17 ♘a4!

Exposing the main weakness of Black's position – the c5 pawn. Now 17...♘d3 is not possible because of 18 ♗xd6 ♕xd6 19 ♘c4 followed by 20 g4, winning a piece.

17...♗d4 18 ♖fd1!

New threats appear – Black's position is as though hanging by a thread.

18...♘b5 19 ♘xb5 ♕xb5 20 ♖xd4! cxd4 21 ♗d2

Now Black loses material, and his slight initiative is only a temporary phenomenon.

21...♖fc8 22 ♕xb4 ♕xb4 23 ♗xb4 ♖c4 24 ♗d2 ♖ac8 25 ♗f1 ♖c2 26 ♗h6 f6 27 ♖d1 g5 28 ♖xd4 ♔f7 29 g4 ♗d7 30 ♗d3 ♖d2 31 ♘c3 ♗xg4 32 h4 ♗f3 33 hxg5 fxg5 34 d6 ♗c6 35 ♗c4+ 1-0

2 Exchange Variation: 6 ♘c3 & 6 ♘f3

1	d4	♘f6
2	c4	g6
3	g3	♗g7
4	♗g2	d5
5	cxd5	♘xd5

In this chapter we consider White's alternatives to 6 e4, which are **6 ♘c3 (2.1)** and **6 ♘f3 (2.2)**.

2.1 (1 d4 ♘f6 2 c4 g6 3 g3 ♗g7 4 ♗g2 d5 5 cxd5 ♘xd5)

---

6 ♘c3

White is not in a hurry to castle, but hopes to strengthen his centre after the exchange of knights at c3. This move order gives Black a couple of additional options, **6...♗e6!? (2.11)** and **6...♘xc3 (2.12)**, whereas the simple **6...♘b6** transposes into the main variations.

2.11 (1 d4 ♘f6 2 c4 g6 3 g3 ♗g7 4 ♗g2 d5 5 cxd5 ♘xd5 6 ♘c3)

6	...	♗e6!?

An interesting idea of Korchnoi. Black wants to occupy the light squares and is unwilling to strengthen the opponent's centre by exchanging on c3.

7	♘f3	0-0
8	0-0	

Too active is **8 ♘e4 ♘a6 9 0-0 c6 10 a3 ♗f5 11 ♘h4 ♗xe4 12 ♗xe4 ♕b6 13 e3 ♖ad8 14 ♕f3 e5 15 dxe5 ♗xe5 16 ♗c2 ♘c5** with an excellent position for Black (Korchnoi-Geller, Curaçao 1962).

8	...	♘c6

Continuing the piece pressure on the centre; 8...c6 and 8...♘a6 can also be considered, but they are more passive.

9	e4	♘xc3
10	bxc3	♗c4
11	♖e1	e5

More passive is **11...e6 12 ♗e3** and **13 ♕a4** with a clear advantage, or **11...♘a5 12 ♕a4 c5 13 ♗g5! f6 14 ♗f4 b5 15 ♕a3 cxd4 16 cxd4 e5 (16...♗f7!** with the idea of ...♘c4) **17 dxe5 fxe5 18 ♖ad1 ♕b6 19 ♘xe5!**, again with advantage to White (Portisch-de Bruycker, Montana 1976).

12	♗a3	exd4!

This exchange sacrifice (essentially forced) enables Black to break up the white centre and gain serious counterplay. Weaker is **12...♖e8 13 d5 ♘a5 14 ♗b4** with a queenside initiative.

Now **13 ♗xf8 ♔xf8 14 ♕a4 b5 15 ♕a6 ♕d7 16 e5 ♖e8** leads to a complicated game with good compensation for Black (Bakic-A.Mikhalchishin, Belgrade 1988).

2.12 (1 d4 ♘f6 2 c4 g6 3 g3 ♗g7 4 ♗g2 d5 5 cxd5 ♘xd5 6 ♘c3)

6	...	♘xc3

7   bxc3   c5
8   e3

Piece support of the centre is less good: **8 ♗e3 ♘c6 9 ♘f3 0–0 10 0–0 ♗e6 11 ♖b1 cxd4 12 ♘xd4 ♗d5** with excellent play for Black (Polulyakhov-Lukin, Podolsk 1990).

8   ...   0–0

There is a more active alternative **8...♘c6 9 ♘e2 ♗d7** (Black can also include 9...♕a5 10 ♕d2 [10 ♗d2 ♕c7] 10...0–0 11 0–0 ♖d8 12 ♕b2 ♗d7 13 ♖b1 ♖ac8 14 ♕a3 b6 15 dxc5 e5!? 16 cxb6 axb6 17 ♕b3 ♕a6 with compensation for the pawn, Peev-Garcia, Cienfuegos 1973) **10 0–0 ♖c8**, with an immediate attack on the white centre:

(a) 11 ♗a3 ♕a5 12 ♕b3 ♕a6 13 ♘f4 b6 14 ♖fe1 ♘a5 15 ♕d1 ♘c4 16 ♗c1 ♕a4 and Black is fine (Geller-Bronstein, Amsterdam 1956);

(b) 11 ♘f4 0–0 12 ♖b1 cxd4 13 cxd4 b6 14 ♗d2 e5! 15 dxe5 ♘xe5 16 ♗b4 ♖e8 17 ♘d5 a5! and again Black stands better (Iskov-Jansa, Svendborg 1981);

(c) 11 dxc5? ♘a5 12 ♗a3 ♗b5! 13 ♕xd8+ ♖xd8 14 ♖fe1 ♗xe2 15 ♖xe2 ♘c4 and Black stands well (Hausner-Stohl, Zlin 1995);

(d) 11 ♖b1 b6 12 dxc5 bxc5 13 c4 ♘a5 14 ♕c2 0–0 15 ♗b2 ♗f5 16 ♗e4

♗e6 with equality (Kirillov-Suetin, USSR 1961);

(e) 11 a4 ♘a5 12 e4 (after 12 d5 0–0 13 ♕c2 ♕b6 14 ♗a3 ♕a6 15 ♖fd1 ♖fd8 Black is fine, Cuellar-Gligoric, Sousse 1967) 12...0–0 13 d5 e6 (13...e5!?) 14 ♖a2 exd5 15 exd5 ♖e8 with equality (Gligoric-Korchnoi, Budva 1967).

9   ♘e2

Less logical is 9 ♘f3 ♕a5 10 ♗d2 ♘c6 11 0–0 ♗f5 12 ♕b3 ♗e4! 13 ♖fd1 b6 14 ♖ac1 ♕a6! with excellent play (Teske-A.Mikhalchishin, Bern 1996).

In this critical position Black has a wide choice: 9...♘d7?! (2.121), 9...♕a5 (2.122) and 9...♘c6 (2.123).

2.121 (1 d4 ♘f6 2 c4 g6 3 g3 ♗g7 4 ♗g2 d5 5 cxd5 ♘xd5 6 ♘c3 ♘xc3 7 bxc3 c5 8 e3 0–0 9 ♘e2)

---

9   ...   ♘d7?!
10 a4!

After **10 0–0 ♖b8 11 e4** (if 11 a4!? b6 12 a5 bxa5 13 ♕a4 ♗a6 14 ♖e1 e5 15 ♗c6 exd4!? 16 ♗xd7 d3 17 ♘f4 ♗xc3 with compensation, Rogozenko-Bologan, Berlin 1995) 11...b5! (weaker is 11...e5 12 ♗e3 b6 13 d5 ♗a6 14 ♖e1 f5 15 f3 ♗c4 16 ♘c1 ♕c7 17 ♘d3 ♗xd3 18 ♕xd3 c4 19 ♕e2 ♖f7 20 a4 when White has a slight advantage, Korchnoi-Mikhalevski, Beer Sheva 1993) 12 ♗e3 ♗a6 13 a3 ♘b6 14 ♖a2 ♘c4 the chances are only with Black (Gligoric-Uhlmann, Moscow 1967).

Now after 10...♖b8 11 a5 b5 12 axb6 axb6 13 0–0 ♗b7 14 e4 cxd4 15 cxd4 ♘c5 16 ♖a7! White's rook on the 7th rank gives him the advantage (Gligoric-Taimanov, Havana 1967).

2.122 (1 d4 ♘f6 2 c4 g6 3 g3 ♗g7 4 ♗g2 d5 5 cxd5 ♘xd5 6 ♘c3 ♘xc3 7 bxc3 c5 8 e3 0–0 9 ♘e2)

---

     9 ...   ♕a5
    10 0–0   ♖d8

10...♘c6 transposes into 2.123, while 10...e5 11 ♕b3 ♕a6 12 ♖e1 ♘c6 13 ♕a3! ♕b6 14 dxc5 ♕c7 15 c4 leaves White with the advantage (Cardoso-Sherwin, Portoroz 1959).

    11 ♕b3

Stronger than 11 a4 ♘d7 12 ♗a3 e5 13 ♕b3 cxd4 14 cxd4 ♘b6 15 ♗c5 ♗e6 when Black does not stand badly (Bakic-Nestorovic, Yugoslavia 1992).

    11 ...   ♘c6

Less good is 11...♕a6 12 ♘f4 c4 13 ♕a3 e6 14 ♕xa6 ♘xa6 15 ♖b1 with advantage (Dely-Lokvenc, Miskolc 1963).

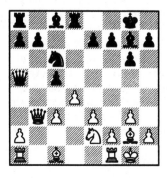

Loeb-Malisauskas (Berlin 1991) now continued 12 a4 ♗g4! 13 f3 ♗d7 14 ♗a3 b6 15 f4 ♖ac8 16 d5 ♘b8 17 ♗b2 c4 with a good game, as the white centre becomes vulnerable.

2.123 (1 d4 ♘f6 2 c4 g6 3 g3 ♗g7 4 ♗g2 d5 5 cxd5 ♘xd5 6 ♘c3 ♘xc3 7 bxc3 c5 8 e3 0–0 9 ♘e2)

---

     9 ...   ♘c6
    10 0–0

Now Black has 10...♕a5 (2.1231) or 10...cxd4 (2.1232).

2.1231 (1 d4 ♘f6 2 c4 g6 3 g3 ♗g7 4 ♗g2 d5 5 cxd5 ♘xd5 6 ♘c3 ♘xc3 7 bxc3 c5 8 e3 0–0 9 ♘e2 ♘c6 10 0–0)

---

    10 ...   ♕a5

    11 a4

This is stronger than:

11 ♕b3 ♗g4 12 ♘f4 (after 12 f3 ♗e6! 13 ♕a3 ♗c4 14 ♕xa5 ♘xa5 15 ♖e1 ♖ac8 16 ♗a3 b6 17 f4 ♖fd8 18 ♔f2 e6 Black does not stand worse, Ilivitsky-Korchnoi, USSR 1952) 12...e5 13 dxe5 ♘xe5 14 h3 (14 ♘d5 ♗e2 15 ♖e1 ♘f3+ leads to an advantage for Black) 14...♗f3 15 ♗xf3 ♘xf3+ 16

♔g2 (Najdorf-Szabo, Zurich 1953), and instead of 16...♘e5 Black should play 16...♕a6 with advantage (Bronstein).

11 ♗d2 ♖d8 (or 11...♗d7!? 12 ♘f4 ♖ae8 13 ♕e2 ♕a4 14 ♘d3 ♕c4 with the better chances, Byrne-Benko, USA 1963/4) 12 ♘c1 ♕c7 13 ♖b1 (13 ♘b3 b6 14 ♕c2 ♗a6 15 ♖fd1 ♖ac8 16 ♖ac1 e5 17 d5 c4! and Black stands better, Szabo-Liptay, Hungary 1962) 13...♗e6 14 ♕a4 ♖ac8 15 ♘d3 ♗f5 16 e4 ♗d7, and the white centre is not very secure (Lutikov-Belyavsky, Riga 1975).

11 ...   ♖d8

11...cxd4 12 cxd4 is weaker:

(a) 12...♕h5 13 ♖b1 ♗h3 14 ♗xh3 ♕xh3 15 ♖xb7 ♖fd8 16 ♗a3 ♗h6 17 ♕c2 ♖ac8 18 ♕e4 and White has the advantage (Korchnoi-Gligoric, Leningrad 1965);

(b) 12...♗e6 (or 12...♗d7 13 ♗a3) 13 ♖b1 ♗c4 14 ♖e1 ♕a6 15 ♘c3 ♖fd8 16 ♘b5 ♖ac8 17 ♗a3 e5 18 ♘d6 with advantage to White (Filip-Fuchs, Czechoslovakia 1958);

(c) 12...♗f5 13 ♗a3 ♖fe8 14 ♖c1 ♕a6 15 ♘f4 and all White's pieces are better placed than Black's.

12 ♖b1!

The game is equal after 12 ♗a3 cxd4 13 cxd4 ♗g4 14 h3 ♗e6 15 ♖b1 ♕a6 16 ♘c3 ♖ac8 17 ♘e4 b6 18 ♘d2 ♗d5 (Peev-Liebert, Lublin 1972).

12 ...   ♕c7

After 12...♕a6 White gains an advantage by 13 ♘f4!, but not 13 ♗a3 cxd4 14 cxd4 ♗g4 15 ♖b5 ♖ac8 16 h3 ♗d7 17 ♘f4 e6 18 ♘d3 ♘xd4! 19 ♗xb7 ♗xb5! 20 ♗xa6 ♗xa6 21 exd4 ♖xd4 with advantage to Black (Rytov-Zhelyandinov, USSR 1979).

13 ♘f4

The game is equal after 13 ♗a3 b6 14 ♘f4 ♗a6 15 ♖e1 ♗c4 16 ♕f3 ♖ac8

17 ♗h3 ♖b8 (Taimanov-Ilivitsky, USSR 1952).

13 ...   cxd4

Kholmov's untested recommendation 13...e6 is probably best.

14 cxd4   ♗f5
15 ♖b5   e5

After 15...b6? 16 ♖xf5 gxf5 17 ♕c2 ♖ac8 18 ♕xf5 White has the initiative (Dementiev-Karasev, USSR 1968).

In Korchnoi-Tseitlin (Beer Sheva 1992) after 16 ♘d5 ♕d7 17 dxe5 ♘xe5 18 e4 ♗e6 19 ♗g5 a6 20 ♖c5 b6 21 ♖c1 ♖db8 22 ♖c7 White maintained some advantage.

2.1232 (1 d4 ♘f6 2 c4 g6 3 g3 ♗g7 4 ♗g2 d5 5 cxd5 ♘xd5 6 ♘c3 ♘xc3 7 bxc3 c5 8 e3 0–0 9 ♘e2 ♘c6 10 0–0)

---

10 ...   cxd4
11 cxd4   ♗f5

After 11...♗e6 Black also stands well:

(a) 12 ♗a3 ♗d5 13 ♗xd5 ♕xd5 14 ♘f4 ♕d7 15 ♕a4 ♖fd8 with equality (Kotov-Keres, USSR 1957);

(b) 12 ♖b1 ♗d5 13 ♗xd5 ♕xd5 14 ♘c3 ♕d7 15 ♕e2 ♖ac8 16 ♗d2 ♖fd8 17 ♖fd1 e6 18 ♗e1 ♘e7 with an excellent game (Dokuchaev-Makarov, Kazan 1995);

(c) 12 ♗b2 ♗d5 13 ♘f4 ♗xg2 14 ♔xg2 ♖c8 15 ♖c1 ♕b6 16 ♕e2 ♖fd8 17 ♖fd1 e6 with complete equality (Vaganian-Szekely, Tallinn 1983). White's centre is immobilised, and there is no evident plan to strengthen his position.

12 ♗a3

Black also stands well after 12 ♕a4 ♕d7 13 ♕a3 ♗h3 14 ♗xh3 ♕xh3 15 ♗b2 ♕f5 (Garcia-Almeida, Andorra 1987).

12	...	♕d7
13	♕b3	

| 13 | ... | ♖fd8 |

In Bernstein-Alekhine (Carlsbad 1923) Black played the more modest **13...♖ab8** 14 ♘f4 ♖fc8 15 ♖ac1 g5!? 16 ♘d3 ♘a5 17 ♕d1 ♘c4 18 ♗c5 b5 19 ♘b4 ♗g4 with a complicated game.

Now after 14 ♖ac1 ♖ac8 15 ♖c5 b6 16 ♖d5 ♕e8 the game is equal (Gligoric-Byrne, Hastings 1967/8), as after the exchange of rooks White's activity evaporates.

2.2 (1 d4 ♘f6 2 c4 g6 3 g3 ♗g7 4 ♗g2 d5 5 cxd5 ♘xd5)

---

6 ♘f3

A sensible idea – White wants to complete his development and only then begin activity in the centre.

6 ... 0–0

The immediate **6...♘b6** is covered in Chapter 3.

7 0–0

Now we consider **7...c5 (2.21)**, **7...♘c6 (2.22)** and **7...♘b6 (2.23)**.

7...c6!? is a rather passive plan, but nevertheless Black exerts pressure on the centre: 8 e4 ♘c7 (8...♘b6 does not allow Black to carry out his plan, and

after 9 h3 ♘a6 10 ♘c3 ♘c7 11 b3 ♘e6 12 ♗e3 c5 [12...f5!? is worth trying] 13 dxc5 ♗xc3 14 ♖c1 White is clearly better, Cvitan-Mayer, Budapest 1990) 9 ♘c3 ♗g4 10 ♗e3 (after 10 ♕b3!? ♕c8 11 ♗e3 ♘ba6 12 ♖ac1 ♖b8 13 ♖fd1 ♕d7 14 ♖d2 White has the advantage, Bewersdorff-Gutman, Germany 1996) 10...♕d6 11 ♕d2 (after 11 h3 ♗xf3 12 ♗xf3 ♖d8 13 ♕b3 ♘ba6 14 ♖fd1 ♕b4 Black has counterplay, Stern-Gutman, Erfurt 1992) 11...♖d8 12 ♖fd1 ♕b4 13 h3 ♗xf3 14 ♗xf3 c5 15 ♘e2 ♕xd2 16 ♖xd2 ♘c6 17 ♖ad1 ♘e6 18 dxc5 ♖xd2 19 ♖xd2 ♘e5 20 ♔g2 ♘c4 21 ♖c2 ♘xb2 22 ♘f4 with some advantage (Dlugy-Gutman, New York 1988).

2.21 (1 d4 ♘f6 2 c4 g6 3 g3 ♗g7 4 ♗g2 d5 5 cxd5 ♘xd5 6 ♘f3 0–0 7 0–0)

---

7 ... c5

A critical and logical attempt to solve the problem of the centre not by piece pressure, but by changing the pawn structure, after which White has: **8 e4 (2.211)**, **8 dxc5 (2.212)** or **8 ♘c3 (2.213)**.

2.211 (1 d4 ♘f6 2 c4 g6 3 g3 ♗g7 4 ♗g2 d5 5 cxd5 ♘xd5 6 ♘f3 0–0 7 0–0 c5)

---

8 e4

This occurs more rarely than the other two continuations, although Botvinnik himself considered it the strongest, and often chose it. In this way White weakens his centre (d4), but by placing his pawn at e5 he seizes space and, most important, restricts the bishop at g7.

8 ... ♘f6

Weaker is **8...♞b6** 9 d5 e6 (9...♝g4 10 h3 ♝xf3 11 ♛xf3 ♞8d7 12 ♛e2 c4 13 ♞c3 ♞c5 14 ♝e3 ♞d3 15 ♖ab1 ♞d7 16 f4 ♖c8 17 e5, Smyslov-Simagin, 28th USSR Ch 1961; Black has the d3 square, but both White's bishops are active) 10 ♝g5! (weaker is 10 ♞c3 exd5 11 ♞xd5 ♞xd5 12 exd5 ♞a6 with an equal game; 10...♝xc3 is also interesting), and now:

(a) 10...♛d7 11 ♞c3 exd5 (11... ♝xc3 12 bxc3 exd5 13 ♞e5! ♛e8 14 ♞d3 dxe4 15 ♞xc5 f5 16 ♛b3+ ♛f7 17 f3 ♛xb3 18 axb3 exf3 19 ♝xf3 ♞c6 20 ♖fe1 leads to an advantage for White, Estrin) 12 ♞xd5 ♞xd5 (after 12...♝xb2 13 ♝f6! White is clearly better) 13 exd5 ♝xb2 14 ♖e1 ♖e8 (if 14...♝xa1 there follows 15 ♛xa1 ♖e8 16 ♖xe8+ ♛xe8 17 ♝f6 with an attack) 15 ♖b1 ♖e1+ 16 ♛xe1 ♝g7 17 ♞e5 with a powerful initiative for White (Boleslavsky);

(b) 10...f6 11 ♝e3 ♞a6 12 ♞c3 ♞c4 (after 12...exd5 13 exd5 ♞c4 14 ♝c1 ♖e8 15 b3 ♞d6 16 ♝f4 ♞c7 17 ♞d2 f5 18 ♖c1 White has the advantage, Fairhurst-Flohr, London 1947) 13 ♝c1 (weaker is 13 ♞d2 ♞xe3! 14 fxe3 exd5 15 exd5 ♝d7 16 a4 ♞b4 17 ♞c4 f5 with equality, Botvinnik) 13...e5! 14 ♞b5! ♝d7 15 a4 ♛b6 16 b3 ♞a5 17 ♖e1 ♞b4 18 ♞a3 a6 19 ♞d2 and White has the advantage (Botvinnik-Novotelnov, Moscow 1947), although the position is very complicated.

9 e5 ♞d5
10 dxc5

Weaker is **10 ♛e2** cxd4 11 ♞xd4 ♞c6 12 ♞xc6 bxc6 13 ♖d1 ♛c7 14 f4 ♛b6+ 15 ♛f2 ♝g4 16 ♖d4 ♖ad8 17 ♞c3 ♞xc3 18 bxc3 f6, when White's strategy is called into question by the undermining of his main e5 point (Tarasov-Zak, USSR 1951).

Now Black has **10...♞b4 (2.2111)**, **10...♞c6 (2.2112)** or **10...♞a6 (2.2113)**.

2.2111 (1 d4 ♞f6 2 c4 g6 3 g3 ♝g7 4 ♝g2 d5 5 cxd5 ♞xd5 6 ♞f3 0–0 7 0–0 c5 8 e4 ♞f6 9 e5 ♞d5 10 dxc5)

10	...	**♞b4**
11	**♞c3**	**♞8c6**
12	**a3**	

Weaker is **12 ♛e2** ♛d3 13 ♖d1 ♛xe2 14 ♞xe2 (Smyslov-Szabo, Hastings 1954/5) – *Game 4*, when 14...♝e6! 15 ♞fd4 ♖fd8 16 ♝g5 ♝xe5 17 ♞xe6 fxe6 would have equalised completely (Neikirch).

12	...	**♞d3**

If **12...♕xd1** 13 ♖xd1 ♘c2 14 ♖b1
♗f5 15 ♘h4, or **12...♘a6** 13 b4 ♘xe5
14 ♘xe5 ♗xe5 15 ♗b2, in each case
with advantage to White.

      13 ♗e3   ♗g4

Not **13...♘xb2** 14 ♕e2 ♘d3 15
♖fd1, when Black has problems.

But now after 14 h3 ♗xf3 15 ♕xf3
♘dxe5 16 ♕e4 ♕d3 17 ♕a4 ♕c4 18
♖ad1 the ending is unpleasant for
Black, in view of White's queenside
advantage and his two active bishops
(Botvinnik-Bronstein, m/19 1951).

**2.2112 (1 d4 ♘f6 2 c4 g6 3 g3 ♗g7
4 ♗g2 d5 5 cxd5 ♘xd5 6 ♘f3 0–0
7 0–0 c5 8 e4 ♘f6 9 e5 ♘d5 10
dxc5)**

---

      10 ...   ♘c6
      11 ♕e2

Very complicated and unclear play
results from the pawn sacrifice **11 ♘a3**
♘db4 12 ♕e2 ♕d3 13 ♕xd3 ♘xd3 14
♖d1 ♘xc5 15 ♗e3 ♘a4 16 ♖d2 ♘xe5
17 ♘xe5 ♗xe5 18 ♘c4 ♗g7 19 ♖c1,
while after **11 a3** the correct continuation is not 11...♘c7? 12 ♕b3 ♘a6 13
♗e3 ♕c7 14 ♘c3 ♗e6 15 ♕a4 with
advantage (Stahlberg-Szabo, Amsterdam 1954), but the simple 11...♗e6!?
12 ♘g5 ♘xe5 13 ♘xe6 fxe6 14 ♕e2
♕d7 with counterplay. Also interesting
is 11...♗g4!? 12 h3 ♗xf3 13 ♗xf3 e6
14 ♗xd5 exd5 15 f4 d4 16 b4 a5 17 b5
♘e7, when Black has play for the pawn,
a line which also awaits a practical
testing.

      11 ...   ♕a5

If **11...♗g4** 12 ♖d1 ♘xe5 13 h3
♗xf3 14 ♗xf3 ♘xf3+ 15 ♕xf3 e6 16
♘c3 ♕a5 17 ♘xd5 exd5 18 ♗e3 with
advantage to White (Gosin-Zelinsky,
USSR 1955).

      12 ♘bd2

Weaker, according to Botvinnik, is
12 ♘fd2 ♘db4! 13 ♘b3 ♕c7 14 f4
♗e6 15 ♘c3 ♖ad8 16 ♗e3 ♘xa2 17
♖xa2 ♗xb3 18 ♖a3 ♗e6 19 ♘b5 ♕b8
20 ♖d1 when the game is unclear,
although it seems to us that here too
White stands better.

Now after 12...♕xc5 13 ♘b3 ♕b6 14
♖d1 e6 15 h4! ♕c7 16 ♖e1 White has
the advantage thanks to his strong e5
pawn, restricting the black bishop
(Botvinnik-Ragozin, training game
1951).

**2.2113 (1 d4 ♘f6 2 c4 g6 3 g3 ♗g7
4 ♗g2 d5 5 cxd5 ♘xd5 6 ♘f3 0–0
7 0–0 c5 8 e4 ♘f6 9 e5 ♘d5 10
dxc5)**

---

      10 ...   ♘a6
      11 ♕e2

After **11 c6** bxc6 12 ♘d4 (12 ♖e1
♕b6 13 ♘c3 ♖d8 14 ♘xd5, and both
14...♖xd5 and 14...cxd5 look satisfactory) 12...♗b7 13 ♖e1 ♕b6 14 ♘c3
♘xc3 (14...♖fd8 15 ♘xd5 cxd5 16 ♗g5
♗f8 17 ♗e3 with a slight advantage for
White) 15 bxc3 c5 16 ♘f3 ♖ad8 17
♕c2 ♘c7 18 ♖b1 ♕a6 the position is
equal (analysis by Boleslavsky).

11 a3 ♘xc5 12 b4 ♘e6 (bad is 12...♘a6 13 ♗b2 ♘b6 14 ♕e2 ♗e6 15 ♖d1 ♕c7 16 ♘bd2 ♕c2 17 ♖ab1 ♗d5 18 ♘d4 ♕a4 19 ♘e4 with a clear advantage to White, Smejkal-Ribli, Leningrad 1977) 13 ♗b2 a5 14 b5 ♕d7 15 ♕e2 ♖d8 16 ♘c3 (after 16 ♘bd2? ♘ef4! Black seizes the initiative, Alekhine-Mikenas, Kemeri 1937) 16...♘xc3 17 ♗xc3 ♕d3 again leads to equality.

11 ... ♘xc5

Deferring the capture is dangerous: 11...♕c7 12 ♖d1 ♕xc5 13 ♘bd2 ♘db4 14 a3 ♘c6 15 ♘e4 ♕b6 16 ♗e3 ♕c7 17 ♖ac1 ♗f5 18 ♗f4 ♕b6 19 b4, and White's advantage is considerable (Olafsson-Cuellar, Moscow 1956).

12 ♖d1

12 ... e6

Or 12...b6:

(a) 13 ♘g5 ♗a6 14 ♕e1 (14 ♕g4 e6 15 ♘c3 h5 16 ♕f3 ♗xe5 17 ♘xd5 exd5 18 ♖xd5 ♕e7 leads only to equality, Oll-Shirov, Tbilisi 1989) 14...e6 15 ♘c3 ♘d3 with a slight advantage to Black;

(b) 13 b4 ♗a6 14 b5 ♗b7 with equality;

(c) 13 ♕c4 e6 (13...♘e3 14 ♖xd8 ♘xc4 15 ♖xf8+ ♔xf8 16 ♘fd2!) 14 ♗g5 ♕c7 15 ♘c3 ♘xc3 16 ♕xc3 a5 17 ♗f6 ♗b7 18 ♗xg7 ♔xg7 19 ♖d6! and

White gains some advantage (Rotstein-Lanka, Cannes 1992).

13 ♗g5!?

After 13 ♗e3 ♕e7 14 ♗d4 b6 15 ♘c3 ♗b7 16 ♘d2 ♘xc3 17 ♗xc3 ♖ad8 the position is equal (Germek-Gligoric, Yugoslavia 1949), while if 13 ♘c3 there follows 13...♘xc3 14 bxc3 ♕c7 15 ♗g5 b6 16 ♕e3 ♗b7 17 ♖d4 ♖ac8 18 ♖c1 ♗xf3 19 ♗xf3 ♘d7 20 ♗f4 g5! with a roughly equal game (Osnos-Averbakh, USSR 1963).

Now after 13...♕a5 14 ♗d2 ♕a4 (14...♕b6 is somewhat better, reducing White's advantage to the minimum) 15 ♘c3 ♘xc3 16 ♗xc3 b6 17 ♘d4 ♗a6 18 ♕e3! (Krogius-Yuferov, St Petersburg 1994) White has the advantage, as the Black pieces stand uncoordinated, and also the unpleasant ♗c6 is threatened.

2.212 (1 d4 ♘f6 2 c4 g6 3 g3 ♗g7 4 ♗g2 d5 5 cxd5 ♘xd5 6 ♘f3 0–0 7 0–0 c5)

---

8 dxc5 ♘a6

The critical move. Others are not in the spirit of the position:

8...♘b4 9 ♘bd2 (9 ♘c3 is also satisfactory) 9...♘8a6 10 a3 ♘c6 11 ♖b1 ♘xc5 12 b4 ♘e6 13 ♗b2 ♘cd4 14

♘xd4 ♘xd4 15 ♘b3 ♘b5 16 ♕c1 ♗xb2 17 ♕xb2 with advantage to White (Trifunovic-Puc, Yugoslavia 1948).

8...♘c6 9 a3 ♗f5 10 ♘bd2 ♘f6 11 ♘c4 ♗e4 12 b4 ♘d5 13 ♗b2 ♗xb2 14 ♘xb2 ♘c3 15 ♕e1, and Black has no compensation for the pawn.

Now White has several possibilities, each leading to a completely different type of position: 9 ♘bd2 (2.2121), 9 ♘g5 (2.2122) and 9 c6! (2.2123).

2.2121 (1 d4 ♘f6 2 c4 g6 3 g3 ♗g7 4 ♗g2 d5 5 cxd5 ♘xd5 6 ♘f3 0–0 7 0–0 c5 8 dxc5 ♘a6)

---

9 ♘bd2

A modest continuation, not without venom – White wants to exploit the hanging black knights and to obtain the slightly more active position.

    9   ...   ♘xc5
   10 ♘b3   ♘e6

Weak is 10...♘a4 11 ♘bd4 ♗d7 12 ♕b3 ♘ab6 13 a4 a5 14 e4 ♘b4 15 e5 ♕e8 16 e6! ♗xa4 17 exf7+ ♖xf7 18 ♕e6 with a strong initiative for the pawn (Kotov-Boleslavsky, Parnu 1947). Now, it is true, the knight at e6 is not badly placed, but the path of the c8 bishop has been firmly blocked.

11 e4

Weaker is 11 ♘bd4 ♘xd4 12 ♘xd4 ♘b6 13 ♘b3 ♘a4 14 ♖b1 ♗f5 15 e4 ♗e6 (Bozic-Andric, Belgrade 1948), although 13 e3 would have clearly been better. The untested 11 ♘g5!? deserves serious consideration.

   11   ...   ♘b6

Or 11...♘b4 12 ♗d2 ♘d3 13 ♕c2 ♘xb2 14 ♖ab1 with compensation for the pawn.

Now 12 ♕e2 ♕c7 13 ♖d1 ♖d8 14 ♗e3 leads to interesting play with some advantage to White, since his pieces are rather more freely placed. This variation needs testing in practice.

2.2122 (1 d4 ♘f6 2 c4 g6 3 g3 ♗g7 4 ♗g2 d5 5 cxd5 ♘xd5 6 ♘f3 0–0 7 0–0 c5 8 dxc5 ♘a6)

---

9 ♘g5

Now Black has 9... ♘db4 (2.21221) or 9...e6!? (2.21222).

Passive is 9...♘dc7 10 ♕c2 ♕d4 11 ♘c3, when he has problems in finding a good post for his queen (Larsen-Szabo, Amsterdam 1954).

2.21221 (1 d4 ♘f6 2 c4 g6 3 g3 ♗g7 4 ♗g2 d5 5 cxd5 ♘xd5 6 ♘f3 0–0 7 0–0 c5 8 dxc5 ♘a6 9 ♘g5)

---

    9   ...   ♘db4
   10 ♘c3

If 10 ♕b3 h6 11 a3 ♘c6 12 ♘f3 ♘xc5 13 ♕c4 b6 14 ♘c3 ♗a6 15 ♕h4 (J.Littlewood-Hollis, Hastings 1962/3) 15...h5 with excellent play for Black.

Here he again has a choice: 10...h6 (2.212211) or 10...♕xd1 (2.212212).

After 10...♘xc5 11 ♗e3:

(a) 11...♘ba6 12 ♕c1 (also strong is 12 ♖c1 h6 13 ♘ge4 ♘xe4 14 ♗xe4

♗h3 15 ♗xb7 with a clear advantage) 12...h6 (or 12...♕e8 13 ♘ge4! ♘e6 14 ♗h6 ♗d7 15 ♗xg7 ♔xg7 16 ♘d5 ♗c6 17 ♕c3+ f6 18 ♖fd1 with a spatial advantage, Wojtkiewicz-Fernandez, Novi Sad 1990) 13 ♖d1 ♕e8 14 ♘ge4 ♘xe4 15 ♗xe4 f5 16 ♗g2 with advantage (Neckar-Pribyl, Czechoslovakia 1994);

(b) 11...♕xd1 12 ♖fxd1 ♘ca6 13 ♖d2 h6 14 ♘f3 ♘c6 (Ilic-Goormachtigh, Gent 1994), when 15 ♖ad1 ♗e6 16 ♘d4 would have given an advantage;

(c) 11...♘e6 12 ♕b3 ♕a5 13 a3 ♘c6 14 ♘xe6 ♗xe6 15 ♕xb7 ♘d4 16 ♕xe7 ♖ab8 17 ♘e4! and Black has no compensation for the material (Geller-Savon, Rovno 1963) – *Game 5*;

(d) 11...♘ca6 12 ♕xd8 ♖xd8 13 ♖fd1 ♖f8 14 ♖ac1 h6 15 ♘ge4 ♗e6 16 a3 ♘c6 17 b4 ♘c7 18 ♘c5 also with the better position for White (Cuellar-Yanofsky, Stockholm 1962).

2.212211 (1 d4 ♘f6 2 c4 g6 3 g3 ♗g7 4 ♗g2 d5 5 cxd5 ♘xd5 6 ♘f3 0–0 7 0–0 c5 8 dxc5 ♘a6 9 ♘g5 ♘db4 10 ♘c3)

10 ...   h6

11   ♘f3

If **11 ♘ge4 ♕xd1** (weaker is 11...f5

12 ♕b3+ ♔h7 13 ♘d2 ♘c6 14 ♕c4 ♘a5 15 ♕b5 ♗d7 16 c6! with advantage, Wojtkiewicz-Hoffman, Bad Zwesten 1997) 12 ♖xd1 f5 13 ♘d2 ♘xc5 14 ♘b3 ♘c2 15 ♖b1 ♘xb3 16 ♗d5+ ♔h7 17 ♗xb3 ♘d4 and Black is excellently placed (Andrianov-Bagirov, USSR 1988).

11 ...   ♗e6

After **11...♕xd1** 12 ♖xd1 ♗e6 (if 12...♘xc5 13 ♗e3 ♘e6 14 ♖ac1 ♘c6 15 b3 ♖d8 16 ♘d5 ♔f8 17 b4 White has the better ending, Helmers-Lobron, Luzern 1979) 13 ♗e3 (according to Boleslavsky, after 13 ♗f4 ♘xc5 14 ♗e5 f6 15 ♗d4 ♖ac8 16 ♘e1 b6 the game is equal, while 13 ♘e1 ♘xc5 14 ♗e3 ♖ac8 15 ♗d4 a5 also leads to equality, Panno-Szabo, Amsterdam 1956) 13...♘c2 14 ♖ac1 ♘xe3 15 fxe3 ♘xc5 16 b4! (weaker is 16 ♘d4 a5 17 ♘cb5 ♖fc8 18 ♖c2 ♗d7 19 ♖dc1 ♘e6 20 b3 ♘xd4 21 ♘xd4 ♖ab8 22 ♔f2 ♗e5 with equality, Larsen-Filip, Moscow 1956) 16...♘a6 (unsatisfactory is 16...♗xc3 17 ♖xc3 ♘e4 18 ♖c7 ♖ac8 19 ♖xb7 ♘c3 20 ♖e1 ♗xa2 21 ♖xa7 with advantage, Ogaard-Olafsson, Reykjavik 1974) 17 a3 ♗b3 (17...♘c7?! 18 ♘d4 ♖ab8 19 ♘xe6 ♘xe6 20 ♘d5 led to an advantage for White in Schmidt-Jasnikowski, Lublin 1988, but after 18...♗xd4! 19 exd4 ♖ab8 20 ♘e4 ♘b5 21 ♘c5 ♗c8 22 a4 ♘d6 23 ♗f3 ♖d8 24 ♔f2 h5 25 b5 ♗g4 26 e4 b6 Black would have held on, Izeta-Vakhidov, Yerevan 1996, and this deserves a serious practical testing) 18 ♖d7 ♖fd8 (after 18...e5 19 ♘d2! ♗e6 20 ♖xb7 ♖fd8 21 ♘de4 Black has problems, Schmidt-Levy, Polanica Zdroj 1969) 19 ♖xd8+ (sharper is 19 ♖xe7 ♖ac8 20 ♘d4 ♗f6 21 ♘xb3 ♗xe7 22 ♗xb7 with somewhat the better chances, Cvitan-Jasnikowski, Warsaw 1990) 19...♖xd8 20 ᐤd4 White has slightly the better ending (Portisch-Kluger, Hungary 1964).

If instead **11...♗f5**, then 12 ᐤh4 (very sharp is 12 ♗e3 ᐤc2 13 ♕c1?! ᐤxa1 14 ♕xa1 ♖c8 15 ♖d1 ♕a5 16 ᐤd4 ᐤb4 17 ᐤxf5 gxf5 18 ♕c1, and White has some threats, Grigorian-Savon, USSR 1971) and now:

(a) 12...♕xd1 13 ♖xd1 (but not 13 ᐤxd1? ♗e6 14 ♗d2 g5 15 ᐤf3 ᐤxa2 with the better game for Black, Hulak-Bagirov, Amsterdam 1989) 13...♗c2 14 ♖d2 g5 15 ♗xb7! and all the black pieces are overloaded (Rokhlin-Estrin, corr. 1968);

(b) 12...♗g4 13 ♗e3 ♕xd1 14 ♖axd1 g5 15 ᐤf3 ᐤc2 16 ᐤd4 ᐤxe3 17 fxe3 ᐤxc5 18 h3 ♗h5 19 g4 ♗g6 (Helmers-Gutman, Renders 1982) and here 20 b4 would have consolidated White's advantage.

After **11...ᐤxc5** 12 ♗e3 ᐤba6 13 ♖c1 ♗d7 14 b4 ᐤe6 15 ♕b3 ᐤac7 16 b5 ♕e8 17 a4 White has the advantage (Mochalov-Gipslis, USSR 1974).

12 ♗f4

12 ♗e3 transposes into variations already considered.

12 ...   ♕xd1

The untried **12...♖c8!?** is worth looking at.

13 ♖fxd1   ᐤxc5
14 ♗e5   f6

After **14...♖fd8** 15 ♗xg7 ♔xg7 16 ᐤd4 ♖xd4 17 ♖xd4 ᐤc2 18 ♖ad1 ᐤxd4 19 ♖xd4 ♖c8 20 f4 b6 Black should hold this slightly inferior ending (Langeweg-Zuidema, Amsterdam 1965).

Now 15 ♗d4 ♖ac8 16 ᐤe1 (if 16 ♖ac1 b6 17 a3 ᐤba6 Black is threatening ...ᐤb3) 16...b6 and Black should be able to equalise (Boleslavsky).

2.212212 (1 d4 ᐤf6 2 c4 g6 3 g3 ♗g7 4 ♗g2 d5 5 cxd5 ᐤxd5 6 ᐤf3 0–0 7 0–0 c5 8 dxc5 ᐤa6 9 ᐤg5 ᐤdb4 10 ᐤc3)

10 ...   ♕xd1
11 ♖xd1   ᐤxc5

11...h6 12 ᐤf3 ᐤxc5 leads to a position from the previous variation.

12 ♗e3   ᐤe6

Weaker is **12...ᐤca6** 13 ♖ac1 h6 14 ᐤge4 ᐤc6 15 a3 ᐤc7 16 b4, when White has a clear advantage (Najdorf-Pachman, Amsterdam 1954).

13 ♖ac1

White should not accept the pawn sacrifice – after **13 ᐤxe6 ♗xe6 14 ♗xb7 ♖ab8 15 ♗e4 f5** Black has good compensation.

13 ...   ᐤc6
14 ᐤd5

Not bad, but somewhat simplifying, is **14 ᐤxe6 ♗xe6 15 b3** (interesting is first 15 ♗xc6 bxc6 16 b3, when the impression is that White is better) 15...♖ad8 16 ᐤd5 ♗b2 17 ♖c2 ♗e5 18 ♖cd2 ♔g7 19 ᐤf4 ♗xf4 20 ♗xf4 ♖xd2 21 ♗xd2 f6 22 ♗e3 with a minimal advantage to White (Darga-Robatsch, Havana 1963).

14 ...   ♗xb2

15 Rb1 ♗e5 16 ♘xe6 fxe6 (weak is 16...♗xe6 17 Rxb7 Rad8 18 f4 ♗d6 19 Rc1 when Black has problems, Geller-Sandor, Gothenburg 1967) 17 ♘b4 with some advantage to White (analysis).

2.21222 (1 d4 ♘f6 2 c4 g6 3 g3 ♗g7 4 ♗g2 d5 5 cxd5 ♘xd5 6 ♘f3 0–0 7 0–0 c5 8 dxc5 ♘a6 9 ♘g5)

---

9 ...   e6!?

A move that became popular comparatively recently. Its main idea is to avoid moving from the centre the powerful d5 knight, although here it is more difficult to regain the c5 pawn. However, White has to spend time defending it, and in the meantime Black manages to develop his pieces in active positions.

10 ♘e4

After 10 ♘c3 ♘xc3 11 bxc3 ♘xc5 12 ♘e4 ♘xe4 13 ♗xe4 ♕c7 14 Rb1 Rb8 15 ♕a4 a6 16 ♗f4 e5 17 ♗e3 b5 Black solved all his problems (Tukmakov-Vaganian, USSR 1983).

10 c6? is bad: 10...bxc6 11 ♘a3 ♘ab4 12 ♘c2 c5 13 a3 ♘c6 14 ♘e3 Rb8! 15 ♘xd5 exd5 16 ♕xd5 ♘d4! with advantage to Black (Schmidt-A.Mikhalchishin, Dortmund 1993).

10 ...   ♗d7!

Black plans to activate his bishop at c6 and thereby strengthen his main strategic point d5. Less good is 10...♕c7 11 ♘bc3 ♘xc3 12 ♘xc3 ♘xc5 13 ♗f4 ♕a5 14 Rc1 Rd8 15 b4! Rxd1 16 bxa5 with advantage to White (Mochalov-Kiss, Matra 1993).

11 ♘bc3

After 11 ♗g5:

(a) 11...♕c7 12 ♘bc3 ♘xc3 13 ♘xc3 ♗c6 14 ♗f4 (stronger is 14 ♕d6 Rfc8 15 Rac1 ♗xg2 16 ♔xg2 ♕xc5 17 ♕xc5 Rxc5 18 ♗e3 Rc4 19 Rfd1 b6 20 Rd7 with somewhat the better game, Itkis-Yuferov, USSR 1983, but the impression is that Black should not have any serious problems) 14...♕c8 15 ♘e4 ♘xc5! the game is equal (Skomorokhin-S.Ivanov, Germany 1996);

(b) 11...f6 12 ♗d2 ♗c6 13 ♘bc3 f5 14 ♘xd5 ♗xd5 15 ♘c3 ♗xg2 16 ♔xg2 ♘xc5 17 Rc1 ♕b6! 18 ♗e3 Rfd8 19 ♕c2 ♗d4 with a good game (Zarkovic-A.Mikhalchishin, Cetinje 1993).

11 ...   ♗c6

White has the advantage after the less logical 11...♘xc3 12 ♘xc3 ♘xc5 13 ♗e3 Rc8 14 Rc1 b6 15 b4 ♘a6 16 ♕b3 ♕f6 17 ♘e4 ♕e7 18 b5 (Fominykh-M.Ivanov, Vladivostok 1995).

12 ♘xd5

After 12 ♗g5 f6 13 ♗d2 f5 14 ♘g5 ♘xc3 15 bxc3 ♗xg2 16 ♔xg2 ♕d5+ 17 ♔g1 h6 18 ♘f3 ♘xc5 Black has no problems (Penichek-Karsa, Copenhagen 1988).

12 ...   exd5

Now 13 ♘d6!? leads to interesting play: 13...♘xc5 14 ♗xd5 ♕d7! 15 ♗xc6 ♕xc6 16 ♘c4 Rfd8 17 ♕c2 ♘e6 with compensation for the pawn.

The alternative is 13 ♘c3 d4 14 ♗xc6 bxc6 15 ♘a4 ♕d5, when the position is equal (A.Mikhalchishin-

Zilberstein, Nikolaev 1981), as Black is splendidly centralised.

**2.2123 (1 d4 ♘f6 2 c4 g6 3 g3 ♗g7
4 ♗g2 d5 5 cxd5 ♘xd5 6 ♘f3 0–0
7 0–0 c5 8 dxc5 ♘a6)**

---

9 c6!   bxc6

By giving back the pawn immediately, White has created a weakness at c6, but Black too has his trumps – good development plus the chance to coordinate his knight at d5, bishop at g7, and rook on the open b-file. Which will outweigh is a question of taste!

10 ♘a3!?

A very interesting decision. The old continuations are weaker:

10 ♘bd2 ♖b8!? (worse is 10...♕c7 11 a3 c5 12 ♘c4 ♗b7 13 ♕c2 with advantage, Botvinnik-Zuidema, Wijk aan Zee 1968, but 10...♘c5 looks satisfactory: 11 ♘c4 ♗a6 12 ♘fe5 ♕c7 13 ♕c2 ♘e6 with complicated play, Donchenko-Gipslis, Dubna 1976 – *Game 6*) 11 ♘c4 ♘c5 12 ♘fe5 ♕c7 13 ♘xc6 ♕xc6 14 ♗xd5 ♕a6 15 ♗f4 ♗h3 16 ♗xb8 ♖xb8 17 ♖c1 ♗xf1 18 ♔xf1 ♘a4 with compensation for the pawn (P.Nikolic-Velimirovic, Kavala 1985).

10 ♘d4!?   ♗b7   11 ♘a3   ♕b6 (11...♖b8 12 ♘b3 leads to a superior position for White, but clearly better is 11...c5!? 12 ♘b3 ♖c8 13 ♘c4 e6 and then ...♘ab4, when Black has no problems) 12 ♘b3 ♖fd8 13 ♗d2 ♕c7 14 ♘c4 ♘b6 15 ♘ba5 ♘xc4 16 ♘xc4 with a slight advantage (Karasev-Savon, USSR 1971).

10 ...   ♕b6

10...♘c5 is very interesting, and 10...e5 11 ♘c4 ♕e7 is also possible. These need to be tried in practice, as the main line is not altogether promising for Black.

11 ♘c4

After 11 e4 ♘db4 12 ♗e3 c5 13 ♘c4 ♕b5 14 ♕e2 ♗e6 15 ♖fc1 ♖fd8 16 a4 ♕e8 17 ♘g5 White has some advantage (Romanishin-Lanka, Yurmala 1983). 15...♘c6! is correct, with play against d4 and equality.

11 ...   ♕c5
12 ♘fe5!

Stronger than 12 ♘fd2 ♗e6! (Yuferov-Gufeld, Barnaul 1969), when Black achieved an active position.

12 ...   ♗e6

Black should have considered supporting his c6 pawn by 12...♗b7 13 e4 ♖fd8! 14 exd5 cxd5.

13 ♕a4   ♕b5
14 ♕xb5   cxb5

Black would appear to have consolidated, but an unexpected tactical resource sets him serious problems: 15 ♘c6! bxc4 16 ♗xd5 ♘f6 17 ♗f3 ♘c5 18 ♗e3! ♘a4 19 ♗d4 with a slight advantage to White (Zhelyandinov-A.Mikhalchishin, Ptuj 1994), since Black clearly has more weaknesses, and the ending after 19...♗xd4 20 ♘xd4 ♖ab8 21 ♘xe6 fxe6 22 b3 is highly unpleasant.

2.213 (1 d4 ♘f6 2 c4 g6 3 g3 ♗g7
4 ♗g2 d5 5 cxd5 ♘xd5 6 ♘f3 0–0
7 0–0 c5)

8   ♘c3!?

A solid plan – White intensifies the piece pressure on the centre and aims to eliminate the active knight at d5, which will result in an open centre and a very tense pawn structure. Black has two main replies: **8...cxd4 (2.2131)** and **8...♘xc3 (2.2132)**.

Sometimes he plays **8...♘c6** 9 ♘xd5 (very passive is 9 e3 ♘xc3 10 bxc3 ♕a5 11 ♗d2 cxd4 12 cxd4 ♕h5 13 ♘h4 ♕xd1 14 ♖fxd1 and White has the advantage, but Black should play 11...♖d8 or 11...♗f5, and in each case he has no problems) 9...♕xd5 10 ♗e3 (after 10 dxc5 ♕xc5 11 ♗e3 Black should play 11...♕b5) 10...cxd4 (if 10...♗f5 11 ♘h4 ♗e4 12 f3 ♗f5 13 ♗f2! ♗d7 14 f4 ♕c4 15 dxc5 and White has the advantage, Osnos-Kamsky, Leningrad 1987, but interesting is 10...♕h5! 11 dxc5 ♗xb2 12 ♖b1 ♗g7 13 ♕a4 ♖b8 14 ♘g5 ♘e5 15 h3 ♗d7 16 ♕xa7 ♗c6! when Black gained compensation for the pawn, Burmakin-Bologan, Kstovo 1997) 11 ♘xd4 ♕a5 (if 11...♕c4 White has 12 b3 ♕a6 13

♘xc6 bxc6 14 ♖c1 ♕xa2 15 ♖xc6 ♗b7 16 ♖c7 with a slight advantage, Bolbochan-Richter, Trenchanske Teplice 1949) 12 ♘xc6 bxc6 13 ♗d2 ♕a6 14 ♕c1 ♖b8 15 ♗c3 ♗xc3 16 ♕xc3 ♕xe2 (Sandor-Kluger, Bucharest 1954), and here White should have played 17 b3 with a slight advantage.

2.2131 (1 d4 ♘f6 2 c4 g6 3 g3 ♗g7
4 ♗g2 d5 5 cxd5 ♘xd5 6 ♘f3 0–0
7 0–0 c5 8 ♘c3)

8   ...   cxd4
9   ♘xd4

If 9 ♘xd5 ♕xd5 10 ♗e3 d3 11 ♘d4 dxe2 12 ♕xe2 ♕a5 13 ♖fd1 (Ortega-Heinicke, Helsinki 1952), and here Black could have played 13...e5 14 ♘b3 ♕c7 15 ♖ac1 ♘c6 or 13...♘a6.

9   ...   ♘xc3
10   bxc3

Of course, White's c3 pawn is weak, but his possession of the b-file plus the powerful d4 knight and active g2 bishop create difficulties for Black. He has two serious alternatives: **10...♘c6 (2.21311)** and **10...♕a5 (2.21312)**.

Other moves are weaker:

10...e5? 11 ♘b5 ♕a5 12 ♘d6 (12 ♕b3 ♗e6 13 c4 ♘c6 14 ♗a3 ♖fd8 15 e3 e4 16 ♖ad1 f5 is unclear, Rubinstein-Tartakower, Vienna 1922, while *ECO* gives an old variation of Alekhine: 12 c4 ♖d8 13 ♕b3 'with advantage', but after 13...♘c6 it is altogether unclear why it is not Black who is better, Alekhine-Felix, Uruguay 1939) 12...♖d8 (12...♕a6 13 ♘xc8 ♖xc8 14 ♖b1 ♘c6 15 ♕d7 e4 16 ♗f4 ♕xa2 17 ♗xe4 ♕e6 18 ♖xb7 and wins, Stahlberg-Mikenas, Buenos Aires 1939, but better is 12...♘c6 13 ♕b3 with only a slight advantage for White) 13 ♘xb7 ♗xb7 14 ♗xb7 ♖xd1 15 ♖xd1 and wins (Estrin).

10...a6? is very slow: 11 ♗a3!? (also 11 ♗e3 ♕c7 12 ♕b3 ♘d7 13 a4 ♖b8 14 ♖fd1 ♗f6?! 15 h4 h5 16 a5 ♗g7 17 ♕a3 ♘f6 18 ♘b3 ♘g4 19 ♕c5! with advantage to White, Loginov-Brunner, Budapest 1993, or 11 ♕b3 ♕c7 12 ♗a3 ♖e8 13 ♖ab1 ♘d7 14 ♖fc1 ♗h6 15 e3 ♖b8 16 c4 e5 17 ♘e2 ♘c5 18 ♕b6 with a slight advantage, Szabo-Kotov, Saltsjöbaden 1948) 11...♖a7 12 ♕b3 b5 13 ♗c5 ♖d7 14 a4! ♕c7 15 ♕b4 bxa4 16 ♖fb1 a5 17 ♕a3! ♕e5 18 ♖b5 and White has the advantage (Ribli-Ljubojevic, Barcelona 1989).

10...♕c7 11 ♕b3 ♘c6 12 ♘xc6 (after 12 ♖d1 ♘xd4 (13 cxd4 ♗g4 14 ♗f4 ♕b6 15 ♗xb7 ♖ab8 16 ♕xb6 axb6 17 f3 White kept the advantage, Szabo-Flohr, Budapest 1950, but 12...♖d8 would have given chances of equality) 12...bxc6 13 ♗f4 ♕a5 (13...e5 14 ♗e3 ♗e6 15 c4 with the better chances for White, Keres-Mikenas, Hastings 1937/8) 14 ♗xc6 ♗e6 15 ♕b7 ♖ac8 16 a4 ♗xc6 17 ♖ac1 and White's position is preferable (Zilberman-Sutovskij, Israel 1994).

10...♘d7 11 ♗a3 ♖e8 12 ♖b1 ♘b6 13 ♘b5 ♗d7 14 ♗c5 ♕c8 15 ♗d4 ♗xb5 16 ♖xb5 ♖d8 with equality

(Vidmar-Szabo, Groningen 1946), but correct was 11 ♕b3! with advantage (Sämisch-Réti, Marianske Lazne 1925). Here White urgently needs to post his rook at d1.

> **2.21311** (1 d4 ♘f6 2 c4 g6 3 g3 ♗g7 4 ♗g2 d5 5 cxd5 ♘xd5 6 ♘f3 0-0 7 0-0 c5 8 ♘c3 cxd4 9 ♘xd4 ♘xc3 10 bxc3)

    10 ...   **♘c6**
A logical developing move.
    11 ♘xc6
This leads by force to a slightly better ending. Future practice may concentrate on:
    11 ♗e3 ♘a5 (weaker is 11...♗d7 12 ♖b1 ♘a5 13 ♘b3 ♘c4 14 ♗d4 ♗c6 15 ♗xc6 bxc6 16 ♕d3 ♘a3 17 ♖bd1 with advantage, Romanishin-Kapengut, Kecskemet 1989) 12 ♖b1 (clearly weak is 12 ♕d3 a6 13 ♖ac1 ♕c7 14 c4 ♗d7 15 ♘b3 ♗f5, when only Black has chances, Bolbochan-Najdorf, Buenos Aires 1950, but 12 ♕c1! ♘c4 13 ♗h6 ♗xh6 14 ♕xh6 e5 15 ♖fd1!? would have given a big advantage) 12...♘c4 13 ♗c1 e5 14 ♘b5 (Romanishin-Benjamin, Groningen 1993 – *Game 7*) and after 14...a6 15 ♕xd8 ♖xd8 16 ♗g5! White would have gained some advantage.
    11 ♖b1!? ♘xd4 12 cxd4 ♕xd4 13 ♗e3 ♕xd1 14 ♖fxd1 ♖b8 15 ♗xa7 ♖a8 16 ♗c5 ♖xa2 17 ♗xe7 ♖e8 18 ♗f3! with somewhat the better chances, although such positions usually transpose into a drawn rook ending, with four pawns against three on one wing (Bany-Schmidt, Poland 1988).
    11 ...   **bxc6**
    12 ♕xd8
White does not really want to develop the black rook, but if 12 ♗xc6

♗h3 13 ♕xd8 (13 ♗g2 ♗xg2 14 ♔xg2 ½-½, Petrosian-Korchnoi, Curaçao 1962) 13...♖axd8 14 ♗g2 ♗xg2 15 ♔xg2 ♗xc3 16 ♖b1 ♖d7 ½-½ (Taimanov-Tal, Leningrad 1977).

12 ♗e3 ♗xc3 13 ♖c1 ♕a5 14 ♕b3 ♗d2 15 ♗xd2 ♕xd2 16 ♖xc6 ♗f5 17 ♖c7 ♖ab8 18 ♕a3 ♖b2 is also equal (Capablanca-Petrov, Buenos Aires 1938).

White also achieves nothing with **12 ♕a4 ♗xc3 13 ♖b1 ♗f5 14 ♖b7 ♕d4 15 ♕a3 a5 16 ♗e3 ♗b4!** (Gutman-Steinbacher, Germany 1986).

More interesting is **12 ♗g5!? ♗xc3 13 ♖c1 ♗f6 14 ♗xf6 exf6 15 ♖xc6 ♖b8 16 ♕a1 ♗e6 17 ♖fc1**, and White has a stable advantage (Yurtaev-Petrienko, Podolsk 1989).

12 ... ♖xd8
13 ♗xc6

13 ... ♗xc3
Or **13...♗h3 14 ♗xa8 ♗xf1 15 ♔xf1 ♗xc3 16 ♖b1 ♖xa8 17 ♖b7** (17 ♗e3 e5=) 17...e6 (worse is 17...♔f8 18 ♗a3 ♗f6 19 e4 with advantage, Smejkal-Adamski, Leipzig 1977) 18 ♗h6 a5 (18...♗g7 19 ♗d2! with the idea of 20 e4 and 21 ♔e2 gave White the advantage in A.Petrosian-Szymchak, Yerevan 1979) 19 a4 ♖d8 20 e4!? (after 20 ♖c7

♗b4 21 e4 ♗d2 22 f4 ♗b4 23 e5 ♗f8 24 ♗g5 ♖b8 25 ♖a7 h6 Black held on, Panchenko-Commons, Plovdiv 1984) 20...♗g7 21 ♗e3 ♗d4 22 ♔e2, and Black has not yet solved all his endgame problems.

14 ♖b1 ♗f5
14...♗h3 leads to a position from the previous note.

15 e4
15 ♖b3 ♖ac8 16 ♖xc3 ♖d6= (Tal).
15...♖ac8 16 ♗b7 ♗h3 17 ♗xc8 ♗xf1 18 ♔xf1 ♖xc8 19 ♗e3 ♖c7 20 ♖c1 a6 and Black held the position (Hübner-Tal, Bugojno 1978).

2.21312 (1 d4 ♘f6 2 c4 g6 3 g3 ♗g7 4 ♗g2 d5 5 cxd5 ♘xd5 6 ♘f3 0-0 7 0-0 c5 8 ♘c3 cxd4 9 ♘xd4 ♘xc3 10 bxc3)

---

10 ... ♕a5
11 ♗e3

11 ♖b1!? is a very interesting idea (Janjgava-I.Sokolov, Belgrade 1988) 11...♕xa2? 12 ♗g5! ♘c6 13 ♘xc6 bxc6 14 ♗xe7 ♖e8 15 ♗xc6 ♗h3 16 ♗xa8 ♗xf1 17 ♕d7 ♖xa8 18 ♕c6 ♖f8 19 ♖xf1 and White gained the advantage, but Black does better to play 11...♘a6 12 ♗e3! with only a slight advantage to White. It is strange that this idea has not been developed.

11 ...   ♘c6

Bad is **11...♕xc3** 12 ♖c1 ♕b4 13 ♖b1 ♕a5 (13...♕d6 14 ♘b5 with advantage) 14 ♖xb7! ♗xb7 15 ♗xb7 ♘a6 16 ♗xa8 ♖xa8 17 ♘c6 ♕c7 18 ♕d5, when White's position is clearly better (Kasparov).

12 ♕b3

Nothing is achieved by **12 ♘xc6** bxc6 13 ♗xc6 ♖b8 14 ♕d5 ♕xc3 15 ♖ac1 ♗e6! with equality (Kasparov).

12 ...   ♕a6!

Black's plan is to develop his queen's bishop, and at the same time he defends his c6 knight. It is illogical to improve White's pawn structure: **12...♘xd4** 13 cxd4 ♖d8 14 ♖fd1 ♕b6 15 ♖ab1 ♗f5 16 ♕xb6 axb6 17 ♖xb6 ♖xa2 18 ♖xb7 with a great advantage (Ivkov-Browne, Amsterdam 1971). No better is **12...♘e5** 13 h3 ♖b8 (13...♗d7 14 ♕xb7 ♖ab8 15 ♘b3! ♖xb7 16 ♘xa5 ♖c7 17 ♗d4 with advantage to White, Tukmakov-Kuznetsov, Edmonton 1989) 14 ♖ab1 ♗d7 15 f4 ♘c6 16 ♘xc6 ♗xc6 17 ♗xc6 ♖bc8! 18 ♕xb7 ♕xc3 19 ♔f2! ♕xc6 20 ♕xc6 ♖xc6 21 ♖b7 e5 22 ♖xa7 with an endgame advantage (Tukmakov-I.Sokolov, Biel 1988).

13 ♖ab1

Less good is **13 ♖fe1** on account of 13...♖d8!= (Kasparov), or **13 ♘xc6** bxc6 14 ♗c5 ♗e6 15 ♕a3 ♕xa3 16 ♗xa3 ♗xc3 17 ♖ac1 ♗f6 18 ♖xc6 ♖ac8 19 ♖a6 ♖c7, and again Black has no problems (Revey-Dlugy, London 1987).

13 ...   ♖d8

After **13...♘xd4** 14 cxd4 (14 ♗xd4 ♖b8 15 ♖b2 b6 16 ♕b4 ♗b7 with an equal game, Csom-Osmanovic, Sarajevo 1981) 14...♕xe2 15 ♕a3 ♗f6:

(a) 16 ♖fe1 ♕g4 (or 16...♕h5 17 d5 ♗h3 18 ♗xh3 ♕xh3 19 ♖xb7 ♖fd8 and Black has some counterplay, Dorfman-Ehlvest, Lviv 1984) 17 d5 ♕d7 18 ♗f4 ♖e8 19 ♖bc1 e5!? 20 dxe6 fxe6 21 ♖ed1 and White has compensation for the pawn (Portisch-Korchnoi, Tilburg 1986);

(b) 16 ♖fc1!? (a more interesting try) 16...♖d8 17 ♖b2 ♕h5 18 h4 ♕g4 19 ♖b4 ♕e6 20 d5! ♖xd5 21 ♗xd5 ♕xd5 22 ♕b3 ♗e6 23 ♖xb7 and Black has insufficient compensation for the exchange (Ribli-Hellers, Tilburg 1993), but 18...♗xd4 19 ♕xe7 ♗e6 20 ♗xd4 ♖xd4 21 ♖xb7 a5! would have led to equality.

14 ♕b2

If **14 ♖fd1** ♘xd4 15 ♗xd4 ♕xe2 16 ♖e1 ♕a6 17 ♖xe7 ♗e6 18 ♕xb7 ♕xa2 with equality, but Kasparov suggests **14 ♖fc1!?**, which has not yet been tried.

14 ...   ♘xd4

15 ♗xd4

After **15 cxd4** ♕a4! 16 ♖fd1 ♗f5 17 ♖bc1 ♖ac8 the game is again equal (Kasparov).

15 ...   e5

Worse is **15...♖b8?** 16 ♗xg7 ♔xg7 17 c4+ ♔g8 18 c5 with advantage (Kasparov).

16 ♗e3!?

After **16 ♗c5 ♖b8 17 ♖fd1 ♗f5!** (Ribli-Kasparov, Luzern 1982), correct is 18 ♗xb7 ♕a5! with equality.

Now 16...♖b8 17 ♖fd1 ♗e6 18 ♖xd8+ ♖xd8 19 ♗xb7 ♕xa2 20 ♕xa2 ♗xa2 21 ♖a1 ♗c4 gives an equal game (Kasparov).

2.2132 (1 d4 ♘f6 2 c4 g6 3 g3 ♗g7 4 ♗g2 d5 5 cxd5 ♘xd5 6 ♘f3 0–0 7 0–0 c5 8 ♘c3)
---

8 ... ♘xc3
9 bxc3 ♘c6

White's main alternatives are **10 dxc5 (2.21321)** and **10 e3 (2.21322)**. He also has several other tries:

10 a4?! ♗e6 11 ♗a3 cxd4 12 ♘xd4 ♘xd4 13 cxd4 ♗xd4 14 ♖b1 ♖b8 15 e3 (15 ♖xb7 ♖xb7 16 ♗xb7 ♕b6 and Black has the advantage) 15...♗f6 16 ♕xd8 ♖fxd8 17 ♖xb7 ♖xb7 18 ♗xb7 a5 19 ♖c1 ♖d2!, and only White can have problems (Miles-Hort, Bugojno 1978).

10 d5 ♘a5 11 ♗g5 b6 12 ♕d3 ♗b7 13 e4 ♕d7 14 ♖ac1 ♖fe8 15 ♖fd1 ♕a4 with an equal game (Palatnik-A.Mikhalchishin, Lviv 1984).

10 ♗e3 ♗e6 (10...cxd4 11 ♘xd4 leads to an earlier variation, while 11 cxd4 ♗e6 12 ♕a4 ♗d5 13 ♖ac1 ♖c8 led to equality in Neb.Ristic-Paunovic, Yugoslavia 1989) **11 ♕a4** (after 11 dxc5 ♗xc3 12 ♖c1 ♗g7 13 ♕a4 ♕a5 14 ♕xa5 ♘xa5 15 ♘d4 ♗xd4! 16 ♗xd4 ♘c6 17 ♗xc6 bxc6 the position is equal, Boleslavsky) 11...cxd4 12 ♘xd4 ♘xd4 13 ♗xd4 ♗xd4 14 cxd4 ♗d5 15 e4 ♗c6 16 ♕b4 ♕d6? 17 ♕b2 e6 (Ljubojevic-Timman, Swift 1986), and here 18 d5! would have given White the advantage, but correct was

16...♕b6! 17 ♕xb6 axb6 18 d5 ♗d7 19 ♖fb1 b5 with a complicated game.

10 ♗a3 cxd4 11 ♘xd4 ♘xd4 12 cxd4 ♗xd4 13 ♖b1 ♗b6 14 ♕xd8 ♖xd8 15 ♗xe7 ♖e8 16 ♗b4 (16 ♗f6 ♖xe2 17 ♖be1? ♗xf2+! and wins) 16...♖xe2 17 ♖be1 ♖xe1 18 ♖xe1 ♗e6 and Black is better (Weldon-Paunovic, New York 1987).

10 ♖b1 ♕a5 11 d5 (after 11 ♕d2 ♖d8 12 e3 e5 13 d5 e4! 14 ♘g5 f5 15 c4 h6 16 ♘h3 ♕xd2 17 ♗xd2 ♘e5 Black has the advantage, Kleinegger-A.Mikhalchishin, Dortmund 1997) 11...♘e5 12 ♘xe5 ♗xe5 13 c4 ♕xa2 14 ♗b2 ♗xb2 15 ♕c2 e5! and White does not have compensation for the pawn (Schneider-Jasnikowski, Naestved 1988).

2.21321 (1 d4 ♘f6 2 c4 g6 3 g3 ♗g7 4 ♗g2 d5 5 cxd5 ♘xd5 6 ♘f3 0–0 7 0–0 c5 8 ♘c3 ♘xc3 9 bxc3 ♘c6)
---

10 dxc5

The critical continuation. White does not win a pawn, of course, but he gives up his weak c3 pawn, and the c5 pawn should restrict Black and give him problems, especially with his b7 pawn.

10 ...   ♕a5

A new idea was seen in Delchev-Tukmakov (Bled 1997): **10...♗xc3!?** 11 ♗h6 ♕xd1 12 ♖axd1 ♖e8 (12...♖d8 is interesting) 13 ♘g5 ♗g7! 14 ♗xg7 ♔xg7 15 ♗d5 f6 16 ♘e6+ ♗xe6 17 ♗xe6 ♖ed8 with an excellent game. This is probably Black's best option.

Less good is **10...♕xd1** 11 ♖xd1 ♗xc3 12 ♖b1 ♖d8 13 ♖xd8+ ♘xd8 14 ♗g5 ♔f8 15 ♗e3! (a pretty move, preparing the following knight manoeuvre) 15...♗d7 16 ♘g5 h6 17 ♘e4 ♗g7 18 ♘d2! ♖b8 19 ♘c4 and White has the advantage (I.Horvath-Brunner, Leukerbad 1992).

11   ♗e3

After **11 ♘d4 ♕xc3** (bad is 11...♖d8? 12 ♗e3 ♕xc3? 13 ♘xc6! ♖xd1 14 ♖axd1 ♗f6 15 ♖d8+ ♔g7 16 ♘xe7! winning, Palatnik-Stohl, Tallinn 1986) 12 ♘xc6 bxc6 the position is equal.

11 ...   ♗xc3

Bad is **11...♖d8** 12 ♕b3 ♗e6 13 ♕xb7 ♖ab8 14 ♕xc6! ♗d5 15 ♘d4 and White stands better (Spraggett-Govin, Saragosa 1992).

12   ♖c1   ♗g7

After **12...♗e6** 13 ♘g5 ♗xa2 14 ♕d7 h6 15 ♘e4 ♗g7 16 ♕xb7 ♖fc8 17

♘d6! ♕c7 (Spraggett-Kudrin, New York 1987) 18 ♕xc7 ♖xc7 19 ♘b5 or 18 ♕a6 would have given White some advantage.

13   ♕b3   ♗e6

If **13...♕a6**, then 14 a4! ♕xe2 15 ♖fd1 with advantage, or even stronger 15 ♕b5! (Vakhidov-Yermolinsky, USSR 1982).

Another possibility **13...♖b8** 14 ♘g5 ♕c7 (or 14...♕a6 15 ♗d5 e6 16 ♗g2 h6 17 ♘e4, and White occupies the important d6 square, Slutzky-Avrukh, Israel 1996) 15 ♗d5! e6 16 ♗g2 ♘d4 17 ♗xd4 ♗xd4 18 ♕a4 also leaves White with an advantage (Boleslavsky).

14   ♕xb7   ♖fc8

15   ♘g5

White gains a slight advantage by 15 ♗f4 ♕xa2 16 ♖fd1 ♕b3 17 ♕a6 h6 (Mikenas-Aronin, USSR 1950), when he should play 18 ♘d2 ♕a2 19 ♕xa2 ♗xa2 20 ♘c4 g5 21 ♗e3, according to analysis by Boleslavsky.

Now after 15...♖ab8 16 ♗xc6 ♖xb7 17 ♗xb7 ♖c7 18 ♘xe6 fxe6 19 c6 White's strong passed pawn gives him a clear advantage (Aronin).

2.21321 (1 d4 ♘f6 2 c4 g6 3 g3 ♗g7 4 ♗g2 d5 5 cxd5 ♘xd5 6 ♘f3 0-0 7 0-0 c5 8 ♘c3 ♘xc3 9 bxc3 ♘c6)

---

10   e3

A rather passive move – White simply reinforces his centre, but there are too many 'holes' in his position, and with the exchange of a pair of knights, Black's problems due to lack of space disappear.

Black's main continuations are **10...♗e6** (2.213211) and **10...♕a5** (2.213212).

10...cxd4 is somewhat weaker: 11 cxd4 ♗e6 12 ♗d2 ♗c4 13 ♖e1 ♖c8 14 ♗c3 ♕d7 15 a4 ♖fd8 16 ♕b1 b6 17 ♕b2 e6?! (correct is 17...♗d5!=) 18 ♘d2 with advantage (Garcia-Gutman, Dortmund 1985).

10...b6?! is very risky: 11 ♘e5 ♘xe5 12 ♗xa8 ♗g4 13 f3 ♗h3 14 ♗e4 ♗xf1 15 ♕xf1 ♘d7 16 f4 with some advantage (Arkell-Perkins, London 1994).

10...♕c7 is possible: 11 ♗b2 (11 ♗a3!? b6 12 dxc5!? ♗a6 13 ♘d4! ♗xf1 14 ♕xf1 ♘xd4 15 cxd4 ♖ab8 16 c6! ♖fd8 17 ♖c1 e6 18 ♕a6 ♗f8 19 ♗b2 and White has more than sufficient compensation for the exchange, Kunsztowicz-Chandler, Germany 1980) 11...♖d8 12 ♘d2 ♗e6 13 ♕e2 ♘a5 14 ♗a3 cxd4 15 cxd4 ♖ac8 16 ♗b4 ♗d5 and the position is equal (Padevsky-Vaganian, Kragujevac 1974).

> **2.213211 (1 d4 ♘f6 2 c4 g6 3 g3 ♗g7 4 ♗g2 d5 5 cxd5 ♘xd5 6 ♘f3 0–0 7 0–0 c5 8 ♘c3 ♘xc3 9 bxc3 ♘c6 10 e3)**

10   ...   ♗e6

Immediately occupying the light squares.

11   ♗a3

After **11 ♕a4** cxd4 12 ♘xd4 (if 12 cxd4? ♕d7 13 ♖d1 ♖fd8 14 ♗b2 ♗g4 15 ♕b3 ♖ac8 Black is better, Aaron-Geller, Stockholm 1962) 12...♘xd4 13 cxd4 ♗d5 the position is completely level.

11 a4 can be met by 11...♖c8 12 ♗a3 ♘a5!? (12...b6!?) 13 ♗xc5 ♘b3 14 ♖b1 ♘xc5 15 dxc5 ♕a5 16 ♘d4 ♗c4 with good compensation (Panno-Neuwald, Sao Paulo 1973).

11 ♘d2 is also passive: 11...cxd4 12 cxd4 ♗d5 13 ♗xd5 ♕xd5 14 ♕b3 ♖fd8 15 ♖b1 ♕xb3 16 ♖xb3 b6 and Black is excellently placed (Spiridonov-Vadasz, Budapest 1976).

11   ...   cxd4
12   cxd4

12 ♘xd4 ♗d5 13 ♘xc6 bxc6 14 ♕a4 ♗xg2 15 ♔xg2 ♕d5+ 16 ♔g1 ♗xc3 17 ♗xe7 ♗xa1 leads to complete equality (Wibe-Smejkal, Siegen 1970).

Mochalov-Yuferov (USSR 1972) continued 12...♖c8 (the immediate 12...♗d5= is also possible) 13 ♕d2 (13 ♕a4 should be tried, as on this square the queen is somewhat more active) 13...♕d7 14 ♖fc1 ♗d5 15 ♖c5 e6 16 ♖xd5 ♕xd5 17 ♗xf8 ♗xf8 18 ♕b2 ♕d7 with an equal game.

> **2.213212 (1 d4 ♘f6 2 c4 g6 3 g3 ♗g7 4 ♗g2 d5 5 cxd5 ♘xd5 6 ♘f3 0–0 7 0–0 c5 8 ♘c3 ♘xc3 9 bxc3 ♘c6 10 e3)**

10   ...   ♕a5
11   ♕b3

11 ♗d2 is more passive: 11...♗f5 (if 11...c4 12 e4 with advantage) 12 ♕e2, and now 12...♗e4 is correct.

11 ♗b2 can be met by 11...♖d8 12 ♘d2 ♕c7 13 ♕c2 ♘a5 14 ♖ab1 (Johner-Alekhine, Zurich 1928), and here Black should have played 14...♖b8 with a good game.

11 ... ♖b8

Less good is **11...♗e6** 12 ♕xb7 ♖fc8 13 ♕b2 cxd4 14 cxd4 ♗c4 15 ♗d2 ♕a6 16 ♖fc1 with a slight advantage (Boleslavsky), or **11...cxd4** 12 cxd4 e5!? 13 ♗d2 (bad is 13 dxe5? ♘xe5 14 ♘xe5 ♗xe5 15 ♗b2 ♗e6 16 ♕c2 ♖ac8 with advantage to Black; 14 ♘d4!?) 13...♕a6 14 dxe5 ♘xe5 15 ♘xe5 (or 15 ♘d4!? ♘c4 16 ♗c3 with advantage) 15...♗xe5 16 ♖ac1, again with a slight advantage.

12 ♘d2!

If **12 ♗a3 ♗e6** 13 ♕b2 cxd4 14 cxd4 ♗d5=, or **12 ♘g5 c4!** 13 ♕b2 ♕xg5 14 ♗xc6 bxc6 15 ♕xb8 ♗h3 16 ♕f4 ♕xf4 17 gxf4 ♗xf1 18 ♔xf1 ♖b8= (Boleslavsky).

12 ... ♗d7

Kashdan-Bogoljubow (Bled 1931) went **12...♕c7** 13 ♗a3 b6, and here 14 ♖fc1 was correct with an unclear game.

13 ♗a3

Nothing is achieved by **13 d5 ♘e5** 14 e4 b5, but **13 ♗b2** followed by 14 ♖fd1 and 15 a4 should be played.

Now Filippov-Bologan (Vladivostok 1995) continued 13...b6 14 ♖fd1 ♖fc8, and after 15 ♗b2 a double-edged battle would have been in prospect.

2.22 (1 d4 ♘f6 2 c4 g6 3 g3 ♗g7 4 ♗g2 d5 5 cxd5 ♘xd5 6 ♘f3 0–0 7 0–0)

7	...	♘c6
8	e4	♘b6
9	d5	♘a5

Not the most accurate move order on Black's part, since it allows White some additional possibilities.

9...♘b8 is too passive: after 10 ♘c3 c6 11 ♘d4 ♘a6 12 ♘c2 cxd5 13 exd5 ♘c7 14 ♖e1 e6 15 dxe6 ♘xe6 16 ♕e2 ♖b8 17 ♗e3 ♗d7 18 ♖ad1 White has the advantage (Djuric-P.Nikolic, Yugoslavia 1985).

10 ♕e1

10 ♕c2!? is good: 10...♘ac4 (after 10...c6!? 11 dxc6 ♕c7 12 ♘c3 ♕xc6 13 ♗g5! or 11...♘xc6 12 ♖d1 ♕c7 13 ♘a3! White has a clear advantage) 11 ♘bd2 (11 ♖d1!?) 11...♘d6 (or 11...♘xd2 12 ♗xd2 with a great advantage) 12 ♖d1 ♗d7 13 e5! (after 13 ♘b3 ♘bc4 14 ♘bd4 c5 15 dxc6 bxc6 16 e5 ♘xe5 17 ♘xe5 ♗xe5 18 ♘xc6 ♗xc6 19 ♗xc6 ♖c8 20 ♗h6 White has some advantage, A.Mikhalchishin-Leonidov, Zhitomir 1977) 13...♗f5 14 ♕b3 ♘e4 15 ♘f1 ♕d7 16 ♗f4 and White has a serious advantage (analysis).

10 ... ♘ac4
11 ♘c3

Here Black has several possibilities:

11...♖e8? 12 b3 ♘e5 13 ♘xe5 ♗xe5 14 ♗g5 ♗g7 15 ♕e3 and White is better (Ilic-Herbrechtsmeier, Kusadasi 1990).

11...♗g4 12 b3 ♘d6 13 e5 ♘dc8 14 ♘h4 with advantage to White (Ilincic-Uhlmann, Hartberg 1991).

11...e5?! 12 b3 ♘d6 13 a4! a5 14 ♗a3 ♖e8 (14...♗d7 or 15...♕e7 is slightly preferable) 15 ♕e2 ♗g4 16 h3 ♗xf3 17 ♕xf3 ♕d7 18 h4! and Black has no real counterplay (Jukic-A.Mikhalchishin, Lienz 1988).

11...c6 12 b3 cxd5!? (a practically forced sacrifice – after 12...♘a5 13 ♗g5 cxd5 14 exd5 ♘xd5 15 ♘xd5 ♕xd5 16 ♖d1 ♕b5 17 a4 ♕a6 18 b4 ♘c4 19 ♕xe7 White has the advantage, Djuric-Rajkovic, Budapest 1990, or 12...♘e5 13 ♘xe5 ♗xe5 14 ♗h6 ♖e8 15 ♖d1 ♕d6 16 ♕e3 and Black has difficulties, Fominykh-Rosenthal, Budapest 1990) 13 bxc4 dxe4 14 ♘g5 f5 15 c5 ♘a4 16 ♗d2 ♘xc5 17 ♗e3 ♘d3 18 ♕d2 h6 19 ♘h3 g5 with a complicated game (Wojtkiewicz-Bonin, New York 1989).

11...e6 12 b3, and now:

(a) 12...♘d6 13 dxe6 ♗xe6 14 e5 ♘f5 15 ♗g5 with advantage, Gutman-Wolff, New York 1987;

(b) 12...♕f6 is too risky: 13 bxc4 ♕xc3 14 ♕xc3 ♗xc3 15 ♖b1 ♘xc4 (15...exd5 16 cxd5 ♖e8 17 ♗d2! ♗g7 18 ♖fe1 with the better game for White, Ilic-I.Ivanov, Saint John 1988) 16 ♗h6 ♗g7 17 ♗xg7 ♔xg7 18 dxe6 and White has some advantage;

(c) 12...♘e5! 13 ♘xe5 ♗xe5 14 ♗b2 ♕e7 15 ♖c1 ♗d7 16 ♕d2 ♖ad8 17 ♖fd1 ♖fe8 18 h4 h5 19 dxe6 ♗xe6 20 ♘d5 ♗xd5 21 exd5 ♕d6 with a good

game for Black (Pigusov-Epishin, Biel 1993).

2.23 (1 d4 ♘f6 2 c4 g6 3 g3 ♗g7 4 ♗g2 d5 5 cxd5 ♘xd5 6 ♘f3 0–0 7 0–0)

---

7 ... ♘b6
8 ♘c3

Other possibilities:

8 e4 ♗g4! 9 d5 c6 10 h3 (after 10 ♘c3 cxd5 11 ♘xd5 ♘c6 12 ♗g5 h6 13 ♗f4 ♖c8 14 h3 ♗e6 Black is better, Peresipkin-Gutman, USSR 1971) 10...♗xf3 11 ♕xf3 (after 11 ♗xf3 cxd5 12 exd5 ♘8d7 13 ♘c3 ♘c4 14 ♖e1 ♖c8 15 ♖b1 ♖e8 16 ♘e4 ♘db6 only White can have problems, Groszpeter-Yrjola, Sochi 1984) 11...♘8d7 12 ♘c3 ♖c8 13 ♖d1 cxd5 14 ♘xd5 ♘xd5 15 exd5 ♘c5 16 ♖b1 b6 17 b3 ♘b7, and Black transfers his knight to d6 and gains counter-chances (Haik-Hulak, Marseille 1987).

8 a4 a5 (after 8...c5 9 a5 ♘c4 10 ♕a4 ♘d6 11 dxc5 ♗d7 12 ♕f4 White has the advantage, Garcia Palermo-Doncevic, Germany 1987) 9 ♘c3 ♘c6 10 ♘b5 ♘b4 11 ♗f4 ♘4d5 12 ♗d2 (12 ♗g5 c6 13 ♘c3 ♗g4 14 h3 ♗xf3 ♘c7! with chances for both sides, Vladimirov-Ye, Asia 1993) 12...♘c4 13 e4 ♘xd2 14 ♕xd2 and White has some advantage.

Now Black's main possibilities are **8...♘a6 (2.231)** and **8...♘c6 (2.232)**. Two rare and rather passive continuations must also be mentioned:

8...c6 9 h3 ♗e6 10 e4 ♕d7 11 ♔h2 ♘a6 12 a4 ♖ad8 13 a5 ♘a8 (13...♘c4? 14 b3) 14 ♗e3 ♘8c7 15 ♕e2 ♕d6 (Baburin-Dvoiris, Russia 1988), and now 16 ♖fd1 should be played, although even then Black has counterplay.

8...a5 9 ♗f4 (less critical is 9 h3 ♘c6 10 d5 ♘b4 11 e4 f5 12 ♘g5 h6 13 a3 ♘a6 14 ♘f3 fxe4 15 ♘h4 g5 16 ♘g6 ♖f6 17 ♕h5 ♗f5 18 ♗xe4 ♕e8 19 ♗xf5 ♖xf5 20 ♖e1 ♔h7 21 ♘f4!? with a complicated game, Wojtkiewicz-Mastrokoukos, Corfu 1991) 9...c6 10 ♕c1 ♘a6 (10...♖e8 11 ♖d1 ♘a6 12 h3 a4 13 e4 ♗d7 14 ♘e5 ♕c8 15 ♔h2 ♖d8 16 ♗g5 with the freer game, Botvinnik-Smyslov, The Hague/Moscow 1948) 11 ♖d1 ♘c7 12 ♗h6 a4 13 h3 ♖a5 14 ♗xg7 ♔xg7 15 ♘e4 f6 16 ♘c5 and Black is deprived of serious counterplay (Furman-Tukmakov, USSR 1969).

2.231 (1 d4 ♘f6 2 c4 g6 3 g3 ♗g7 4 ♗g2 d5 5 cxd5 ♘xd5 6 ♘f3 0–0 7 0–0 ♘b6 8 ♘c3)

8   ...   ♘a6

A fairly logical continuation, which removes the knight from a possible attack d4-d5, but, on the other hand, reduces the pressure on the centre. Black wishes to play ...c7-c5 after due preparation.

9   ♗f4

Also possible is **9 b3** c6 10 ♗b2 ♘c7 11 ♕c2 a5 12 ♖fd1 ♗f5 13 e4 ♗g4 14 h3 ♗xf3 15 ♗xf3 with a slight advantage (Gheorghiu-Poch, Mar del Plata 1971), or **9 e4** ♗g4 10 d5 ♕d7 11 ♕b3 ♗h3 12 ♗e3 and White's chances are again preferable (Bertok-Lundquist, Reggio Emilia 1978). In both cases one senses a lack of pressure on the centre by Black.

9   ...   c5

9...c6 is more passive: 10 ♕c1 ♗g4 11 ♖d1 ♖e8 12 ♗h6 ♗f6 13 ♘g5 ♕c7 14 h3 ♗c8 15 ♘f3 and Black has problems with space (Boleslavsky-Malich, Budapest 1965).

10   d5

The alternative is **10 dxc5** ♘xc5 11 ♕c1 ♘ca4 (11...♗d7 12 ♗h6 ♗c6 13 ♗xg7 ♔xg7 14 ♕e3 ♘cd7 15 ♖fd1 ♕e8, Davis-Popovic, Vrsac 1989, and here 16 ♖d4!? would have given an advantage; if 11...♘ba4 12 ♗e5!?) 12 ♘xa4 ♘xa4 13 ♗e5 ♗xe5 14 ♘xe5 ♕d4 15 ♕c7 ♕xb2 16 ♕xe7 ♗e6 17 ♘d3 ♕xe2 18 ♘f4 and Black has problems (Cvitan-Lehmann, Budapest 1990).

10   ...   c4

It is risky to accept the pawn sacrifice: **10...♗xc3** 11 bxc3 ♕xd5 12 ♕c1 ♕h5 13 h4! f6 14 e4 c4 (14...e5!? 15 ♗h6 ♖d8 16 ♘h2 ♕e2 with the idea of ...♕c4-f7 is the only alternative worth trying, Vilela) 15 e5! ♘c5 16 ♗h6 ♖d8 17 ♕e3 ♘e6 (17...♘d3 18 exf6) 18 exf6 exf6 19 ♖ad1 ♘d5 20 ♕e4! and White has a great advantage (Rodriguez-Vilela, Cuba 1989).

11   ♕d2!

If **11 e4** ♗g4 12 ♕d2 ♗xf3 13 ♗xf3 ♘c5 14 ♖ad1 ♘bd7 15 ♗e2 ♖c8 (Savchenko-Dvoiris, Simferopol 1988), and here White should have played 16 ♗xc4 ♘xe4 17 ♘xe4 ♖xc4 18 ♕e2 with advantage.

Malaniuk-Dvoiris (Simferopol 1988) now continued 11...♗xc3 (if 11...♗g4

12 ♘e5) 12 bxc3 ♕xd5 13 ♘d4 ♕a5 14 ♖ab1 ♗d7 (or 14...♖d8 15 ♖fd1 e5 16 ♗g5 with pressure) 15 ♗xb7 ♖ad8 16 ♗h6 ♖fe8 17 ♕e3 ♘c7 18 ♘c6 with the initiative for White thanks to Black's weakness on the dark squares.

> **2.232 (1 d4 ♘f6 2 c4 g6 3 g3 ♗g7 4 ♗g2 d5 5 cxd5 ♘xd5 6 ♘f3 0–0 7 0–0 ♘b6 8 ♘c3)**

8 ... ♘c6
Here we consider: **9 ♗f4 (2.2321)** and **9 d5 (2.2322)**.

> **2.2321 (1 d4 ♘f6 2 c4 g6 3 g3 ♗g7 4 ♗g2 d5 5 cxd5 ♘xd5 6 ♘f3 0–0 7 0–0 ♘b6 8 ♘c3 ♘c6)**

9 ♗f4
A fairly logical developing move, but Black has sufficient possibilities, and in particular the d4 pawn is too valuable to be given up.

9 ... ♘xd4
The plan with **9...♗g4** is fundamentally incorrect: 10 d5 ♗xf3 (or 10...♘a5 11 ♘e5 ♗f5 12 e4 ♗c8 13 ♘d3 e6 14 dxe6 ♗xe6 15 ♘c5 with strong pressure, Miralles-Damljanovic, Vrsac 1989) 11 ♗xf3 ♘d4 (after 11...♘e5 12 ♗g2 c6 13 e4 cxd5 14 exd5 ♘ec4 15 ♕e2 ♖c8 16 ♖ac1 ♕d7 17 b3 ♘d6 18 ♗e5 White has the advantage Dzindzichashvili-Tisdall, Hastings 1977) 12 ♗g2 e5 13 dxe6 ♘xe6 14 ♗xb7 ♖b8 15 ♗a6 with advantage.

9...e6 is possible: 10 ♕c1 (after 10 e3 h6 11 h4 ♘b4 12 ♕d2 ♘4d5 13 e4 ♘xf4 14 ♕xf4 ♕d6! 15 ♕d2 c6 the position is equal, Miralles-Kasparov, Paris 1989; if 10 ♖c1 h6 11 b3, then 11...a5 with the idea of 12...a4 or 12...♕d7 is correct) 10...♘xd4 11 ♘xd4

♕xd4 12 ♗xb7 (after 12 ♖d1 ♕c4 13 ♗xb7 ♖ad8 14 ♗f3 c6 15 ♗h6 ♖xd1+ 16 ♘xd1 ♕xc1 17 ♗xc1 ♘d5 the game is equal, Donchev-Ftacnik, Prague 1985; White cannot achieve anything by exchanging the d4 and b7 pawns) 12...♖ab8 13 ♖d1 (if 13 ♗g2 ♘a4 Black seizes the initiative, Dzindzichashvili-Grigorian, USSR 1972; after 13 ♗f3 ♖fc8 14 ♘b5 ♕a4 15 ♗c6 ♗d5 16 ♗xd5 ♘xd5 17 ♘c3 ♘xf4 18 gxf4 ♕a5 Black has a slight advantage, Gavrikov) 13...♕b4 14 ♗f3 ♘a4 15 ♘xa4 ♕xa4 16 b3 ♕a6 17 ♗h6 ♗xh6 18 ♕xh6 ♖fd8 19 ♖dc1 ♕a3 with equality (Lechntinsky-Stohl, Czechoslovakia 1985). In view of the weakness of his queenside, White has no chance of an advantage.

10 ♘xd4 e5

After **10...♗xd4** 11 ♘b5 ♗xb2 12 ♖b1 ♕xd1 13 ♖fxd1 ♗g7 14 ♘xc7 ♖b8 15 ♘d5 e5 (15...♘xd5? 16 ♗xd5 e5 17 ♗e3 b6 18 ♗c5 and wins) 16 ♗g5 ♗e6! (16...♘xd5 17 ♗xd5 ♗f5 18 e4 ♗g4 19 ♖dc1 ♖fc8 20 ♖xc8+ ♗xc8 21 ♗d8 and White has a great advantage) 17 ♘xb6 axb6 18 a3 White has some advantage (Vainstein).

11 ♘c6
Or **11 ♘db5?!** exf4 12 ♕xd8 ♖xd8:

(a) 13 ♘xc7? ♖b8 14 ♖fd1 (14 gxf4 is risky in view of 14...♗g4, with more than sufficient compensation for the pawn) 14...♗g4 15 h3 ♗xc3 16 hxg4 ♗e5 with advantage to Black (Liabotro-Tisdall, Oslo 1986);

(b) 13 ♖fd1 ♗d7 14 ♘xc7 ♖ac8 15 ♘7d5 ♘xd5 16 ♘xd5 ♗a4 17 b3 ♗xa1 18 ♖xa1 ♖xd5 19 ♗xd5 ♗c6 and Black holds on (Chiburdanidze-Brustman, Yerevan 1996).

Now 11...♕xd1 12 ♘e7+ ♔h8 13 ♖fxd1 exf4 14 ♘xc8 ♖axc8 15 ♗xb7 ♖b8 16 ♗a6 fxg3 17 hxg3 ♗xc3 (or 17...♖fd8 18 ♖ac1 c6 19 ♖xd8+ ♖xd8 20 ♗d3 f5, also with an equal game, Helmers-Ftacnik, Aarhus 1983) 18 bxc3 ♘a4 19 ♖d5 ♖b2 20 ♖a5 ♘xc3 21 ♔f1 led to a roughly equal ending in Karasev-Tukmakov (USSR 1970).

> **2.2322 (1 d4 ♘f6 2 c4 g6 3 g3 ♗g7 4 ♗g2 d5 5 cxd5 ♘xd5 6 ♘f3 0-0 7 0-0 ♘b6 8 ♘c3 ♘c6)**

9 d5

The main position of this variation. White plays to seize space, but in so doing he opens up the bishop at g7 and allows various attacks on his centre. Black's two main possibilities are

9...♘b8 (2.23221) and 9...♘a5 (2.23222).

> **2.23221 (1 d4 ♘f6 2 c4 g6 3 g3 ♗g7 4 ♗g2 d5 5 cxd5 ♘xd5 6 ♘f3 0-0 7 0-0 ♘b6 8 ♘c3 ♘c6 9 d5)**

9 ...   ♘b8

This old continuation is less logical and active than the main move 9...♘a5, but it is better than might appear at first sight.

10 e4   c6

Here White has several alternatives:

11 ♘d4 (the least promising) 11...e6 (weaker is 11...♘a6 12 ♘c2 cxd5 13 exd5 ♘c7 14 ♖e1 with advantage, Djuric-Z.Nikolic, Novi Sad 1985) 12 ♘b3 exd5 13 exd5 cxd5 14 ♘xd5 ♘c6 with equal chances (Smyslov).

11 ♕b3 cxd5 (11...♘a6 12 ♖d1 cxd5 13 exd5 ♗f5 14 ♗e3 ♖c8 15 ♗d4 ♘c5 16 ♕b5 leads to an advantage for White, Palatnik-Krnic, Krk 1976, while 11...e6 also allows him the better game after 12 ♗g5 f6 13 dxe6 ♕e7 14 ♗f4 ♗xe6 15 ♕c2 ♘8d7 16 ♘d4 ♗f7 17 ♖ad1 ♘e5 18 ♗c1 ♖fd8 19 f4 c5 20 ♘f5) 12 ♘xd5 ♘xd5 13 exd5 ♘d7 14 ♗e3 ♘f6 (14...♘b6 15 ♖fd1 ♗d7 16 a4 with the better game, Vidmar-Germek,

Yugoslavia 1947) 15 ♖ad1! ♘e8 16 ♖fe1 ♘d6 17 ♗g5, and the pressure on e7 gives White an appreciable advantage (Nesis-Ortel, corr. 1980).

11 ♗g5 h6 12 ♗f4 cxd5 (12...♗g4 13 h3 e5!? 14 dxe6 ♗xe6 15 ♕c1 g5 16 ♗e5 ♗xe5 17 ♘xe5 with advantage, first tried in Z.Ilic-Djuric, Svetozarevo 1990) **13 ♘xd5 ♘xd5 14 exd5 e6 15 ♕c1 g5 16 ♗e5 exd5 17 ♗xg7 ♔xg7 18 h4** with serious compensation for the pawn (Yurkov-Muratov, USSR 1967).

2.23222 (1 d4 ♘f6 2 c4 g6 3 g3 ♗g7 4 ♗g2 d5 5 cxd5 ♘xd5 6 ♘f3 0–0 7 0–0 ♘b6 8 ♘c3 ♘c6 9 d5)

---

9 ...   ♘a5

The main continuation, which occurs in 90% of cases.

10 e4

Other variations are unpromising for White, and so their consideration is of purely theoretical significance:

10 ♘d4?! e5! **11 ♘b3 ♘ac4 12 e4 ♕e7** (12...f5! is equally good) **13 ♕e2 ♗d7 14 ♘d2 ♘d6 15 a4 f5** with a complicated game (Birnboim-Rechlis, Beer Sheva 1987).

10 ♘g5 (the idea is to manoeuvre the knight via e4 to c5 and support the pressure on Black's queenside, but it obviously requires a great expenditure of time) **10...c6 11 dxc6 ♘xc6 12 ♘ge4 ♗f5** (12...♘c4!? is also possible; clearly worse is 12...h6 13 ♘c5 ♘d7 14 ♘d3 ♘de5 15 ♘xe5 ♕xd1 16 ♖xd1 ♘xe5 17 b3 with an obvious advantage to White, Bagirov-Szymczak, Kirovakan 1978) **13 ♗f4 ♕c8 14 ♖c1 ♘d4 15 ♖e1 ♖e8** with an equal game (Stangl-Mohr, Altensteig 1989).

10 ♗e3 (an interesting attempt to infuse fresh spirit into this variation,

although rather unnatural) **10...♗xc3** (after 10...♘ac4 11 ♗d4 ♘xb2 12 ♕b3 White has the more promising position) **11 ♗xb6 axb6 12 bxc3 c6 13 e4 ♗g4 14 ♕d4 ♗xf3 15 ♗xf3 cxd5 16 exd5 ♖c8 17 ♖ab1 ♖c4 18 ♕xb6 ♖xc3** with an obvious draw (Fominykh-Stohl, Rimavska Sobota 1991).

10 ...   c6

The main position of this basic variation. Black has no reason to defer the thematic ...c7-c6, e.g. **10...♗g4 11 ♗g5 h6 12 ♗f4 ♘ac4 13 ♕c2 c6 14 a4 cxd5 15 a5 ♘d7 16 ♘xd5** and White has the advantage (Z.Ilic-Herbrechts-meier, Rovinj 1981).

Now the main variations are **11 ♖e1 (2.232221)**, **11 ♗f4 (2.232222)** and **11 ♗g5 (2.232223)**. After other moves Black does not experience any difficulties:

11 h3 ♗xc3 (11...♘ac4 12 ♕e2 ♗d7 13 ♖d1 cxd5 14 exd5 ♖c8 15 ♘d4 ♘d6 16 ♗f4 ♖e8 17 ♖ac1 ♖c4 18 ♘f3 ♕c8 19 ♘e5 ♖c5 20 ♘e4 gives White the better game, Baburin-Chuchelov, Novosibirsk 1989) **12 bxc3 cxd5 13 exd5 ♘xd5 14 ♗h6 ♖e8 15 ♘e5 ♗e6 16 c4 ♘b6 17 ♕e1! ♘bxc4 18 ♕c3 f6 19 ♖fe1 ♖c8 20 ♖ad1** with an attack (Bronstein-Lputian, Ubeda 1996).

11 ♘g5?! h6 (better than 11...cxd5 12 exd5 ♗f5 13 h3 ♖c8 14 ♖e1 h6 15 ♘ge4 ½-½, Marovic-Hort, Rovinj/Zagreb 1970) 12 ♘h3 cxd5 13 exd5 ♗f5 14 ♘f4 ♘ac4 15 ♘fe2 ♕d7 16 ♖e1 ♖ad8 with somewhat the better chances for Black (Marovic-Smyslov, Rovinj/Zagreb 1970).

11 dxc6?! ♘xc6 (or 11...♕xd1 12 ♖xd1 ♘xc6 13 ♖b1 ♗g4 14 h3 ♗xf3 15 ♗xf3 ♘d4 and Black stands better, Stolyar-Lederer, Beer Sheva 1990) 12 ♗f4 ♗e6 13 ♕c1 ♗g4! 14 ♗h6 ♗xf3 15 ♗xf3 ♖c8 16 ♖d1 ♘d4 17 ♗xg7 ♔xg7 18 ♕f4 ♘c4 with the initiative for Black (Webb-Banas, Decin 1977).

11 ♘d4?! (an ineffective loss of time – this allows Black to open the position by interposing ...e6 or ...e5, whereas White's options are limited, since dxe6 is not possible) 11...cxd5 12 exd5 e6 (12...e5! is also possible: 13 ♘b3 ♘ac4 14 a4 ♘d6 15 ♕e2 ♗f5 16 ♖d1 ♕c7 17 ♗e3 ♕c4 with advantage to Black, Reshevsky-Kavalek, New York 1972) 13 ♘b3 (13 ♘de2 exd5 14 ♘xd5 ♗g4! is somewhat weaker) 13...♘xd5! (13...♘xb3 14 axb3 exd5 15 ♘xd5 ♗e6 16 ♘xb6 ♕xb6 17 ♗e3 ♕b5 and Black has only equality, Priehoda-Plachetka, Trnava 1986) 14 ♘xd5 exd5 15 ♕xd5 (15 ♗xd5 ♘c6 also favours Black, Hjartarson-P.Popovic, Belgrade 1987) 15...♕xd5 16 ♗xd5 ♘c6! 17 ♘c5 ♘d4 18 ♔g2 ♖d8 with an appreciable advantage to Black (Tibensky-Stohl, Novi Smokovec 1990).

2.232221 (1 d4 ♘f6 2 c4 g6 3 g3 ♗g7 4 ♗g2 d5 5 cxd5 ♘xd5 6 ♘f3 0–0 7 0–0 ♘b6 8 ♘c3 ♘c6 9 d5 ♘a5 10 e4 c6)

---

11 ♖e1

The idea of this move is to exert pressure on e7 after the usual opening of the e-file. It used to occur earlier, but for a long time was overshadowed by the main continuation 11 ♗g5. Recently it once again appeared, but Black, after some initial failures, found a convincing way to equalise.

11 ... ♖e8!

The most useful move. Black defends his e7 pawn and supports ...e7-e6, which is especially effective when the white queen is developed at e2.

Other moves are less good:

11...cxd5?! (the most unfortunate reply to 11 ♖e1) 12 exd5 ♘ac4 (12...e6 13 ♗g5! f6 14 ♗e3 ♘xd5 15 ♘xd5 ♕xd5 16 ♕xd5 exd5 17 ♘d4 ♖d8 18 ♘b5! also brings no relief, Vadasz-Weinstein, Budapest 1976) 13 ♗g5 (White should avoid 13 ♘d4?! e5 14 ♘f3 ♖e8 15 b3 ♘d6 when Black, by blockading the d5 pawn, achieves an ideal position, Hug-Altyzer, Zurich 1989) 13...♖e8, and now:

(a) 14 ♕b3 ♗f5 (also weak is 14...h6 15 ♗f4 g5 16 ♗e5 g4 17 ♗f1 ♘xe5 18 ♘xe5 with advantage to White, Kozma-Jansa, Czechoslovakia 1977) 15 ♖ad1 ♕d7 (as usual in these positions, 15...♘xb2 16 ♕xb2 ♘a4 17 ♘xa4

♗xb2 18 ♘xb2 is dangerous) 16 ♗f4?
♗g4 17 ♖c1 ♖ac8 18 ♘e5 ♘xe5 19
♗xe5 ♗xe5 20 ♖xe5 ♘c4 21 ♖ee1
♘d2! with advantage to Black
(Kharitonov-Dvoiris, Gorky 1989), but
White should have played 16 ♘d4! with
the better game;

(b) 14 ♕e2 ♗g4 (or 14...h6 15 ♗xe7
♕d7 16 d6 ♘xd6 17 ♖ad1 with
advantage) 15 ♖ad1 h6 16 ♗f4 g5 17
♗c1 and Black has many weaknesses
on the kingside.

11...♘ac4!? 12 ♕e2 (in Gabdrakh-
manov-Urban, Beskidy 1991, White
played the weaker 12 a4 a5 13 ♕b3
♕d6 14 ♕c2 ♗g4 15 h3 ♗xf3 16 ♗xf3
♕b4 and Black gained the advantage)
12...♗g4 (12...cxd5?! transposes into
the previous variation) 13 dxc6 (13 h3
is worth trying) 13...bxc6 14 h3 ♗xf3
15 ♗xf3, and now instead of 15...a5?!
16 ♗g5 ♕d6 17 ♕c2 with some
advantage to White (Yurtaev-Belov,
Podolsk 1989), exerting pressure on the
queenside by 15...♕d6 16 ♗f4 ♕b4
would have given Black the better
game.

11...♗g4 (unconvincing; logically,
White should gain the advantage) 12 h3
♗xf3 13 ♕xf3 ♖c8 (or 13...♘ac4 14 b3
♘e5 15 ♕e2 cxd5 16 exd5 ♖c8 17 ♗d2
with advantage) 14 ♗f4 ♘ac4
(14...cxd5 15 exd5 ♘ac4 16 b3 ♗xc3
17 ♕xc3 ♘d6 ♘a3 18 ♕b2 ♘c2 19
♗h6 also leads to an advantage for
White) 15 b3 ♘e5 16 ♕e3 cxd5 17
♘xd5 ♘bd7 18 ♖ac1! ♖xc1 19 ♖xc1 e6
20 ♖c8! and White is better (Khari-
tonov-Timoshchenko, USSR 1989).

12 ♗g5

After **12 h3** ♗xc3 13 bxc3 cxd5 14
exd5 ♕xd5 15 ♗a3 White has
compensation for the pawn, but not
more. David-Schmidt (Polanica Zdroj

1989) ended in a draw after 15...♕xd1
16 ♖axd1 ♘c6 17 ♘d4 ♗d7! 18 ♘xc6
♗xc6 19 ♗xe7 ♗xg2 20 ♔xg2 ♖ac8 21
♗f6.

12   ...   h6
13   ♗f4   ♘ac4

13...cxd5 14 exd5 ♘ac4 is also good.
White must move his queen, but where
to? The variations 15 ♕e2 e5 16 dxe6
♖xe6 17 ♖ad1 ♕f8 18 ♕c2 ♖xe1+ 19
♖xe1 ♗e6 and 15 ♕b3 g5!? (or 15...e5
16 dxe6 ♗xe6 17 ♖ad1 ♕c8 18 ♘d4)
16 ♗e5 ♘xe5 17 ♘xe5 ♘d7!? favour
Black. That only leaves 15 ♕c1, but this
too is unsatisfactory because of 15...g5
16 ♗e5 ♘xe5 17 ♘xe5 and now after
17...♘d7?! 18 ♘c4 White has the
advantage (Palatnik-David, Hradec
Kralove 1989), but 17...e6! 18 dxe6
♖xe6 19 ♘f3 ♗d7 would have given
Black excellent chances.

14 ♕b3

Or **14 ♕e2** g5 15 ♗c1 cxd5 16 exd5
♗g4 17 ♕e4 ♕d7 18 a4 ♖ac8 19 a5
♘d6 with advantage to Black
(Shestoperov-Khasin, USSR 1973).

14   ...   e5
15   dxe6   ♗xe6
16   ♕c2

Or **16 ♖ad1** ♕e7 17 ♕c2 ♕b4, again
with equality.

16...♗g4! (very precise; if 16...♕e7 17 b3 ♘a3 18 ♕c1! and White is slightly better) 17 b3 ♗xf3 18 ♗xf3 ♕f6! 19 ♘e2 ♘e5 20 ♗g2 g5 21 ♗xe5! ½-½ (Baburin-Janjgava, USSR 1989). According to Janjgava, after 21...♕xe5 22 ♖ad1 ♖ad8 23 f4 ♕b2 the game is equal.

2.232222 (1 d4 ♘f6 2 c4 g6 3 g3 ♗g7 4 ♗g2 d5 5 cxd5 ♘xd5 6 ♘f3 0–0 7 0–0 ♘b6 8 ♘c3 ♘c6 9 d5 ♘a5 10 e4 c6)

---

11 ♗f4

The modern continuation, the idea of which is to play ♖ac1 and b2-b3 as soon as possible. In the variation 11 ♗g5 h6 12 ♗f4 this is hard to achieve, since at any moment Black can attack the bishop at f4 by ...g6-g5. But it is obvious that by including ...h7-h6 Black simultaneously both strengthens and weakens his position. The drawbacks are that the activity of his dark-square bishop is restricted by the need to defend the pawn, and that White is granted additional attacking chances on the kingside.

11 ... cxd5

The best reply.

11...♘ac4 12 ♕e2 (too sharp is 12 b3 ♗xc3 13 bxc4 ♗xa1 14 ♕xa1 cxd5 15 cxd5 f6 16 ♘d4 ♗d7 17 e5 ♖c8, when White's attack comes to a halt, Neverov-Beshukov, St Petersburg 1996) 12...♗g4 (12...cxd5 transposes into the main line) 13 h3 e5 14 dxe6 ♗xe6 15 ♖ac1 h6 16 g4 g5 17 ♗g3 ♘d7 18 ♖fd1 gives White the advantage (Lin Weiguo-Ftacnik, Bejing 1996), but after the correct 16...♕f6 the position is very unclear.

11...e5 12 dxe6 ♗xe6 13 ♕c2 ♘ac4 14 ♖ad1 ♕c8 15 b3 ♘a3 16 ♕c1 leads to an advantage for White (Greenfeld-Svidler, Haifa 1996).

11...♗g4 also fails to equalise: 12 h3 ♗xf3 13 ♕xf3 cxd5 14 exd5 ♘ac4 15 b3 ♘d6 16 ♖ac1 ♖c8 17 ♖fe1 (Z.Ilic-Nestorovic, Svetozarevo 1990).

With **11...h6** Black transposes into the main variation 11 ♗g5 h6 12 ♗f4 a tempo down. Z.Ilic-Georges (Lenk 1991) continued 12 ♕c1 cxd5 13 ♘xd5 ♘xd5 14 exd5 g5 15 ♗e5 f6 16 ♗c7 ♕xd5 17 ♖d1 ♕b5 18 ♘d4 ♕b4 19 a3 ♕a4 20 b3 with advantage.

11...♗xc3 must also be considered, but here too after 12 bxc3 cxd5 13 ♗h6 ♖e8 (premature is 13...dxe4 14 ♗xf8 ♕xd1 15 ♖fxd1 exf3 16 ♗h6 ♗g4 17 h3 with advantage to White) 14 ♕d4 f6 15 ♖ad1 White has an excellent attacking position.

12 exd5 ♘ac4

After **12...♗xc3** 13 bxc3 ♕xd5 (or 13...♘xd5 14 ♗h6 ♖e8 15 ♕d4 ♘f6 16 ♘e5 with compensation, Euwe-Seewald, corr. 1981) 14 ♖e1 ♕xd1 15 ♖axd1 the critical position of the 11 ♗f4 variation is reached. Now after 15...♖e8 (or 15...♘c6 16 ♘d4) 16 ♗g5 White has the initiative for the sacrificed pawn.

13 ♕e2

If **13 ♕b3** Black should play 13...e5. If 13...♘xb2, then 14 ♕xb2 (preferable to 14 a4 ♘2xa4 15 ♘xa4 ♗xa1 16 ♖xa1 ♕xd5 17 ♕xd5 ♘xd5 with a good game, D.Werner-Hünerkopf, Germany 1983) 14...♘a4 15 ♘xa4 ♗xb2 16 ♘xb2 and, as usual in such positions, the three pieces are stronger than the queen.

Now Black has these possibilities:

13...♗d7 14 ♖ac1 ♖c8 15 b3 ♘d6 16 ♘e5 (16 ♗e5!?) 16...♖xc3 17 ♖xc3 ♗b5 18 ♖c4 f6 with a complicated game (Jansa-Scholl, Amsterdam 1973).

13...♖e8 14 ♘e5 ♘xe5 15 ♗xe5 ♗xe5 16 ♕xe5 ♘c4 17 ♕e2 ♘d6 ½-½ (Ilic-Ilincic, Zlatibor 1989).

13...e5 14 dxe6 ♗xe6 15 ♖fd1 ♕c8 16 ♖ac1 ♖e8 17 b3 with advantage.

13...♗g4 14 ♖ac1 ♖c8 15 b3 ♘d6 16 ♗e5 ♗h6 17 ♖cd1 ♘d7 18 ♗d4 ♘f5, and Black is not badly placed.

2.232223 (1 d4 ♘f6 2 c4 g6 3 g3 ♗g7 4 ♗g2 d5 5 cxd5 ♘xd5 6 ♘f3 0-0 7 0-0 ♘b6 8 ♘c3 ♘c6 9 d5 ♘a5 10 e4 c6)

---

11 ♗g5

The most popular position in the 9 d5 variation.

Black has the following possibilities: **11...cxd5 (2.2322231)**, **11...♘ac4 (2.2322232)** or **11...h6 (2.2322233)**.

11...♗g4 was not recommended earlier, because of the possibility after 12 h3 ♗xf3 13 ♕xf3 of b2-b3. C.Hansen-Kasparov (Thessaloniki 1988) continued 13...cxd5 (13...h6 is considered in section 2.2322233) 14 ♘xd5 ♘xd5 15 ♖ad1! ♕c7 (if 15...♕b6 16 exd5 ♖fe8 17 b3 with advantage) 16 exd5 ♗xb2 17 ♖fe1 ♖fe8 18 ♖xe7! ♖xe7 19 d6 ♖e1+! 20 ♖xe1 ♕xd6 21 ♖e7 ♖f8 22 ♕d5! with a powerful position for White.

2.2322231 (1 d4 ♘f6 2 c4 g6 3 g3 ♗g7 4 ♗g2 d5 5 cxd5 ♘xd5 6 ♘f3 0-0 7 0-0 ♘b6 8 ♘c3 ♘c6 9 d5 ♘a5 10 e4 c6 11 ♗g5)

---

11   ...   cxd5

This is not as good as the other two main possibilities, since it allows White to remove the central tension immediately.

12 ♘xd5

This move is ineffective if 11...h6 12 ♗f4 is included, as e7 is not attacked, and Black has the possibility after 12...cxd5 13 ♘xd5 of 13...♘ac4 (see section 2.2322233).

12   ...   ♘xd5
13   exd5   ♗xb2

The interesting **13...f6!?** 14 ♗f4 e5 15 dxe6 ♗xe6 has not been tried.

14 ♖e1!

An unpleasant move to meet. Less good is **14 ♖b1 ♗f6** 15 ♗xf6 exf6 16 ♕d4 (16 d6 ♗f5) 16...♗f5 17 ♖bc1 ♕d6 18 ♖fe1 ♖fd8, when only White has problems (Giddins-Janjgava, Hastings 1989/90).

14   ...   ♗f6?!

Gelfand considers that **14...f6** 15 ♗h6 ♗xa1 16 ♗xf8 ♔xf8 17 ♕xa1 needs testing.

15 ♗xf6 exf6

And now, instead of **16 ♖c1?!** (Ivanchuk-Gelfand, Tilburg 1990), White could have gained a clear advantage by **16 d6! ♗e6** (16...♘c4 17 ♕d4 ♘xd6 18 ♖ad1) 17 ♕d4.

2.2322232 (1 d4 ♘f6 2 c4 g6 3 g3 ♗g7 4 ♗g2 d5 5 cxd5 ♘xd5 6 ♘f3 0–0 7 0–0 ♘b6 8 ♘c3 ♘c6 9 d5 ♘a5 10 e4 c6 11 ♗g5)

---

11 ... ♘ac4

Black plays actively on the queenside, with the idea after ...h7-h6

of playing ...e7-e5 without removing the tension in the centre. However, modern experience shows that things do not go so smoothly here for Black as they used to. Two replies are encountered:

12 ♕e2 h6 13 ♗f4 e5 (after 13...g5 14 ♗c1 cxd5 15 ♘xd5 ♗g4 16 h3 ♗xf3 17 ♗xf3 ♖c8 18 ♖b1 e6 19 ♘e3 ♕e7 20 ♖d1 ♖c7 21 b3 ♘a3 22 ♗xa3 ♕xa3 23 e5! White has attacking chances, Akopian-Lputian, Yerevan 1995) 14 dxe6 (White loses too much time with 14 ♗c1 cxd5 15 ♘xd5 ♘xd5 16 exd5 ♘d6 17 ♖d1 ♗g4 18 h3 ♗xf3 19 ♕xf3 ♖c8 20 ♕e2 ♘f5 21 ♗e3 ♘d4 when Black has no reason for complaint, Stempin-Aagaard, Lyngby 1990) 14...♗xe6, and now:

(a) 15 ♖fd1 ♕e7 16 ♘d4 (weaker is 16 b3?! g5! 17 ♗d2 ♘xd2 18 ♕xd2 ♗g4 19 ♖ac1 ♖ad8 20 ♕e3 ♖fe8 with advantage to Black, Vadasz-Honfi, Budapest 1983) 16...♖fd8 17 ♘xe6 ♕xe6 18 ♖xd8+ ♖xd8 19 ♖d1 ♖d7 20 ♖xd7 ♕xd7 21 b3 ♕d4 22 bxc4 ♕xc3 23 ♗f1 ♔h7 24 e5! ♕a3 ½-½ (Z.Ilic-Hulak, Cetinje 1985);

(b) 15 ♖ad1 ♕c8 16 ♕c2 (16 ♘d4 ♗h3 17 ♖fe1 ♗xg2 18 ♔xg2 ♖d8 leads to equality, Konopka-Pribyl, Prague 1987) 16...g5 17 ♗c1 ♗g4 18 ♖d3 ♖d8 19 ♖fd1 ♕c7 20 b3 and White retains a slight advantage (Akopian-Yermolinsky, USA 1996).

12 ♕c1! ♗g4 (after 12...cxd5!? 13 ♘xd5 ♘xd5 14 ♕xc4 ♘b6 15 ♕b4 White has the advantage, Mikhalchishin), 13 b3 (clearly better than 13 dxc6 bxc6 14 h3? [correct is 14 ♖d1 ♕c8 with equality] 14...♗xf3 15 ♗xf3 ♕d6! and Black is better, Smejkal-Hulak, Zagreb/Rijeka 1985) 13...♗xf3 14 ♗xf3 ♘e5 15 ♗g2 cxd5 16 ♘xd5

♘c6 17 ♖d1 ♘xd5 18 exd5 ♘d4 19 ♕d2 and White is better (A.Mikhalchishin-Kindermann, Palma de Mallorca 1989), but 19 ♕c5! is even stronger, when Black has great problems.

> **2.2322233 (1 d4 ♘f6 2 c4 g6 3 g3 ♗g7 4 ♗g2 d5 5 cxd5 ♘xd5 6 ♘f3 0–0 7 0–0 ♘b6 8 ♘c3 ♘c6 9 d5 ♘a5 10 e4 c6 11 ♗g5)**

11   ...   h6

The most interesting continuation. Black immediately drives the bishop from its active position, but as has already been mentioned, this has both positive and negative aspects.

12   ♗f4

Theory does not consider an alternative to this move, but Ubilava-Kozul (Tbilisi 1988) went 12 ♗e3 ♘ac4 (12...cxd5 13 ♗xb6 axb6 14 ♘xd5 ♗xb2 seems more purposeful) 13 ♗d4 (with the idea of sacrificing a pawn to exchange the dark-square bishops and exploit the weakened position of the black king) 13...♘xb2 (Black also fails to equalise by 13...e5 14 dxe6 ♗xe6 15 ♗xg7 ♔xg7 16 b3) 14 ♕b3 ♗xd4 15 ♘xd4 ♘2c4 16 ♖fd1 with splendid compensation for the pawn.

Now Black has a choice: **12...♗g4 (2.23222331)**, **12...♘ac4 (2.23222332)** or **12...cxd5! (2.23222333)**, modern theory demonstrating that the last of these gives the best equalising chances.

Also **12...g5** (a provocative move, the virtues of which are seen after the automatic reaction 13 ♗c1 cxd5 14 exd5 e5 15 dxe6 ♗xe6) 13 ♗e5, and now:

(a) 13...♗xe5 14 ♘xe5 ♕d6 15 f4! cxd5 16 exd5 ♘bc4 17 ♘e4 and Black's position collapses (Wojtkiewicz-R.Rodriguez, Bacolod 1991);

(b) 13...g4 14 ♗xg7 gxf3 15 ♗xh6 fxg2 16 ♖e1 ♖e8 17 e5 ♗f5 (17...♘xd5 18 ♕h5 ♔h7 19 ♖e4 and wins) 18 e6 ♘xd5 19 ♖e5, and White has a strong attack after both 19...fxe6 20 ♕h5 ♔h7 21 ♘xd5 ♗g6 (21...cxd5 22 ♖xf5! exf5 23 ♗f4+) 22 ♕g5 cxd5 23 ♖xe6 ♖g8 24 ♕h4 with a decisive advantage, or 19...♗g6 20 ♕f3! f6 21 ♕g4 ♔h7 22 ♖h5 (analysis by Ftacnik).

> **2.23222331 (1 d4 ♘f6 2 c4 g6 3 g3 ♗g7 4 ♗g2 d5 5 cxd5 ♘xd5 6 ♘f3 0–0 7 0–0 ♘b6 8 ♘c3 ♘c6 9 d5 ♘a5 10 e4 c6 11 ♗g5 h6 12 ♗f4)**

12   ...   ♗g4

This move is less flexible, as White has not played ♕e2.

13   ♕c1!

13 h3 ♗xf3 (after 13...e5 14 ♗e3 ♗xf3 15 ♕xf3 ♘ac4 16 dxc6 bxc6 17 ♖ad1 ♕e7 18 ♗c1 ♖fd8 19 ♖xd8+ ♖xd8 20 ♖d1 White has slightly the better pawn structure, Romanishin-Buturin, Lviv 1996) 14 ♕xf3, and now:

(a) 14...g5 15 ♗c1 cxd5 16 exd5 ♕d7 17 b3! ♖ac8 18 ♗d2 ♘c6 19 dxc6 ♕xd2 20 ♘e4 ♕a5 21 cxb7 ♖b8 22 ♖ac1 with advantage (Makarov-Tunik, USSR 1990);

(b) 14...♘ac4 15 dxc6 (15 b3) 15...bxc6 16 ♖ad1 ♕c8 17 b3 ♘e5 18 ♕e2 c5 19 ♘d5 and again White is better (Bielicki-L.Bronstein, Argentina 1989);

(c) 14...cxd5 15 exd5 ♖c8 (Black should avoid 15...♘ac4 16 b3 ♘d6 17 ♖fe1) 16 ♖ad1! (in important move; 16 ♖ac1 ♘ac4 17 b3 g5! leads to unnecessary complications) 16...♘ac4 17 ♗c1 with a slight but adequate advantage to White (Ehlvest-Ftacnik, Haninge 1990).

Greenfeld-Korchnoi (Beer Sheva 1993) now continued 13...cxd5 14 exd5 ♗xf3 (after 14...g5 15 ♗e5 ♗xf3 16 ♗xg7 White has the advantage) 15 ♗xf3 g5 16 ♗d2 ♘ac4 17 ♖d1 ♖c8 (17...♘d7!?) 18 ♗e1 ♕d6 (again 18...♘d7!? is interesting) 19 ♖b1!? and here 19...♖fd8 or 19...♘d7 would have led to a complicated game (*Game 8*).

2.23222332 (1 d4 ♘f6 2 c4 g6 3 g3 ♗g7 4 ♗g2 d5 5 cxd5 ♘xd5 6 ♘f3 0–0 7 0–0 ♘b6 8 ♘c3 ♘c6 9 d5 ♘a5 10 e4 c6 11 ♗g5 h6 12 ♗f4)

---

12 ...   ♘ac4

For many years the question was whether this thematic move should be played immediately, or after first exchanging on d5. In modern tournaments the second option is more often seen.

13 b3!

This strong discovery of Romanishin, the most unpleasant reply for Black, is not possible after the exchange in the centre, as the d5 pawn is hanging. Other moves do not give an advantage:

13 ♕e2 e5!, transposing into variation 2.2322232.

13 ♕b3 e5 14 ♗c1 cxd5 15 exd5 ♘d6 16 ♗e3 ♘bc4 with advantage to

Black (Reshevsky-D.Byrne, New York 1970).

13 ♕c2 cxd5 14 ♘xd5 e5 15 ♘xb6 ♕xb6 16 ♗xh6 ♗xh6 17 ♕xc4 ♗e6 18 ♕e2 ♖fd8 and Black has sufficient compensation (Agdestein-Ostenstad, Oslo 1990).

13 ...   ♗xc3

If **13...♘d6** 14 ♖c1 cxd5 (14...♗xc3 transposes into the A.Petrosian-K.Grigorian game, given below) 15 exd5 ♗g4 16 h3 ♗xf3 17 ♕xf3 with the more comfortable position for White (Stangl-Orgovan, Budapest 1990).

13...g5 14 bxc4 gxf4 is insufficient for equality: 15 ♕b3! (stronger than 15 ♕d3 cxd5 16 cxd5 fxg3 17 fxg3 ♗g4 18 ♖ac1 ♖c8 with an equal position, Romanishin-Gulko, Kiev 1973) 15...fxg3 (dubious is 15...e6?! 16 ♖ad1 exd5 17 exd5 cxd5 18 c5 with a big advantage, Romanishin-Spiriev, Sibenik 1990) 16 hxg3 cxd5 (16...♕d6 17 ♖ac1 ♕c5 18 ♘e2 e5 19 ♘e1 cxd5 is also unconvincing; despite the draw agreed in Ilic-Lalic, Cetinje 1987, White is better) 17 cxd5, and now:

(a) 17...♗d7 18 ♖ac1 (18 ♖ad1 ♖c8 19 e5 ♖c5! 20 ♖d4 ♕c7 with a complicated position) 18...♖c8 19 ♘e2! (with the idea of ♘f4-h5; less good is

19 ♘b5 ♗xb5 20 ♕xb5 ♕d6 21 ♕a5 ♘c4 22 ♕xa7 b5 intending 23...♖a8, when Black has compensation for the material) 19...♖xc1 (after 19...♗a4 20 ♕e3 ♗b5 21 ♖xc8 ♕xc8 22 ♖c1 ♕b8 23 ♘ed4 White is a little better) 20 ♖xc1 ♕b8 21 ♘f4 ♖c8 22 ♖xc8+ ♗xc8 23 ♕a3! with advantage (A.Mikhalchishin-Ragozin, Sibenik 1990);

(b) 17...e6 18 ♖ad1 exd5 19 exd5 ♗g4 20 ♕b4! h5 21 d6, and the wedge at d6 makes Black's position very difficult (A.Mikhalchishin-G.Timoshchenko, Tbilisi 1978).

14   ♖c1   ♘b2

Black's choice is very restricted: **14...♘d6?!** 15 ♖xc3 ♘xe4 16 ♖d3! ♘xd5 17 ♗xh6, and he soon encounters problems on the kingside (A.Petrosian-K.Grigorian, Yerevan 1980).

Probably no one will risk playing **14...cxd5.** After 15 ♖xc3 (but not 15 exd5 ♘xd5! 16 ♗xh6 ♘cb6! and White stands badly) 15...dxe4 16 bxc4 ♕xd1 17 ♖xd1 exf3 18 ♗xf3 White has strong pressure on the opponent's position.

15   ♕c2!

The crushing effect of this subtle blow is not obvious. The earlier **15 ♕e2** also gives White a good game after 15...♗g7 16 ♗e5 ♗xe5 17 ♘xe5 cxd5 18 exd5 ♘xd5 19 ♕xb2. Ilic-Vareille (Dijon 1987) continued 19...e6?! 20 ♖fe1! ♕f6 21 ♕d2 h5 22 ♖c4 b6 23 g4 hxg4 24 ♘xg4 ♕d8 25 ♕h6 and White soon won by a direct attack.

15   ...   ♗g7
16   ♗e5   ♗xe5
17   ♘xe5   cxd5
18   exd5   ♘xd5

18...♗f5 does not significantly improve the position. After 19 ♕xb2 ♕d6 20 g4! ♗d7 21 ♖fe1 ♖ac8 22 ♖cd1 ♖c7 23 ♕d2 ♔g7 24 ♕d4 ♔h7 25 ♖e3 ♗c8 26 ♖h3 Black encountered serious problems on the kingside (Jirovsky-David, Czechoslovakia 1991).

Romanishin-Kindermann (Debrecen 1990) continued 19 ♘xg6 ♘b4 20 ♕e4 ♖e8 21 ♘e5 ♕d2 22 ♖xc8 and White won. Interestingly, this analysis by Romanishin dates back to 1974.

2.23222333 (1 d4 ♘f6 2 c4 g6 3 g3 ♗g7 4 ♗g2 d5 5 cxd5 ♘xd5 6 ♘f3 0-0 7 0-0 ♘b6 8 ♘c3 ♘c6 9 d5 ♘a5 10 e4 c6 11 ♗g5 h6 12 ♗f4)

12   ...   cxd5!
13   exd5

13 ♘xd5 has been tried in many games, but the final assessment after

Black's best reply is that White not only does not gain any advantage, but even has problems:

(a) 13...♘c6?! 14 ♕c1! ♘xd5 15 exd5 ♘b4 16 ♗xh6 ♘xd5 17 ♗xg7 ♔xg7 18 ♖d1 e6 19 ♘e5! ♕a5 20 ♘g4 ♖h8 21 ♕c4! with advantage (Ilic-Modr, Prague 1980);

(b) 13...♘xd5 14 exd5 and now:

(b1) 14...♘c4? 15 ♕c1 ♘b6 (15...g5 16 ♗xg5 hxg5 17 ♕xc4 g4 18 ♘h4 ♗xb2 19 ♖ae1 and White has an obvious advantage, Romanishin-Kupreichik, USSR 1972; 15...♘xb2 16 ♗xh6 ♘d3 17 ♕d2 with a great advantage, A.Mikhalchishin-Passerotti, Rome 1977) 16 ♗xh6 ♘xd5 17 ♖d1 e6 18 ♗xg7 ♔xg7 19 ♖d4! with advantage to White (Jurek-Pribyl, Czechoslovakia 1984);

(b2) 14...♗g4 is better, with equalising chances after 15 ♖c1 (or 15 h3 e5! 16 ♗d2 ♗xf3 17 ♕xf3 ♖c8 18 ♖ac1 ♘c4 19 ♗b4 ♖e8 20 b3 a5 21 ♗e1 ♘d6 with equality, Demina-Qin, Subotica 1991, or 15 ♕a4!? ♗xf3 16 ♗xf3 ♖c8 17 ♖ac1 ♕b6 18 b3 and White is slightly better, Makarov-Nestorovic, Belgrade 1993) 15...♖c8 16 ♖xc8 ♕xc8 17 ♕e2 ♕f5 18 h3 ♗xf3 19 ♗xf3 g5 20 ♗c1 ♘c4 21 ♗e4 with advantage to White (Tischer-Dueball, Germany 1982);

(c) 13...♗g4 14 h3 ♗xf3 15 ♕xf3 ♘xd5 16 exd5 ♘c4 17 ♕b3 ♘d6 18 ♖fe1 ♕d7 19 h4 ♖fc8 20 ♖ad1 and White is slightly better (Adorjan-Milos, Szirak 1987);

(d) 13...♘ac4!, when with accurate play Black should parry all the opponent's threats:

(d1) 14 ♘c7?! ♖b8 15 ♕xd8 ♖xd8 16 ♖ad1 (16 ♘d5 e5!) 16...♗g4 17 ♘d5 e5 18 ♘xb6 ♖xd1 19 ♖xd1 ♘xb2! 20 ♖d2 exf4 with advantage to Black (Pastircak-Hort, Czechoslovakia 1984);

(d2) 14 ♕b3 e5! (weak is 14...♘xd5 15 exd5 ♘d6 [15...e5 16 ♗xh6!] 16 ♖fe1 ♖e8 17 ♖ad1 a6 18 ♖d2 ♖b8 19 ♘d4 ♗d7? 20 ♘e6! with a decisive advantage, Ilic-Banas, Virovitica 1981) 15 ♘xb6 ♕xb6! 16 ♗xh6! (16 ♕xc4? exf4) 16...♗xh6 17 ♕xc4 ♕xb2 18 ♖ab1 ♕a3 19 ♘xe5 ♗e6 with active play on the queenside (Shpilker-Krasenkov, USSR 1987) – *Game 9*;

(d3) 14 ♘xb6 ♕xb6 15 ♕c1 ♗e6 16 ♗xh6 ♗xb2 17 ♕f4 ♗xa1 18 ♗xf8 (Helmers-Yrjola, Helsinki 1984) 18...♖xf8 19 ♖xa1 ♕b2 with the better chances for Black.

13 ...   ♘ac4

Oratovsky-Zalkind (Jerusalem 1996) saw the very interesting innovation **13...e6** 14 dxe6 ♗xe6 15 ♗e5?! ♘c6 16 ♗xg7 ♔xg7 17 b3 ♕xd1 18 ♖fxd1 ♖fd8 and Black has no particular problems. 15 ♕c1 g5 16 ♖d1 is stronger for White.

14 ♕e2

As already mentioned, **14 b3?** does not work because of 14...♗xc3 (in Magerramov-Banas, Trnava 1981, Black missed this opportunity and had the worse position after 14...♘d6? 15 ♗e5 ♘d7 16 ♗xg7 ♔xg7 17 ♖e1) 15 ♖c1 ♘xd5 16 ♗xh6 ♘cb6! (16...♘b2!? 17 ♕e2 ♖e8 18 ♖xc3 ♘xc3 19 ♕e5 f6 20 ♕xc3 ♘d3 21 ♖d1 ♗f5 22 g4 ♖c8 23 ♕d2 ♘xf2 is unclear) 17 ♗xf8 ♕xf8 with advantage to Black.

After **14 ♕b3 g5** (14...e5!?) 15 ♗c1 (15 ♗e3 ♘xe3 16 fxe3 ♗xc3 17 bxc3 ♕xd5 solves all Black's problems, Poor-Douven, Budapest 1989) 15...♗f5 16 h4 g4 17 ♘d2 ♗d3 18 ♖e1 ♘e5 Black has active play (Nippgen-Meyer, Germany 1984).

Not long ago this was a popular position. Black has **14...♗g4** (2.232223331), **14...e5** (2.232223332) or **14...g5** (2.232223333).

He should avoid **14...♘xb2**:

(a) 15 ♘e5!? ♘2a4 (after 15...g5 16 ♕xb2 gxf4 17 gxf4 ♗f5 18 ♖ad1 White has the advantage, Muco) 16 ♘xa4 ♘xa4 17 ♖ac1 ♘b6 18 ♖fd1 with compensation for the pawn (Muco-Thomson, Thessaloniki 1988);

(b) 15 ♕xb2 ♘a4 16 ♘xa4 ♗xb2 17 ♘xb2 and the three pieces are stronger than the queen (Wojtkiewicz-Skalik, Warsaw 1989).

2.232223331 (1 d4 ♘f6 2 c4 g6 3 g3 ♗g7 4 ♗g2 d5 5 cxd5 ♘xd5 6 ♘f3 0–0 7 0–0 ♘b6 8 ♘c3 ♘c6 9 d5 ♘a5 10 e4 c6 11 ♗g5 h6 12 ♗f4 cxd5 13 exd5 ♘ac4 14 ♕e2)

---

14   ...   ♗g4

This is one of the positions where this move is effective. Now White must play carefully, as Black is threatening the unpleasant 15...♖c8 with strong pressure on the queenside.

15 ♖ac1

15 h3?! is a loss of time, and after 15...♗xf3 16 ♗xf3 ♖c8 17 ♖ac1 g5 18

♗e3 ♘xe3 19 ♕xe3 ♘c4 20 ♕e2 ♕a5 21 d6! ♘xd6 22 ♕xe7 ♘f5 23 ♕xb7 ♖b8 24 ♕d5 ♕xd5 it led to a draw in Ilic-Roos (Orange 1989).

15 b3 leads to a complicated game with the better chances for Black after 15...♗xc3 16 ♖ac1 ♘xd5 17 ♗xh6 ♘cb6 18 ♖xc3 ♘xc3 19 ♕e5 f6 20 ♕xc3 ♖f7, and after the exchange of blows White has insufficient compensation (Foigel-Neverov, USSR 1987).

Xu Jun-Timoshchenko (Belgrade 1987) now continued 15...♖c8 (if 15...g5 16 b3!) 16 b3 ♘d6 17 ♗e5 ♘d7 18 ♗xg7 ♔xg7 19 ♖fe1 ♖e8 20 ♕b2 ♗xf3 21 ♗xf3 ♘f6 with a roughly equal position.

2.232223332 (1 d4 ♘f6 2 c4 g6 3 g3 ♗g7 4 ♗g2 d5 5 cxd5 ♘xd5 6 ♘f3 0–0 7 0–0 ♘b6 8 ♘c3 ♘c6 9 d5 ♘a5 10 e4 c6 11 ♗g5 h6 12 ♗f4 cxd5 13 exd5 ♘ac4 14 ♕e2)

---

14   ...   e5

A fashionable idea. Black takes radical measures to avoid the potential pressure on the e-file, but all the central files will now be opened, and it turns out that White is better prepared for this.

15 dxe6

15 ♗c1?! is pointless. After 15...♖e8 (15...♗g4 is also possible) 16 ♘d2 Black prematurely agreed to a draw in Dorfman-Stohl (Amsterdam 1990). He should have continued 16...♘d6 17 ♘de4 ♘f5 with clearly the better chances.

15 ...   ♗xe6
16 ♖fd1   ♕c8

16...♕e7 17 ♘d4 is clearly better for White.

17 ♖ac1   g5

The position after **17...♖e8 18 b3!** is uncomfortable for Black:

(a) 18...g5 19 ♗xg5 hxg5 (19...♗g4 20 ♗e3 ♘xe3 21 fxe3 ♗xc3?! 22 ♖d3) 20 bxc4 ♗xc4 21 ♕c2 g4 22 ♘g5 with advantage (Stohl);

(b) 18...♗g4 19 ♕f1 ♘b2 20 ♘b5 ♕f5 21 ♘fd4! (21 ♘d6 ♕h5 22 ♘xe8 ♖xe8 23 ♖e1 is bad in view of 23...♖xe1 24 ♘xe1 ♗e2 25 g4 ♕xg4 26 f3 ♕xf4 and Black wins) 21...♕h5 22 ♖d2 with a decisive advantage to White (Stohl);

(c) 18...♗h3 19 ♕f1 ♗xg2 20 ♔xg2 ♘b2 21 ♘b5 ♕f5 22 ♘d6 ♕h5 23 ♘xe8 ♖xe8 24 ♖e1 and White wins (Ilic-Chabanon, Bern 1989).

18 ♗e5!

White maintains the tension. After **18 ♗e3?!** ♘xe3 19 ♕xe3 ♖e8 20 ♘d4 ♗g4 Black seizes the initiative.

18 ...   ♘xe5

18...g4 is tactically unjustified: 19 ♗xg7 gxf3 20 ♗xf3 ♔xg7 21 b3 ♘a3 22 ♘b5! (Neat) and White wins.

Wojtkiewicz-Stohl (Werfen 1990) now continued 19 ♘xe5 ♕c7 20 ♘d3 ♕e7 21 b4 with the positional threat of ♘c5. Black with difficulty maintained the balance, but White stands slightly better.

2.232223333 (1 d4 ♘f6 2 c4 g6 3 g3 ♗g7 4 ♗g2 d5 5 cxd5 ♘xd5 6 ♘f3 0-0 7 0-0 ♘b6 8 ♘c3 ♘c6 9 d5 ♘a5 10 e4 c6 11 ♗g5 h6 12 ♗f4 cxd5 13 exd5 ♘ac4 14 ♕e2)

14 ...   g5
15 ♗c1

This position first appeared in tournament games in the 1960s, and the majority of theoretical assessments in this line are based on old examples of that period.

Black has two possibilities: the old **15...♗g4** (2.2322233331) and the more fashionable **15...e5** (2.2322233332).

2.2322233331 (1 d4 ♘f6 2 c4 g6 3 g3 ♗g7 4 ♗g2 d5 5 cxd5 ♘xd5 6 ♘f3 0-0 7 0-0 ♘b6 8 ♘c3 ♘c6 9 d5 ♘a5 10 e4 c6 11 ♗g5 h6 12 ♗f4 cxd5 13 exd5 ♘ac4 14 ♕e2 g5 15 ♗c1)

15 ...   ♗g4
16 h3   ♗h5

Black's pieces are extremely active, which compensates for the weakness of his kingside. His practical results have been better than the appearance of his position. White has several options:

17 g4 ♗g6 and now:

(a) 18 ♘d2 ♖c8 19 ♘de4 ♕d7 with equality (Gufeld-Taimanov, USSR 1969);

(b) 18 ♖d1 ♖c8 (18...♕c7 19 ♘d4 ♕e5 20 b3 ♕xe2 ½-½, de Boer-Van Mil, Denmark 1991) 19 ♘d4 ♘d6 20 f4?! gxf4 21 ♗xf4 ♘bc4 22 b3? ♕b6! 23 ♔h1 ♘b2 24 ♕xb2 ♗xd4 25 ♖ac1 ♘e4 and Black wins (Stangl-Roze, Germany 1990);

(c) 18 h4 (the most active try) 18...♕d7 19 hxg5 ♕xg4 (weak is 19...hxg5 20 ♘xg5 ♘e5 21 ♘ge4, Vladimirov-Tseitlin, Leningrad 1970) 20 gxh6 ♗f6 21 ♖e1 ♖ac8 22 ♘e4 ♕xe4 23 ♕xe4 ♗xe4 24 ♖xe4 ♘xd5 25 ♘d2 ½-½ (Krogius-Hort, Varna 1969).

17 ♖e1 ♖e8 18 a4 a5 19 g4 ♗g6 20 h4 (this is similar to the previous game, Krogius-Hort, but with the moves a4 a5 and ♖e1 ♖e8 included):

(a) 20...♕d7 21 hxg5 ♕xg4 22 gxh6 ♗f6 and White has 23 ♘e4!, but Black can avoid this by 22...♖xc3 23 bxc3 ♘xd5 24 ♘d2 ♕xe2 25 ♖xe2 ♘xc3 26 ♖e1 ♘b6 with a probable draw;

(b) 20...e6! (aiming for a complicated ending) 21 hxg5 exd5 22 ♕xe8+ ♕xe8 23 ♖xe8+ ♖xe8 and Black's chances are not worse (Krogius-Tukmakov, Leningrad 1971).

17 ♖d1 (the most recent and best move – White supports his d-pawn and after ...g5-g4 he has the possibility of ♘d4, solving the problem of pressure on the a1-h8 diagonal; however, there are few practical examples, and so it is premature to draw conclusions) 17...♖c8 (White may also encounter 17...♖e8 with the idea of 18 ♘e4 or 18 g4 ♗g6 19 h4; this last move avoids the complications of 19 ♘d4 e6) 18 g4 (18 a4 is careless and allows 18...♘xb2!; Ruban-Lucke, Miskolc 1990, continued 19 ♗xb2 ♗xc3 20 g4 ♗g6 21 ♘e5 and now instead of 21...♗h7? 22 ♘c6! Black can achieve a good game with 21...♗xb2 22 ♕xb2 ♕d6! 23 ♘xg6 fxg6!) 18...♗g6 19 ♘d4 ♕d7 (19...♘d6 is more accurate, preventing White from playing his dark-square bishop to its best position) 20 b3 ♘d6 21 ♗b2 ♖fe8 22 a4 a5 23 ♖ac1 with the better chances for White (Stangl-Luecke, Altensteig 1989).

2.2322233332 (1 d4 ♘f6 2 c4 g6 3 g3 ♗g7 4 ♗g2 d5 5 cxd5 ♘xd5 6 ♘f3 0–0 7 0–0 ♘b6 8 ♘c3 ♘c6 9 d5 ♘a5 10 e4 c6 11 ♗g5 h6 12 ♗f4 cxd5 13 exd5 ♘ac4 14 ♕e2 g5 15 ♗c1)

---

15 ...　　　　e5

This is more accurate than **15...e6**, although in this case too White can go in for the main variation with the exchange of pawns. But he can also follow Wojtkiewicz-Kindermann (Debrecen 1990) and gain the advantage by 16 h4! g4 17 ♘h2 exd5 18 ♘xg4 d4 19 ♘xh6+ ♗xh6 20 ♗xh6 dxc3 21 ♖ad1 ♕f6 22 ♗xf8 ♔xf8 23 bxc3 ♗e6 24 ♖d4.

15...♗f5!? is a new possibility: 16 ♖d1 ♕d7 17 h4 gxh4 18 ♘xh4 ♗h7 19

♔h2 ♖ac8 20 ♗h3 f5 21 ♔g2 ♘xb2 with a sharp game (Zhelyandinov-A.Mikhalchishin, Ptuj 1995), although the authors prefer White's position.

16 dxe6

Black has no reason for concern if White avoids this exchange: 16 ♘d2 ♘d6 17 ♘de4 ♘xe4 18 ♘xe4 f5 19 ♘c3 ♗d7 20 ♗e3 ♖c8 with an unclear situation, but where Black has more threats (Pigusov-Gavrikov, Moscow 1990).

16 ...   ♗xe6

We have a position from variation 2.232223332 (p.63) with the inclusion of ...g5 and ♗c1. It is hard to state categorically whom this inclusion favours. Here are some practical examples:

17 ♖d1 ♕c8 18 h4 (in Hjartarson-Popovic, Belgrade 1989, White played the superficial 18 ♘d4?! and lost after 18...♗g4 19 ♗f3 ♗h3! 20 ♘d5 ♘xd5 21 ♗xd5 ♖d8! 22 ♘c6 bxc6 23 ♗xc4 ♕f5 24 ♗d3 ♕e5) 18...♖e8 (Popovic suggested 18...♗g4 19 hxg5 ♘e5 with a complicated game) 19 hxg5 hxg5 20 ♗xg5 ♘xb2 21 ♕xb2 ♕xc3 (21...♗xc3 is too risky: 22 ♕c1 ♗xa1 23 ♕xa1 with the threat of 24 ♗h6) 22 ♕xc3 ♗xc3 with equality (Wojtkiewicz-Stohl, Warsaw 1990).

17 h4 (this is stronger; White is threatening to capture twice on g5, attacking the queen) 17...g4 18 ♘h2 ♕c8 19 ♘e4!? (19 ♖d1 ½-½, Pribyl-David, Czechoslovakia 1990). Now 19...♖e8?! allows White a strong attack after 20 ♗xh6! ♗xh6 21 ♘f6+ ♔h8 22 ♘xe8 ♕xe8 23 b3 with advantage (Lagunov-Berndt, Berlin 1990). According to analysis by Lagunov, 19...♗f5 20 f3! gxf3 21 ♕xf3 ♗xe4 22 ♕xe4 is also better for White. For a final assessment of 17 h4, a practical testing of 19...♖d8 is needed.

Game 4
Smyslov-Szabo
Hastings 1954/5

1 d4 ♘f6 2 ♘f3 g6 3 g3 ♗g7 4 c4 0-0 5 ♗g2 d5 6 cxd5 ♘xd5 7 0-0 c5

This is what Smyslov writes: 'A good continuation – Black wants to open the diagonal for his bishop and to shake somewhat White's position in the centre.'

8 e4

The most active attempt to gain an advantage in the centre, but also with the logical idea after e4-e5 of restricting Black's main piece – the bishop at g7.

8...♘f6

After 8...♘b6 9 d5 ♗g4 10 h3 ♗xf3 11 ♕xf3 ♘8d7 12 ♕e2 c4 13 ♘c3 ♘c5 14 ♗e3 ♘d3 15 ♖ab1 ♘d7 16 f4! White has a serious advantage (Smyslov-Simagin, 28th USSR Ch 1961).

9 e5 ♘d5 10 dxc5 ♘b4

10...♘a6 is stronger. At the 1954 Olympiad in Amsterdam, Szabo against Stahlberg tried 10...♘c6 11 a3 ♘c7?! 12 ♕b3 ♘a6 13 ♗e3 ♕c7 14 ♘c3 ♗e6 15 ♕a4 and encountered problems; however 11...♗e6!? 12 ♘g5 ♘xe5 13

♘xe6 fxe6 14 ♕e2 ♕d7 would have been stronger. But 11 ♕e2 is better for White: 11...♕a5 (11...♗g4 12 ♖d1 ♘xe5 13 h3!) 12 ♘bd2 ♕xc5 13 ♘b3 ♕b6 14 ♖d1 e6 15 h4 ♕c7 16 ♖e1 h6 17 ♗d2 a5 18 ♖ac1 with advantage (Botvinnik-Ragozin, Moscow 1951).

11 ♘c3 ♘8c6 12 ♕e2?!

White played more strongly in Botvinnik-Bronstein (m/19 1951): 12 a3 ♘d3 13 ♗e3 ♗g4 14 h3 ♗xf3 15 ♕xf3 ♘dxe5 16 ♕e4 ♕d3 17 ♕a4 ♕c4 18 ♖ad1 with the better ending. Now Black has a forced, but adequate reply.

12...♕d3 13 ♖d1 ♕xe2 14 ♘xe2 ♘xe5?!

In the opinion of Neikirch, 14...♗e6! 15 ♘fd4 ♖fd8 16 ♗g5 ♗xe5 17 ♘xe6 fxe6 would have equalised.

15 ♘xe5 ♗xe5 16 ♗h6 ♖e8 17 ♖d2

As a result of the simplification, an ending has arisen with the better chances for White, thanks to his superior development and queenside pawn majority. Black's defence is not at all easy.

17...♘c6 18 ♘f4 ♗f5 19 ♖e1 ♗g7?!

19...f6 looks stronger, leaving the bishop at its strong post in the centre.

20 ♗xg7 ♔xg7 21 a3 g5

Black does not sense the danger and chooses an ineffective method of de-

fence. He should have played 21...♖ad8 with the idea after 22 ♗xc6 bxc6 23 ♖xd8 ♖xd8 24 ♖xe7 g5! of gaining counterplay for the pawn. White's correct reply would be 22 ♖ed1.

22 ♘d5 ♖ed8 23 ♖ed1 ♗g4 24 f3 ♗e6 25 b4

25 ♘c7 was weaker: after 25...♗b3 26 ♘xa8 ♗xd1 White has nothing special.

25...h6

Weaker was 25...♖d7 26 ♘f4! ♖xd2 27 ♘xe6+ fxe6 28 ♖xd2 ♖d8 29 ♖xd8 ♘xd8 30 f4! with advantage to White.

26 ♔f2 ♖d7 27 ♘c3 ♖xd2+ 28 ♖xd2 ♖d8

Less good was 28...a5 29 b5 ♘e5 30 f4 ♘c4 31 ♖d4 when White has clearly the better position.

29 ♖xd8 ♘xd8 30 f4

There is little material on the board, but White's queenside superiority and bishop at g2 give him a great advantage.

30...gxf4 31 gxf4 ♗b3 32 ♔e3 ♔f6 33 b5 e5

After 33...♔e6 White wins by 34 c6 ♔d6 35 b6! ♘xc6 36 ♗xc6.

34 ♘e4+ ♔e6

35 c6!

This little combination crowns White's strategy on the queenside.

35...exf4+ 36 ♔xf4 bxc6

In any case a piece is lost – after 36...♔e7 there follows 37 ♘c5.

37 ♘c5+ ♔d6 38 ♘xb3 cxb5 39 h4 ♘c6 40 ♗xc6 ♔xc6 41 ♔g4!

The correct way to realise the advantage – the knight copes with the black pawns, while the king goes to the h-pawn.

41...b4 42 axb4 ♔b5 43 ♘d4+ 1–0

Game 5
Geller-Savon
Rovno 1963

---

1 d4 ♘f6 2 c4 g6 3 g3 ♗g7 4 ♗g2 d5 5 cxd5 ♘xd5 6 ♘f3 0–0 7 0–0 c5 8 dxc5 ♘a6

9 ♘g5

With the idea of piece play in the centre. Another positional idea is 9 c6 bxc6, creating a weakness at c6, but at the same time opening the b-file for Black and supporting his knight at d5.

9...♘db4

In recent times Black has tried 9...e6 here and achieved a reasonable game – cf. the analysis.

10 ♘c3 ♘xc5

After 10...h6 11 ♘f3 ♕xd1 12 ♖xd1 ♗e6 13 ♗e3 ♘c2 14 ♖ac1 ♘xe3 15

fxe3 ♘xc5 16 b4 ♘a6 17 a3 ♗b3 18 ♖d7 ♖fd8 19 ♖xe7 ♖ac8 20 ♘d4 ♗f6 21 ♘xb3 ♗xe7 22 ♗xb7 ♗g5 23 ♔f2 ♖e8 24 ♖c2 ♗xe3+ 25 ♔f3 White gained an endgame advantage in Cvitan-Jasnikowski (Warsaw 1990). For a more detailed study of the variation see the analysis section.

11 ♗e3 ♘e6

After 11...♘ba6 12 ♕c1! ♕e8!? 13 ♘ge4! ♘e6 14 ♗h6 ♗d7 15 ♗xg7 ♔xg7 16 ♘d5 ♗c6 17 ♕c3+ f6 18 ♖fd1 White has the advantage (Wojt-kiewicz-Fernandez, Novi Sad 1990).

12 ♕b3 ♕a5 13 a3 ♘c6

13...♘a6 is clearly less logical.

14 ♘xe6 ♗xe6 15 ♕xb7 ♘d4 16 ♕xe7 ♖ab8

At the cost of two pawns Black has activated his pieces, and at first sight has gained some play, but now White returns the material, in exchange for which he gains the initiative.

17 ♘e4! ♘xe2+ 18 ♔h1 ♕f5

If 18...♖xb2 Black did not care for 19 ♘f6+ ♔h8 20 ♘e8!

19 ♖ad1!

Again pawns do not matter – it is the initiative plus development that are important.

19...♖xb2 20 ♖d8!

Now 21 ♕xf8+ ♗xf8 22 ♗h6 is threatened, so that Black's reply is forced.

20...♖b8 21 ♖xb8 ♖xb8 22 ♕xa7 ♕b5 23 a4

Now the rook's pawn is bound to decide the outcome.

23...♕b2 24 a5 ♘d4 25 h3 ♗c4 26 ♖c1 ♘e2 27 ♖d1 ♕b3 28 ♖e1 ♖d8 29 ♕c7 ♖d1 30 ♕c8+ ♗f8 31 ♗c5! ♖xe1+ 32 ♔h2 1–0

> ## Game 6
> ## Donchenko-Gipslis
> *Dubna 1976*

1 d4 ♘f6 2 c4 g6 3 g3 ♗g7 4 ♗g2 d5 5 ♘f3 0–0 6 cxd5 ♘xd5 7 0–0 c5 8 dxc5 ♘a6 9 c6

A very interesting, although double-edged plan in this critical position, where White has a wide choice of different strategic plans: 9 ♘bd2, 9 e4 and 9 ♘g5. In return for the weakness of the c6 pawn and the c5 square, Black gains play on the b-file and interesting coordination of his bishop at g7 and knight at d5.

9...bxc6 10 ♘bd2 ♘c5

In Yuferov-Gufeld (Barnaul 1969) Black first brought out his queen by 10...♕b6!?, and after 11 ♘c4 ♕c5 12 ♘fd2 ♗e6 13 a3 ♖fd8 14 ♕a4 ♕b5 15 ♕c2 ♖ab8 the arrangement of his pieces looks very harmonious. Therefore White does better to play 12 ♘fe5! ♗e6 13 ♕a4, as in Zhelyandinov-Mikhalchishin (Ptuj 1994), when Black has to concern himself with how to equalise.

11 ♘c4 ♗a6 12 ♘fe5 ♕c7 13 ♕c2?!

White underestimated his opponent's reply. Serious consideration should have been given to 13 ♘xc6 ♗xc4

(13...e6!? is interesting) 14 ♗xd5 ♗xd5 (after 14...♖ad8 15 ♘xd8 ♖xd8 16 ♗xc4! White stands better after sacrificing his queen) 15 ♕xd5 ♖fc8 16 ♕xc5 ♕xc6 17 ♕xc6 ♖xc6 18 ♖e1 ♖c2 when Black has compensation for the pawn.

13...♘e6!

Now White's d4 square is weak.

14 ♘f3 ♖ab8 15 a3

15 ♗d2 can be met by 15...♗xc4 16 ♕xc4 ♖xb2, but 15...♘b4 is also possible.

15...♖fd8 16 ♖d1 c5 17 e4 ♘b6!

Lifting the blockade. The pseudo-active 17...♘c3?! 18 ♖xd8+ ♖xd8 19 ♗f1 is less good.

18 ♘e3 ♖xd1+ 19 ♘xd1

After 19 ♕xd1 ♖d8 20 ♘d5 ♘xd5 21 exd5 ♗b7 White has problems.

19...♕d8! 20 ♗f1 ♗xf1 21 ♔xf1 ♘d4 22 ♘xd4 cxd4

Now Black has acquired a passed pawn, and if 23 ♗f4 he has 23...d3! 24 ♕c7 ♕xc7 25 ♗xc7 ♖c8 26 ♗xb6 axb6 when the ending is very unpleasant for White.

23 ♗d2 d3 24 ♕b3 ♕d4 25 ♘c3?

The last chance was 25 ♕b4! ♕d7! 26 ♔g2 a5, although here too Black has the advantage.

25...♘d7!

After this strong manoeuvre White's position becomes critical.

26 ♕a2 ♘e5! 27 ♗f4

Slightly better is 27 ♗e3 ♕d7 28 ♔g2 ♕g4!

27...♘g4! 28 ♘d1 ♕xe4 29 ♔g1 ♕e1+ 30 ♔g2 ♖xb2! 31 ♕d5

After 31 ♘xb2 there follows 31...♕xf2+ 32 ♔h3 ♕xh2+ 33 ♔xg4 ♕h5 mate.

31...♖xf2+! 32 ♘xf2 ♕xf2+ 33 ♔h3 h5

Simpler was 33...♕xh2+ 34 ♔xg4 h5+ 35 ♔g5 ♕h3, forcing mate.

34 ♖h1 ♕e2 35 ♔h4 ♘f2 0–1

Game 7
Romanishin-Benjamin
Groningen 1993

---

1 d4 ♘f6 2 ♘f3 g6 3 c4 ♗g7 4 ♘c3 0–0 5 g3 d5 6 cxd5 ♘xd5 7 ♗g2 c5 8 0–0

The Grünfeld Defence has been reached here in a rather cunning way. Before Ribli's games the variation with ♘c3 was considered fairly harmless, but in the last 15 years a number of interesting plans for White have been found. It has to be admitted that the main point of these set-ups – using the coordination of the bishop at g2 and the rook at b1 against the b7 pawn – is very logical and promising.

8...♘xc3

A sharp alternative is 8...cxd4 9 ♘xd4 ♘xc3 10 bxc3 ♕a5 11 ♗e3 ♘c6 12 ♕b3 ♕a6 13 ♖ab1 ♘xd4 14 cxd4 ♕xe2 15 ♕a3 ♗f6 16 ♖fc1!? (White also has good compensation after 16 ♖fe1) 16...♖d8 17 ♖b2 (17 d5 ♕h5! 18 h4 ♗g4 with an unclear game) 17...♕h5 18 h4 (Ribli-Hellers, Tilburg 1993), and here 18...♗xd4 19 ♕xe7 ♗e6 20 ♗xd4 ♖xd4 21 ♖xb7 a5 would have led to equality.

The most correct approach is 10...♘c6 11 ♘xc6 bxc6 12 ♕xd8 ♖xd8 13 ♗xc6 ♗xc3 14 ♖b1 ♗f5 15 e4 ♖ac8 16 ♗b7 ♗h3 17 ♗xc8 ♗xf1 18 ♔xf1 ♖xc8 19 ♗e3 ♖c7 20 ♖c1 a6 and Black equalised (Hübner-Tal, Bugojno 1978).

9 bxc3 ♘c6 10 ♗e3!?

Another method of play, radically changing the pawn structure, is also not at all bad: 10 dxc5 ♕a5 11 ♗e3 ♗xc3 12 ♖c1 ♗g7 13 ♕b3 ♕a6 14 a4! ♕xe2 15 ♖fd1 (15 ♕b5 is also good) 15...a5 16 ♖d2 ♕a6 17 ♗f1 ♕a7 18 ♗c4 with excellent compensation for the pawn (Vakhidov-Yermolinsky, Tashkent 1982).

10...cxd4

This looks natural, whereas 10...♘a5?! gives White a clear advantage after 11 ♕c1 cxd4 12 cxd4 (12 ♘xd4!? is more logical) 12...♗e6 13 ♗h6 ♖c8 14 ♕f4 ♕c7 15 ♕h4 (Rossolimo-Michel, Mar del Plata 1950). Also the interesting 10...♗e6 has yet to be tried.

11 ♘xd4

Weaker is 11 cxd4 ♗e6 12 ♕a4 ♗d5 13 ♖ac1 ♖c8 when Black has no problems (Neb.Ristic-Paunovic, Yugoslavia 1989).

11...♘a5

Black decides on immediate play against the c3 pawn and the c4 square. If 11...♗d7 12 ♖b1 ♘a5 13 ♘b3! ♘c4 (13...♘xb3 14 ♕xb3 ♗c6 15 ♗xc6 bxc6 16 ♖fd1 with a slight advantage to White) 14 ♗d4 ♗c6 15 ♗xc6 bxc6 16 ♕d3 with the better game (Romanishin-Kapengut, Kecskemet 1989).

12 ♖b1!?

Also good is 12 ♕c1 ♘c4 13 ♗h6 ♗xh6 14 ♕xh6 e5 15 ♖fd1! when Black has problems.

12...♘c4 13 ♗c1 e5 14 ♘b5 ♕e7

After 14...♕xd1 15 ♖xd1 ♗g4 16 f3 ♗e6 17 ♘c7 ♖ad8 18 ♗g5! White has the advantage, while if 14...a6 there follows 15 ♕xd8 ♖xd8 16 ♘c7 ♖a7 17 ♗g5 f6 18 ♗d5+ with advantage.

15 ♕d5!

This centralising move clarifies White's advantage.

15...♘b6 16 ♕d6?!

But White should not have exchanged queens. After 16 ♕b3! ♗e6 17 ♗a3 ♕d7 18 ♕c2 he would have maintained a great advantage.

16...♕xd6 17 ♘xd6 ♗e6 18 ♖a1?!

Better was 18 ♗a3! ♗xa2 19 ♖b2 ♗d5 20 c4! ♗xg2 (20...♗c6 21 c5 ♘a4 22 ♖xb7! with advantage to White) 21

♔xg2 when White has unpleasant threats.

18...♘a4 19 ♗a3 ♘xc3 20 ♘xb7 ♖fb8

After 20...♘xe2+ 21 ♔h1 e4! the play is very unclear.

21 ♘c5 ♗d5 22 ♗xd5 ♘xd5 23 ♖ac1 ♗f8

Two other possibilities were 23...♘b4 and 23...a5.

24 ♖fd1 ♘b6

Weaker is 24...♘b4 25 ♘d7 ♘xa2 26 ♘xb8 ♘xc1 27 ♖d8, winning.

25 ♖d3! ♖c8

After 25...♖d8 Black would have equalised.

26 ♘e4 ♗xa3

26...♖xc1+ looks simpler.

27 ♖xc8+ ♖xc8 28 ♖xa3 ♖c7?

And here 28...♖c4! looks more active.

29 ♘f6+ ♔h8 30 g4!

Despite the small number of pieces, the ending is highly unpleasant for Black.

30...h6 31 h4 ♖b7 32 ♖a5! ♖e7 33 g5 hxg5 34 hxg5 ♔g7 35 ♖c5 e4 36 a4! ♖b7 37 ♖b5 a6 38 ♖b4 a5 39 ♖b5 ♖b8 40 e3!

In view of complete *zugzwang*, Black resigned.

Game 8
Greenfeld-Korchnoi
Beer Sheva 1993

1 d4 ♘f6 2 c4 g6 3 ♘f3 ♗g7 4 g3 0–0
5 ♗g2 d5 6 cxd5 ♘xd5 7 0–0 ♘c6 8 e4
♘b6 9 d5 ♘a5 10 ♘c3

This move order gives White an additional possibility, although it is not especially dangerous for Black: 10 ♕e1 ♘ac4 11 ♘c3 e6 12 b3 ♘e5 13 ♘xe5 ♗xe5 14 ♗b2 ♕e7 15 ♖c1 ♗d7 16 ♕d2 ♖ad8 17 ♖fd1 ♖fe8 18 h4 h5 19 dxe6 ♗xe6 20 ♘d5 ♗xd5 21 exd5 ♕d6 with an equal game (Pigusov-Epishin, Biel 1993). At present this is the latest word in theory.

10...c6 11 ♗g5 h6

The attempt by Black to include the exchange leads to an interesting pawn sacrifice: 11...cxd5 12 ♘xd5! ♘xd5 13 exd5 ♗xb2 14 ♖e1! ♗f6 (14...f6!? 15 ♗h6 ♗xa1 16 ♗xf8 ♔xf8 17 ♕xa1 with compensation for the pawn) 15 ♗xf6 exf6 (Ivanchuk-Gelfand, Tilburg 1990), and here 16 d6 ♗e6 17 ♕d4! would have led to a serious advantage for White.

12 ♗f4 ♗g4

12...cxd5 is stronger: 13 exd5 (for 13 ♘xd5 see *Game 9*, Shpilker-Krasenkov, USSR 1987) 13...♘ac4 14 ♕e2 e5 15 dxe6 ♗xe6 16 ♖fd1 ♕c8 17 ♖ac1 g5 18 ♗e5! ♘xe5 19 ♘xe5 ♕c7 and White has only a minimal advantage (Wojtkiewicz-Stohl, Werfen 1990), whereas 12...♘ac4 13 b3! ♗xc3 14 ♖c1! is dangerous for Black: 14...♘b2 15 ♕c2 ♗g7 16 ♗e5 ♗xe5 17 ♘xe5 cxd5 18 exd5 ♘xd5 19 ♘xg6! ♘b4 20 ♕e4! ♖e8 21 ♘e5 ♕d2 22 ♖xc8! 1-0 (Romanishin-Kindermann, Debrecen 1990).

13 ♕c1!?

After 13 h3 ♗xf3 14 ♕xf3 cxd5 15 exd5 ♖c8 16 ♖ad1! ♘ac4 17 ♗c1 White has a minimal advantage (Ehlvest-Ftacnik, Haninge 1990), but Black has the strong idea of 13...e5! 14 hxg4 exf4, equalising.

13...cxd5 14 exd5 ♗xf3

Weak is 14...g5 15 ♗e5! ♗xf3 16 ♗xg7 ♗xg2? (16...♔xg7 17 ♗xf3 ♘ac4 is better) 17 ♗xh6 ♔h7 18 ♕xg5 ♖g8 19 ♕h4, winning.

15 ♗xf3 g5!? 16 ♗d2 ♘ac4 17 ♖d1 ♖c8

Activating the other knight by 17...♘d7!? came into consideration.

18 ♗e1

18...♕d6?

The start of an incorrect plan. 18...♘xb2 did not work: 19 ♕xb2 ♗xc3 (after 19...♘a4 20 ♘xa4 ♗xb2 21 ♘xb2, as in other positions after a similar queen sacrifice, White stands better) 20 ♗xc3 ♘a4 21 ♕xb7 ♘xc3 22 ♖d3 with advantage, but 18...♕d7 19 ♖b1 ♕f5 or 18...♘e5 19 ♗g2 ♘bc4 20 b3 ♘d6 was correct, with good counterplay, although 18...♘d7 could also be considered.

19 ♖b1

Essential, as after 19 ♕c2 Black could now have played 19...♘xb2 20

♕xb2 (if here 20 ♘xa4? ♗xb2 21 ♘xb2 ♕f6!, winning a piece) 20...♘a4 21 ♕xb7 ♘xc3, when he seizes the initiative.

19...f5?

Continuing the same risky plan – 19...♖fd8 or 19...♘d7 was much stronger.

20 ♕c2! ♘e5 21 ♗g2 f4

Black's last chance was 21...♘bc4, although even here his position is clearly inferior.

22 ♕b3!

Now Black's position collapses in view of the numerous weaknesses.

22...♔h8

After 22...fxg3 23 hxg3 ♘f3+? 24 ♗xf3 ♖xf3 25 ♘e4! White has a decisive advantage.

23 ♘b5 ♕g6 24 d6 exd6

Again 24...fxg3 was slightly better.

25 ♘xa7 fxg3?!

But now this loses quickly, although after 25...♖c2 26 ♖xd6 (or 26 ♕xb6) 26...♕xd6 27 ♕xc2 White is close to a win.

26 ♘xc8 gxf2+ 27 ♗xf2 ♘xc8 28 ♕xb7 ♘g4 29 ♗g3 ♗d4+ 30 ♔h1 ♘e3 31 ♗e4 1–0

Game 9
Shpilker-Krasenkov
USSR 1987

---

1 d4 ♘f6 2 c4 g6 3 ♘f3 ♗g7 4 g3 0–0 5 ♗g2 d5 6 cxd5 ♘xd5 7 0–0 ♘b6 8 ♘c3 ♘c6 9 d5 ♘a5 10 e4 c6 11 ♗g5 h6 12 ♗f4 cxd5 13 ♘xd5!?

This deviation from the main variation leads to a somewhat different type of position. The idea is that after ...♘ac4 White plays b2-b3, and the knight at c3 is not 'hanging' in any of the variations.

13...♘ac4!?

Black avoids positions with a pawn at d5. After 13...♘xd5 14 exd5 ♘c4 there follows 15 ♕c1! ♘xb2 16 ♗xh6 ♘d3 17 ♕d2 with a big advantage (A.Mikhalchishin-Passerotti, Rome 1977), while if 14...g5 White even has 15 ♗e5 g4 16 ♗xg7 gxf3 17 ♕xf3 ♔xg7 18 b4!

14 ♕b3!

In Pastircak-Hort (Czechoslovakia 1984) White played the unfortunate 14 ♘c7?! ♖b8 15 ♕xd8 ♖xd8 16 ♖ad1 (after 16 ♘a6? e5 17 ♘xb8 exf4 the knight is trapped) 16...♗g4 17 ♘d5 e5 18 ♘xb6 ♖xd1 19 ♖xd1 ♘xb2! 20 ♖d2 exf4 and ended up in a difficult position. The most interesting here is 14 b3!? ♗xa1 15 ♕xa1, which has not yet been tried in practice.

14...e5!

A very strong strategic blow. After 14...♘xd5 15 exd5 ♘d6 16 ♖fe1 White has an advantage typical of the given variation in view of the weakness of the e7 pawn.

15 ♘xb6 ♕xb6! 16 ♗xh6!

White too rises to the occasion – 16 ♕xc4? is bad because of 16...exf4.

16...♗xh6 17 ♕xc4 ♕xb2 18 ♖ab1 ♕a3 19 ♘xe5 ♗e6!

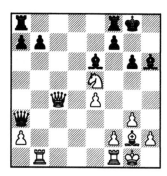

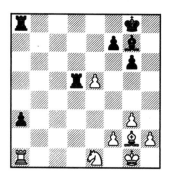

Black has sacrificed a pawn and obtained excellent play in view of the weakness of the a2 pawn, and in addition the white bishop is blocked by the pawn at e4. Now White should not have gone into an ending, but played 20 ♕b5.

20 ♕b4 ♕xb4 21 ♖xb4 ♗g7! 22 ♘f3 a5 23 ♖xb7 ♗xa2 24 e5!

White tries to restrict the black bishops, with the support of which the a-pawn is advancing irrepressibly. In principle, this play is typical of the Grünfeld Defence.

24...a4 25 ♖b2

The best way for White to combat the a-pawn was by 25 ♖a1 ♗e6 26 ♘d4.

25...♗c4 26 ♖a1 a3 27 ♖b4 ♗d5 28 ♖b5 ♖fd8 29 ♖xd5 ♖xd5 30 ♘e1?

White has devised a good saving operation, but he carries it out inaccurately. Correct was 30 ♘g5! ♖xe5 31 ♗xa8 ♖a5 32 ♖xa3 ♖xa3 33 ♗d5 ♖a5 34 ♗xf7+ ♔f8 35 f4 with a drawn ending.

30...♖xe5! 31 ♗xa8 ♖a5 32 ♖a2

Now 32 ♖xa3 ♖xa3 33 ♗d5 ♖a1 34 ♔f1 ♗c3 does not work, as Black wins the knight at e1.

32...♖xa8 33 ♔f1 ♗f8 34 ♔e2 ♔g7 35 ♔d1?

35 h4! was better, although the ending is very difficult – White's main piece, his rook, is too restricted by the passed a-pawn.

35...g5! 36 h3 ♔g6 37 ♘d3 ♔f5 38 f3 ♗d6 39 g4+

White is forced to weaken his pawns, which leads to loss of material.

39...♔f6 40 ♘f2 ♔e5 41 ♘e4 ♗e7 42 ♔e2 ♔f4 43 ♘f2 ♖a6 44 ♘d3+ ♔g3 45 ♘f2 ♖b6! 46 ♘e4+ ♔xh3 47 ♖d2 ♖b2

Black goes into a won ending with bishop against knight, and things end in *zugzwang*.

48 ♖xb2 axb2 49 ♘c3 ♗b4 50 ♘b1 ♔g2 51 ♔e3 ♔f1 52 ♔d3 ♔f2 53 ♔c4

If 53 ♔e4 Black wins by 53...f6 54 f4 ♔g3 55 fxg5 fxg5 56 ♔f5 ♔h4.

53...♗e1 0–1

3 Exchange Variation: 6 ♘f3 ♘b6

1	d4	♘f6
2	c4	g6
3	g3	♗g7
4	♗g2	d5
5	cxd5	♘xd5
6	♘f3	♘b6!
7	0–0	♘c6!

Experts consider this to be the most accurate move order for Black, avoiding the various lines with d4-d5 and e2-e4. White must either sacrifice a pawn by 8 ♘c3 (3.1), which however does not promise him any particular advantage, or else play 8 e3 (3.2).

3.1 (1 d4 ♘f6 2 c4 g6 3 g3 ♗g7 4 ♗g2 d5 5 cxd5 ♘xd5 6 ♘f3 ♘b6 7 0–0 ♘c6)

---

8 ♘c3 ♘xd4

The pawn sacrifice should be accepted. Weaker is 8...♗g4 9 d5 ♗xf3 10 ♗xf3 ♘e5 11 ♗g2 0–0 12 ♗f4 c6 13 ♕b3 cxd5 14 ♘xd5 ♘xd5 15 ♗xd5 ♘c6 (Kuzmin-Balashov, Moscow 1979) and here White should have played 16 ♖fd1 ♘d4 17 ♕xb7 with advantage.

8...0–0 9 e3 transposes into the main line (section 3.22).

9 ♘xd4 ♕xd4

Worse is 9...♗xd4 10 ♘b5 ♗e5 11 ♕xd8+ ♔xd8 12 ♖d1+ ♘d7 13 ♗e3 with the initiative, since the black king is prevented from castling.

10 ♘b5

In the event of 10 ♕xd4 ♗xd4 11 ♘b5 ♗e5 12 ♗f4 ♗xf4 13 gxf4 0–0 14 ♘xc7 ♖b8 15 ♘b5 ♗d7 16 ♘d4 ♘c4 Black has no problems (Dzindzichashvili-Wolff, USA 1993), but the sharp 13...♔d8 14 ♖fd1+ ♘d7 15 ♖d2 c6 16 ♘d4 a5 17 ♖c1 e6 18 ♖c3 ♔e7 19 a3 ♘f6 is also possible, when Black gradually develops, retaining his extra pawn (Sturua-Makarov, Helsinki 1992).

More interesting is 10 a4!? ♕xd1 11 ♖xd1 c6 12 a5 ♘c4 13 a6 0–0 14 axb7 ♗xb7 15 ♖d7 ♗c8 16 ♖xe7 ♖b8 17 ♖exa7 ♗e6 with advantage to White, although whether it is enough to win is not clear (Davies-Liss, Israel 1994).

10 ... ♕c5!

There is also 10...♕c4 (weaker is 10...♕xd1 11 ♖xd1 ♗e5 12 ♗f4) 11 a4!? (earlier White used to play 11 ♕b3 0–0 12 ♕xc4 ♘xc4 13 ♘xc7 ♖b8 14 ♘d5 ♗e6 [after 14...♖e8 15 ♗f4 e5 16 ♗g5 ♘xb2 17 ♘c7 ♖f8 18 ♗e7 White is better, Pigusov-Cvitan, Tilburg 1994] 15 ♘xe7+ ♔h8 with equality, Ornstein-Smejkal, Skopje 1972) 11...0–0 12 b3 ♕g4 13 ♗e3 (Fominykh-Krasenkov, Elista 1996), and here Black should have played 13...♗xa1 14 ♕xa1 c6! 15 ♘c7 ♗f5! 16 ♘xa8 ♖xa8 17 ♕e5 with an unclear game (Krasenkov).

Tukmakov-Gavrikov (Gijon 1988) now continued 11 a4 ♘xa4! 12 ♕xa4 ♗d7 13 ♗xb7 ♗xb5 14 ♕a5 (an equal ending results from 14 ♗e3 ♗xa4 15 ♗xc5 ♖b8 16 ♗f3 ♗b3! 17 ♗xa7 ♖d8 18 ♗c6+ ♔f8 19 ♗c5 ♗f6 20 ♖a7 ♔g7, Skomorokhin-A.Mikhalchishin, Lviv 1996, or 17 ♗c6+ ♔f8 18 ♖xa7 ♗e5 and 19...♔g7) 14...♖b8 15 ♗e3 ♕f5 16 ♕xc7 0–0 (after 16...♗e5!? 17 ♗c6+ ♔f8 18 ♗h6+ ♔g8 19 ♕xe7 ♗xc6 20 ♖fd1 ♗f6 21 ♕d6 ♖c8 22 ♖ac1 White regains his piece, Neat) 17 ♖a5 ♗e5! and Black equalised (Skomorokhin-A.Mikhalchishin, Lviv 1996).

3.2 (1 d4 ♘f6 2 c4 g6 3 g3 ♗g7 4 ♗g2 d5 5 cxd5 ♘xd5 6 ♘f3 ♘b6 7 0–0 ♘c6)

8   e3

Now Black has **8...e5 (3.21)** or the main variation **8...0–0 (3.22)**.

3.21 (1 d4 ♘f6 2 c4 g6 3 g3 ♗g7 4 ♗g2 d5 5 cxd5 ♘xd5 6 ♘f3 ♘b6 7 0–0 ♘c6 8 e3)

8   ...   e5
9   ♘c3

9 dxe5 is not so active, but may also be dangerous: 9...♕xd1 10 ♖xd1 ♘xe5

---

11 ♘xe5 (after 11 ♘d4 c6 White simply has nothing, Polugayevsky-Letelier, Mar del Plata 1962) 11...♗xe5 12 ♘c3 (weaker is 12 ♘d2 c6 13 ♘f3 ♗g7 14 ♘d4 ♗g4! 15 f3 ♗d7 16 ♗d2 c5 17 ♘b3 ♘a4 with advantage to Black, Hübner-Kasparov, Cologne 1992, or 12 ♘a3 c6 13 ♖b1 0–0 14 b3 ♗e6 15 ♗b2 ♗xb2 16 ♖xb2 ♖fd8 17 ♖bd2 ♖xd2 18 ♖xd2 a5! with the initiative, Semkov-Dvoiris, Sochi 1982) 12...0–0 (interesting is 12...c6!? 13 e4 ♗g4 14 f3 ♗e6 15 ♗h6 ♖d8 16 f4 ♖xd1+ 17 ♖xd1 ♗xc3 18 bxc3 f5 with a reasonable game, Garcia-Fernandez, Spain 1991) 13 e4 ♗g7 (Black does not have to withdraw his bishop so early – after 13...♗e6 14 f4 ♗xc3 15 bxc3 ♖fd8 16 ♖d4 c5 17 ♖xd8+ ♖xd8 18 ♗e3 ♘a4 he is not badly placed, Gudmundsson-Grunberg, Reykjavik 1982, or 13...c6 14 f4 ♗g7 15 e5 f6! 16 exf6 ♗xf6 and White has not managed to restrict the black bishops, Todorcevic-Fernandez, Ibercaja 1996) 14 ♗e3 ♗g4 15 f3 ♗e6 16 ♗d4 (P.Nikolic-Anand, Linares 1997), and here 16...♖fd8 would have given chances of holding the ending (*Game 10*).

Now we consider **9...exd4 (3.211)** and **9...♗g4 (3.212)**.

3.211 (1 d4 ♘f6 2 c4 g6 3 g3 ♗g7 4 ♗g2 d5 5 cxd5 ♘xd5 6 ♘f3 ♘b6 7 0–0 ♘c6 8 e3 e5 9 ♘c3)

9   ...   exd4
10   exd4

The exchange of a pair of knights normally eases Black's defence: **10 ♘xd4 ♘xd4 11 exd4 0–0** (the position is also equal after 11...c6 12 d5 cxd5 13 ♘xd5 0–0 14 ♘c3 ♕xd1 15 ♖xd1 ♗g4 16 ♖f1 ♘c4, Najdorf-Olafsson, Bled 1961) 12 d5 ♗f5 13 a4 (Vukic-Ilincic,

Cetinje 1990) 13...♘c4 or 13...♖e8 14 ♕b3 a5 with an equal game.

10 ... 0–0
11 ♗g5

11 ... ♗f6
Less good is **11...♕d7** 12 ♘e4 (but not 12 ♖e1 h6 13 ♗e3 ♖d8 14 ♕e2 ♕e7 15 ♖ad1 ♗e6 with only equality, Brunner-Hellers, Biel 1993) 12...♘d5 13 ♘c5 (and not 13 ♕d2 f6 14 ♗h6 b6 15 ♗xg7 ♔xg7 16 ♖fe1 ♗b7 17 h4 ♖ae8 18 ♔h2 ♖e7 again with an equal game, Talanin-Kazhgaleev, Kstovo 1996) 13...♕d6 14 ♖c1! with a strong initiative.

Even worse is **11...f6** 12 ♗f4 ♗e6 13 ♖e1 ♗f7 14 ♖c1 a6 15 ♘d2! g5 16 ♗e3 f5 17 ♘b3 ♕f6 18 d5 ♖ad8 19 ♗c5 with advantage (Jasnikowski-Kaminski, Germany 1993).

12 d5
The untried 12 ♗h6 comes into consideration.

12 ... ♗xg5
13 ♘xg5 ♕xg5
14 dxc6 bxc6
15 ♗xc6

Perhaps it is worth considering the pawn sacrifice **15 ♖e1** or **15 ♕c1** – in any case the c6 pawn is hopelessly weak.

15 ... ♗h3
16 ♖e1

It was worth centralising by **16 ♗xa8** ♗xf1 17 ♕xf1 ♖xa8 18 ♖d1! when the black knight is somewhat restricted, although after 18...♖d8 it is doubtful whether White could squeeze anything out of the position.

16 ... ♖ad8
17 ♕c1

Stronger was 17 ♘e4 with some advantage to White, whereas if **17 ♕f3** ♗g4.

17...♕xc1 18 ♖axc1 ♖d2 19 b3 ♖fd8 with equality (Rechlis-Miles, Ostende 1993).

> **3.212 (1 d4 ♘f6 2 c4 g6 3 g3 ♗g7 4 ♗g2 d5 5 cxd5 ♘xd5 6 ♘f3 ♘b6 7 0–0 ♘c6 8 e3 e5 9 ♘c3)**

9 ... ♗g4
10 h3
After **10 d5** e4!? (if 10...♘e7 11 e4 c6 12 h3 ♗xf3 13 ♕xf3 cxd5 14 ♘xd5 Black should transpose into the main line by 14...0–0, but not 14...♘c6 15 ♕a3! ♗f8 16 ♕d3 with advantage to White, Blees-A.Mikhalchishin, Hungary 1989) 11 ♘xe4 (after 11 dxc6 ♕xd1 12 ♖xd1 exf3 13 cxb7 ♖b8 14 ♗f1 ♖xb7 15 ♗b5+ ♔e7 Black's chances are not worse) 11...♕xd5 12 ♕xd5 ♘xd5 13 h3 ♗xf3 14 ♗xf3 0–0–0 15 ♘c5 b6 Black has a serious lead in development (Julanpera-Kasparov, simul. 1988).

10 ... ♗xf3
11 ♗xf3
After 11 ♕xf3 exd4 12 exd4 0–0 13 d5 ♘e5 14 ♕d1 ♖e8 15 a4 ♘bc4 16 b3 ♘d6 17 ♖a2 ♕f6 18 ♘e4 ♘xe4 19 ♗xe4 ♖ad8 Black has an excellent game (Langeweg-Hort, Wijk aan Zee 1975).

Now after 11...exd4 12 exd4 0–0 13 d5 ♘d4 14 ♗g2 ♖e8 15 h4 ♘c4 16 b3 ♘d6 17 ♗g5 ♕d7 18 ♖c1 h6 19 ♗f4 ♖e7 Black has a good game, since his knights excellently control the centre (Janjgava-A.Mikhalchishin, Pavlodar 1987).

> **3.22 (1 d4 ♘f6 2 c4 g6 3 g3 ♗g7 4 ♗g2 d5 5 cxd5 ♘xd5 6 ♘f3 ♘b6 7 0–0 ♘c6 8 e3)**

**8 ...   0–0
9 ♘c3**

Now Black's main options are 9...a5 (3.221), 9...♖e8 (3.222) and 9...e5 (3.223).

9...♗e6 10 b3 is a very rare continuation:

(a) 10...a5 11 ♘g5 ♗f5 12 ♘ge4 e5 13 d5 ♘b4 and Black is not badly placed (Loeffler-Pribyl, Germany 1994), but 12 ♗a3! was stronger;

(b) 10...h6 11 ♗b2 a5 12 ♘e1 a4! 13 ♘xa4 ♘xa4 14 bxa4 ♗d5 15 ♗xd5 ♕xd5 16 ♕b3 ♕e4 17 ♖c1 and White is better (Ribli-Romanishin, Novi Sad 1982);

(c) 10...♕c8!? 11 ♗b2 ♗h3 12 ♖c1 (better 12 ♕e2 with the idea of 13 ♖fd1,

preparing d4-d5) 12...♗xg2 13 ♔xg2 ♖d8 (another typical plan, involving the exchange of light-square bishops; its drawback, of course, is that it has little influence on the centre) 14 ♕e2 e5 15 dxe5 ♘xe5 16 ♘xe5 ♗xe5 17 ♘e4 ♕f5 with equality (Kharitonov-Zaichik, Vilnius 1978).

> **3.221 (1 d4 ♘f6 2 c4 g6 3 g3 ♗g7 4 ♗g2 d5 5 cxd5 ♘xd5 6 ♘f3 ♘b6 7 0–0 ♘c6 8 e3 0–0 9 ♘c3)**

9 ...   a5
Smyslov's favourite plan. The idea is to create play on the queenside, seizing as much space as possible, and only then to launch an attack in the centre. Its drawback, of course, is that it defers the play in the centre.

White's main responses are: 10 b3 (3.2211), 10 ♕e2 (3.2212) and 10 d5 (3.2213).

The simple prevention of Black's play by **10 a4?** gives his knight the important b4 square after 10...e5 11 d5 ♘b4, while after **10 ♗d2** a4 11 ♖c1 ♗e6 12 ♕c2 ♘b4 13 ♕e4 c6 14 a3 ♗f5 15 ♕h4 ♘d3 the black pieces are excellently placed (Katetov-Smyslov, Moscow 1946).

> **3.2211 (1 d4 ♘f6 2 c4 g6 3 g3 ♗g7 4 ♗g2 d5 5 cxd5 ♘xd5 6 ♘f3 ♘b6 7 0–0 ♘c6 8 e3 0–0 9 ♘c3 a5)**

10 b3
A logical but harmless continuation, allowing Black the opportunity for a counter in the centre.

10 ...   e5!
10...♗d7 is more passive: 11 ♗a3 ♕c8 12 ♖c1 ♗h3 13 ♘g5 ♗xg2 14 ♔xg2 ♘b4 15 ♕f3 and White has a

serious spatial advantage (Zak-Tukmakov, France 1991).

The author of this plan himself played **10...♘b4 11 ♗b2 a4 12 ♘xa4 ♘xa4 13 bxa4 ♘d5** in Benko-Smyslov (Budapest-Moscow 1949); now 14 a5! ♖xa5 15 a4 ♘b4 16 ♘e5 would have led to complicated play – *Game 11*.

11　♗a3　　♖e8

12　♘xe5

If **12 dxe5 ♘xe5 13 ♘d4 c6 14 ♕c2 ♘d5 15 ♘xd5 cxd5 16 ♖ac1 a4 17 ♗b4** with advantage (Sokolsky), but it would have been correct to include the exchange of queens 12...♕xd1 with an equal game.

Novikov-Lukin (USSR 1972) now continued 12...♘xe5 13 dxe5 ♕xd1 14 ♖fxd1 ♗xe5 15 ♖ac1 a4 16 ♗c5 axb3 17 axb3 ♗g4 with equality.

3.2212 (1 d4 ♘f6 2 c4 g6 3 g3 ♗g7 4 ♗g2 d5 5 cxd5 ♘xd5 6 ♘f3 ♘b6 7 0–0 ♘c6 8 e3 0–0 9 ♘c3 a5)

10　♕e2　　e5!?

After **10...♗e6 11 ♖d1 ♗c4 12 ♕c2 a4** (if 12...e6 13 b3 White is better, Boleslavsky) **13 ♘e4 e5! 14 ♘c5 exd4 15 ♘xd4 ♘xd4 16 exd4 ♗d5! 17 ♘xb7 ♕f6** Black has strong pressure in the

centre and on the queenside for the sacrificed pawn, but 13 e4! is better, as in the Levenfish-Kopylov game.

After **10...♗g4 11 h3 ♗e6 12 ♖d1 ♗c4 13 ♕c2 a4 14 e4 f5 15 ♗e3 ♘b4 16 ♕b1 ♕c8 17 ♘e5** Black has problems due to his lack of space (Levenfish-Kopylov, USSR 1947).

Now after 11 dxe5 ♘xe5 12 ♘d4 a4 13 ♖d1 ♕e7 14 h3 ♖d8 15 ♖b1 c5 16 ♘db5 ♗e6 (Todorcevic-Agdestein, Marseille 1987) Black has a reasonable game. He has solved all his centre and development problems.

3.2213 (1 d4 ♘f6 2 c4 g6 3 g3 ♗g7 4 ♗g2 d5 5 cxd5 ♘xd5 6 ♘f3 ♘b6 7 0–0 ♘c6 8 e3 0–0 9 ♘c3 a5)

10　d5　　　♘b4

If **10...♗xc3** there follows 11 dxc6 ♕xd1 12 ♖xd1 ♗f6 13 ♘d4 bxc6 14 ♗xc6 ♖b8 15 b3 and then 16 ♗b2, and in view of the weakness at c7 White has the better chances.

11　e4　　　c6

If **11...e6 12 a3 ♘a6 13 ♗g5 f6 14 ♗e3 ♘c4 15 ♗c1 ♖e8 16 h4 exd5 17 exd5 ♘d6 18 ♘d4** and White is better (Skomorokhin-Nemet, Szekszard 1994).

12　a3　　　♘a6

13 dxc6

If **13 ♗e3 ♘c4 14 ♗d4 e5!** 15 dxe6 ♗xe6 16 ♗xg7 ♕xd1, equalising (Akhmilovskaya-Chiburdanidze, Sofia 1986). But **13 ♗f4 cxd5 14 exd5 ♘c5** is interesting, with an unclear position.

13 ... bxc6

14 ♕c2

14 ... ♕c7

White has the advantage after 14...♗g4 15 h3 ♗d7 16 ♖d1 ♕c8 17 ♔h2 c5 18 ♗e3 (Keene-Smyslov, Moscow 1975). Black's problem throughout the variation is his weak c-pawn and badly placed knight at a6.

15 ♖d1

Less good is **15 ♘a4 ♘xa4 16 ♕xa4 ♖b8 17 ♕c2 ♖b5 18 ♖d1 ♕b6** and Black has no problems (Reshevsky-Olafsson, Dallas 1957).

Kochiev-Tseshkovsky (Baku 1977) now continued 15...♖b8 16 h3 a4!? 17 ♘xa4 ♘xa4 18 ♕xa4 ♘c5 19 ♕c2 ♘b3 20 ♖b1 ♘xc1 21 ♖dxc1 ♕a7 with some compensation for the pawn.

3.222 (1 d4 ♘f6 2 c4 g6 3 g3 ♗g7 4 ♗g2 d5 5 cxd5 ♘xd5 6 ♘f3 ♘b6 7 0–0 ♘c6 8 e3 0–0 9 ♘c3)

9 ... ♖e8

A useful waiting move – Black prepares ...e7-e5 and invites White to make a move, and White does not have any especially useful moves. His main options are **10 ♘e1 (3.2221)**, **10 ♖e1 (3.3222)** and **10 d5 (3.2223)**. Other possibilities:

10 b3 e5 11 dxe5 ♘xe5 12 ♘xe5 ♕xd1 (if 12...♗xe5 13 ♗b2 c6 14 ♕c2 ♗d7 15 ♖ad1 ♕e7 16 ♕c1 ♕c5 17 ♕a1 ♗f5 and Black has no problems, Jeric-Fogarasi, Budapest 1993) 13 ♖xd1 ♗xe5 14 ♗b2 c6 15 ♖d2 f5 16 ♖ad1 (the game is equal after 16 ♖e1 ♗e6 17 f4 ♗g7 18 e4 ♖ad8 19 ♖ed1 ♖xd2 20 ♖xd2 fxe4, Damljanovic-Kozul, Cetinje 1991) 16...♗e6 17 h3 ♗g7 18 ♘e2 a5 19 ♘f4 with a minimal advantage (Gufeld-Rogers, Wellington 1988). White has complete control of the central file, but Black retains possibilities of play on the queenside.

10 ♕e2 e5 11 dxe5 ♘xe5 12 ♘xe5 ♗xe5 13 ♖d1 ♕e7 14 e4 h5!? (Black has eliminated the d-pawn, so White's only chances involve advancing his e- and f-pawns, whereas Black has a queenside majority; if 14...c6 15 f4 ♗g7 16 ♗e3 ♗e6 17 ♕f2 with slightly the better game for White, Smyslov-Cvitan, New York 1987) 15 ♗e3 ♗e6 16 ♗d4 ♗xd4 17 ♖xd4 c5 18 ♖d2 ♖ad8 with an equal position (Smyslov-Korchnoi, Beer Sheva 1990).

10 h3 (a modest move, which does not aim for anything serious or immediate) 10...a5!? 11 ♖b1 a4 12 ♘e1 ♗f5! 13 e4 ♗d7 (13...♗c8 is also good, avoiding occupying d7) 14 ♘c2 e5 15 dxe5 (weaker is 15 d5 ♘d4 16 ♗e3 c5 with advantage to Black) 15...♘xe5 16 f4 ♘ec4 17 ♕f3 ♕e7 with an excellent game for Black (Speelman-Short, London 1991).

3.2221 (1 d4 ♘f6 2 c4 g6 3 g3 ♗g7 4 ♗g2 d5 5 cxd5 ♘xd5 6 ♘f3 ♘b6 7 0–0 ♘c6 8 e3 0–0 9 ♘c3 ♖e8)

10 ♘e1

An interesting knight manoeuvre – the idea is to uncover the bishop at g2 and to use the knight to strengthen the queenside.

10 ... e5

After **10...a5!?** 11 ♘d3 ♘b4 12 ♘c5 c6 13 a3 ♘a6 14 ♘d3 ♗e6 Black managed to equalise in Foisor-Rogers (Saint John 1988), but 11 b3 was stronger.

11 d5 ♘a5
12 e4

Or **12 ♘c2** :

(a) 12...c6 13 e4 cxd5 14 exd5 ♘ac4 15 b3 ♘d6 16 ♗b2 e4 17 ♖b1 ♘d7 18 ♘e3 and White is better (Furman-Jansa, Leningrad 1970); even stronger is 13 b4! ♘ac4 14 dxc6 e4 15 ♘d4 f5 16 ♕b3 bxc6 17 ♖d1 with advantage (Vaganian-Kozul, Toronto 1990);

(b) 12...♘ac4 13 e4 ♘d6 14 b3 ♗d7 15 ♗b2 f5 16 exf5 gxf5 17 f4 exf4 18 ♖xf4 with a slight advantage (Korchnoi-Hort, Luhacovice 1969);

(c) 12...e4! 13 ♘xe4 ♘xd5 14 ♘d4 ♘c4! 15 b3 ♘e5 16 ♗b2 ♕e7 17 ♕d2 ♖d8! when White's queen is in an unpleasant pin, and only he has problems (A.Mikhalchishin-Kozul, Portoroz 1993).

12 ... c6

If **12...♘ac4** 13 a4! a5 14 b3 ♘d6 15 ♘d3 f5 16 ♘c5 ♕e7 (Vaganian-Chandler, Thessaloniki 1984), and here 17 ♖a2! with the idea of 18 ♖c2 would have given White the advantage.

13 a4!

This is stronger than 13 ♗e3 ♘ac4 14 ♗xb6 ♘xb6 15 dxc6 bxc6 16 ♘c2 ♕e7 17 ♕e2 a5 with equality (Burmakin-S.Farago, Balatonbereny 1993).

The old **13 ♘c2** cxd5 14 exd5 ♘ac4 (also good is 14...f5!? 15 ♕e2 ♘ac4 16 b3 ♘d6 17 ♖d1 ♗d7 18 a4 a6 19 ♗b2 h5! seizing the initiative, Dizdarevic-Rogers, Biel 1987) 15 b3 (perhaps stronger is 15 a4 ♗f5 16 a5 ♘c8 17 ♘e3 ♘8d6 18 ♕a4 b5! 19 axb6 axb6 with chances for both sides, Damljanovic-Ftacnik, New York 1987) 15...♘d6 16 a4!? (16 ♗b2!? ♗d7 17 ♘e3 f5 leads to a complicated game, Kharitonov-Lputian, Simferopol 1988, but 16 ♗e3!? is better) 16...e4 17 ♗b2 h5 18 ♕d2 ♗g4 with an unclear position (P.Nikolic-Ftacnik, Naestved 1985).

13 ... cxd5
14 exd5 f5

If **14...♗f5** 15 g4 ♗d7 16 ♘e4 h6 (Loginov-Gorbatov, St Petersburg 1994), and here correct was 17 b3 with advantage.

15 ♘d3 ♘bc4
16 ♖b1 e4
17 ♘f4 ♗d7

If **17...♕b6** 18 ♘b5 a6 19 b3! axb5 20 bxc4 ♘xc4 21 ♖xb5 ♕a6 22 d6! ♘xd6 23 ♕b3+ ♘f7 24 a5 with the initiative for the pawn (Loginov-I.Horvath, Budapest 1993).

Now 18 d6!? ♗xc3 19 ♕d5+ ♔g7 20 bxc3 ♕f6 21 ♗e3 ♘xe3 22 fxe3 b6 leads to a complicated game (Loginov-I.Horvath, Budapest 1994).

> **3.2222 (1 d4 ♘f6 2 c4 g6 3 g3 ♗g7 4 ♗g2 d5 5 cxd5 ♘xd5 6 ♘f3 ♘b6 7 0–0 ♘c6 8 e3 0–0 9 ♘c3 ♖e8)**

10 ♖e1   e5

10...a5 is possible: 11 b3 (11 ♘d2 e5 12 d5 ♘e7 13 ♘b3 a4 14 ♘c5 a3 15 e4 axb2 16 ♗xb2 ♘c4 also did not achieve anything in Rohde-Kudrin, USA 1988) 11...e5 12 dxe5 ♘xe5 13 ♘xe5 ♕xd1 14 ♖xd1 ♗xe5 15 ♗b2 c6 16 ♖ab1 ♗g7 17 h3 ♗f5 18 e4 ♗e6, and Black held on (Hulak-Tal, Moscow 1990).

11 d5   ♘a5

Possible is **11...♘e7** 12 e4 ♗g4 13 ♕b3 ♗xf3 14 ♗xf3 c6 15 ♗e3 cxd5 16 exd5 ♘f5 17 ♖ad1 ♘d6 18 ♘b5 ♘bc8 19 ♘xd6 ♘xd6 20 ♗c5 ♖e7 21 ♕b4, and White has some advantage (Timman-Ftacnik, Prague 1990).

12 e4   c6

13 ♗g5

Weaker is **13 a4** cxd5 14 exd5 ♗g4 15 h3 ♗xf3 16 ♗xf3 f5 17 ♗e2 e4 18 ♗b5 ♗xc3! 19 bxc3 ♖e5 with an excellent game for Black (Lesiege-Wolff, Montreal 1993).

Now after 13...f6 14 ♗e3 ♘ac4 15

dxc6 ♘xe3 (after 15...bxc6 16 ♗c1 ♕xd1 17 ♖xd1 ♗f8 18 b3 ♘a3 19 ♗b2 ♗g4 20 ♖ac1 White is slightly better, Kasparov-Perec, simul. 1988) 16 ♕xd8 ♖xd8 17 cxb7 ♗xb7 18 ♖xe3 ♗h6 19 ♖ee1 ♘c4 20 ♖ad1 ♗f8 Black has compensation for the pawn in the form of the serious activity of his pieces (Karpov-Kasparov, Amsterdam 1988).

> **3.2223 (1 d4 ♘f6 2 c4 g6 3 g3 ♗g7 4 ♗g2 d5 5 cxd5 ♘xd5 6 ♘f3 ♘b6 7 0–0 ♘c6 8 e3 0–0 9 ♘c3 ♖e8)**

10 d5   ♘a5

Bad is **10...♘b4** 11 e4 c6 12 ♕b3 ♘a6 (12...♘d3 13 ♗e3 cxd5 14 ♖fd1 ♘xb2 15 ♕xb2 ♘a4 16 ♘xa4 ♗xb2 17 ♘xb2 and White's three pieces are stronger than the queen, Ivanchuk) 13 ♗e3 cxd5 14 ♖fd1! ♗d7 15 exd5 ♕c7 16 ♘g5! with advantage (Ivanchuk-Lputian, Lviv 1987).

11 ♘d4   ♗d7

The critical position of the variation, where White has several different plans, the main being **12 e4 (3.22231)** and **12 a4 (3.2232)**. Others:

12 b3 (a modest continuation that allows Black to equalise immediately) 12...c5!? (12...c6 comes to the same thing) 13 dxc6 ♘xc6 14 ♘xc6 ♗xc6 15 ♗xc6 ♕xd1 (the game is also equal after 15...bxc6 16 ♗b2 c5 17 ♕e2 c4! 18 bxc4 ♕c8 19 ♘d5 ♗xb2 20 ♘xb6 axb6 21 ♕xb2, Damljanovic-Kozul, Bled 1991) 16 ♖xd1 bxc6 (Black's pawns are somewhat broken, but by the advance of his a-pawn and pressure on the b-file he succeeds in eliminating White's initiative) 17 ♗d2 a5 ½-½ (Ljubojevic-Kasparov, Barcelona 1989).

12 b4 (with the idea of seizing space – a very logical and interesting plan, against which Black has to find the only correct response) 12...♘ac4 13 a4 (if 13 h3 c6 14 dxc6 ♗xc6 15 ♗xc6 bxc6 16 ♖b1 ♕c8 17 ♕g4 e6 18 h4 c5 with equality, Razuvaev-Timoshchenko, USSR 1988) 13...a5 (bad is 13...c6? 14 ♕b3! cxd5 15 a5 e5 16 ♘de2 with advantage) 14 b5 ♕c8 15 ♖e1 (again the exchange of bishops favours Black – he increases his living space and weakens the d5 pawn) 15...♗h3 16 ♗h1 ♕g4! 17 ♘ce2 (more critical is 17 ♗f3 ♕d7 18 ♘e4 ♖ad8 19 ♘c5 ♕c8 20 ♕b3, with a complicated game where White is still slightly better, Zhidkov-Stohl, Slovakia 1990) 17...♖ad8 18 ♕b3 ♕d7 with a complicated game (Portisch-Kasparov, Reykjavik 1988). The black knight at c4 'restrains' White's position, and ...e7-e6 is threatened, breaking up the centre.

12 ♘b3 ♘xb3 13 axb3 c6 14 dxc6 (after 14 e4 cxd5 15 exd5 ♘c8 16 ♗e3 ♘d6 17 ♗d4 ♗xd4 18 ♕xd4 ♕b6 19 ♕d1 a5 Black has a good game, Jukic-Kozul, Pula 1994) 14...♗xc6 15 e4 ♕xd1 16 ♖xd1 ♖ad8 17 ♗e3 ♘c8 18 f3 a6 (in the resulting ending White has slightly the freer game, but the doubled b-pawns deny him any real winning chances; Black also has no particular

problems after 18...f5 19 exf5 gxf5 20 ♔f2 a6 21 ♗f1 e6 with equality, Yusupov-Kasparov, Belgrade 1989) 19 ♔f2 ♘d6 20 ♗f1 ♘b5 with equality (Yusupov-Stohl, Germany 1996).

12 ♕e2, and now:

(a) 12...♕c8 13 ♖d1 c5 (possible is 13...c6 14 dxc6 ♘xc6 15 ♘xc6 ♗xc6 16 e4 ♕e6 17 ♗e3 ♕c4! with an excellent game, Kosic-Kozul, Novi Sad 1992, but better is 14 e4 cxd5 15 exd5 ♘ac4 16 b3 ♘d6 17 ♗b2 ♗g4 18 f3 ♗h3 19 ♖ac1, retaining some advantage, Neckar-S.Mohr, Zurich 1987) 14 ♘b3 ♘xb3 15 axb3 a6! 16 e4 e6 17 d6 ♗c6 18 h4 with advantage to White (Lein-Ftacnik, Palma de Mallorca 1989);

(b) 12...c6 (stronger) 13 dxc6 ♘xc6 14 ♘xc6 ♗xc6 15 ♗xc6 bxc6 16 ♖d1 ♕c8 17 ♗d2 ♕e6 18 ♗e1 h5! (a good idea – White must be diverted from creating pressure on the c6 pawn) 19 ♖ac1 h4 with good counterplay (Korchnoi-Kasparov, Tilburg 1989).

3.22231 (1 d4 ♘f6 2 c4 g6 3 g3 ♗g7 4 ♗g2 d5 5 cxd5 ♘xd5 6 ♘f3 ♘b6 7 0–0 ♘c6 8 e3 0–0 9 ♘c3 ♖e8 10 d5 ♘a5 11 ♘d4 ♗d7)

---

12 e4

And now Black has: **12...c6** (3.222311) or **12...c5!?** (3.222312).

> **3.222311** (1 d4 ♘f6 2 c4 g6 3 g3 ♗g7 4 ♗g2 d5 5 cxd5 ♘xd5 6 ♘f3 ♘b6 7 0–0 ♘c6 8 e3 0–0 9 ♘c3 ♖e8 10 d5 ♘a5 11 ♘d4 ♗d7 12 e4)

12 ...   c6
13   b3

After **13 dxc6 ♘xc6 14 ♘xc6 ♗xc6 15 ♕b3 ♕d3 16 ♗e3 ♖ac8 17 ♖fd1 ♕a6 18 ♗d4 ♕a5** the game is equal (Hjartarson-Kasparov, Barcelona 1989), while if **13 ♘de2** Black has 13...e6 14 h3 exd5 15 exd5 ♘ac4 16 a4 ♘d6 17 ♗f4 ♘bc4 18 b3 ♘e5 19 ♗e3 ♖c8 20 ♖c1 b6 when everything is in order (Petrov-Letelier, Halle 1995).

13   ...   cxd5

Or **13...c5!?** 14 ♘de2 e6 15 ♗b2 exd5 16 exd5 ♗g4 (Landenbergue-Miralles, Luzern 1989), and here after 17 ♖e1! White has the advantage.

13...♖c8!? is interesting: 14 ♗e3 cxd5 15 ♘xd5 ♘c6 16 ♖c1 ♘xd4 17 ♖xc8 ♗xc8 18 ♗xd4 ♗xd4 19 ♕xd4 ♗e6 and Black held on (Kinsman-de Boer, Dieren 1990).

14   exd5   ♖c8!

Earlier Black used to attack the centre immediately, but then White stands better thanks to his control of the c-file: **14...e6** 15 dxe6 ♗xe6 16 ♗e3 ♗d5 (less good is 16...♘d5 17 ♘xe6 ♘xe3 18 ♕xd8 ♖exd8 19 ♘xd8 ♘xf1 20 ♖d1! ♗xc3 21 ♔xf1 with advantage, Pigusov-Yermolinsky, USSR 1987) 17 ♖c1 ♗xg2 18 ♔xg2 ♘d5 19 ♘xd5 ♕xd5+ 20 ♘f3, and now:

(a) 20...♕xd1 21 ♖fxd1 ♖e7 22 b4 ♘c6 23 b5 ♘e5 24 a4 ♘xf3 25 ♔xf3 b6 26 ♖c6 ♗e5 27 ♗h6 f6 28 ♗e3 and Black was unable to solve his endgame problems (Cvitan-Huzman, Moscow 1989);

(b) 20...♕e4 21 ♕d7! ♖e7 (21...♖ed8 22 ♕c7 ♘c6 23 ♕xb7 also leads to a great advantage for White) 22 ♖c8+ ♖xc8 23 ♕xc8+ ♖e8 24 ♕d7 ♘c6 25 ♖d1! ♗f8 26 ♗g5! ♘e5 27 ♕d5! and again Black has problems (Cvitan-Timoshchenko, Pula 1989);

(c) 20...♕b5!? 21 ♖c5 ♕a6 22 ♖c7! (less good is 22 ♖d5 ♘c6 23 ♕d2 ♖ad8 24 ♗g5 ½-½, Stempin-Novak, Warsaw 1990) 22...♖ad8 23 ♕c2 ♘c6 24 ♖d1 ♖xd1 25 ♕xd1 ♖d8 26 ♕f1! with the better game (C.Hansen-Khalifman, Wijk aan Zee 1991).

15   ♕d2

If **15 ♗b2 ♘bc4!** 16 bxc4 ♕b6! 17 ♘e6 (better 17 ♘a4! ♗xa4 18 ♕xa4, Kabatianski-Tumenok, USSR 1990, and now 18...♘xc4!? 19 ♗c3 ♗xd4 would have led to an unclear game) 17...♘xc4 18 ♘xg7 ♘xb2 19 ♕c2 (Kharitonov-Makarov, Elista 1994) 19...♔xg7 20 ♖ab1 ♗f5 with an excellent game.

15   ...   e6!?

Black also stands well after **15...e5** 16 ♘de2 e4 17 ♗b2 ♘ac4 18 bxc4 ♘xc4 19 ♕c2 ♗g4! (Ilincic-Kozul, Cetinje 1991).

16 ☖b1

Bad is **16 dxe6 ♗xe6 17 ♘xe6 ☖xe6** with a good game for Black.

Now after 16...♘xd5 17 ♘xd5 exd5 18 ♗b2 ♘c6 19 ♗xd5 ♗h3! 20 ♗xc6 bxc6 21 ☖fd1 ♕d5 Black has the advantage (Ilincic-Makarov, Arandjelovac 1993).

> **3.222312 (1 d4 ♘f6 2 c4 g6 3 g3 ♗g7 4 ♗g2 d5 5 cxd5 ♘xd5 6 ♘f3 ♘b6 7 0–0 ♘c6 8 e3 0–0 9 ♘c3 ☖e8 10 d5 ♘a5 11 ♘d4 ♗d7 12 e4)**

12 ... c5!?

This immediately solves all Black's problems.

13 ♘b3

13 ... ♘xb3

Possibly better is **13...♘a4!? 14 ♕c2 ♘xc3 15 bxc3 ♗a4 16 ♕b2 ♕b6 17 ☖b1 ♘c4 18 ♕a1 ♕c7** with a complicated game, where Black has excellent chances (Ribli-Wolff, Groningen 1993)

14 ♕xb3 c4

Less good is **14...e6 15 ♗e3 exd5 16 exd5 c4 17 ♕b4 ♗f5 18 ☖fe1 ♗d3 19 a4** with advantage (Liptay-Yermolinsky, Tbilisi 1986).

15 ♕d1

If **15 ♕c2 e6 16 dxe6 ♗xe6**, holding the position (Kharitonov-Podgaets, USSR 1985).

15...e6 16 ♗f4 exd5 17 exd5 ♗f5 18 ♕d2 ♗d3 19 ☖fe1 ♕d7 with an equal game (Jukic-Vukanovic, Sibenik 1989).

> **3.22232 (1 d4 ♘f6 2 c4 g6 3 g3 ♗g7 4 ♗g2 d5 5 cxd5 ♘xd5 6 ♘f3 ♘b6 7 0–0 ♘c6 8 e3 0–0 9 ♘c3 ☖e8 10 d5 ♘a5 11 ♘d4 ♗d7)**

12 a4

A very serious attempt to disrupt the coordination of the black knights on the queenside.

12 ... ☖c8

Less good is **12...c5** 13 dxc6 ♘xc6 14 a5 ♘c4 (14...♘xd4 15 exd4 ♘c4 16 ♗xb7 ☖b8 17 a6 ♗h3 18 ☖e1 ♘a5 19 ♗h1 ♘b3 20 ☖a4 ♘xd4 21 ♗e3 with advantage, Agdestein-Wolff, Baguio 1987) 15 a6 ☖b8 (or 15...♕c8 16 ♕b3 ♘d6 17 ♕d5 and again White is better, Pigusov-Riemersma, Dordrecht 1988) 16 axb7 ♗xd4 17 exd4 ☖xb7 18 ♘e4 with the initiative (Vaganian-Kudrin, Marseille 1987).

But **12...♕c8!?** is possible: 13 ♘b3 ♘xb3 (13...♘bc4!? is more interesting, with complicated play) 14 ♕xb3 c6 15 a5 ♘xd5 16 ♘xd5 cxd5 17 ♗xd5 ♗e6 18 e4! ♗xd5 19 exd5 ♕d7 with equality (Gritsak-A.Mikhalchishin, Lviv 1995).

13 ♘b3

Black has no problems after 13 ♖e1 c5! 14 dxc6 bxc6 15 ♘e4 c5 16 ♘xc5 ♖xc5 17 b4 ♗xd4! 18 exd4 ♖xc1 with the better game (Loginov-S.Horvath, Kecskemet 1992).

If 13 ♖a2 c5 14 dxc6 ♘xc6 15 a5 ♘c4 16 a6 bxa6 17 ♖xa6 ♘xd4 18 exd4 ♖b8 19 ♖xa7 ♘xb2 20 ♕e2 ♗xd4 21 ♖xd7 ♕xd7 22 ♗xb2 ♖ec8 and with difficulty Black held on (Loginov-Soffer, Budapest 1994). But his play can be improved: 14...♗xc6! 15 ♘xc6 bxc6 16 ♕c2 ♘d5 17 ♘xd5 cxd5 18 ♕d3 ♕b6 19 b4 ♘c6!, and again White has nothing (Loginov-Khalifman, St Petersburg 1994).

13 ...   ♘bc4

Strangely enough, the knight at a5, restraining the a-pawn, stands well.

14 ♘xa5

After 14 ♘c5 c6 15 ♘xd7 ♕xd7 16 dxc6 ♕xd1 17 ♖xd1 bxc6 18 ♗f1 ♖ed8 Black stands well, since he has blockaded the opponent's queenside (Ninov-Ftacnik, Stara Zagora 1990).

Now after 14...♘xa5 15 e4 c6 16 ♗g5 cxd5 17 exd5 ♘c4 18 ♖a2 ♕a5 Black has excellent game, since the pressure exerted by his pieces on b2 and c3 is very unpleasant (Podgaets-Lputian, Kharkov 1985).

3.223 (1 d4 ♘f6 2 c4 g6 3 g3 ♗g7 4 ♗g2 d5 5 cxd5 ♘xd5 6 ♘f3 ♘b6 7 0–0 ♘c6 8 e3 0–0 9 ♘c3)

9 ...   e5

The most direct and natural continuation in the battle with White's

centre. The drawback to the move is that the dark-square bishop may be shut out of play for a long time. However, the white bishop at g2 also does not come into play. The resulting structures are more similar to certain lines of the King's Indian.

10 d5

Less critical is 10 dxe5 ♘xe5 11 ♘xe5 ♗xe5 12 ♕c2 c6 13 b3 ♕e7 14 ♗b2 ♖e8 15 ♔h1 ♗g7 16 e4 ♗d7 17 a4!? ♗e6 with equality (Sion Castro-Leko, Leon 1994).

Now Black has: **10...e4!? (3.2231), 10...♘e7 (3.2232)** or **10...♘a5 (3.2233)**.

3.2231 (1 d4 ♘f6 2 c4 g6 3 g3 ♗g7 4 ♗g2 d5 5 cxd5 ♘xd5 6 ♘f3 ♘b6 7 0–0 ♘c6 8 e3 0–0 9 ♘c3 e5 10 d5)

10 ...   e4!?

An unexpected invention by GM Gennady Kuzmin, employed in the Akhmilovskaya-Chiburdanidze match (Sofia 1985). Black wants at any cost to maintain the activity of his bishop; the pawn sacrifice gives him pressure on the b-file and good piece coordination.

11 dxc6

Other continuations are worse: **11
♘d2 ♘xd5** and Black has no problems,
or **11 ♘h4 ♗xc3 12 dxc6 ♗f6 13 ♗xe4
♕xd1 14 ♖xd1 bxc6 15 ♗xc6 ♖b8** with
active play for the pawn (Adorjan).

11 ... ♕xd1

Black has to go into the endgame – if
11...exf3 12 ♕xf3 bxc6 13 ♕xc6 ♗g4
(13...♖b8 14 ♖d1 ♕e7 15 e4 with
advantage) **14 h3 ♗e6 15 ♕c5 ♖b8 16
♖d1 ♕c8 17 ♔h2 ♘c4 18 ♘d5 ♗xd5
19 ♖xd5 ♘xb2 20 ♖b1 ♘a4 21 ♖xb8
♕xb8 22 ♕c2** and White has the
advantage (Adorjan).

12 ♖xd1

12 ♘xd1 is passive, and Black has a
good game after 12...exf3 13 ♗xf3
bxc6 14 ♗d2 (14 ♗xc6 ♖b8 15 ♗d2
♗a6 16 ♖e1 ♘c4 17 ♗c3 ♗xc3 18
♘xc3 ♖xb2 with an excellent position)
14...♖b8 15 ♗c3 ♗xc3 16 ♘xc3 ♘c4!
17 ♗xc6 ♗h3 18 ♖fc1 ♘e5 and Black
holds the ending (Cvitan-C.Horvath,
Nova Gorica 1997).

12 ... exf3
13 ♗xf3 bxc6
14 ♗xc6

14 ♘e2 is a serious alternative, but
after 14...♗d7 (14...♖b8 is rather
worse: 15 ♘d4 c5 16 ♘c6 ♗b7 17 ♔g2
♗xc6 18 ♗xc6 ♘c4 19 ♖d7 ♖fc8 20
♖d5 ♘xb2 21 ♗xb2 ♗xb2 22 ♖ad1 c4
23 ♖c5 with advantage, Pytel-Saucey,
France 1989) 15 ♘d4 ♖ad8 Black has
an excellent game, while if **14 ♗d2
♘c4** with equality (Nogueiras-Leko,
Cienfuegos 1997).

14 ... ♖b8
15 ♘d5

White has several other
continuations:

15 ♘b5 ♘c4! 16 ♘xc7 (16 ♘xa7?
♗g4 17 f3 ♗e6! 18 e4 ♘xb2 19 ♗xb2
♗xb2 and Black's chances are better;

16 a4 ♗g4!? 17 f3 ♗h3 with serious
compensation for the sacrificed material, Adorjan; 16 ♘d4 ♖d8 17 ♗f3 ♖b6
18 b3 ♘e5 19 ♗e2 c5 20 ♘c2 ♖xd1+
21 ♗xd1 ♗f5 22 ♗b2 ♖d6 and Black is
better, Dugandzic-Prizmic, Croatia
1995) 16...♘xb2 17 ♗xb2 ♖xb2 and
Black has a slight advantage (Adorjan).

15 ♗b5 ♗g4 16 ♖d2 (16 ♗e2 ♗xe2
17 ♘xe2 ♘c4 with equality) 16...♘c8!
and 17...♘d6 with a very sharp game
(Chiburdanidze).

15 ♗f3 ♘c4 16 ♘d5 ♗e6 (or
16...♘xb2 17 ♗xb2 ♗xb2 18 ♖ab1
♗e6=) 17 ♘xc7 ♘xb2 18 ♗xb2 ♗xb2
19 ♘xe6 fxe6 20 ♗g4 ♗xa1 21 ♗xe6+
♔g7 22 ♖xa1 ♖b2 with equality
(Sorokina-Behl, Budapest 1996).

15 ... ♘xd5!?

In the main game Akhmilovskaya-
Chiburdanidze (Sofia 1986) the reasonable **15...♘c4** was played: 16 ♘e7+ (16
♘xc7 ♘xb2 17 ♗xb2 ♗xb2 18 ♖ab1
♗f5 19 e4 ♗g4 20 ♖d3 ♗e5 with an
equal game, Chiburdanidze) 16...♔h8
17 ♘xc8 ♖fxc8 18 ♗a4 ♘xb2 19 ♗xb2
♖xb2! and Black equalised.

16 ♖xd5

16 ♗xd5 ♗g4 17 ♖d2 ♖fd8 18 f3
c6! or 18...♗e6!, in both cases with
equality (Adorjan).

Now after 16...♗h3 17 ♖b1 ♖fd8! or 17...♗f5! Black has no difficulties (Adorjan).

3.2232 (1 d4 ♘f6 2 c4 g6 3 g3 ♗g7 4 ♗g2 d5 5 cxd5 ♘xd5 6 ♘f3 ♘b6 7 0-0 ♘c6 8 e3 0-0 9 ♘c3 e5 10 d5)

---

10 ...   ♘e7

Black's plan is to attack and centre and weaken the d5 pawn by ...c7-c6, transfer his knight to the blockade square d6, and try to activate his g7 bishop after ...e5-e4.

11 e4   ♗g4

After 11...♘c4 12 b3 ♘d6 13 ♗b2 h6 14 ♘e1 White has the advantage, as after 15 ♘d3 he can choose between the plan of ♘c5 or f2-f4 (Lengyel-Fazekas, Kecskemet 1962).

Now White has a wide choice of plans: **12 h3 (3.22321), 12 a4 (3.22322)** and **12 ♕b3 (3.22323)**.

3.22321 (1 d4 ♘f6 2 c4 g6 3 g3 ♗g7 4 ♗g2 d5 5 cxd5 ♘xd5 6 ♘f3 ♘b6 7 0-0 ♘c6 8 e3 0-0 9 ♘c3 e5 10 d5 ♘e7 11 e4 ♗g4)

---

12 h3   ♗xf3

13 ♕xf3

Less logical is **13 ♗xf3** c6 14 a4 (14 ♕b3 cxd5 15 ♘xd5 ♘bxd5 16 exd5 ♘f5 17 ♗g2 ♘d4 gives Black the better chances, Murey-Ribli, Reykjavik 1975) 14...cxd5 15 exd5 ♘f5 (stronger is 15...♘c4 16 b3 ♘d6 with an excellent game, Keene-Uhlmann, Hastings 1970/1 – *Game 12*) 16 a5 ♘c4 17 a6 ♖b8 18 ♘e4 ♘cd6 19 axb7 ♖xb7 20 ♖a6 ♘xe4 21 ♗xe4 ♘d4 with a good game (Veremeichik-Mochalov, USSR 1975).

13 ...   c6

14 ♖d1

The centre must be maintained – after **14 dxc6** ♘xc6 15 b3 ♘d4 16 ♕d3 ♖c8 Black is excellently placed (Mochalov-Deiko, Minsk 1987).

14 ...   cxd5

15 ♘xd5

If **15 exd5** ♘f5 16 d6 ♖b8 17 ♗e3 ♘d4 18 ♗xd4 exd4 19 ♘b5 ♘c4 with equality (Zilberman-Bagirov, Moscow 1983).

15 ...   ♘exd5

The other capture **15...♘bxd5** is also possible: 16 exd5 (less good is 16 ♗g5 h6 17 ♖xd5 ♕e8 18 ♗xe7 ♕xe7 19 ♗f1 ♖fd8 20 ♗c4 ♖xd5 when Black equalises, Tukmakov-Timoshchenko Ashkhabad 1978), and now:

(a) 16...♘f5 17 d6 ♘d4 (more accurate is 17...♖b8 18 h4! ♕d7 19 ♗h3! ♘d4 20 ♖xd4 ♕xh3 21 ♖d1 ♕e6 22 ♗g5! with some advantage, Adla-Ricardi, Buenos Aires 1990) 18 ♕xb7 ♕xd6 19 ♗e3!? a5 20 ♕xa8! ♖xa8 21 ♗xa8 ♕b8 22 ♗e4 ♕xb2 23 ♖ab1 and White has an appreciable advantage (Orr-I.Ivanov, Thessaloniki 1988);

(b) 16...♕d6 17 ♕b3 (17 ♗d2!? ♘f5 18 ♖ac1 ♖fd8 19 ♔h2 h5 20 ♕b3 ♖d7 21 ♗b4 with advantage, Drasko-Popovic, Yugoslavia 1989; less good is

17 ♗e3 ♘f5 18 ♖ac1 ♖fc8 19 ♖xc8+ ♖xc8 with equality, Van der Sterren-Schmidt, Dortmund 1989) 17...♘f5 (better than 17...♖fc8 18 ♗d2 ♘f5 19 ♖ac1 ♕d7!? 20 d6! with advantage, Stempin-Schmidt, Polanica Zdroj 1989) 18 ♗d2 ♘d4 19 ♕b4 ♕f6 20 ♗e4 a5! with equality (Anic-Peek, Lugano 1989).

15...♘c6 is interesting: 16 ♗d2 (after 16 ♕d3 ♘d4 17 ♗e3 ♘xd5 18 exd5 ♕d7 19 ♖ac1 ♖fc8, Jasnikowski-Kiss, Germany 1996, 20 f4!? would have given a slight advantage) 16...♘d4 17 ♕d3 ♘xd5 18 exd5 ♕b6 19 ♗c3 (Stempin-Malisauskas, Poland 1989) 19…♖fe8 with approximate equality. In general this set-up looks more logical than the capture on d5, but for more serious conclusions further experience is required.

16   exd5   ♕d6

The queen is not the best blockader, but it is there only temporarily.

17   ♕b3

Possible is **17 a4** ♘c8 18 ♗e3 ♘e7? (more logical is 18...♕b4!? 19 ♖ac1 ♖d8 20 ♗c5 ♕xb2, when 21 d6 is not possible because of 21...♘xd6) 19 ♖dc1 b6 20 ♕e2 ♖ac8 21 ♕a6 with advantage (McNab-Botterill, Bath 1987).

17   ...   ♖fc8

If 17...♖fd8 18 ♗g5 ♖d7 19 a4 h6 20 ♗e3 ♖ad8 21 a5 ♘c8 22 a6 and White is clearly better (Jukic-Batas, Balaton-bereny 1986).

18   ♗d2

Weaker is **18 a4** a5 19 ♗g5 f6 20 ♗e3 ♘c4 21 ♖ac1 ♘xe3, when Black even stands slightly better (A.Mikhalchishin-Kinsman, France 1989).

Now 18...♗f8 19 ♖ac1 ♖xc1 20 ♗xc1 ♕d7! (Black changes blockaders and eliminates White's initiative) 21 ♗e3 ♗d6 22 a3 ♖c8 leads to an equal game (Tukmakov-A.Mikhalchishin, Nikolaev 1981).

3.22322 (1 d4 ♘f6 2 c4 g6 3 g3 ♗g7 4 ♗g2 d5 5 cxd5 ♘xd5 6 ♘f3 ♘b6 7 0–0 ♘c6 8 e3 0–0 9 ♘c3 e5 10 d5 ♘e7 11 e4 ♗g4)

---

12   a4

With the intention of taking the initiative on the queenside and in some cases of weakening Black's pawn structure; in addition the knight from b6 will be forced to take up an insecure post at c4.

12   ...   c6
13   a5   ♘c4

More passive, but no weaker, is **13...♘bc8** 14 a6 bxa6 15 h3 ♗xf3 16 ♕xf3 cxd5 17 ♘xd5 ♘xd5 18 ♖d1 ♕b6 19 ♖xd5 ♘e7! when the knight goes via c6 to d4, ensuring equality (Janjgava-Semeniuk, USSR 1989).

Now we consider **14 ♕b3!?** (**3.223221**) and **14 a6!?** (**3.223222**).

> **3.223221** (1 d4 ♘f6 2 c4 g6 3 g3 ♗g7 4 ♗g2 d5 5 cxd5 ♘xd5 6 ♘f3 ♘b6 7 0-0 ♘c6 8 e3 0-0 9 ♘c3 e5 10 d5 ♘e7 11 e4 ♗g4 12 a4 c6 13 a5 ♘c4)

14 ♕b3!?

By sacrificing two pawns White aims for a big lead in development. The quieter **14 ♕a4** is also possible: 14...b5 15 ♕b4 cxd5 16 exd5 ♖b8 17 ♘g5 ♘f5 18 b3 ♕d6! 19 ♕xd6 ♘cxd6 20 h3 ♗h5 21 g4 e4 22 ♗b2 with advantage (Lechtinsky-Blees, Kecskemet 1989), but 16...a6 is better.

14 ...   ♘xa5

Weaker is **14...cxd5** 15 ♘xd5 ♘xd5 16 ♕xc4 ♘e7 17 ♗g5 h6 18 ♖fd1 ♕e8 19 ♗e3 ♕c6 20 ♕b4 with advantage (Tukmakov-Semeniuk, USSR 1987). Gavrikov's suggestion of **14...♘d6!?** has not yet been tested.

15 ♕a2

Bad is **15 ♕a4** b6 16 b4 ♘c4 17 dxc6 (Lengyel-Bagirov, Sarajevo 1980) 17...♕d3 18 ♕b3 ♗xf3 19 ♗xf3 ♘xc6 with advantage to Black.

15	...	b6
16	b4	♘b7
17	♗g5	c5
18	d6	

After **18 bxc5?!** ♘xc5 19 d6 (19 ♘d2 h6 20 ♗e3 ♘b7! leads to an advantage for Black, Hulak-Henley, Indonesia 1983) 19...♕xd6 20 ♖fd1 ♕c7 21 ♘b5 ♕c6! 22 ♗xe7 ♕xb5 23 ♗xf8 ♖xf8! 24 ♕xa7 ♘xe4 Black's chances are better (Ljubojevic).

18 ...   ♕xd6

This is stronger than **18...♘xd6?!** 19 bxc5 (bad is 19 ♘d5? ♘xd5 20 ♗xd8 ♘xb4 21 ♕b2 ♖fxd8, when Black has more than enough for the queen, Azmaiparashvili-Gavrikov, USSR 1980) 19...♘dc8 20 ♕a3! and White has the initiative (Spraggett-Ftacnik, New York 1980), whereas weaker is 20 ♘d5 ♕d7!? 21 ♘xe7+ ♘xe7 22 cxb6 axb6 23 ♕xa8 ♖xa8 24 ♖xa8+ ♘c8 25 ♘d2 with a complicated game (Baburin-Berebora, Dier, 1990).

Now after 19 ♖fd1 ♕c7 20 ♘b5 ♕c6 21 ♘xa7 ♕c7 Black has a good game (Ninov-Knobel, Dortmund 1989).

> **3.223222** (1 d4 ♘f6 2 c4 g6 3 g3 ♗g7 4 ♗g2 d5 5 cxd5 ♘xd5 6 ♘f3 ♘b6 7 0-0 ♘c6 8 e3 0-0 9 ♘c3 e5 10 d5 ♘e7 11 e4 ♗g4 12 a4 c6 13 a5 ♘c4)

14 a6!?

Again a temporary pawn sacrifice, this time with a different idea – White wants to break up Black's queenside pawns.

14　...　　bxa6

Also possible is **14...cxd5** 15 exd5 (or 15 axb7 ♖b8 16 exd5 ♖xb7 17 ♕a4 ♕c8 18 ♘g5 ♘b6 19 ♕a2 ♖d7 20 ♗e3 h6 21 ♘ge4 ♘bxd5 22 ♘xd5 ♘xd5 23 ♖fc1 ♕d8 24 ♗c5 ♖e8 25 ♘d6!? with a very complicated game, Greenfeld-Kozul, Ljubljana 1989) 15...♘d6 16 ♕a4 (16 axb7!? ♘xb7 17 ♗e3 with advantage should be considered) (Vladimirov-Zilberstein, USSR 1975), and now correct was 16...♗xf3! 17 ♗xf3 bxa6 18 ♕xa6 ♘ef5 intending 19...♘d4 with good counterplay.

15　♕b3

If **15 ♖xa6** Black equalises by 15...cxd5 16 exd5 ♘f5, but not 16...e4 17 ♘xe4 ♕xd5 18 ♘f6+ ♗xf6 19 ♖xf6 when White has the advantage (Vaulin-Berebora, Budapest 1990), or **15 h3** ♗xf3 16 ♗xf3 cxd5 (16...a5!?) 17 exd5 ♘d6 18 ♖xa6 ♘ef5 19 ♕a4 ♖e8 with equality (Schulz-Panzer, Germany 1992).

15　...　　cxd5
16　exd5

After **16 ♘xd5** ♘xd5 17 ♕xc4 ♘b6 18 ♕xa6 ♗e6 19 ♗g5 ♕d6 20 ♘d2 ♖fc8 the position is equal (Hausner-Smejkal, Germany 1995).

16　...　　♘d6

In such positions the knight has more of a future from the blockading square. Less logical is **16...♘b6** 17 ♘h4! ♖b8 18 ♕a2 h6 19 h3 ♗c8 20 ♖d1! g5 21 ♘f3 ♘f5 22 ♘e1 ♘d4 23 ♗e3 when White has the initiative (Portisch-Smejkal, Reggio Emilia 1985).

17　♖xa6　　♗c8
18　♖a2　　♘ef5!

Black controls d4, and the bishop at g7 is not blocked in. White must play something like 19 ♗d2 and then ♖c1, but in any case Black has sufficient counterplay (Smejkal-Doncevic, Germany 1986).

3.22323 (1 d4 ♘f6 2 c4 g6 3 g3 ♗g7 4 ♗g2 d5 5 cxd5 ♘xd5 6 ♘f3 ♘b6 7 0–0 ♘c6 8 e3 0–0 9 ♘c3 e5 10 d5 ♘e7 11 e4 ♗g4)

12　♕b3　　c6
13　♘h4

For a certain time this unusual manoeuvre caused Black considerable problems. After avoiding the exchange of bishop for knight, White wants to push back the black bishop with h2-h3 and thus reduce its scope.

Black has no problems after **13 ♗e3** cxd5 14 exd5 ♖c8 15 ♘d2 ♘f5 16 ♗xb6 axb6 17 ♕b4 ♘d4 (Ree-Timman, Wijk aan Zee 1975), or **13 ♗g5** h6 14 ♗e3 cxd5 15 exd5 ♘f5 16 ♗c5 ♖e8 17 h3 ♗xf3 18 ♗xf3 ♘d7 (Vokac-Votava, Prague 1992) in each case with equality.

13　...　　cxd5

If **13...♕d7** 14 ♗e3 cxd5 15 exd5 ♘bc8 16 h3! ♗f5 17 ♖fd1 h5 18 ♘a4! with advantage to White (Dominte-Schneider, Hungary 1990).

14　exd5　　♘ec8

Weak is **14...♖c8?** 15 ♗g5 h6 16 d6! and wins, but possible is **14...h6** 15 h3

♗c8 16 ♖d1 g5 17 ♘f3 g4 18 hxg4 ♗xg4 19 ♖e1 ♗xf3 20 ♗xf3 ♘f5 (Vukic-Popovic, Tuzla 1981), and here 21 ♗e3 would have given White the advantage.

Other ideas are 14...♕d7 15 ♗e3 ♘ec8 16 a4 ♘d6 17 ♗xb6 axb6 18 ♕xb6 f5 with some compensation for the pawn (Schinzel-Pribyl, Hradec Kralove 1978), or 14...♕c8 15 ♗g5 ♘f5 16 ♘xf5 ♗xf5 17 ♖ac1 ♕d7 18 ♖fd1 and again White is slightly better (Podgaets-Malisauskas, Klaipeda 1983).

15　a4

If **15 h3** ♗d7 16 ♘e4 (or 16 a4 ♘d6 17 a5 ♘bc4 18 ♕b4 b6! 19 a6 ♖c8 with a complicated game, Ionescu-Schmidt, Thessaloniki 1988) 16...♗a4 17 ♕b4 ♗c2 (Kharitonov-A.Mikhalchishin, USSR 1981), and here White should have played 18 ♘c5 ♘d6 with chances for both sides.

15　...　♘d6
16　a5　♘bc4

After the less active 16...♘bc8 17 h3 ♗d7 18 ♗e3 f5 19 ♘f3 h6 20 ♗c5 ♖e8 Black has difficulty holding the position (Vukic-Popovic, Bela Crkva 1982).

17　♕b4　♖c8

After 17...b6 18 b3 (18 a6 ♖c8 19 h3, Vukic-Marangunic, Yugoslavia 1977,

and here 19...♗h5! was correct with an unclear game) 18...bxa5 19 ♕a4 ♗d7 20 ♕a2 ♘b6 21 ♕xa5 White has some advantage (Vukic-Jansa, Kragujevac 1984).

Now 18 h3 ♗h5! 19 ♖a2 g5 20 g4! ♗xg4? 21 hxg4 gxh4 22 b3 h3 23 ♗xh3 ♕h4 leads to a sharp game, but the impression is that White is slightly better (Vukic-Ftacnik, Banja Luka 1983). However, correct was 20...gxh4 21 gxh5 f5! 22 b3 e4! with excellent counterplay – Black is fully developed, he has opened up his bishop, and has carried out the optimum plan with ...f7-f5 and ...e5-e4.

> **3.2233 (1 d4 ♘f6 2 c4 g6 3 g3 ♗g7 4 ♗g2 d5 5 cxd5 ♘xd5 6 ♘f3 ♘b6 7 0–0 ♘c6 8 e3 0–0 9 ♘c3 e5 10 d5)**

10　...　♘a5

This is a completely different plan of counterplay – the idea is similar, in that the centre is attacked by ...c7-c6, but then the knight from a5 takes up an active post at c4. Its drawback, of course, is the temporary slight lack of coordination of the knights at a5 and b6.

11　e4

White occupies the centre and temporarily restricts the black knight on the edge of the board. However, the e4/e5 structure is not very favourable with the bishop at g2, and in addition White slightly weakens the dark squares, so that his spatial advantage is not very important.

11 ᐁd2 is an interesting try: 11...f5 (better is 11...c6 12 ᐁb3 ᐁxb3 13 ♕xb3 ᐁxd5 14 ᐁxd5 cxd5 15 ♗xd5 ♕e7, equalising, Dautov) 12 e4 ᐁac4 13 b3 ᐁxd2 14 ♕xd2 and White has the freer game (Dautov-Ragozin, USSR 1987).

11 ...   c6

Less good is **11...♗g4** 12 h3 (or 12 b3 c6 13 ♗a3 ᐢe8, Vaganian-Sigurjonsson, Hastings 1974, and now 14 d6 would have given an advantage) 12... ♗xf3 13 ♗xf3 c6 14 b4 ᐁac4 15 dxc6 bxc6 16 ♕b3 with advantage to White.

12 ♗g5

This continuation occurs in 99 cases out of 100. Some alternatives:

12 d6!? ♗g4 13 b3 ᐁc8 14 ♗a3 ♕d7 15 ♕d3 b6 16 h3 ♗xf3 17 ♗xf3 c5 and the d6 pawn is cut off from the other forces.

12 ᐢe1 cxd5 (there is also 12...ᐢe8 13 ♗f1 cxd5 14 exd5 ♗g4 15 ♗b5 ♗d7 with an unclear game, Cebalo, but the logical 14...ᐁac4 is better) 13 exd5 ♗g4 14 ♕d3 ♗xf3! 15 ♕xf3 f5 16 ᐢd1 ᐢc8 17 ♕e2 ♔h8 18 ᐢb1 ᐢf7! 19 h4 ᐁac4 with approximate equality (Furman-Averkin, USSR 1969).

12 ♗e3 cxd5 13 exd5 ᐁac4 14 ♗c5 ᐢe8 15 ᐁd2 ♗f5 16 ᐁxc4 ᐁxc4 17 ♕e2 ᐁd6 18 g4! ♗c8 19 ᐢac1 e4 with a complicated game (Leski-Anic, France 1991).

12 ᐁe1!? cxd5 13 exd5 ᐁac4 14 ᐁd3 ♗f5 15 ᐢe1 ᐢc8 and Black has

active piece play (Zhidkov-Ragozin, Vladivostok 1994).

12 ᐁd2 cxd5 13 exd5 f5 14 ᐁb3! ᐁac4 15 a4 (after 15 ♕e2 e4 16 ᐢd1 ♗d7 17 ᐁd4 ᐢc8 18 a4 ᐁe5 19 a5 ᐁbc4 the black knights dominate the centre, S.Farago-Krasenkov, Hungary 1989) 15...e4 (15...ᐁd6 16 a5 ᐁbc4 is stronger) 16 a5 ᐁd7 17 f3 exf3 18 ᐢxf3 ᐁde5 19 ᐢf2 ♔h8 20 h3 ♕e7 21 ᐢe2 with some advantage to White (Agdestein-Yrjola, Nordic 1992).

12 ...   f6

Again an automatic reply, although earlier Black was not especially successful with:

12...♕d6 13 ᐁe1!? h6 14 ♗c1 ᐢd8 15 ᐁc2 cxd5 16 exd5 (Gavrikov-Tseshkovsky, USSR 1982), and here 16...♗f5 should have been played, but here too White is slightly better;

12...♕d7 13 a4 (also good are two other continuations, with which Podgaets twice gained an advantage: 13 ♕e1 cxd5 14 ᐁxd5 ᐁxd5 15 ♕xa5 ᐁb6 16 ᐢac1 ♕e6 17 b3, Podgaets-Vaganian, USSR 1971, and 13 ᐢc1 h6 [13...cxd5 14 exd5 ᐁac4 15 b3 ᐁd6 16 a4 a5 17 ♗e3 with a big advantage] 14 ♗e3 ᐁac4 15 ♗c5 ᐢd8 16 b3 ᐁd6 17 a4 ♕c7 18 a5 ᐁd7 19 ♗xd6 ♕xd6 20

dxc6, Podgaets-Pioch, Tbilisi 1974)
13...cxd5 14 exd5 ♕g4 15 ♗e7 ♖e8 16
h3 ♕d7 17 ♗b4 ♘ac4 (Gulko-
Kupreichik, USSR 1972), and here 18
a5 would have given White the better
chances.

13 ♗e3   cxd5

Now the play divides into two
branches: **14 ♗xb6** (3.22331) and **14
exd5** (3.22332).

3.22331 (1 d4 ♘f6 2 c4 g6 3 g3
♗g7 4 ♗g2 d5 5 cxd5 ♘xd5 6 ♘f3
♘b6 7 0-0 ♘c6 8 e3 0-0 9 ♘c3 e5
10 d5 ♘a5 11 e4 c6 12 ♗g5 f6 13
♗e3 cxd5)

---

14 ♗xb6

White gives up his bishop, but gains
control of d5, although with the
symmetrical structure it is very hard to
demonstrate an advantage.

14 ...   ♕xb6

Weak is **14...axb6** 15 ♕xd5+ ♔h8 16
♖fd1 ♕e7 17 ♕b5 ♕c5 18 ♖d5 ♕c7 19
♖ad1 ♘c6 (or 19...♗g4 20 h3 ♗xf3 21
♗xf3 and White is better) 20 h3 with
advantage (Smejkal-Lombardy, Siegen
1980).

15 ♘xd5   ♕d8
16 ♖c1

A logical developing move, but even
so, here too there are alternatives:

16 b4!? ♘c6 17 ♕b3 ♗e6 18 ♖fd1
f5 with advantage to Black (Plachetka-
Petran, Stary Smokovec 1973), while 17
♖c1 transposes into section 3.223311.

16 h3 ♗e6 17 ♕a4 ♖f7 18 ♖fd1 ♖d7
19 ♖d2 ♗xd5 20 exd5 ♖c8 21 ♗f1 a6
22 ♖ad1 b5 23 ♕e4 ♗h6 with a very
complicated game (Tukmakov-Ragozin,
Helsinki 1992).

16 ♕c1 ♗g4 17 ♖d1 ♗xf3 18 ♗xf3
♘c6 19 ♕e3 ♘d4 20 ♖ac1 ♖f7 21 ♗g2

♕f8 22 f4 ♖e8 with a complicated game
(Podgaets-Notkin, Moscow 1995).

16 ...   ♘c6

After **16...f5** 17 ♘c7 ♕xd1 18 ♖fxd1
♖b8 19 ♘g5 ♗h6 20 h4 ♘c6 (Cvitan-
Conquest, Bern 1992) 21 ♖c5! ♗xg5 22
hxg5 fxe4 23 ♗xe4 ♗g4 24 ♖e1 would
have given an advantage (Conquest),
while if **16...♗g4?** White has 17 ♖c7
♖f7 18 ♖xf7 ♔xf7 19 ♘xe5+, winning
(Cvitan-Sanchez, Mexico 1983).

Now there are two ways of pro-
ceeding: **17 b4** (3.223311) with play on
the queenside, and **17 ♕b3** (3.223312),
developing an initiative on the other
side of the board.

3.223311 (1 d4 ♘f6 2 c4 g6 3 g3
♗g7 4 ♗g2 d5 5 cxd5 ♘xd5 6 ♘f3
♘b6 7 0-0 ♘c6 8 e3 0-0 9 ♘c3 e5
10 d5 ♘a5 11 e4 c6 12 ♗g5 f6 13
♗e3 cxd5 14 ♗xb6 ♕xb6 15
♘xd5 ♕d8 16 ♖c1 ♘c6)

---

17 b4   ♗g4

After **17...a6** 18 ♕b3 (if 18 a4 f5! 19
b5 axb5 20 axb5 fxe4 21 bxc6 bxc6 22
♘xe5 cxd5 23 ♘c6 ♕d7 24 ♕xd5+
♕xd5 25 ♘e7+ ♔h8 26 ♘xd5 ♖a2
Black has reasonable compensation,
Mayorov-Gavrikov, Klaipeda 1983, but

22...♕xd5 would have equalised) 18...♔h8 19 ♕e3! f5 20 ♘b6 ♖b8 21 ♖fd1 ♕e7 22 ♘xc8 ♖bxc8 23 a3 White has some advantage (Hulak-Popovic, Zlatibor 1989).

17...f5?! is strongly met by 18 exf5 (after 18 b5 fxe4 19 bxc6 bxc6 20 ♘xe5 ♕xd5 21 ♘xc6 ♕xd1 22 ♖fxd1 ♖e8 Black holds on, Vladimirov-Karasev, St Petersburg 1997) 18...e4 19 f6! ♗h6 20 ♖xc6 exf3 21 ♖d6! fxg2 22 ♖e1! with a decisive advantage (A.Maric-Howell, Hastings 1994).

18   ♕b3

18   ...   ♗xf3

After 18...♔h8 19 b5 ♗xf3 20 bxc6 bxc6 21 ♖xc6 ♗e2 22 ♖e1 ♗h5 23 ♖c7 White has the advantage (Berg-Tisdall, Skei 1994).

19 ♘e7+ ♔h8 20 ♘xc6 bxc6 21 ♗xf3 ♕b6 22 ♕c3 a5 with equality (Janjgava-Georgadze, Simferopol 1988).

3.223312 (1 d4 ♘f6 2 c4 g6 3 g3 ♗g7 4 ♗g2 d5 5 cxd5 ♘xd5 6 ♘f3 ♘b6 7 0-0 ♘c6 8 e3 0-0 9 ♘c3 e5 10 d5 ♘a5 11 e4 c6 12 ♗g5 f6 13 ♗e3 cxd5 14 ♗xb6 ♕xb6 15 ♘xd5 ♕d8 16 ♖c1 ♘c6)

---

17   ♕b3   ♖f7

18   ♖fd1   ♗e6
19   h4

Weaker is **19 ♕a4 ♖d7 20 h4 ♔h8** when the position is completely unclear (Portisch-Schmidt, Bath 1973), or **19 ♕e3 ♕f8 20 ♖c5 ♖d8 21 ♕c3 ♖dd7 22 b4 ♔h8** with the threat of ...f6-f5 (Donner-Van Mil, Amsterdam 1982), or **19 ♕b5 ♕f8 20 ♕f1 ♗g4 21 ♖c3 ♖d8 22 ♗h3 ♗xf3 23 ♖xf3 ♘d4 24 ♖xd4 exd4 25 ♗e6** with a complicated game (Kapetanovic-Blees, Belgrade 1988).

19   ...   h6

After **19...♖d7? 20 ♗h3! f5 21 ♘g5 ♗xd5 22 ♖xd5! ♖xd5 23 exd5 ♘d4 24 ♕xb7** White has a strong attack (Baburin-Pribyl, Schaan, 1996), while if **19...♔h8** there follows 20 ♔h2 ♖d7 21 ♗h3! f5 22 h5 ♕e8 23 ♕a4! with advantage (Podgaets-Dvoiris, Kharkov 1985).

There is also **19...♗h6 20 ♖c3 ♔h8 21 ♔h2 ♕e8 22 ♗h3 ♗xh3 23 ♔xh3 ♕e6+ 24 ♔g2** and again White is better (S.Hansen-Korchnoi, Biel 1992), while Borovikov-Shmuter (Nikolaev 1992) went **19...g5!? 20 hxg5 fxg5 21 ♕e3 ♗h6 22 b4! ♕f8 23 ♘xg5 ♘d4**, and here White could have played 24 ♖c4 with advantage.

20   h5

20 ♔h2 with the idea of ♗h3 is also interesting.

Now after 20...g5 21 ♕a4 ♕e8 22 ♘e3 White has some advantage thanks to the weakening of Black's kingside, especially the f5 square (Dorfman-Yrjola, Helsinki 1986).

3.22332 (1 d4 ♘f6 2 c4 g6 3 g3 ♗g7 4 ♗g2 d5 5 cxd5 ♘xd5 6 ♘f3 ♘b6 7 0–0 ♘c6 8 e3 0–0 9 ♘c3 e5 10 d5 ♘a5 11 e4 c6 12 ♗g5 f6 13 ♗e3 cxd5)

---

14   exd5

White gains an isolated d5 pawn, which he will aim to advance further and open up his bishop at g2. If he succeeds with this idea, he will gain the advantage, but Black has a serious plan of counterplay – transferring his knight to d6 or ...f7-f5 and ...e4-e4.

We consider: **14...♗g4 (3.223321)**, **14...♘ac4 (3.223322)** and **14...♖f7 (3.223323)**.

Weak is **14...♖e8** 15 ♘d2 f5 16 ♗xb6 ♕xb6 17 ♕a4 ♖d8 18 b4 (½-½, Helmers-Yrjola, Gjovik 1985), but after 18...♕d4 19 ♕xa5 b6 20 ♕a3 ♕xd2 21 ♖fd1 ♕g5 22 ♘b5 what is Black to do?

3.223321 (1 d4 ♘f6 2 c4 g6 3 g3 ♗g7 4 ♗g2 d5 5 cxd5 ♘xd5 6 ♘f3 ♘b6 7 0–0 ♘c6 8 e3 0–0 9 ♘c3 e5 10 d5 ♘a5 11 e4 c6 12 ♗g5 f6 13 ♗e3 cxd5 14 exd5)

---

14   ...   ♗g4
15   ♗c5

There is also **15 h3** ♗xf3 16 ♗xf3 (no better is 16 ♕xf3 f5 17 ♖fd1 ♘ac4 18 ♗c5 ♘xb2 19 ♗xf8 ♕xf8 with an excellent game for Black, Rukavina-Shmuter, Pula 1994) 16...f5, and now:

(a) 17 ♖c1 ♖f7 18 b3 e4 19 ♘xe4?! fxe4 20 ♗xe4 ♖d7 and White does not have complete compensation for the piece (Pigusov-Krasenkov, USSR 1987);

(b) 17 ♗e2!? ♖c8 18 d6 ♔h8 19 ♘b5 ♘ac4 20 ♗xb6! axb6 21 d7 ♖c6 22 ♗xc4 ♖xc4 23 ♕d2 and the passed d-pawn is very dangerous (Janosi-Danek, corr. 1989).

15 ♖c1 is well met by 15...f5! 16 d6 ♔h8 17 ♗xb6 ♕xb6 18 ♕d5 ♗xf3 19 ♗xf3 e4 (Bykhovsky-Krasenkov, USSR 1988) and here 20 ♘a4! ♕d4 21 ♕xa5 exf3 would have led to an unclear game.

15	...	♖f7
16	b3	f5
17	♗b4	♘ac4!?

By tactical means Black tries to coordinate his forces. After 17...♘c8 18 ♕e1 ♗xf3 19 ♗xf3 ♘d6 20 ♗e2 e4 21 ♖d1 White has the advantage.

| 18 | bxc4 | e4 |
| 19 | ♖c1 | ♕d7 |

If **19...exf3** 20 ♗xf3 ♗xf3 21 ♕xf3 ♘xc4 22 ♘b5 ♘e5 23 ♕b3 and Black faces difficulties (Ionov-Urban, Katowice 1991).

Now after 20 ♘b1 exf3 21 ♗xf3 ♗xf3 22 ♕xf3 f4 23 g4 Black has insufficient compensation for the pawn (Vaganian-Kasparov, Barcelona 1989).

3.223322 (1 d4 ♘f6 2 c4 g6 3 g3
♗g7 4 ♗g2 d5 5 cxd5 ♘xd5 6 ♘f3
♘b6 7 0–0 ♘c6 8 e3 0–0 9 ♘c3 e5
10 d5 ♘a5 11 e4 c6 12 ♗g5 f6 13
♗e3 cxd5 14 exd5)

14 ... ♘ac4

This is more correct – the knight must be urgently transferred from the edge of the board to the blockading square d6. **14...♘bc4** is not altogether logical: 15 ♗c5 ♘d6 16 ♘d2 b6 17 ♗b4 f5 18 ♖e1 ♘ab7 19 a4 ♖e8 20 ♗f1 with some advantage (Matlak-Stohl, Stary Smokovec 1991).

15 ♗c5 ♖f7

If **15...♘d6** 16 ♕b3 ♘bc4 17 ♘b5 f5 18 ♘xd6 ♘xd6 19 ♕a3 e4 20 ♗xd6 exf3 21 ♗xf3 ♗xb2 22 ♕xb2 ♕xd6 23 ♖ac1 with advantage (Brook-Stepak, Netanya 1987).

16 b3

Or **16 ♘d2** and now:

(a) 16...f5 17 ♘xc4 ♘xc4 18 ♕e2 ♘d6 19 ♖ac1 ♕f6 20 ♘b5 ♘xb5 21 ♕xb5 b6 22 ♕e8+ ♗f8 23 ♗xf8 ♖xf8 24 ♕c6 and White is a little better (Tukmakov-Lalic, Sochi 1987);

(b) 16...♗g4? 17 ♕xg4 ♘xd2 18 ♖fd1 f5 19 ♕b4 ♘bc4 20 ♘b1! winning (Schöbel-Roschlan, Germany 1992);

(c) 16...♗f5?! 17 ♘xc4 ♘xc4 18 ♕e2 ♘d6 19 g4 ♗c8 20 ♖fd1 ♗f8 21 h3 ♗d7 22 ♖ac1 ♗c8 23 ♗xd6! ♗xd6 24 ♘e4 and White succeeds in lifting the blockade at d6 (Krogius-M.Pribyl, Berlin 1996);

(d) 16...♗f8 17 ♗xf8 ♕xf8 18 b3 ♘d6 19 a4 ♗f5 20 a5 ♘d7 21 b4 ♗d3 22 ♖e1 f5 with an unclear game (Gligoric-Savon, Skopje 1971).

16 ... ♘d6

17 a4

There is also the new idea 17 ♘d2 f5 18 ♖c1 ♘e8 (18...e4 19 ♗xd6 ♕xd6 20 ♘b5 ♕d8 21 d6 with advantage) 19 d6! and if White succeeds in advancing his pawn to d6, he always has the advantage (Loginov-Orlov, St Petersburg 1996).

17 ... ♗g4

If **17...♗f8** White gains the advantage by 18 h3, restricting the bishop at c8.

18 a5 ♘bc8

19 ♕d2

White also gains the advantage by **19 h3!** ♗xf3 20 ♗xf3 f5 21 ♗g2!, when he is ready to meet ...e5-e4 with f2-f3 (Stein-Kupreichik, Sochi 1970).

19 ... ♗f8

If **19...♗xf3** there follows 20 ♗xf3 f5 21 ♗g2 ♖d7 22 ♖fd1 ♖b8 23 ♗b4 with some advantage (Pigusov-Conquest, Dordrecht 1988).

20 ♘e1

Weaker is **20 b4** ♖c7 21 ♕d3 ♗xf3 22 ♗xf3 ♖b8 23 ♖fd1 b6, when Black has a good game (Griffin-Frois, Haifa 1989).

Now after 20...♗f5 21 ♗e3 ♗d7 22 ♘d3 White has some advantage thanks in particular to the weakness of the c5 square (Tukmakov-Gavrikov, Riga 1985).

3.223323 (1 d4 ♘f6 2 c4 g6 3 g3 ♗g7 4 ♗g2 d5 5 cxd5 ♘xd5 6 ♘f3 ♘b6 7 0–0 ♘c6 8 e3 0–0 9 ♘c3 e5 10 d5 ♘a5 11 e4 c6 12 ♗g5 f6 13 ♗e3 cxd5 14 exd5)

| 14 | ... | ♖f7 |
| 15 | ♗c5 | |

If 15 ♘d2 ♘ac4 16 ♘xc4 ♘xc4 17 ♗c5 (17 ♕e2!? ♘xe3 18 fxe3 ♕b6 19 ♖ad1 ♗h6 with a complicated game, Petz-Vegh, Germany 1990) 17...♘xb2 18 ♕b3 ♘d3 19 ♗a3 f5 20 ♖ad1 e4 21 ♖xd3 exd3 22 d6 and White has play for the exchange (Hansen-Tisdall, Helsinki 1986).

15 b3 ♗g4 16 ♗c5! is interesting, transposing into the previous variation.

| 15 | ... | f5 |

If 15...♗g4 16 b3, again transposing into the previous variation.

| 16 | ♕c1! | |

An excellent idea of Gutman. White removes his queen from the d-file and to strengthen his position plays his rook to d1. Less good is 16 ♗b4 ♘ac4 17 ♘d2 e4 (17...♘xb2 18 ♕c2 ♘2c4 19 ♘xc4 ♘xc4 20 ♘b5 with sufficient compensation for the pawn) 18 ♘xc4 ♘xc4 19 ♕e2 ♘e5 20 ♖fd1 ♗d7 with a good game (Kupreichik-Gavrikov,

Minsk 1987), or 16 ♘d2 e4 17 ♘b3 ♘ac4 18 ♕e2 ♘e5 19 ♖ad1 ♘bc4 20 ♘d4 b6 21 ♘c6 ♕e8 22 ♘xe5 ♘xe5 23 ♗d4 ♗b7 with equality (Gligoric-Gavrikov, Moscow 1989).

| 16 | ... | e4 |

Bad is 16...h6 17 ♖d1 ♗d7 18 b4 ♘ac4 19 a4 a5 20 bxa5 ♖xa5 21 ♗b4 ♖a6 22 a5 with a clear advantage.

Now after 17 ♘g5 ♖c7 18 b4 ♘bc4 19 ♖d1! ♗xc3 20 ♕xc3 ♕xg5 21 ♗d4! (also good is 21 ♗e3!? ♕d8 22 bxa5 ♘xe3 23 ♕xe3 ♕d6 24 f3 when White is slightly better, A.Mikhalchishin-Gavrikov, Budapest 1989) 21...♗d7 (A.Mikhalchishin-Ftacnik, Palma de Mallorca 1989) White's correct continuation was 22 bxa5 ♕e7 23 ♖ab1!? with advantage.

Game 10
P.Nikolic-Anand
Linares 1997

1 d4 ♘f6 2 c4 g6 3 ♘f3 ♗g7 4 g3 d5 5 cxd5 ♘xd5 6 ♗g2 ♘b6 7 0–0 ♘c6 8 e3 e5 9 dxe5!?

This rather quiet transition into an endgame is not without its dangers for Black. White wants to seize space in the centre, restrict the dark-square bishop by f2-f4 and e4-e5, and exploit the d-file, while Black has a queenside pawn majority.

9 ♘c3 is more ambitious:

(a) 9...exd4 10 exd4 0–0 11 ♗g5 ♕d7 12 ♖e1 h6 13 ♗e3 ♖d8 14 ♕e2 ♕e7 15 ♖ad1 ♗e6 and Black equalised, although this can hardly be called model play by White (Brunner-Hellers, Biel 1993);

(b) 9...♗g4!? 10 h3 ♗xf3 11 ♗xf3 exd4 12 exd4 0–0 13 d5 ♘d4 14 ♗g2 ♖e8 15 h4 ♘c4 16 b3 ♘d6 17 ♗g5

♕d7 18 ♖c1 h6 19 ♗f4 ♖e7 and Black has everything in order (Janjgava-A.Mikhalchishin, Pavlodar 1987).

9...♕xd1 10 ♖xd1 ♘xe5 11 ♘xe5 ♗xe5 12 ♘c3

More passive is 12 ♘d2 c6 13 ♘f3 ♗g7 14 ♘d4 ♗g4! 15 f3 ♗d7 16 ♗d2 c5 17 ♘b3 ♘a4! 18 ♗c3 ♘xc3 19 bxc3 b6 with advantage to Black (Hübner-Kasparov, Cologne 1992). In general White has only one strategic threat – to play f2-f4 and e4-e5, blocking in the bishop at g7.

12...0–0

12...c6!?, analogous to Kasparov's play, is interesting: 13 e4 ♗g4 14 f3 ♗e6 15 ♗h6 ♖d8 16 f4 ♖xd1+ 17 ♖xd1 ♗xc3 18 bxc3 f5! 19 a4 ♔f7 20 ♖b1 ♖b8 with a complicated game (Garcia-Fernandez, Spain 1991).

13 e4 ♗g7

Stronger is 13...♗e6 14 f4 ♗xc3 15 bxc3 ♖fd8 16 ♖d4 c5 17 ♖xd8+ ♖xd8 18 ♗e3 ♘a4 when Black is not badly placed (Gudmundsson-Grunberg, Reykjavik 1982), or 13...c6 14 f4 ♗g7 15 e5 f6 16 exf6 ♗xf6, again with equality (Todorcevic-Fernandez, Ibercaja 1996). In general, for the moment there is nothing to herald any problems for Black.

14 ♗e3 ♗g4

If 14...♘c4 15 ♗c5 ♘xb2 (15...♖e8 16 ♘d5) 16 ♗xf8 ♘xd1? 17 ♗xg7 White wins, but better is 16...♔xf8 17 ♖dc1 (17 ♖d8+ ♔e7 achieves nothing) 17...♘d3 18 ♖c2 ♘b4, with a draw by repetition.

15 f3 ♗e6

Weak is 15...♘c4 16 ♗d4 ♘xb2? 17 ♗xg7 ♘xd1 18 ♗xf8 ♘xc3 19 ♗b4, winning.

16 ♗d4

White changes plan slightly; after the exchange of bishops it will be easier for him to exploit the central file.

16...♗xd4+?

An artificial plan – 16...♖fd8 is obviously more logical.

17 ♖xd4 c5?

Here too it was more logical to exchange the other rook by 17...♖fd8 18 ♖ad1 ♖xd4 19 ♖xd4 c6, and then bring the king to e7.

18 ♖d3 ♖ad8 19 ♖ad1 ♖xd3 20 ♖xd3 ♘c4

20...f6 might have been tried, with the idea of bringing the king to e7 as quickly as possible.

21 b3 ♘e5 22 ♖d6 ♘c6 23 f4

If 23 ♘a4 Black equalises by 23...c4 24 ♘c5 cxb3 25 axb3 ♖d8.

23...♖c8?!

23...♖b8 should have been played, with the idea of freeing the knight.

24 e5 c4 25 bxc4 ♗xc4 26 ♗d5!?

26 ♗xc6 was hardly sufficient for a serious advantage.

26...♗xd5 27 ♘xd5 ♔g7 28 ♖d7 ♖d8 29 ♖xd8 ♘xd8 30 ♔f2

Despite its apparent simplicity, the knight ending is very difficult for Black. His king is cut off, and its white opponent can make straight for the queenside.

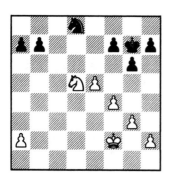

30...♘c6 31 ♔e3 g5 32 ♔e4 gxf4 33 gxf4 b5 34 ♘c7! b4

34...♘b4 is bad because of 35 a3.

35 ♘a6! ♔g6 36 f5+ ♔g5 37 f6 h5 38 h4+!

The pawn cannot be taken because of 39 e6.

38...♔g6 39 ♔d5 1-0

Black's position is quite hopeless.

Game 11
Benko-Smyslov
Moscow v. Budapest 1949

---

1 d4 ♘f6 2 c4 g6 3 ♘f3 ♗g7 4 g3 d5 5 cxd5 ♘xd5 6 ♗g2 0-0 7 0-0 ♘b6 8 ♘c3 ♘c6 9 e3 a5!?

The idea of Smyslov's unusual plan is to divert White's attention from the centre and to activate his two knights on the flank.

10 b3

After 10 a4? e5 11 d5 ♘b4 the black knight is excellently placed, while if 10 ♗d2 a4 11 ♖c1 ♗e6 12 ♕c2 ♘b4 13 ♕e4 c6 14 a3 ♗f5 15 ♕h4 ♘d3 Black has an excellent game (Katetov-Smyslov, Moscow 1946).

10...♘b4

Nowadays 10...e5! is preferred: 11 ♗a3 ♖e8 12 ♘xe5 ♘xe5 13 dxe5 ♕xd1

14 ♖fxd1 ♗xe5 15 ♖ac1 a4 with good play (Novikov-Lukin, USSR 1972).

11 ♗b2

11...a4!? 12 ♘xa4 ♘xa4 13 bxa4 ♘d5!

The knight makes a lengthy manoeuvre with the aim of picking up the a4 pawn and occupying there an impregnable position.

14 ♘e5

14 a5!? ♖xa5 15 a4 ♘b4 16 ♘e5 would have led to a very complicated game.

14...♘b6 15 ♘d3?!

15 ♖b1 ♘xa4 16 ♗a1 looks better.

15...♘xa4 16 ♗a3

Here too 16 ♖b1 came into consideration.

16...♗e6!

Activity in the Grünfeld Defence is important above all else.

17 ♕c1

Bad is 17 ♗xb7? ♘c3! when White wins, but 17 ♘c5 ♘xc5 18 ♗xc5 b6! 19 ♗xa8 ♕xa8 20 ♗xe7 ♖e8 21 ♗g5 ♗h3 22 f3 ♗xf1 23 ♕xf1 c5! looks more active, with a very complicated game.

17...c6 18 ♖d1 ♖e8 19 ♘c5 ♘xc5 20 ♗xc5 ♖a6!

20...♗xa2? was bad because of 21 ♕b2! with advantage to White, but now this move is threatened, since Black can defend his bishop and his b7 pawn with ...♛a8.

21 a3 ♝d5 22 ♕c2

Weakening the centre by 22 e4 ♝b3 23 ♖d3 ♝a4 was bad, but 22 ♝xd5 ♕xd5 23 ♖b1 b5 24 ♕c2 looks better with a complicated game.

22...♝xg2 23 ♔xg2 b6 24 ♝b4

24...c5!

White underestimated this blow – if 25 dxc5 there follows 25...♕a8+ 26 c6 ♝xa1 27 ♖xa1 b5 28 ♖c1 ♖c8 and wins.

25 ♝c3 cxd4 26 ♝xd4 ♕a8+ 27 e4

After 27 ♔g1 ♝xd4 28 ♖xd4 ♖xa3 29 ♖xa3 ♕xa3 30 ♕c6 ♖b8 31 ♕c7 ♕a1+ 32 ♔g2 ♕a8+ 33 e4 e6 Black has good chances of realising his extra pawn.

27...♖c8 28 ♕d3 ♖a4! 29 ♝xg7 ♔xg7 30 f3?

A slightly inferior position is difficult to defend, but one should not create additional weaknesses. Therefore 30 ♖e1 was better.

30...♕a5! 31 h4

After 31 ♕d7 ♖c2+ 32 ♔h1 ♕h5 Black wins.

31...♖c3 32 ♕d7 ♖axa3 33 ♖xa3 ♕xa3 34 ♕d4+ f6 35 ♕xb6 ♖c2+ 0–1

Game 12
Keene-Uhlmann
Hastings 1970/1

1 d4 ♘f6 2 c4 g6 3 g3 ♝g7 4 ♝g2 d5 5 cxd5 ♘xd5 6 ♘f3 0–0 7 0–0 ♘c6 8 ♘c3 ♘b6 9 e3 e5 10 d5 ♘e7 11 e4 ♝g4

Black wants to give up his bishop (in general it is hard to find any other useful function for it) with the idea of gaining time to attack the centre, and also of countering his lack of space (for which he should exchange as many pieces as possible). He then transfers his badly placed knight at b6 to the good blockading square d6.

12 h3 ♝xf3 13 ♝xf3?!

White should not waste time. Therefore 13 ♕xf3 was necessary, and if 13...c6 14 ♖d1 – cf. the analysis.

13...c6 14 a4

14 ♕b3 cxd5 15 ♘xd5 should have been tried.

14...cxd5 15 exd5 ♘c4

The knight aims for the blockading square.

16 b3 ♘d6!

Black resists the provocation: 16...e4? 17 ♘xe4 ♝xa1 18 bxc4 with a powerful position for the exchange.

17 ♗a3 ♘ef5 18 ♘e4!

A fierce battle for the d6 square is in progress, but there is also another factor – the bishop at g7 is better than the one at f3.

18...♖e8 19 ♖c1 ♗f8 20 ♗b2

White avoids the exchange of the dark-square bishops. After 20 ♘xd6 ♘xd6 21 h4 f5 Black has complete domination.

20...♘xe4 21 ♗xe4 ♘d6 22 ♗g2 ♗g7!

Now it is evident that White cannot avoid the exchange of bishops, and he has to play with a 'bad' bishop against a powerful knight at d6.

23 h4

Maric recommends 23 f4! as being the best chance, with the variation 23...e4 24 ♗xg7 ♔xg7 25 ♕d4+ ♕f6 26 ♕xf6+ ♔xf6 27 ♖c7 and advantage to White.

However, after 23...♕b6+! 24 ♔h1 exf4 25 ♗xg7 ♔xg7 26 ♖xf4 ♖e3 Black simply has a won position.

23...e4! 24 ♗xg7 ♔xg7 25 ♗h3

With the idea of controlling the c-file – after 25 ♕d4+ ♕f6 26 ♕xf6+ ♔xf6 27 ♖c7 ♖ac8 28 ♖fc1 ♖xc7 29 ♖xc7 ♖e7! or 29...♔e5 the ending is very difficult for White.

25...♕f6 26 ♖c7 ♖e7 27 ♖xe7 ♕xe7 28 ♕d4+ ♕f6 29 ♕e3

White can on no account exchange queens.

29...a6 30 ♖c1?

White plays on the open c-file, but this is pointless – 30 f3! was better, undermining Black's pawn structure.

He would have had to find 30...exf3 31 ♖xf3 ♕a1+ 32 ♖f1 ♖e8! 33 ♕f4 ♕e5 with advantage.

30...♖e8 31 ♖c7 ♖e7 32 ♖xe7 ♕xe7

The resulting ending is clearly in Black's favour, as the superiority of the knight over the bishop is enormous.

33 ♕c3+ ♕f6 34 ♕c5

After the exchange of queens things would be even worse for White.

34...♕e5 35 ♔h2 ♔f6

The immediate flank play 35...h6 and 36...g5 was simpler.

36 b4 ♔g7 37 ♔g2 h6 38 ♔h2 g5 39 hxg5 hxg5 40 ♗d7 ♔g6 41 b5 axb5 42 ♗xb5

After 42 axb5 e3! 43 ♕xe3 ♕xe3 44 fxe3 ♔f6 and 45...♔e5 Black would have won easily.

42...♘f5 43 ♕f8

If 43 ♗d7 there would have followed 43...♘d4 44 ♗g4 ♔g7 and ...f7-f5.

43...♕xd5 44 ♕g8+ ♘g7 45 ♗e8 g4 46 ♗b5 ♕d2 47 ♕c8 ♕xf2+ 48 ♔h1 ♕xg3 49 ♕xb7 ♕f3+ 50 ♔g1 ♕e3+ 51 ♔f1 g3 52 ♕c6+ ♘e6 0-1

4 Main Variation with 5 ♘f3

1	d4	♘f6
2	c4	g6
3	g3	♗g7
4	♗g2	d5
5	♘f3	

We now move on to consider variations where White avoids the capture cxd5. This allows Black various options in the centre – he can support it with pieces or with pawns, for example by ...c7-c6, or he can cede the centre by exchanging on c4.

In the present chapter we consider **5...dxc4 (4.1)** and **5...0–0 (4.2)**.

Variations where Black supports his d5 pawn with ...c7-c6 are covered in Chapters 5 and 6.

4.1 (1 d4 ♘f6 2 c4 g6 3 g3 ♗g7 4 ♗g2 d5 5 ♘f3)

5	...	dxc4

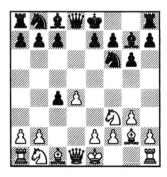

By conceding the centre, Black allows White a spatial advantage, but retains the option of attacking it in various ways. This exchange is possible now or after castling, which, however, is of no particular significance. The exchange on the 5th move gives White one additional possibility, which, however, is not particularly good for him.

6 ♕a4+

White can also choose other moves:

6 0–0 (a pawn sacrifice similar to the Catalan Opening, but with the bishop at g7 it is not sufficiently effective; Black has no problems with his king, and in addition he has strong play against the d4 pawn) 6...c6, and now:

(a) 7 ♘e5? ♘g4 8 f4 0–0 9 e3 ♘xe5 10 fxe5 c5 and Black takes the initiative (P.Nikolic-Anand, Munich 1994);

(b) 7 ♘a3 b5 8 ♘e5 ♘d5 9 ♘c2 ♗b7 10 e4 ♘b6 11 ♕f3 0–0 12 ♘g4 ♕e8 13 ♘h6+ ♔h8 14 e5 ♘8d7 15 ♖e1 ♘d5 16 b3 and White merely has some compensation for the pawn (Kharlov-I.Horvath, Vienna 1996);

(c) 7 ♘c3 0–0 8 e4 b5 9 ♖e1 a6 10 e5 ♘d5 11 a4 ♘xc3 12 bxc3 ♗e6 13 axb5 cxb5 14 ♘g5 ♗d5 15 e6!? (Lesiege-Kozul, Toronto 1990), and here 15...♗xg2 16 exf7+ ♔h8 17 ♔xg2 ♕d5+ would have led to an unclear game;

(d) 7 a4 0–0 8 ♘a3 ♗e6 9 ♘g5 ♗d5 10 e4 h6 11 exd5 hxg5 12 dxc6 ♘xc6 13 ♗xg5 ♕xd4 14 ♗xc6 ♕xd1 15 ♖axd1 bxc6 with equal chances (Adianto-Tkachiev, Djakarta 1996).

6 ♘bd2 and now:

(a) 6...c3? 7 bxc3 0–0 (or 7...c5 8 0–0 cxd4 9 cxd4 0–0 10 ♗b2 ♘c6 11 e4 b6 12 d5 ♘a5 13 ♕e2 with the initiative, Trifunovic-Gligoric, Moscow 1947) 8 ♗a3 ♘d5 9 c4 ♘b6 10 c5 ♘6d7 11 0–0 ♖e8 12 ♘c4 and White has a great spatial advantage (Sveshnikov-Georgadze, Rostov 1976);

(b) 6...b5 7 a4 c6 8 ♘e5 ♘d5 9 0–0 0–0 10 ♘e4 a6 11 b3? (11 ♘c5 was correct, with a sharp game) 11...♗f5! 12 bxc4 ♗xe4 13 ♗xe4 ♘c3 14 ♕d3 ♕xd4! with advantage to Black (Todorcevic-Kozul, Cetinje 1991).

6 ♘a3 c5 (6...0–0 7 ♘xc4 ♗e6 8 b3 a5 9 0–0, P.Nikolic-Romanishin, Novi Sad 1982, and now 9...♗d5!? transposes into variations considered later, while after 6...♗e6 7 0–0 ♗d5 8 ♕c2 ♘c6 9 e3 a5 10 ♘xc4 ♘b4 the game is equal, A.Petrosian-Buturin, Lviv 1995) 7 0–0 (weaker is 7 ♘xc4 ♘c6 8 ♕a4 cxd4 9 ♘xd4 ♕xd4 10 ♗xc6+ bxc6! 11 ♕xc6+ ♕d7 12 ♕xa8 0–0 13 ♘a5 ♕b5 14 ♕xa7 ♗a6 and Black has a strong initiative, A.Maric-Brustman, Yerevan 1996) 7...♘c6 (7...cxd4 8 ♘xd4 0–0 9 ♘xc4 ♘bd7 10 a4 ♘g4 11 e3 ♘ge5 12 ♘xe5 ♘xe5 13 ♕b3 with a clear advantage to White, Schmidt-Savon, Yerevan 1976) 8 dxc5 ♕a5 9 ♘d4 (9 ♘xc4 ♕xc5 10 b3 ♕h5 with equality, Savon) 9...0–0 10 ♘xc6 bxc6 11 ♘xc4 ♕xc5 12 b3 ♘d5 13 ♗a3 ♕b5 14 ♖c1 with some advantage to White (Karpov-Popovic, Belgrade 1996).

6 ... ♘fd7!

By playing his knight to the queenside Black intensifies the pressure on the d4 pawn, after which it is only White who can have difficulties.

The alternatives are weaker:

6...♘bd7 7 0–0 ♘d5 8 ♕xc4 ♘7b6 9 ♕c2 0–0 10 a3 ♗d7 11 ♘bd2 ♗a4 12 b3 ♗b5 13 ♘e4 ♘d7 14 ♗b2 with a slight but clear advantage (Bronstein-Klaman, USSR 1977).

6...c6 7 ♕xc4 ♗e6 (7...0–0 8 ♘c3 ♘bd7 9 0–0 ♘b6 10 ♕d3 ♗e6 11 ♖d1 ♗c4 12 ♕c2 ♗a6 13 e4 ♕c8 14 b3 and

White has a spatial advantage, Stoltz-Pilnik, Bled 1950) 8 ♕c2 ♗f5 (after 8...♗d5 9 ♘bd2 0–0 10 0–0 ♘a6 11 a3 ♘c7 12 b3 ♕c8 13 ♗b2 White has a slight advantage, Barcza-Yanofsky, Marienbad 1948) 9 ♕a4 ♘bd7 10 0–0 0–0 11 ♘c3 a5 with an equal game (Andersson-Hort, Buenos Aires 1980).

6...♘c6? 7 ♘e5 0–0 8 ♘xc6 bxc6 9 ♕xc6 ♖b8 10 ♕xc4 ♗e6 11 ♕c5 and Black has no compensation for the pawn (Espig-Romanishin, Dortmund 1991).

7 ♕xc4

If 7 ♘bd2 c5 (7...♘c6 8 ♘xc4 0–0 9 0–0 ♗xd4 10 ♘xd4 ♘xd4 11 ♗h6 ♖e8 12 ♖fd1 e5 with a complicated game, Pigusov-Hoelzl, Budapest 1989; 7...0–0 transposes into the main line) 8 ♘xc4 cxd4 9 ♗g5 0–0 10 ♕a3 ♘c6 11 ♖d1 h6 with advantage to Black (Poddubny-Yermolinsky, Leningrad 1987.

7 ... ♘c6
8 0–0

Less good is 8 ♘g5 0–0 9 d5 ♘ce5 10 ♕h4 h6 11 ♘h3 g5 12 ♕b4 ♘b6 13 ♘c3 ♗xh3 with advantage to Black (Karasev-Antoshin, USSR 1970).

8 ... ♘b6
9 ♕c2 ♘xd4

9...♗xd4 10 ♘xd4 ♘xd4 11 ♕d2 0–0 12 ♖d1 looks risky (Gudmundsson-

Pilnik, Amsterdam 1950), but 12...c5 13 e3 ♘e6 14 ♕c2 is worth testing, with an unclear position.

If 9...0–0 10 ♖d1 (10 e3?! ♗f5 11 e4 ♗g4 12 d5 ♗xf3 13 dxc6 ♗xg2 14 ♔xg2 bxc6 15 ♕xc6 ♕d6 with advantage to Black, Kan-I.Horvath, Budapest 1995) 10...♗f5 11 ♕b3 (11 e4 ♗g4 12 d5 ♗xf3 13 ♗xf3 ♘d4 14 ♕d3 e6 15 ♘c3 exd5 16 exd5 ♕f6 17 ♗g2 ♖ad8 18 ♗f4 ♘e6 also leads to equality, Grabarczyk-Jansa, Germany 1996) 11...a5 12 ♘a3 a4 13 ♕c3 e5! 14 ♗g5 exd4 15 ♕d2 ♕d7 with an excellent game (Smyslov-Stean, Teesside 1975).

Now after 10 ♘xd4 ♕xd4 11 ♕xc7 ♕c4 12 ♕xc4 ♘xc4 13 ♘c3 ♗d7 14 ♖d1 ♗xc3 15 bxc3 0–0–0 Black has no problems (Savon-Grigorov, Varna 1982).

4.2 (1 d4 ♘f6 2 c4 g6 3 g3 ♗g7 4 ♗g2 d5 5 ♘f3)

> 5 ...   0–0
> 6 0–0

Apart from the main variation 6...dxc4 Black also has several not very common continuations, leading to completely different types of positions. We consider: **6...♘c6!? (4.21)**, **6...c5 (4.22)**, **6...e6 (4.23)** and **6...dxc4 (4.24)**.

After 6...a5 7 cxd5 ♘xd5 8 e4 ♘b6 (8...♘f6 9 ♘c3 ♗g4, attacking the centre, looks no less logical) 9 h3 c6 (Black could try 9...♘c6 10 d5 ♘b4 with the idea of attacking the centre by ...c7-c6, as well as the sharp 9...f5!?) 10 ♘c3 ♘a6 11 ♗f4 ♗e6 12 ♖e1 ♕d7 13 ♔h2 ♖fd8 14 ♕c1 ♖ac8 15 ♖d1 White has a solid centre and a slight advantage (Simagin-Korchnoi, 22nd USSR Ch 1955). However, it is not at all easy to

breach Black's position. White must carry out a plan of creating some weakness in the opponent's position, which most probably should be the advance f2-f4-f5.

4.21 (1 d4 ♘f6 2 c4 g6 3 g3 ♗g7 4 ♗g2 d5 5 ♘f3 0–0 6 0–0)

> 6 ...   ♘c6!?

In rejecting the main variation 6...dxc4, Black wishes to avoid strengthening his opponent's centre, but he has to contend with a very sharp and unpleasant reply.

> 7 ♘e5!?

After this the play takes on outlines typical of the Catalan Opening, but again the bishop's position at g7 and the attack on d4, in contrast to the Catalan, are in favour of Black.

If White wants to transpose into the main variation with **7 cxd5 ♘xd5 8 ♘c3** (8 e4 is better), then there is Epishin's very interesting idea of 8...e6!? 9 e4 ♘xc3 10 bxc3 e5! 11 d5 ♘a5 12 ♗a3 ♖e8 13 ♗b4 ♘c4 14 ♘d2 ♘d6 15 c4 a5 16 ♗a3 b6 with a complicated game (Vukic-Djuric, Becici 1993), or 8...♘xc3 9 bxc3 e5!? 10 e3 (10 d5 ♘a5 11 e4 c6 12 ♗g5 f6 13 ♗e3 b6 and Black stands well, Stempin-Epishin, Warsaw 1990) 10...♗e6 11 ♗a3 ♖e8 12 ♘d2 ♖b8 13 ♖e1 f5 with an excellent game (Cvitan-Epishin, Warsaw 1990).

If **7 ♘bd2**, then:

(a) 7...♘e4 8 cxd5 ♘xd2 9 ♗xd2 ♕xd5 10 ♗c3 ♕d6 11 ♕d2 ♗g4 12 ♖fd1 ♖fd8 13 d5 (Kurajica-Schoen, Oberwart 1991), and here 13...♗xf3! 14 ♗xf3 ♗xc3 15 ♕xc3 ♘e5 leaves White with only a minimal advantage;

(b) 7...♗e6 8 cxd5 ♗xd5 9 e3 ♘e4 10 ♕c2 f5 11 ♘c4 ♘d6 12 ♘fe5 ♗xg2 13 ♔xg2 ♘f7 14 ♕b3 ♕d5+ with equality (Vaulin-Berebora, Budapest 1993);

(c) 7...a5 8 b3 ♘e4 (or 8...♗g4 9 ♗b2 ♗xf3 10 ♗xf3 e6 11 ♖c1 ♖e8 12 a3 ♘e7 13 e3 c6 14 ♕e2 ♘f5 with equality, Rivas-Schoen, Debrecen 1992) 9 ♗b2 ♗e6 10 e3 f5 11 ♕e2 ♗f7! 12 cxd5 ♗xd5 13 ♘xe4 ♗xe4 (Georgiev-Topalov, Elenite 1994), and here the best continuation 14 ♘g5 ♗xg2 15 ♔xg2 e6! 16 ♘xe6 ♕d5+ 17 ♕f3 ♕xe6 18 d5 ♘e5! 19 dxe6 ♘xf3 would have led to an equal rook ending.

The original **7 ♘a3!?** a5 8 cxd5 ♘xd5 9 e4 ♘b6 10 ♘b5 ♗g4 11 ♗e3 ♘c4 leads to the better game for Black (Gutman-Sax, Biel 1976).

7 e3 dxc4 8 ♘a3 has also been tried: 8...♗g4? 9 h3 ♗f5 10 ♘xc4 ♕c8 11 ♔h2 ♖d8 12 ♕e2 h6 13 ♖d1 ♗e4 14 b3 with advantage to White (Bareev-J.Polgar, Geneva 1996), but better is 8...♗e6 9 ♘g5 ♗g4 10 f3 ♗d7 11 ♘xc4 h6 with equality.

    7 ...   dxc4!

7...♘xe5 8 dxe5 ♘g4 9 cxd5 ♘xe5 10 ♘c3 gives White a great advantage.

    8 ♘xc6   bxc6

    9 ♗xc6

The alternative is 9 ♘a3 ♗e6 10 ♕c2 (or 10 ♗xc6 ♖b8 11 ♗f3 ♗d5 12 ♕c2 ♗xf3 13 exf3, Vladimirov-Lipski, Poland 1978, and after 13...♕xd4 14 ♖d1 ♕c5 15 ♗e3 ♕c6 Black would have equalised) 10...♘d5 11 ♖d1 ♘b4 12 ♕c3 c5!? 13 ♗xa8 ♕xa8 14 ♕e1 (14 ♘xc4 ♘c6 15 e3 ♖d8 with unpleasant pressure) 14...♗h3 15 d5 c3! 16 bxc3 ♘xd5 and Black regains the material (Miles-Honfi, Baden 1981).

Now Black has doubled pawns, but the open b-file and the weakness at d4 give him good counter-chances.

    9 ...   ♖b8

After 9...♗h3 10 ♖e1 ♖b8 White can transpose into the main line by 11 ♘c3, but more accurate is 11 ♘a3 ♘d5 12 ♘xc4 ♘b4 13 ♗e4 ♗e6! 14 a3 ♗xc4 15 axb4 ♕xd4 with equality (Sveshnikov-A.Mikhalchishin, Volgodonsk 1981).

    10 ♘c3

After 10 ♘a3 ♗e6 Black stands well.

    10 ...   ♗b7!?

A positional decision, but, depending on a player's tastes, he can also choose the older and sharper **10...♗h3** 11 ♖e1 (of course White should play 11 ♗g2 ♗xg2 12 ♔xg2 ♘d5, but here Black has an excellent game) 11...♘g4!, and now:

(a) 12 d5 ♕c8!? 13 ♗f4 g5! 14 ♗xg5 ♕f5 15 ♗f4 ♖xb2 16 ♖c1 ♗e5 17 f3 ♗xf4 18 gxf4 ♘e3 19 ♕a4 ♔h8 with a decisive attack (Dautov-Schoen, Germany 1996);

(b) 12 e3 e5! 13 ♗f3 (13 d5 e4! 14 ♘xe4 ♘e5 15 f3 ♗f5 16 ♘f2 c3! 17 e4 cxb2 also gives Black the advantage, Kapelan-Jansa, Vrsac 1975; here too White should exchange bishops by 13 ♗g2 ♗xg2 14 ♔xg2 exd4 15 exd4 ♘h6 16 ♕a4! ♕xd4 17 ♗e3 ♕f6 18 ♖ad1 ♘f5 19 ♗xa7 ♖xb2 20 ♘d5 with chances of equalising) 13...exd4 14 exd4 ♘xf2!! 15 ♔xf2 ♗xd4+ 16 ♖e3 ♖e8 17 ♘d5 ♗c5 18 b4 cxb3 19 ♗a3 ♗xe3+ 20 ♘xe3 b2 with a decisive advantage for Black (Quinteros-Portisch, Manila 1974) – *Game 13*.

11 ♗f3

If 11 ♕a4 ♕xd4 12 ♖d1 ♗xc6 13 ♕xc6 ♕b6 14 ♕xc4 ♖fd8 with a good game for Black, while after 11 ♗xb7 ♖xb7 12 e3 c5 13 dxc5 ♕c7 14 ♕f3 ♖fb8 he has strong pressure.

Hübner-J.Polgar (Dortmund 1996) now continued 11...♗xf3 12 exf3 ♘d5 13 ♕e2 ♘b4 (13...♗xd4 is also good) 14 ♕xc4 ♘c2 15 ♖b1 ♖b4 16 ♕d5 ♘xd4 17 ♗e3 and here 17...e5 would have supported the knight at d4 and equalised completely.

4.22 (1 d4 ♘f6 2 c4 g6 3 g3 ♗g7 4 ♗g2 d5 5 ♘f3 0–0 6 0–0)

---

6 ...   c5!?

An attempt by GM Lev Gutman to solve immediately the problem of the centre. The drawback to the move, of course, is that it is symmetric, which usually makes it difficult for the second player to obtain active play.

7 dxc5

7 cxd5 transposes into positions from section 2.212.

7 ...   ♘a6

It is not worth continuing the symmetry: 7...dxc4 8 ♘a3 (8 ♕a4 ♕d5 9 ♘a3 ♕xc5 10 ♕xc4 ♕xc4 11 ♘xc4 ♘c6 12 ♘ce5 ♘xe5 13 ♘xe5 ♘g4 and White has nothing, Bilek-Liptay, Hungary 1963) 8...c3 9 ♘b5! ♘a6 10 ♘xc3 ♘xc5 11 ♗e3 ♘ce4 12 ♘xe4 ♘xe4 13 ♕a4 with advantage to White (Pirc-Pilnik, Mar del Plata 1956).

8 ♘c3

Again **8 cxd5** transposes into positions from section 2.212.

8 ...   dxc4

9 c6

After **9 ♕a4 ♘xc5 10 ♕xc4 b6! 11 ♖d1 ♕e8 12 ♘e5 ♗a6 13 ♕h4 ♗b7** Black is not worse (Root-Gutman, Lone Pine 1981), or **9 ♕xd8 ♖xd8 10 ♘e5** (no better is 10 c6 bxc6 11 ♘e5 ♘b4 12 a3 ♘fd5! 13 ♘xc6 ♘xc6 14 ♗xd5 ♗b7 15 ♗xc4 ♖ac8 with full compensation for the pawn, Garcia-Stahlberg, Mar del Plata 1946) 10...♘xc5 11 ♗e3 ♘fe4 12 ♘xe4 ♘xe4 13 ♘xc4 f5 14 ♖ac1 ♗e6 and again Black stands well (Haukford-Gutman, London 1984).

9 ...   ♘b4!

10 ♕a4

If **10 cxb7 ♗xb7 11 ♕a4 a5 12 a3**, then 12...♗c6.

   10 ...   ♘xc6
   11 ♕xc4   ♗g4

Here Black has a wide choice. **11...♕b6** is interesting, as is **11...h6** with idea of 12...♗e6 or 12...♕a5.

Sveshnikov-Gutman (Ashkhabad 1978) continued 12 ♗e3 ♕a5 13 ♖fd1 ♖ac8 14 ♕b5 ♕xb5 15 ♘xb5 a6 16 ♘bd4 ♘xd4 17 ♘xd4 e5 with equality in the endgame.

4.23 (1 d4 ♘f6 2 c4 g6 3 g3 ♗g7 4 ♗g2 d5 5 ♘f3 0–0 6 0–0)

---

   6 ...   e6!?

Transposing into positions from some hybrid of the Catalan. The similar idea **6...b6!?** 7 ♘e5 ♗b7 8 ♘c3 e6 has not been tried in practice.

   7 ♘c3

7 ♘bd2 is more passive: 7...♘a6!? 8 b3 c5 9 ♗b2 ♘e4 (simpler is 9...b6 10 ♖c1 ♗b7 11 ♕c2 ♘b4 12 ♕b1 dxc4 13 a3 cxd4 14 ♖xc4 ♘c6 15 ♘xd4 ♘xd4 16 ♖xd4 ♕e7 with equality, Akopian-Lputian, Altensteig 1989) 10 cxd5 exd5 11 ♕c1 ♗h6 12 dxc5 ♘axc5 13 ♕c2 ♗f5 14 ♘xe4 ♘xe4 15 ♕d1 (Kakhiani-Gaprindashvili, Tbilisi 1990), and here 15...♘f6 (with the idea of ...♗e4) 16 ♕d4 ♗g7 would have led to a good game for Black.

Not at all bad for White is **7 ♕c2** ♘c6 8 ♖d1 ♘e4 9 ♘c3 ♘xc3 10 ♕xc3 ♘e7 11 ♗f4 (11 b4!? ♗d7 12 a4 ♕e8 13 b5 a6 14 ♘e5 axb5 15 cxd5 ♘xd5 16 ♗xd5! b4 17 ♕xc7 ♗xe5 18 dxe5 exd5 19 ♗h6 with the better chances for White, Rashkovsky-Kurajica, Dojran 1991) 11...f6!? 12 cxd5 ♘xd5 13 ♕b3 ♘xf4 14 gxf4 c6 15 ♖dc1 with some advantage for White (Tukmakov-

Kurajica, Yugoslavia 1991). Of course, Black should continue his own line with 7...b6 and 8...♗b7.

   7 ...   dxc4

Possible is **7...a6!?** 8 ♘e5 c6 9 ♕d3 b5 10 cxd5 cxd5 11 ♗g5 h6 12 ♗d2 ♘fd7 13 f4 with equality (Andersson-Kamsky, Reggio Emilia 1991); after 13...♗b7 Black threatens 14...♘c6 with an excellent game.

Somewhat weaker is **7...b6** 8 ♗g5 ♗b7 9 ♘e5 h6 10 ♗xf6 ♗xf6 11 cxd5 exd5 12 f4 ♕d6 13 e4! with advantage to White (Kharlov-Schmittdiel, Leeuwarden 1992).

7...♘e4 is also not very logical: 8 ♗f4 ♘c6 9 ♖c1 a6 10 a3 ♖e8 11 b4 a5 12 ♘b5! ♕d6 13 ♘xd6 cxd6 14 cxd5 exd5 15 b5 and White has the advantage (Pigusov-Lputian, Sochi 1987).

   8 ♕a4

If **8 ♘e5**, then 8...♕e7 9 ♘xc4 ♖d8 with the idea of 10...c5 is possible.

   8 ...   a6

After this Csom-Ftacnik (Romania 1982) continued 9 ♕xc4 b5 10 ♕b3 ♗b7 11 a4 c6 12 ♗g5 ♕b6 13 ♗xf6 ♗xf6 14 ♘e4 ♗e7 15 a5 ♕a7 16 ♕c3 with some advantage to White in view of the weakness of Black's c5 square and his c6 pawn.

4.24 (1 d4 ♘f6 2 c4 g6 3 g3 ♗g7 4 ♗g2 d5 5 ♘f3 0–0 6 0–0)

   6 ...   dxc4
   7 ♘a3

The most logical move – at c4 the knight will strengthen White's control of the central e5 square, although at the same time his control of d5 and e4 is slightly weakened. Other continuations are weaker:

7 ♘e5 (a 'Catalan' move, but whereas in the Catalan Black's reply would have no point, here it opens an attack on the d4 pawn by the bishop at g7) 7...♘e8! 8 ♘a3 (8 ♗f4 may be better, although then White has to reckon with tricks such as ...g6-g5) 8...c5! 9 ♗e3 cxd4 10 ♗xd4 ♘d6 11 ♘exc4 (worse is 11 ♖c1?! ♗e6 12 ♘f3 ♗h6! 13 e3 ♘c6 with advantage to Black, Romanishin-Kozul, Yugoslavia 1993) 11...♗xd4 12 ♕xd4 ♘xc4 13 ♕xc4 ♕b6 14 ♕b5 (or 14 ♕c3 ♘c6 15 ♗xc6 bxc6 16 ♘c4 ♕b5 17 a4 ♕d5 18 ♖fd1 ♕e6 with equality, Romanishin-Hellers, Malmo 1993) 14...♘c6 15 ♕xb6 axb6 16 ♖fc1 ♗d7 with an equal game (Romanishin-Ftacnik, Groningen 1991).

7 ♕a4 (here capturing on c4 with the queen merely assists the rapid development of the black pieces) 7...♘c6 (also logical is 7...♘fd7 8 ♕xc4 ♘b6 9 ♕c5 ♘c6 10 ♖d1 ♗g4 11 d5 ♘e5 with the better prospects for Black, Joksic-Doncevic, Zurich 1987) 8 ♖d1 ♘d7 9 ♕xc4 ♘b6 10 ♕b3 (10 ♕c2 ♗f5 11 ♕d2 e5! 12 dxe5 ♕xd2 13 ♗xd2 ♘xe5 with a good game for Black, Sygulski-Pribyl, Yurmala 1987) 10...a5! 11 ♘c3 a4 12 ♕c2 ♗f5 13 ♕d2 and here 13...a3 would have led to an excellent game (Ivkov-Andersson, Wijk aan Zee 1971).

Now Black has: **7...a5 (4.241),** **7...♘a6 (4.242), 7...♘c6 (4.243)** or **7...c3 (4.244).**

4.241 (1 d4 ♘f6 2 c4 g6 3 g3 ♗g7 4 ♗g2 d5 5 ♘f3 0–0 6 0–0 dxc4 7 ♘a3)

   7 ...   a5!?
The favourite weapon of GM Gutman.

   8 ♘xc4

After 8 ♘e5 ♘fd7 9 ♘exc4 ♘c6 (or 9...c6 10 d5!? ♖a6!? 11 ♗f4 cxd5 12 ♕xd5 ♘c6 13 ♖fd1 e5 14 ♗e3 ♕f6, Ravikumar-Sveshnikov, Hastings 1995, and here 15 ♘b5 would have led to an advantage for White) 10 d5 ♘b4 11

♗d2 c6 12 dxc6 ♘xc6 13 ♕e1 ♘de5 14 ♖d1 ♘xc4 15 ♘xc4 ♕c7 16 ♗c3 ♗xc3 17 ♕xc3 ♗e6 the position is equal (Ilinsky-Gutman, Moscow 1979).

    8   **...**   **♗e6**

    9   **b3**

After **9 ♘e3** a4 10 ♕d3 ♘c6 11 ♗d2 ♘d5 12 ♖fc1 (Reshevsky-Gutman, Beer Sheva 1982) correct is 12...♘xe3 13 ♗xe3 ♗d5 with counterplay, while if **9 ♘fe5** ♗d5 10 f3 ♘fd7 11 ♘e3 (Egger-Fette, Krumbach 1991) Black should play 11...♘xe5 12 dxe5 (12 ♘xd5 ♘ec6 with advantage) 12...♗c6 13 f4 ♗xg2 14 ♔xg2 ♘c6 with an excellent game.

    9   **...**   **c5!**

9...♗d5 transposes into section 4.2433.

The immediate **9...a4!?** 10 ♘g5 ♗d5 11 e4 ♗c6 12 ♖e1 (12 d5 ♗b5 13 ♖b1 is probably better) 12...axb3 13 ♗b2!? bxa2 14 d5 ♗b5 15 ♕b3 ♗xc4 16 ♕xc4 h6 17 ♘h3 ♘bd7 18 ♖xa2 ♘b6 19 ♕b3 ♖xa2 20 ♕xa2 ♕a8 led in Timoshchenko-Gutman (Ashkhabad 1978) to a position where White has some compensation for the pawn.

    10   **♗b2**   **♘c6**

    11   **♘ce5**

Interesting is **11 dxc5** ♗xc4?! 12 bxc4 ♘e4 13 ♗xg7 ♕xd1 14 ♖fxd1 ♔xg7 15 ♖db1 ♘xc5 16 ♖b5, and Black has problems.

Georgiev-Gutman (Wijk aan Zee 1984) continued 11...a4 (11...♗d5!?) 12 bxa4 ♕b6 13 ♖b1 ♗xa2 14 dxc5 ♕xc5 15 ♖a1 ♗d5 with equality. Gutman's idea deserves serious practical testing.

4.242 (1 d4 ♘f6 2 c4 g6 3 g3 ♗g7 4 ♗g2 d5 5 ♘f3 0–0 6 0–0 dxc4 7 ♘a3)

---

    7   **...**   **♘a6!**

A move 'to the side', but the plan, to attack the centre by ...c7-c5, is in general a fairly logical one.

White replies **8 ♘e5** (4.2421) or **8 ♘xc4** (4.2422).

4.2421 (1 d4 ♘f6 2 c4 g6 3 g3 ♗g7 4 ♗g2 d5 5 ♘f3 0–0 6 0–0 dxc4 7 ♘a3 ♘a6)

---

    8   **♘e5**   **c5**

After **8...♘e8!?** 9 ♘axc4 ♘d6 10 d5 ♗f5 11 ♗e3 ♘b4 12 ♗c5 ♘a6 13 ♗a3? ♘xc4 14 ♘xc4 b5! 15 ♘e3 b4 Black had the advantage in P.Nikolic-Ye (Moscow 1994). Correct was 13 ♗d4 with a complicated game.

    9   **dxc5**   **♘xc5**

    10   **♗e3**   **♕c7**

    11   **♘exc4**   **♘g4!**

Weaker is 11...♗e6 12 ♘b5 ♕d7 13 ♕xd7 ♘fxd7 14 ♖ac1 ♖ac8 15 ♘xa7 ♖a8 16 b4 ♖xa7 17 bxc5 ♖xa2 (Schmidt-Polajzer, Bled 1995), and here 18 ♗xb7 would have given White the advantage.

    12   **♗f4**

If **12 ♘b5** ♘xe3 13 ♘xc7 ♘xd1 14 ♘xa8 ♘xb2 15 ♘xb2 ♗xb2 16 ♖ab1 ♗e5 17 ♖fc1 b6, and the knight cannot escape without loss of material.

P.Nikolic-Mecking (Sao Paulo 1991) now continued 12...e5 13 ♗g5 h6 14 ♗d2 ♖d8 15 ♕c1 ♕e7 16 h3 ♘f6 17 ♗xh6 ♗xh6 18 ♕xh6 e4 19 ♖ad1 ♗e6, when Black had some compensation for the pawn.

4.2422 (1 d4 ♘f6 2 c4 g6 3 g3 ♗g7 4 ♗g2 d5 5 ♘f3 0–0 6 0–0 dxc4 7 ♘a3 ♘a6)

---

8 ♘xc4 c5

White plays **9 dxc5 (4.24221)** or **9 b3 (4.24222)**.

4.24221 (1 d4 ♘f6 2 c4 g6 3 g3 ♗g7 4 ♗g2 d5 5 ♘f3 0–0 6 0–0 dxc4 7 ♘a3 ♘a6 8 ♘xc4 c5)

---

9 dxc5 ♗e6

After **9...♘xc5 10 ♗e3 ♗e6** (if 10...♘ce4 11 ♘d4 b6 12 ♘c6 ♕e8 13 ♘4e5 ♗b7 14 ♖c1 ♘d6 15 b4 ♘d7 16 ♘xd7 ♕xd7 17 ♗f4 ♗f6 18 ♕d2 White is slightly better, Puc-Leban, Yugoslavia 1965, but Boleslavsky's recommendation of 11 ♕a4 ♗d7 12 ♕b3 is more accurate) 11 ♖c1 ♖c8 12 b3 ♘d5 13 ♗d4 ♘b4 14 ♕d2 ♗xd4 15 ♕xb4 (15 ♘xd4? ♘xa2! 16 ♖cd1 ♗xc4 17 ♕xa2 ♗d5! 18 ♘b5 ♕b6 with an excellent game) 15...♗f6 16 ♖fd1 ♕c7 17 ♘d4 ♗xd4 18 ♖xd4 b6 Black calmly holds the position (Adianto-Ye, Djakarta 1994).

10 ♘ce5

After **10 ♘fe5 ♘xc5** (bad is 10...♘d5? 11 c6! b5 12 ♘d7!, and Black loses material) 11 ♗e3 ♖c8 12 ♖c1 ♘fd7 (12...♗d5!?) 13 ♘xd7 ♕xd7 14 ♕xd7 ♘xd7 15 ♘a5 ♗xb2 the game is equal (Matlak-Jansa, Karvina 1995).

If **10 ♕xd8 ♖fxd8 11 ♘a5 ♗d5 12 ♗e3 ♘e4** (12...♘g4!? is sharper) 13 ♖ad1 ♘exc5 14 ♘d4 ♗xg2 15 ♔xg2 ♘a4 16 ♘xb7 ♖db8 with an equal ending (P.Nikolic-Smejkal, Sarajevo 1983).

10 ... ♘xc5
11 ♗e3 ♕a5

Somewhat weaker is **11...♖c8 12 ♖c1 ♘ce4** (12...♘fe4!?) 13 ♕a4 a6 14 ♘d3 ♘d6 15 ♘c5 and White stands better (Pirc-O'Kelly, Bled 1950), or **11...♘fe4 12 ♖c1 ♖c8** (if 12...♕a5 13 ♕d4 ♕xa2 14 ♖xc5 ♘xc5 15 ♕xc5 ♕xb2 16 ♗d4 with a slight advantage, Barcza-Zilberstein, Lipetsk 1968) 13 ♕c2!? (13 b4? ♕xd1 14 ♖fxd1 ♘a4!) with the threat of 14 b4 or 14 ♖fd1.

12 ♗d4

After **12 ♕e1 ♕xe1 13 ♖fxe1 ♖ac8 14 ♘g5 ♗d5 15 ♗h3 ♖c7 16 ♖ac1 ♘a6 17 ♖xc7 ♘xc7 18 ♖c1 ♘b5 19 a4 ♘d6** the position is equal (Kurajica-Smejkal, Smederevska Palanka 1982).

Now after **12...♗d5 13 e3** (Timman-Henley, Arnhem 1983), either 13...♘e6 or 13...♖fd8 would have led to an equal game.

4.24222 (1 d4 ♘f6 2 c4 g6 3 g3 ♗g7 4 ♗g2 d5 5 ♘f3 0–0 6 0–0 dxc4 7 ♘a3 ♘a6 8 ♘xc4 c5)

---

9 b3 ♗f5

Again a typical plan of using the light squares in the centre, which should secure Black sufficient counterplay.

After 9...♘d5 10 ♗b2 b5 (10...♘b6 11 ♘e3 ♖b8 12 ♖c1 ♘d7 13 ♕d2 cxd4 14 ♘xd4 ♘e5 15 ♖fd1 leads to an advantage for White, Kurajica-Nurkic, Tuzla 1983) 11 ♘ce5 ♗b7 12 dxc5 ♘xc5 13 ♘c6! White has the advantage (Kurajica-Ftacnik, Banja Luka 1983).

After 9...♗e6 10 ♗b2 ♖c8 (if 10...♕c8 11 ♖c1 ♖d8 12 e3 ♗h3 13 ♕e2 ♗xg2 14 ♔xg2 ♕f5 15 ♖fd1 ♖ac8 16 d5! the tactics are in White's favour, Abramovic-Mitrovic, Niksic 1996) 11 ♖c1 ♖c7 (more logical is 11...♗d5 12 e3 e6 13 ♕e2 ♕e7 14 ♖fd1 ♖fd8 15 ♗a3 ♗f8 16 ♘ce5 ♕e8 17 ♘g5!, but here too White has the initiative, Svidler-Liss, Israel 1996) 12 dxc5 ♘xc5 13 ♕xd8 ♖xd8 14 ♘d4 ♗d7 15 ♘e5 ♘e8 16 ♘xd7 ♖dxd7 17 ♖cd1 ♖c8 18 e3 ♖cd8 19 ♗a3 Black is again slightly worse (Romanishin-Greenfeld, Ljubljana 1995).

10 ♗b2   ♗e4
11 ♖c1

After 11 ♕d2 ♕c7 12 ♖ad1 ♖ad8 13 ♕e3 cxd4 14 ♘xd4 ♗xg2 15 ♔xg2 ♘b4 16 ♕f3 ♘xa2 17 ♖a1 ♘b4 18 ♖xa7 ♘fd5 19 e4 ♗xd4! 20 ♗xd4 ♘c6 the position is completely equal (Andersson-Stohl, Prague 1996).

11 ...   ♖c8

Perhaps no weaker is 11...cxd4 12 ♕xd4 ♕xd4 13 ♘xd4 ♖fd8 (13...♗xg2!? is stronger) 14 f3 ♗d5 15 ♘a5 ♘g4 (better 15...b6! 16 ♘ac6 ♗xc6 17 ♘xc6 ♖d2 with equality) 16 fxg4 ♗xg2 17 ♔xg2 ♗xd4 18 ♗a3 ♖d7 19 ♖fd1 ♖ad8 20 ♖d3 ♗b6 (20...♗f6 21 ♘xb7) 21 ♖xd7 ♖xd7 22 ♖c8+ ♔g7 23 ♘c4 with a slight advantage to White (Georgiev-Stohl, Dortmund 1991).

Also good, however, is 11...b6!? 12 ♕d2 ♕d5 13 ♖fd1 ♖ad8 14 dxc5 ♘xc5 15 ♕xd5 ♖xd5 16 ♘fe5 ♖xd1+ 17 ♖xd1 ♗xg2 18 ♔xg2 ♖c8 and Black holds on (Abramovic-Nesterovic, Tivat 1995).

12 ♕d2

If 12 ♗h3, then not 12...♖c7 13 ♘g5 ♗f5 14 ♗xf5 gxf5 15 dxc5 with advantage (Adorjan-Szekely, Hungary 1992), but 12...e6 13 dxc5 ♖xc5 14 ♕xd8 ♖xd8 15 ♖fd1 ♖cd5 16 ♖xd5 ♗xd5 17 ♘d4 ♘b4 with equality (Adorjan).

12 ...   b6

After 12...♕d5 13 ♖fd1 ♕h5?! (13...♖fd8 14 ♕e1 is rather more logical, but here too the black queen feels uncomfortable) 14 h3! cxd4 (after 14...♗h6 15 ♘e3 ♘d5 16 g4 ♗xe3 17 fxe3 ♕h6 18 g5 ♕h5 19 dxc5 Black has great problems) 15 ♗xd4 ♖fd8 16 ♘ce5! ♖xc1 17 ♕xc1 ♗xf3 18 ♗xf3! White has a great advantage (Karpov-J.Polgar, Wijk aan Zee 1998 – *Game 14*).

Sorry-Kekki (Helsinki 1989) now continued 13 ♖fd1 ♖c7 (13...♕d5 is equally good) 14 ♕f4 ♕a8 15 dxc5 ♖xc5 16 ♘ce5 ♖xc1 17 ♕xc1 ♘c5 18 b4 ♘e6 with an equal game.

4.243 (1 d4 ♘f6 2 c4 g6 3 g3 ♗g7
4 ♗g2 d5 5 ♘f3 0–0 6 0–0 dxc4 7
♘a3)

7 ...   ♘c6

With this move Black begins a plan of piece pressure on White's centre. In addition, he wants to exploit his control of the light-square complex d5 and e4. Modern theory does not consider this plan the strongest, but its few supporters have a weighty argument – this is what Bobby Fischer himself liked to play, and at the present time it has again become fashionable – cf. *Game 15* (P.Nikolic-Piket, Wijk aan Zee 1996).

8 ♘xc4   ♗e6
9 b3

The most logical. Less good is 9 ♘ce5 ♗d5 or 9 ♘e3 ♘d5, exchanging a pair of minor pieces, which favours Black with his slightly cramped position.

Here Black has several fundamentally different plans: 9...♕c8!? (4.2431), 9...a5 (4.2432) and 9...♗d5 (4.2433).

4.2431 (1 d4 ♘f6 2 c4 g6 3 g3 ♗g7
4 ♗g2 d5 5 ♘f3 0–0 6 0–0 dxc4 7
♘a3 ♘c6 8 ♘xc4 ♗e6 9 b3)

9 ...   ♕c8!?

Preparing the exchange of light-square bishops, as well as ...♖d8, attacking the d4 pawn.

10 ♖e1

Preparing to answer ...♗h3 with ♗h1, avoiding the exchange of bishops. White should not fall in with his opponent's plans: 10 ♗b2 ♗h3 11 ♖c1 ♖d8 12 e3 ♗xg2 13 ♔xg2 ♕e6 14 ♕e2 a5 15 a3 ♘e8!? 16 ♖fe1 h6 17 ♕c2 ♖d7 18 ♘cd2 f5 with a good game for Black (Vadasz-Martz, Wijk aan Zee 1975).

Now after 10...♖d8 11 ♗b2 ♗d5 12 e3 a5 13 ♘cd2 ♘e4 14 ♘xe4 ♗xe4 15 ♕e2 a4 16 ♗c3 axb3 17 axb3 (Smyslov-Pilnik, Amsterdam 1956) and 17...♕d7 White has nothing special. This plan is very logical, and therefore it is hard to understand why it is not more popular.

4.2432 (1 d4 ♘f6 2 c4 g6 3 g3 ♗g7
4 ♗g2 d5 5 ♘f3 0–0 6 0–0 dxc4 7
♘a3 ♘c6 8 ♘xc4 ♗e6 9 b3)

9 ...   a5

Fischer considered this plan to be the most logical – without further ado Black seizes space and creates targets to attack on the queenside, which looks very logical with the bishop at e6, giving Black additional possibilities.

10 ♗b2

10 a4 transposes to variation 4.2433.

10 ... a4

Somewhat premature, allowing White to set up a strong centre. **10...♗d5** is probably better, again transposing into variation 4.2433.

11 ♘g5

After 11 ♘fe5 ♘xe5 12 dxe5 ♘g4 (12...♘d5!? is possible) 13 ♗xb7 ♖b8?! (13...♖a7 14 ♗f3 ♗xc4! 15 bxc4 ♘xe5 leads to equality) 14 ♘a5 ♕xd1 15 ♖fxd1 axb3 16 axb3 ♘xe5 17 ♖ab1 ♗f5 18 ♖bc1 White has some advantage (Szabolcsi-Rezsek, Budapest 1992).

11 ... ♗d5

After **11...♗xc4** 12 bxc4 a3 13 ♗c3 h6 14 ♘h3 ♘e8 (14...♘d7 followed by 15...♘b6, attacking the white pawns, is also interesting) 15 e3 e5 16 d5 ♘a5 17 c5 b6 18 ♕d2 ♘c4 19 ♕e2 ♘b2! Black created counterplay (Nikoladze-Arakhamia, Tbilisi 1990).

12 e4 ♗xc4

13 bxc4 h6

Weaker is **13...e5** 14 d5 ♘a5 15 ♖c1 ♖e8 16 c5 when White has the advantage (Gofstein-Kupreichik, USSR 1976) or **13...a3** 14 ♗c3 ♘d7 15 e5 ♘b6 16 e6, also with advantage to White (Csom-Lukacs, Hungary 1972), but not 16 ♗xc6 bxc6 17 ♕b3 ♕c8 18 ♗b4 f6! 19 exf6 ♗xf6 with excellent counterplay (Schlosser-Konopka, Czechoslovakia 1993).

14 ♘h3 a3

15 ♗c3 ♘d7

16 ♖c1!?

There was complicated play after 16 e5 ♘b6 17 ♖b1 ♘a4 in Ilievsky-Fischer (Skopje 1967), where the future World Champion had to fight for equality.

Now after 16...e5 17 d5 (Portisch-Ilievsky, Skopje 1968) 17...♘e7 18 ♗b4! White has the advantage.

4.2433 (1 d4 ♘f6 2 c4 g6 3 g3 ♗g7 4 ♗g2 d5 5 ♘f3 0–0 6 0–0 dxc4 7 ♘a3 ♘c6 8 ♘xc4 ♗e6 9 b3)

---

9 ... ♗d5

10 ♗b2 a5

Now **10...♕c8** is not so logical:

(a) 11 ♘e3 ♗e4 12 ♘e5 ♗xg2 13 ♔xg2 ♘xe5 14 dxe5 ♖d8 15 ♕c2 ♘g4 16 ♘xg4 ♕xg4 17 ♖ad1 with some advantage (P.Nikolic-Dvoiris, Sochi 1982), although after 17...c6 Black should be able to hold on;

(b) 11 ♖c1 ♖d8 12 e3 ♕e6 13 ♖e1 ♘e4 14 ♕e2 f5 15 ♖ed1 ♖ac8 16 ♘e1! with advantage to White (Timoshchenko-Rychagov, Barnaul 1988);

(c) 11 e3 and now:

(c1) 11...♖d8 12 ♕e2 a5 (or 12...♕e6 13 ♖ac1 a5 14 ♘ce5! ♘e4 15 ♘d3! ♕d6 16 ♘fe5 with a central advantage, Pfleger-G.Garcia, Camaguey 1974) 13 a3 h6 14 ♖ac1 ♕e6 15 ♖fd1 ♗e4 16 ♗f1! and White has some advantage (Padevsky-Whiteley, Nice 1974);

(c2) 11...a5 12 ♖c1 ♖d8 13 a3 ♗h6!? 14 ♕e2 ♕e6 15 ♖fe1 ♖a6 16 ♕f1 ♘e4

17 ♘fd2 ♘xd2 18 ♘xd2 ♗xg2 19 ♕xg2 and White has rather the better game due to his greater control of space (Makarov-Semeniuk, Russia 1991).

Now White's main continuations are 11 a4 (4.24331), 11 e3 (4.24332) and 11 ♖c1 (4.24333).

Nikolic's favourite continuation 11 ♘e3 is not so good here – after 11...♗e4 12 ♘e5 ♗xg2 13 ♔xg2 ♘d5 14 ♕c1 (or 14 ♘xc6 ♘xe3+ 15 fxe3 ♕d5+ 16 ♖f3 ♕xc6 17 ♖c1 ♕d7 18 ♕c2 c6 19 ♕c4 e6 and Black took the initiative, A.Zaitsev-Kupreichik, USSR 1969) 14...♘xe3+ 15 ♕xe3 ♗xe5 16 dxe5 ♕d5+ 17 ♕f3 ♖fd8 18 ♖fc1 a4 Black gained an advantage in P.Nikolic-Popovic (Vrsac 1981).

4.24331 (1 d4 ♘f6 2 c4 g6 3 g3 ♗g7 4 ♗g2 d5 5 ♘f3 0–0 6 0–0 dxc4 7 ♘a3 ♘c6 8 ♘xc4 ♗e6 9 b3 ♗d5 10 ♗b2 a5)

---

11 a4!?
Rather primitively forestalling Black's queenside play, although, of course, the b3 pawn becomes weak.
11 ... ♘b4

After **11...e6** 12 ♖c1 ♖a6 13 e3 ♕b8 14 ♗a3 ♖d8 15 ♖e1 ♖a8 16 ♗f1 White

has the advantage (Spassky-Bronstein, USSR 1963).

More interesting is **11...♖b8!?** 12 e3 b5 13 axb5 ♖xb5 14 ♘fd2 ♗xg2 15 ♔xg2 e6 16 ♕f3 ♘d5 17 ♖fc1 ♘db4 and Black equalised (Georgiev-Dvoiris, Moscow 1994).

11...♘e8?! is original: 12 ♘fe5 ♗xg2 13 ♔xg2 f5 14 ♘xc6 ♕d5+ 15 f3 bxc6 16 ♕c2 with advantage to White (Kengis-Rychagov, Barnaul 1988).

Also possible is **11...♕b8** 12 e3 ♖d8 13 ♕e2 e6 14 ♖fc1 ♘e4 15 h4 b5! with counterplay (Kurajica-P.Nikolic, Pula 1991).

12 e3
After **12 ♘fe5** c6 13 ♘d3 ♗xg2 14 ♔xg2 b5! 15 ♘ce5 ♕d5+ 16 f3 ♘xd3 17 ♕xd3 ♘d7 18 ♘xd7 ♕xd7 19 ♖fc1 ♖fb8 the game is equal (Kurajica-Henley, Indonesia 1982).

12...♗e4 13 ♘e1 ♗xg2 14 ♔xg2 (Kurajica-Rogers, Reggio Emilia 1985), and here 14...c6 and 15...♘d7 was correct, threatening ...b7-b5 and creating counterplay on the queenside.

4.24332 (1 d4 ♘f6 2 c4 g6 3 g3 ♗g7 4 ♗g2 d5 5 ♘f3 0–0 6 0–0 dxc4 7 ♘a3 ♘c6 8 ♘xc4 ♗e6 9 b3 ♗d5 10 ♗b2 a5)

---

11 e3   a4
12 ♕e2   ♖a6!?

12...♘e4 is also interesting: 13 ♖fc1 f5 14 ♘e1 ♘f6 15 f3 ♗h6 with a complicated game (Panno-Mecking, Manila 1976).

12...♕c8 is also good: 13 ♘e1 (13 ♖fc1!?) 13...♗xg2 14 ♔xg2 axb3 15 axb3 ♖xa1 16 ♗xa1 ♕f5 17 ♘d3 ♖a8 18 ♗b2 (Garcia-Miles, Bajamo 1986), and here 18...♕d5+ would have given Black a slight advantage.

Vukic-Korchnoi (Sarajevo 1976) continued 13 ♖fc1 ♖e8 14 ♘e1 ♗xg2 15 ♘xg2 ♘d5 16 ♘e1 e6 17 ♘d3 ♕a8 with a promising position for Black.

4.24333 (1 d4 ♘f6 2 c4 g6 3 g3 ♗g7 4 ♗g2 d5 5 ♘f3 0–0 6 0–0 dxc4 7 ♘a3 ♘c6 8 ♘xc4 ♗e6 9 b3 ♗d5 10 ♗b2 a5)

---

11 ♖c1

Now Black has **11... ♕c8 (4.243331)** or **11...a4! (4.243332)**.

4.243331 (1 d4 ♘f6 2 c4 g6 3 g3 ♗g7 4 ♗g2 d5 5 ♘f3 0–0 6 0–0 dxc4 7 ♘a3 ♘c6 8 ♘xc4 ♗e6 9 b3 ♗d5 10 ♗b2 a5 11 ♖c1)

---

11 ...   ♕c8

11...♕b8, with the same idea, is weaker: 12 a3 ♖d8 13 e3 ♘e4 14 ♕c2 a4 15 b4 ♘a7 16 ♘fe5 ♘f6 17 e4 and White has the better game (Barcza-A.Zaitsev, Hungary 1969).

12 a3

After **12 ♘e3 ♗e4 13 ♘e5 ♗xg2 14 ♔xg2** (Miles-Schmid, London 1980), 14...♘xe5 15 dxe5 ♖d8 16 ♕c2 ♘g4 17 ♘xg4 ♕xg4 18 f3 ♕e6 19 ♕xc7 a4! would have led to equality.

12 ...   ♖d8

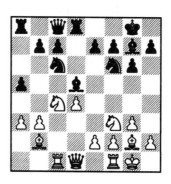

13 e3 ♕e6 14 ♕c2 (if 14 ♘g5 ♕g4 15 ♕xg4 ♘xg4 16 ♗xd5 ♖xd5, equalising) 14...♘e4! 15 ♖fe1 f5 16 ♖e2 ♕f7 with equality (Speelman-Nunn, London 1986).

4.243332 (1 d4 ♘f6 2 c4 g6 3 g3 ♗g7 4 ♗g2 d5 5 ♘f3 0–0 6 0–0 dxc4 7 ♘a3 ♘c6 8 ♘xc4 ♗e6 9 b3 ♗d5 10 ♗b2 a5 11 ♖c1)

---

11 ...   a4!

A positional pawn sacrifice – White gains an extra pawn, although it is doubled – in return for which Black gains a clear plan of pressure on the a4 and a2 pawns.

12 bxa4

12 ♘e3 ♗e4 can be included: 13 bxa4 (also interesting is 13 ♘e5!? ♗xg2 14 ♔xg2 ♘b4 15 bxa4 ♖a7 16 ♕b3 with advantage, Lazic-David, Bardejov 1996) 13...♖a6, and now:

(a) 14 ♕b3 ♕a8 15 ♘e5 ♗xg2 16 ♘xg2 ♖xa4 17 ♘xc6 bxc6 18 a3 ♘e4 19 ♖fd1 c5 with an excellent game for Black (Podzielny-Banas, Trnava 1984);

(b) 14 ♘e5 is somewhat stronger: 14...♗xg2 15 ♘xg2 ♕d5 16 a3, (P.Nikolic-Ftacnik, Pula 1997), although here too Black has equality after 16...♖fa8 17 f3 ♖xa4 18 e4 ♕b5.

12 ... ♖a6

Black has sacrificed a pawn, but has gained a target to attack and comfortable development for his rook and queen.

12...♘e8 is also interesting: 13 e3 (13 ♘fe5 ♗xg2 14 ♔xg2 ♗xe5! 15 dxe5 ♕xd1 16 ♖fxd1 ♖xa4 is equal, Petrosian-Belyavsky, USSR 1975) 13...♘d6 14 ♘fd2 ♘xc4 15 ♘xc4 ♗xg2 16 ♔xg2 ♕d5+ 17 ♔g1 (Csom-Adamski, Bath 1973), and here 17...♖fb8! was correct with a complicated game.

12...♕b8, with a similar idea, is weaker: 13 ♘fe5 ♗xg2 14 ♔xg2 ♘xe5 15 dxe5 ♖d8 16 ♕b3 ♘d7 17 e6! and Black has a bad position (Gorelov-M.Ivanov, Moscow 1995), while **12...♖a7** is too artificial: 13 ♘fe5 ♘a5 14 ♗xd5 ♕xd5 15 ♘xa5 (15 f3!?) 15...♕xa5 16 ♖c5! with a great advantage to White (Podgaets-Krogius, Moscow 1973).

Now White has **13 ♘fe5 (4.2433321)** or **13 a3 (4.2433322)**.

Less critical is **13 ♘e3 ♗e4** 14 ♘e5 ♗xg2 15 ♔xg2 ♘d7!? (15...♕a8 is also good) 16 ♘xc6 bxc6 17 ♗a3 ♘b6! with a good game for Black (Rotstein-Buturin, Lviv 1996).

4.2433321 (1 d4 ♘f6 2 c4 g6 3 g3 ♗g7 4 ♗g2 d5 5 ♘f3 0–0 6 0–0 dxc4 7 ♘a3 ♘c6 8 ♘xc4 ♗e6 9 b3 ♗d5 10 ♗b2 a5 11 ♖c1 a4 12 bxa4 ♖a6)

13	♘fe5	♗xg2
14	♔xg2	♕a8

Less good is **14...♕d5+** 15 f3 ♖fa8 16 e4 ♕d8 17 ♘xc6 ♖xc6 18 a5 ♘e8 19 ♕b3 with a great advantage to White (Buturin-Chudinovskikh, Smolensk 1992), or **14...♘d7** 15 ♘xc6 ♖xc6 16 ♕b3 ♕a8 17 ♔g1 ♘b6 18 ♘xb6 ♖xb6 19 ♕a3 with the better game for White (Ilivitsky-Szabo, Gothenburg 1955). **14...♘xe5** is also unsatisfactory: 15 dxe5 ♘d7 16 a5 b5 17 axb6 cxb6 18 ♕d5! with advantage (Quinteros-Kavalek, Las Palmas 1974).

15 ♘xc6

After **15 ♔g1 ♖xa4** 16 a3 ♘e4 17 ♕c2 ♘d6 18 ♘xd6 exd6 19 ♘xc6 bxc6 20 ♕xc6 ♗xd4 a draw is imminent (P.Nikolic-Yermolinsky, Wijk aan Zee 1997), but interesting is 16...♘xe5!? 17 dxe5 ♖d8 18 ♕c2 ♘d5 19 e4 b5 20 ♘d2 ♘b6 with a complicated game.

15 ... bxc6

With **15...♖xc6** 16 ♔g1 ♕a6 17 ♕b3 Black deviates from the correct course.

16   ♔g1

After **16 a5 c5+ 17 ♔g1 ♖d8 18 e3** cxd4 **19 exd4 c5** Black equalises (Vogt-Ghizdavu, Bucharest 1974). Also good is **19...♘e4 20 ♕f3 ♗xd4 21 ♗xd4 ♖xd4** (P.Nikolic-Piket, Wijk aan Zee 1996) – *Game 15*.

16   ...   ♖xa4
17   a3   ♘d7

Also satisfactory is **17...♖b8 18 ♗a1 ♘d7 19 ♕c2 c5** with equality (Antunes-Atalik, Pula 1997).

Now after **18 ♘e5 ♘xe5 19 dxe5 ♖b8 20 ♖c2 e6 21 ♕d7 ♖a5!** Black equalised (Karpov-Piket, Tilburg 1996).

4.2433322 (1 d4 ♘f6 2 c4 g6 3 g3 ♗g7 4 ♗g2 d5 5 ♘f3 0–0 6 0–0 dxc4 7 ♘a3 ♘c6 8 ♘xc4 ♗e6 9 b3 ♗d5 10 ♗b2 a5 11 ♖c1 a4 12 bxa4 ♖a6)

---

13   a3   ♕a8
14   a5

Or **14 ♘e3** and now:

(a) **14...♖xa4 15 ♘xd5 ♘xd5 16 ♕b3 ♘b6 17 ♖c2 e6 18 ♖fc1 ♖d8 19 e3 ♗f8 20 ♘g5!** ♗xa3 **21 ♘xe6!** and White has a strong attack (Todorcevic-Marinkovic, Belgrade 1991);

(b) **14...♗e4 15 ♕b3 (15 ♘e5 ♗xg2 16 ♔xg2 ♖xa4 17 ♘xc6 bxc6 18 ♔g1 ♖b8** with an equal game, Schmidt-Gheorghiu, Bath 1973) **15...e6 16 ♘e5 ♖b6! 17 ♕a2 ♗xg2 18 ♔xg2 ♕xa4 19 ♘3c4 ♖a6** and Black equalises (Schulz-David, Germany 1992).

14   ...   ♖d8

Another plan is also good. After **14...♖c8 15 ♘e3 ♖xa5 (15...♗e4!?** is also possible) **16 ♘xd5 ♘xd5 17 e3 e6 18 ♘d2 ♖a7! 19 ♕b3 ♘a5 20 ♕c2 ♖a6 21 ♕d3 c5! 22 ♖c2 cxd4 23 ♖xc8+ ♕xc8 24 ♗xd5 exd5 25 ♗xd4 ♗xd4 26**

♕xd4 ♘c4 complete calm reigns on the board (Martinovic-Howell, Groningen 1995).

15   ♕e1!?

After **15 e3 ♘e8 16 ♕e2 ♘xa5 17 ♘cd2 ♘b3** the position is equal (Forintos-Milev, Hungary 1959).

Bönsch-Pribyl (Leipzig 1990) now continued **15...e6 16 e3 ♖c8 17 ♕e2 ♘xa5 18 ♘xa5 ♖xa5 19 ♘e5 ♗xg2 20 ♔xg2**, and here Black should have played **20...c5!** with equality.

4.244 (1 d4 ♘f6 2 c4 g6 3 g3 ♗g7 4 ♗g2 d5 5 ♘f3 0–0 6 0–0 dxc4 7 ♘a3)

---

7   ...   c3

Black does not want to allow the knight to go to c4, but in so doing he strengthens White's centre.

8   bxc3   c5

Now White has several options: **9 ♕b3 (4.2441), 9 ♘c4 (4.2442), 9 ♘e5 (4.2443)** and **9 e3 (4.2444)**.

Of other continuations we must mention:

9 ♖b1 (a fairly logical plan – White removes his rook from the long diagonal and threatens a possible dxc5, but the move does nothing to strengthen his centre) 9...♘c6 10 ♘e5 (10 ♘c4? ♗e6 11 ♘ce5 ♗d5 12 ♘xc6 ♗xc6 13 ♕b3 ♗e4 14 ♖b2 ♖c8 leads to the better game for Black, Georgadze-Romanishin, Moscow 1987, while 10 dxc5? is strongly met by 10...♘d5) 10...♘d5 11 ♕b3 (after 11 ♘xc6 bxc6 12 ♕b3 cxd4 13 cxd4 ♗e6 14 ♕c2 ♗xd4 15 ♗h6 ♗g7 the game is equal, Schneider-I.Horvath, Linz 1992) 11...♘xe5 12 dxe5 (12 ♗xd5 cxd4 13 cxd4 ♘c6) 12...♗e6 13 c4 (13 ♖d1 ♘xc3! 14 ♖xd8 ♗xb3 15 ♖xa8 ♖xa8 16 ♖xb3 ♘xe2+ and Black has an excellent game) 13...♘b4 14 f4 ♖b8 15 ♗e3 b5! 16 ♗xc5 bxc4 17 ♕e3 a5 with an equal game (Sveshnikov-Tukmakov, Frunze 1981).

9 ♗b2 (this rather passive strengthening of the centre cannot cause Black any serious problems) 9...♘c6 10 ♘c4 ♗e6 11 ♘fe5 (after 11 ♘cd2 ♗d5 Black is excellently placed) 11...♖c8 (11...♗d5 is also good) 12 ♗xc6 bxc6 13 ♕d3 cxd4 14 cxd4 c5! with an excellent game (Remmler-Baikov, Moscow 1990).

4.2441 (1 d4 ♘f6 2 c4 g6 3 g3 ♗g7 4 ♗g2 d5 5 ♘f3 0–0 6 0–0 dxc4 7 ♘a3 c3 8 bxc3 c5)

---

9 ♕b3

A continuation introduced by Bulgarian players. White wants to support his centre with his rook from d1 while keeping the b7 pawn under attack, but the position of the queen at b3 is also vulnerable.

9 ...   ♘c6

Risky is 9...♘e4 10 ♖d1 cxd4 11 cxd4 ♗e6 12 ♕c2 ♗d5 13 ♘e5 f5 14 f3 ♘d6 15 e4 fxe4 16 fxe4 ♗e6 17 ♗b2 ♘d7 18 ♘xd7 ♕xd7 19 e5 when White

is clearly better (Speelman-Howell, London 1987).

10 ♖d1

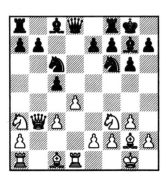

This move order is the point of White's set-up, but now Black has the possibility, by driving back the queen, of occupying the light squares.

10 ...   ♘a5!

Bad is 10...cxd4 11 cxd4 ♕d5 12 ♘e5! ♕xb3 13 axb3 ♘xe5 14 dxe5 ♘d7 15 f4 ♘c5 16 b4 ♘b3 17 ♖b1 ♗e6 18 ♗e3 with a great advantage to White (Georgiev-Van Mil, Wijk aan Zee 1984).

11 ♕b2

Bad is 11 ♕c2? ♗f5 12 ♕b2 ♗e4, when Black seizes the initiative (Voiska-Chiburdanidze, Dubai 1986).

11 ...   cxd4!

Possible, although less good, is 11...♗e6 12 ♘g5 ♗d7 13 ♗f4 h6 14 ♘e4 ♘xe4 15 ♗xe4 g5 16 ♗c1 ♗a4 with an unclear position (Timoshchenko-Chekhov, Riga 1988).

After 11...♗f5 12 ♗d2 ♕b6 13 ♕c1? (better is 13 ♕xb6 axb6 14 ♘e5 ♖fd8 15 ♗e1 cxd4 16 cxd4 ♘g4 17 ♘f3 ♘c6 18 ♘b5 ♗c2 19 ♖d2 ♗a4 with counterchances, Velikov-Miralles, Marseille 1990) 13...♖ac8 14 ♗e3 ♘g4! 15 dxc5 ♕a6 16 ♗d4? (16 ♘d4 ♖xc5 and Black stands well) 16...e5 17 h3 ♗h6! Black has a clear advantage (Gutman-Douven, Lugano 1989).

But **11...♗d7** is illogical: 12 dxc5 ♕c7 13 ♗e3 ♖fd8 14 h3 ♗a4 15 ♖d4 with a serious advantage for White (Tatai-Ricardi, Thessaloniki 1984).

12   cxd4   ♗f5

Also possible is **12...♗e6** 13 ♗f4 ♗d5 14 ♖ac1 ♖c8 15 ♖xc8 ♕xc8 16 ♖c1 ♕d7! 17 ♘e5? (17 ♘b5=) 17...♕a4! 18 ♗xd5 ♘xd5 with a slight advantage for Black (Kirov-Honfi, Budapest 1987).

13   ♗d2

After 13 ♗f4 ♗e4 14 ♗e5 ♕d7 the game is equal.

Now after 13...♗e4 14 ♖ac1 ♘c6 15 ♘c4 ♖c8 16 ♗e1 b6 the black pieces completely control the centre. If 17 ♘ce5 ♖c7 18 ♕a3 ♕c8 and 19...♕b7 Black stands better, while after 17 ♕a3 (Ninov-I.Sokolov, Graz 1987) he could have gained the advantage by 17... ♗xf3 18 ♕xf3 ♘xd4 19 ♕d3 ♘d7! 20 ♗c3 b5 (Sokolov).

4.2442 (1 d4 ♘f6 2 c4 g6 3 g3 ♗g7 4 ♗g2 d5 5 ♘f3 0–0 6 0–0 dxc4 7 ♘a3 c3 8 bxc3 c5)

---

9   ♘c4   ♘c6

Interesting is **9...♗e6** 10 ♘ce5 cxd4 11 cxd4 ♗d5 12 ♗a3 ♘c6 13 ♕d3 ♖e8 14 ♖fc1 ♖c8 with an unclear game (Pigusov-Nenashev, USSR 1987).

Now White has **10 ♗a3** (4.24421), **10 ♘ce5** (4.24422) or **10 ♘fe5** (4.24423).

4.24421 (1 d4 ♘f6 2 c4 g6 3 g3 ♗g7 4 ♗g2 d5 5 ♘f3 0–0 6 0–0 dxc4 7 ♘a3 c3 8 bxc3 c5 9 ♘c4 ♘c6)

---

10   ♗a3

The development of the bishop at a3 usually gives Black various tactical possibilities, as is also the case here.

10   ...   ♗e6

Also good is **10...♘d5** 11 ♖c1 ♘b6! 12 ♘ce5 ♘xe5 13 ♘xe5 ♗xe5! 14 dxe5 ♕c7 15 c4 (15 f4 ♘c4!) 15...♖d8 16 ♕b3 ♗e6 17 ♕e3 ♖ac8, and Black is excellently placed (Plachetka-Ftacnik, Trnava 1983).

Shapiro-Thorsteins (New York 1989) now continued 11 ♘ce5 ♘xe5 12 ♘xe5 ♘d5 13 ♗xc5 ♖c8 14 c4 ♘c3 15 ♕d3 (or 15 ♕c2 ♗xe5 16 ♕xc3 etc.) 15...♗xe5! 16 ♕xc3 ♖xc5 17 dxe5 b6 (or 17...♕c7 18 ♕e3 ♕xe5 19 ♕xe5 ♖xe5 20 ♗xb7 ♖b8 with an excellent game, Espig-S.Mohr, Germany 1991) 18 f4 ♖xc4 19 ♕a3 ♕d4+ 20 ♔h1 ♖c2, and the black pieces penetrate into White's position.

4.24422 (1 d4 ♘f6 2 c4 g6 3 g3 ♗g7 4 ♗g2 d5 5 ♘f3 0–0 6 0–0 dxc4 7 ♘a3 c3 8 bxc3 c5 9 ♘c4 ♘c6)

---

10   ♘ce5   ♘d5

Also possible is **10...♗f5!?** 11 ♗b2 (after 11 ♘xc6 bxc6 12 ♘e5 ♘e4 13

Wd3! the position is double-edged, Kasparov) 11...♗e4 (11...♗e6 has also been tried: 12 ♘xc6 bxc6 13 ♘e5 ♗d5 14 f3 cxd4 15 cxd4 ♘d7 with an unclear game, Sapis-Trapl, Ulan-Bator 1988) 12 e3 **Wc7** 13 **We2** ♘xe5 14 ♘xe5 ♗xg2 15 ♔xg2 ♘e4 16 f3 ♘d6 17 ♖ac1 ♖fd8 18 ♖fd1 **Wa5** with equality (Schussler-Kasparov, Graz 1981).

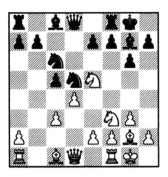

11   Wb3

If 11 ♗b2 ♘xe5 12 ♘xe5 ♗xe5! 13 dxe5 ♗e6 14 c4 ♘b6 15 ♗xb7 ♖b8 16 ♗e4 ♘xc4 17 ♗c3 **Wxd1** 18 ♖fxd1 ♘b2! 19 ♖d2 ♘a4 with an excellent game (Arkell-Lukin, Leningrad 1989).

Harmless is 11 ♗d2 ♘xe5 (less good is 11...♗e6 12 e4 ♘b6 13 ♘xc6 bxc6 14 dxc5 ♘c4 15 ♘d4 ♘xd2 16 **Wxd2** ♗c4 17 ♖fd1 **Wa5**, Shaboian-Hachian, USSR 1991, 18 e5! **Wxc5** 19 f4 with the better position for White) 12 ♘xe5 ♘b6 13 ♗f4 ♘d5 ½-½ (Smyslov-Kasparov, Moscow 1981).

Gutman-Wolff (Paris 1987) now continued 11...♘xe5 12 ♘xe5 ♘b6 13 **Wd1** (this move signifies the failure of White's idea) 13...♗xe5! (a typical manoeuvre in such positions – Black gives up his important bishop, but White is unable to exploit the weakness of the dark squares, and his pawn weaknesses are very perceptible) 14 dxe5 **Wc7** 15 f4 ♗e6 16 **We1** ♖ad8 17 ♗f3, and here 17...♘a4 18 g4 ♗d5 would have led to an advantage for Black.

4.24423 (1 d4 ♘f6 2 c4 g6 3 g3 ♗g7 4 ♗g2 d5 5 ♘f3 0–0 6 0–0 dxc4 7 ♘a3 c3 8 bxc3 c5 9 ♘c4 ♘c6)

---

10   ♘fe5   ♘d5
11   ♗b2   .

After 11 ♘xc6 bxc6 12 ♗b2 ♖b8 (12...♗e6 transposes into variations considered later) 13 **Wd2** ♗a6 14 ♘e5 **Wb6** 15 ♗a3 ♗xe5 16 ♗xc5 **Wa5** 17 ♗xd5 cxd5 18 ♗b4 **Wc7** 19 dxe5 **Wxe5** the game is equal (Hjartarson-Yermolinsky, Leningrad 1984).

Now we consider **11...♘xe5** (4.244231) and **11...♗e6** (4.244232).

4.244231 (1 d4 ♘f6 2 c4 g6 3 g3 ♗g7 4 ♗g2 d5 5 ♘f3 0–0 6 0–0 dxc4 7 ♘a3 c3 8 bxc3 c5 9 ♘c4 ♘c6 10 ♘fe5 ♘d5 11 ♗b2)

---

11   ...   ♘xe5
12   ♘xe5   ♗xe5!

Again Black gives up his important bishop, but more important is the fact that White cannot exploit this weakness, and the e5 knight must be eliminated. **12...♘b6?** fails to 13 f4! **Wc7** 14 ♗a3 c4 15 e4 with advantage (Zaichik-Cvitan, Tbilisi 1986).

13   dxe5   ♗e6!

Less good is **13...♘b6?** 14 **Wxd8!** (but not 14 e6? ♗xe6 15 ♗xb7 ♖b8 16 ♗f3 **Wxd1** 17 ♖fxd1 ♘a4 with advantage to Black, Fernandez-Ragozin, Linares 1995) 14...♖xd8 15 ♗c1! ♗g4 16 ♗xb7 ♗xe2 17 ♖e1 ♖ab8 18 ♗g2

♗c4 19 e6! with advantage (Miles-Ninov, Amsterdam 1988).

14   ♕c2

More passive is **14 ♕c1** ♕c7 15 f4 ♘b6 16 e4 ♘c4 17 ♖f2 ♘xb2 18 ♕xb2 ♗c4 and Black stands better (S.Mohr-Ninov, Dortmund 1989), or **14 e4** ♘b6 15 ♕c2 ♘c4 16 ♖ad1 ♕c7 17 ♗c1 ♘xe5 18 f4 ♘c6 with advantage (Rivera-de la Villa, Linares 1991).

Now after 14...♕c7 15 e4 ♘b6 16 f4 ♗c4 17 ♖fe1 ♖ad8 18 ♗c1 ♗d3 19 ♕f2 ♘c4 20 g4 ♕a5 Black has the advantage, since White does not have any serious attacking chances, and his weaknesses are hard to defend (A.Petrosian-Kaidanov, Moscow 1987).

4.244232 (1 d4 ♘f6 2 c4 g6 3 g3 ♗g7 4 ♗g2 d5 5 ♘f3 0–0 6 0–0 dxc4 7 ♘a3 c3 8 bxc3 c5 9 ♘c4 ♘c6 10 ♘fe5 ♘d5 11 ♗b2)

---

11   ...   ♗e6
12   ♘xc6

After **12 e3** ♕c7 13 ♘xc6 bxc6 14 ♕c1 ♖ab8 15 ♗a3 cxd4 16 cxd4 ♘b4 17 ♘d2 ♘xa2! 18 ♕c5 ♖fc8 19 ♘e4 ♗f8 Black has the advantage (Smyslov-Gulko, Tilburg 1992), while if **12 ♖c1** he can play 12...♖c8 13 ♕a4 a6 14

♕a3 ♘xe5 15 ♘xe5 ♗xe5 16 dxe5 ♘b6 with an excellent game (Karlsson-Hellers, Haninge 1990).

12   ...   bxc6
13   ♘e5

In general, as all the examples show, White should not allow ...♗xe5, and therefore he does better to avoid this knight move. After **13 ♕c2** ♕c7 14 e3 cxd4 15 cxd4 c5 16 dxc5 ♕xc5 17 ♗xg7 ♔xg7 the game is equal (Andersson-Balashov, Buenos Aires 1980), while **13 ♕a4** can be met by 13...♖b8 14 ♖ac1 cxd4 (14...♕c7!?) 15 cxd4 ♖b4 16 ♕c2 (Orso-Csom, Hungary 1977) and here 16...c5! was correct.

13   ...   ♗xe5!

The correct decision – with the bishop blockaded at b2 Black can always give up his dark-square bishop. Weaker is **13...♕c7?** 14 ♘d3 ♖ab8 15 e4 ♘f6 16 ♗c1! ♕a5 17 ♗f4 when White stands better (Simic-Honfi, Baden 1987).

Now after 14 dxe5:

(a) 14...♕b8? 15 ♕c1 ♘b6 16 c4 (16 ♗xc6 ♘c4 17 ♗xa8 ♕xa8 with some compensation) 16...♘a4 (16...♘xc4 17 ♗c3 ♕c7 18 f4 ♘b6 19 e4 with compensation for the pawn) 17 ♖b1 ♘xb2 (17...♕c7 18 f4 ♘xb2 19 ♕xb2 ♗xc4

20 ♖bc1 with some advantage to White) 18 ♗xc6! and White has the advantage, P.Nikolic-Kozul, Ljubljana 1989);

(b) 14...♕c7! 15 e4 ♘b6 16 f4 ♗c4 17 ♖f2 ♖ad8 18 ♕g4 ♘a4 19 ♗f1 ♗d3! 20 ♗xd3 ♖xd3 Black occupies the important file and stands better (Modr-A.Mikhalchishin, Dortmund 1990).

4.2443 (1 d4 ♘f6 2 c4 g6 3 g3 ♗g7 4 ♗g2 d5 5 ♘f3 0–0 6 0–0 dxc4 7 ♘a3 c3 8 bxc3 c5)

---

9 ♘e5 ♘c6!

Thanks to this active resource Black exchanges the central e5 knight and intensifies the pressure on d4. After this move was found, the variation began to develop intensively in the late 1970s.

The quieter 9...♘d5 is also possible:

(a) 10 ♗b2 ♘c6 11 e4 (11 ♘ac4 transposes into variation 4.24423) 11...♘b6 12 f4 ♘xe5 13 fxe5 ♗d7 14 ♖b1 ♖c8 15 ♗a1 ♗a4 16 ♕e2 ♕d7 17 h4 ♖c7 18 ♔h2 e6 with approximate equality (P.Nikolic-Damljanovic, Belgrade 1989);

(b) 10 ♗d2 ♘c6 11 ♘ac4 (or 11 ♘xc6 bxc6 12 ♖c1 cxd4 13 cxd4 ♗xd4 14 ♗h6 ♗g7 with an equal game, Csom-Gaprindashvili, Olot 1973) 11... cxd4 12 cxd4 ♘xd4 13 ♗a5 ♘b6! 14 ♖b1 ♗xe5 (14...♘c6!? is interesting) 15 ♘xe5 ♕d6 16 ♗c3 ♕xe5 17 ♗xd4 ♕h5 with complications (A.Petrosian-S.Ivanov, USSR 1990);

(c) 10 ♕b3! ♘xc3! (weaker is 10... ♘b6 11 ♖d1 ♗e6 12 d5 ♗d7 13 ♘xd7 ♘8xd7 14 ♖b1 with advantage, Kozlov-Baikov, Roslavl 1989) 11 ♕xc3 cxd4 12 ♕c5 ♘a6 13 ♕b5 ♘c7 14 ♕a5 b6 15 ♘c6 bxa5 16 ♘xd8 ♖xd8 17 ♗xa8 ♘xa8 18 ♖b1 ♗a6 19 ♖e1 ♘b6 with an active game for Black (Kalinichev).

9...♘fd7 is somewhat more passive: 10 ♘xd7 (the natural 10 ♗f4!? is worth trying) 10...♘xd7 11 ♘c4 (11 ♖b1 cxd4 12 cxd4 ♘b6 with an equal game, Norwood-Conquest, Calcutta 1996) 11...♘b6 12 ♘xb6 axb6 13 ♗e3 ♕c7 14 ♕b3 ♖a6 and Black is excellently placed (Martinovsky-Benko, New York 1991).

The modern 9...♘bd7 10 ♖b1 ♘xe5 11 dxe5 ♘g4 12 ♕xd8 (12 f4 ♕a5!) 12...♖xd8 13 f4 ♖b8 (Nadanian-Hachian, Yerevan 1995) would have led to an advantage for White after 14 h3 ♘h6 15 g4 ♗e6 16 c4.

10 ♘xc6

The critical 10 ♘ac4 ♘d5 leads to variation 4.24423, while 10 ♕a4!? ♘d5! 11 ♘xc6 bxc6 transposes into the main line.

10 ... bxc6
11 ♕a4

11 ♕d3?! is incorrect: 11...♘d5 12 ♖d1 ♕a5 13 ♗b2 ♖b8 14 ♕c2 ♖xb2! 15 ♕xb2 ♘xc3 16 ♖d3 cxd4 17 ♗xc6 ♗a6 with the initiative for Black (Granda-Kasparov, Dubai 1986).

After 11 ♗xc6 ♗h3 12 ♗xa8 (if 12 ♖e1 ♖c8 13 ♗f3 ♘d5 14 ♕b3, then 14...♘xc3! 15 ♗b7 ♖b8 16 ♗f4 ♕xd4! 17 ♗xb8 ♖xb8 and Black seizes the initiative, Alburt-Olafsson, New York 1990, or 12 ♗g2 ♗xg2 13 ♔xg2 ♘d5 14 ♗b2 ♖b8 15 ♖b1, Trichkov-Pribyl, Czechoslovakia 1996, and here 15... cxd4 16 cxd4 ♕a5! would have given Black the advantage) 12...♕xa8 13 f3 ♗xf1 14 ♔xf1 ♘d5 15 ♕d2 ♘xc3! 16 ♘c2 cxd4 Black has a great advantage (Rotstein-Cvitan, Bad Worishöfen 1996).

Another idea is the rather passive 11 ♘c2 ♘d5 12 ♗d2 ♗a6 13 ♖c1 ♖b8 14 ♖e1 ♖b2 15 e4 ♘b6 16 e5 ♗b5, again with advantage to Black (Beyer-Himmel, Germany 1992).

11 ...   ♘d5

12 ♕xc6

After 12 ♗b2 ♖b8 13 ♖ab1 ♖xb2!? 14 ♖xb2 ♘xc3 15 ♕xa7 cxd4 16 ♗xc6 ♗g4 17 ♖e1 e5 18 ♘b1 e4 (Kapelan-Cvitan, Vrsac 1989) Black gained counterplay, although the quieter 13...♕b6!? 14 ♗a1 ♕a6! is also good, with strong play on the light squares.

12 ...   ♗e6!

13 ♕xc5

13...♘xc3! 14 e3 ♘e2+ 15 ♔h1 ♘xd4! 16 ♖b1 ♖c8 17 ♕xa7 ♘c6 18 ♕a4 ♗xa2! with a roughly equal game (Notaros-Paunovic, Cetinje 1993).

4.2444 (1 d4 ♘f6 2 c4 g6 3 g3 ♗g7 4 ♗g2 d5 5 ♘f3 0-0 6 0-0 dxc4 7 ♘a3 c3 8 bxc3 c5)

---

9 e3!?

This entire variation for White was under a cloud until the mid-1980s, when Hungarian players, and in particular GM Adorjan, revived it by devising this seemingly unpretentious continuation. The idea of it – strengthening the centre to the maximum – is clear, and it is not easy for Black to combat such a

structure. He has several plans – counterplay with ...e7-e5 or play aimed at seizing the light squares.

9 ...   ♘c6

9...♘bd7? is unnatural: 10 ♘c4 ♘d5 11 ♗b2 ♕c7 12 ♕e2 ♘5b6 13 ♖ac1 ♘xc4 14 ♕xc4 b5?! 15 ♕xb5 ♖b8 16 ♕e2 ♕a5 17 ♗a1 and Black has no compensation for the pawn (Weischede-Erker, Dortmund 1992), but **9...♘d5!?** is interesting: 10 ♗b2 ♕a5 11 ♕e2 ♘b6 12 ♖ac1 ♗g4 13 h3 ♗xf3 14 ♗xf3 ♘c6 15 ♕b5 ♕xb5 16 ♘xb5 ♘c4 17 ♖c2 ♖ac8 with an excellent game for Black (A.Petrosian-Tukmakov, Yerevan 1996). This idea of Tukmakov, a great expert on the Grünfeld, should be given a more serious practical testing.

Now White's main continuations are **10 ♗b2** (4.24441) and **10 ♕e2** (4.24442).

After 10 ♘c4 ♗e6 11 ♘ce5 ♘xe5 12 ♘xe5 ♗d5 13 ♖b1 ♗xg2 14 ♔xg2 (Gyimesi-Derevyagin, Stokerai 1996) 14...♕c7 or 14...b6 would have given Black a good game, since White's centre does not especially restrict the black pieces.

If **10 ♖b1**:

(a) 10...♖b8 11 c4?! (a very risky plan) 11...♗f5 12 ♖b5 ♘e4! 13 ♗b2

♘b4 14 ♕b3 a6 15 ♖xb4 cxb4 16 ♕xb4 b5 and White has no compensation for the exchange (Kalinichev-Zezulkin, Podolsk 1990);

(b) 10...♘d5 (even stronger) 11 ♗d2 ♗f5! 12 ♖b2 (12 ♖xb7 ♕a5! 13 ♘c4 ♕a6) 12...♗e4 13 ♕a4 ♘b6 14 ♕d1 ♕d5 with a clear advantage (Kurajica-P.Nikolic, Yugoslavia 1988).

> **4.24441 (1 d4 ♘f6 2 c4 g6 3 g3 ♗g7 4 ♗g2 d5 5 ♘f3 0–0 6 0–0 dxc4 7 ♘a3 c3 8 bxc3 c5 9 e3!? ♘c6)**

10 ♗b2

Now Black has several possibilities: **10...e5!?** (4.244411), **10...♗f5** (4.244412) and **10...♕c7** (4.244413).

There is also **10...♕a5** 11 ♘d2 (11 ♕e2 transposes into section 4.24442) 11...♗g4 (less good is 11...cxd4 12 cxd4 ♕b4 13 ♘ac4 ♗e6 14 ♕b3 ♕xb3 15 axb3 with the better ending for White, Panno-Chiburdanidze, Aruba 1992) 12 f3 ♗e6 13 ♘b3 ♕b6 14 dxc5 ♕c7 and Black has insufficient compensation for the pawn (Zysk-Luecke, Germany 1992).

> **4.244411 (1 d4 ♘f6 2 c4 g6 3 g3 ♗g7 4 ♗g2 d5 5 ♘f3 0–0 6 0–0 dxc4 7 ♘a3 c3 8 bxc3 c5 9 e3!? ♘c6 10 ♗b2)**

10 ... e5!?

A sharp continuation with the idea of breaking up White's centre by a temporary pawn sacrifice. The same idea played a little later does not work: **10...a6** 11 ♕e2 e5 12 ♘xe5 ♘xe5 13 dxe5 ♘g4 14 f4 f6 15 h3 ♘h6 16 exf6 ♕xf6 17 g4 and White has a clear advantage (Kirov-de Boer, Dieren 1990).

11 ♘c4

The pawn sacrifice should not be accepted because of **11 ♘xe5 ♘xe5** 12 dxe5 ♘g4 13 c4 ♘xe5 14 ♕b3 ♕d2! 15 ♗xe5 ♗xe5 16 ♖ad1 ♕b4 17 ♖d5 ♗f6 18 ♖b1 ♗e6 19 ♖dd1 (Nogueiras-Howell, Matanzas 1993), and here 19...♕a5 would have led to an unclear game.

11 ... exd4

11...♗g4 is very interesting: 12 ♕b3 (12 ♘cxe5 ♘xe5 13 dxe5 ♘d7 leads to equality) 12...♗e6 13 ♕a4 ♕d7 (after 13...exd4 14 cxd4 cxd4 15 ♘xd4 ♘d5 16 ♘xc6 bxc6 17 ♖ad1 White has the advantage) 14 dxc5 (Kir.Georgiev-Stohl, Dortmund 1991), and now 14...b5 15 cxb6 axb6 16 ♕b5 ♘a5 17 ♕xd7 ♘xd7 18 ♘xa5 ♖xa5 would have given Black excellent play for the pawn.

Closing the centre by **11...e4** 12 ♘fe5 ♘xe5 13 ♘xe5 h5, 13...b6 or 13...♗e6 leads to a position that has yet to be tested in practice.

12 cxd4 cxd4

Also possible is **12...♗e6** 13 ♕e2 cxd4 14 ♘xd4 ♘xd4 15 ♗xd4 ♖e8 16 ♖ad1 ♕e7 17 ♘a5 ♕a3! with reasonable counterplay for Black (Froehlich-Luke, Germany 1995).

Now after 13 ♘xd4 ♘xd4 14 ♗xd4 ♗e6 the position is equal, as with the elimination of the pawn centre White's pieces do not stand much better than Black's.

4.244412 (1 d4 ♘f6 2 c4 g6 3 g3 ♗g7 4 ♗g2 d5 5 ♘f3 0–0 6 0–0 dxc4 7 ♘a3 c3 8 bxc3 c5 9 e3!? ♘c6 10 ♗b2)

---

    10 ...   **♗f5**
    11 ♕e2

If White begins fighting for the light squares with **11 ♘d2**, then:

(a) 11...♗g4 (also not bad is 11...♖c8!? followed by 12...b6, or 11...♕c8 followed by 12...♖d8 or 12...♘h3) 12 f3 ♗e6 13 ♘b3 cxd4 14 cxd4 ♕b6 15 ♖f2 ♖fd8 16 ♘c5 ♗d5 17 e4? ♗xa2! 18 ♘a4 ♕b3 19 ♕xb3 ♗xb3 20 ♘c5 ♘a5 and Black is a pawn up (Skomorokhin-Smith, Voronezh 1991);

(b) there is also the logical plan of 11...cxd4 12 cxd4 ♕d7 13 ♘b3 ♗h3 14 ♘c5 ♕c8 15 ♖c1 ♗xg2 16 ♔xg2 b6 17 d5!? bxc5 18 ♖xc5 ♕f5! with equality (J.Horvath-Kozul, Velden 1994).

    11 ...   **♗e4**
11...♕a5 12 ♖fd1 ♗e4 transposes into variation 4.2444211.

11...e5!? is a slightly different attempt to liquidate White's centre:

(a) 12 ♖fd1 e4! 13 ♘e5 (after 13 ♘d2 ♗g4 14 f3 exf3 15 ♘xf3 ♖e8 White's centre is blockaded) 13...♘xe5 14 dxe5 ♘d7 15 g4!? ♗e6 16 ♗xe4 ♕h4 17 f4 ♗xg4 18 ♗f3 ♗xf3 19 ♕xf3 ♘b6 20 c4 f6!, and by attacking the centre Black obtains good play (Konopka-Lagunov, Germany 1993);

(b) 12 ♘c4 e4 (if 12...exd4 13 cxd4 cxd4 14 ♘xd4 ♘xd4 15 ♗xd4 ♕e7 16 ♕b2 ♗e4 17 ♗xe4 ♕xe4 18 ♘d6 with advantage, Bandza-Ivanov, Katowice 1993) 13 ♘fe5 ♘xe5 14 ♘xe5 h5 15 h3 ♕c8 16 ♔h2 ♘d7 17 ♘c4 ♕c7 18 ♔g1 ♖fe8 19 ♖fc1 ♘b6 with an unclear position (Dumitrache-I.Horvath, Solin 1995), whereas 15 c4! would have given White a slight advantage, since he still stands better in the centre, and the e4 pawn is rather weak.

    12 ♖fd1
The most natural. Other moves are less logical:

12 ♖fc1 ♕a5 13 ♘c4 ♕a6 14 ♗f1 ♗d5 15 ♘fd2 ♘e4 16 ♘xe4 ♗xe4 17 ♘d2 ♕xe2 18 ♗xe2 ♗f5 19 ♗f3 ♖ac8 20 ♗a3 b6 with equality (Bischoff-Grunberg, Hannover 1991).

12 ♘c4 ♗d5 13 ♖fd1 ♕c7 14 ♘cd2 cxd4 15 cxd4 ♕b6! 16 ♗a3 ♘e4 17 ♕d3 ♘xd2 18 ♖xd2 ♕a5 19 ♖b1 ♖fb8 and again Black has no particular problems (Stempin-W.Schmidt, Poland 1990).

    12 ...   **cxd4**
If **12...♕a5** there can follow 13 c4 or 13 ♗f1 followed by 14 ♘d2.

Now after 13 exd4! ♕a5 14 c4 e6 15 ♘b5 a6 (P.Nikolic-W.Schmidt, Novi Sad 1990, went 15...♖fd8? 16 a4 ♗xf3 17 ♗xf3 ♖d7 18 d5 exd5 19 cxd5 ♘e7 20 d6 ♘f5 21 ♖ab1! and White gained a great advantage) 16 ♘d6 ♗xf3 17 ♗xf3 White has a slight advantage, since the hanging pawns seriously restrict Black's possibilities (Nikolic).

> **4.244413 (1 d4 ♘f6 2 c4 g6 3 g3 ♗g7 4 ♗g2 d5 5 ♘f3 0–0 6 0–0 dxc4 7 ♘a3 c3 8 bxc3 c5 9 e3!? ♘c6 10 ♗b2)**

**10	...	♕c7**
**11	♕e2**

11 c4 is premature: 11...♖d8 12 ♕e2 ♗f5 13 ♖fd1 ♕c8 14 ♘b5 cxd4 15 exd4 a6 16 ♘c3 b6 17 d5 ♘a5 18 ♘d2 ♖a7 19 ♖ac1 ♗h6! with the initiative for Black (Shipman-Henao, New York 1992).

White also achieves nothing with **11 ♘d2 ♖d8 12 ♕e2 e5 13 dxc5 ♘a5 14 c6 ♘xc6 15 ♘b5 ♕b6 16 a4 ♗g4 17 f3 ♗e6** (Sisniega-Henao, Bogota 1991).

**11	...	e5**
**12	♘b5**

After **12 ♖ac1?!** ♖e8 13 ♘b5 ♕b8 14 dxc5 ♘e4! 15 ♖fd1 ♗f8 Black has an excellent game (A.Petrosian-A.Mikhalchishin, Lviv 1997).

**12	...	♕b8**

After **12...♕a5** 13 ♘xe5 (A.Mikhalchishin-Schaefer, Bern 1996) Black could have gained some counterplay by 13...♘xe5 14 dxe5 ♘g4 15 f4 ♘xe3!

16 ♕xe3 ♕xb5, although whether it is serious is doubtful.

**13	dxc5!?**

In Adorjan's opinion **13 ♘xe5 ♘xe5 14 dxe5 ♕xe5 15 c4 ♕e7 16 ♘c3 ♗g4 17 f3 ♗e6 18 e4** with the idea of ♘d5 also gives an advantage.

Adorjan-Fogarasi (Hungary 1995) now continued 13...e4 14 ♘fd4 ♗g4 15 ♕c2 ♕e5 16 ♘d6! ♕xc5 17 ♘xe4 (also good is 17 ♘xb7 ♕d5 18 ♘xc6 ♕xc6 19 ♘a5 with a clear advantage, Adorjan) 17...♘xe4 18 ♕xe4 with advantage to White.

> **4.24442 (1 d4 ♘f6 2 c4 g6 3 g3 ♗g7 4 ♗g2 d5 5 ♘f3 0–0 6 0–0 dxc4 7 ♘a3 c3 8 bxc3 c5 9 e3!? ♘c6)**

**10	♕e2**

Black's main options are **10...♗f5** (4.244422) and **10...♕a5** (4.244422).

Less good is **10...♗g4?!** 11 h3 ♗e6 12 ♗b2 ♕c8 13 ♔h2 ♗d5 14 c4!? ♗e4 15 ♖fd1 ♖d8 16 d5 ♘b8 17 ♘b5 with advantage to White (Ginting-Miles, Adelaide 1990).

10...♘e4?! is a risky move at a time when Black has insufficient control of the centre: 11 ♗b2 cxd4 (after 11...♕a5

12 ♖fc1 ♗g4 13 ♕c2! White has the advantage, Antonov-Krivonogov, Moscow 1996) 12 ♘xd4! ♘c5 13 ♖fd1! (less good is 13 ♘xc6! bxc6 14 ♗xc6 ♖b8 with counterplay) 13...♕b6 14 ♖ab1 ♘a4 15 ♗a1 ♕c5 16 ♘c4 a6 17 ♖bc1 with advantage (Rashkovsky-Gislason, Reykjavik 1994), and it is not clear how Black can develop his queenside, although simpler is 17 ♗xc6 bxc6 18 ♖b4 and if 18...e5 19 ♘b3, winning the knight (Neat).

But **10...♗e6!?** is more interesting: 11 ♗b2 (11 ♘g5 ♗g4! 12 ♕b5 ♕b6! with a complicated game) 11...♗d5 12 ♖fd1 cxd4 13 exd4 e6 14 c4 ♗xf3 15 ♗xf3 ♖e8 16 ♘c2 ♕b6 17 ♘e3 ♖ad8 with a double-edged position (Vorisek-Aronian, Pardubice 1996).

4.244421 (1 d4 ♘f6 2 c4 g6 3 g3 ♗g7 4 ♗g2 d5 5 ♘f3 0–0 6 0–0 dxc4 7 ♘a3 c3 8 bxc3 c5 9 e3!? ♘c6 10 ♕e2)

---

10 ...   ♗f5

White's main options are **11 ♖d1 (4.2444211)** and **11 ♗b2 (4.2444212)**.

After **11 ♘c4 ♖c8** (stronger is 11...♘d5! 12 ♗b2 ♘b6! with equality) 12 ♗a3 ♘e4 13 ♖fc1 cxd4 (the very interesting 13...b5!? has yet to be tried) 14 cxd4 ♗e6 15 ♘fe5 (if 15 ♖ab1 ♗d5) 15...♘xe5 16 ♘xe5 ♖xc1+ (16...♗d5 17 ♕b5 is unpleasant for Black) 17 ♖xc1 ♘d6 the game is equal (Steingrimsson-Schmidt, Biel 1990).

4.2444211 (1 d4 ♘f6 2 c4 g6 3 g3 ♗g7 4 ♗g2 d5 5 ♘f3 0–0 6 0–0 dxc4 7 ♘a3 c3 8 bxc3 c5 9 e3!? ♘c6 10 ♕e2 ♗f5)

---

11 ♖d1   ♗e4!

Possible is **11...♖c8** 12 ♗b2 cxd4 13 cxd4 ♕a5 14 h3 ♗e4 15 ♕b5 a6 16 ♕xa5 ♘xa5 17 ♘e5 b5 with equality (Pers-Douven, Groningen 1991).

12 ♗b2

Less good is **12 ♘c4** cxd4 (or 12...♘a5! 13 ♘cd2 ♗c2 14 ♖f1 ♘d5 with advantage to Black, Abramovic-J.Horvath, Tivat 1995) 13 cxd4 ♖c8 14 ♗a3 ♘d5 15 ♖ac1 ♘a5! 16 ♗b2 ♘b4 17 ♘xa5 ♕xa5 18 a3 ♖xc1 19 ♖xc1 ♘d3 with advantage to Black (Panchenko-Cvitan, Bern 1994).

12 ...   ♕b6!

After **12...cxd4** 13 exd4 e6 (or 13...♕a5 14 c4 e6 15 ♘b5 ♖fd8 16 a4 ♗xf3 17 ♗xf3 ♖d7 18 d5 exd5 19 cxd5 ♘e7 20 d6 ♘f5 21 ♖ab1!) 14 c4 ♖e8 15 ♘e5 ♗xg2 16 ♔xg2 ♖c8 17 f4 White has a spatial advantage (Drasko-Popovic, Novi Sad 1995).

13 ♘c4

Interesting is **13 ♖d2!?** ♖fd8 14 ♖ad1 cxd4 15 exd4 ♗h6 16 ♘c4 ♕a6 17 ♘e3 ♕xe2 18 ♖xe2 ♖ac8 with an equal ending (P.Nikolic-Kozul, Yerevan 1996).

13 ...   ♕a6
14 ♗f1   ♖fd8

After **14...cxd4** 15 exd4 ♖ac8 16 ♘fd2 ♗f5 17 ♕e1 ♕a4 the position is equal (Korotylev-Zviagintsev, Russia 1994).

15 ♘fd2　♗c2
16 ♖dc1　♗a4
17 ♘b3　♘d7!

After 17...b6 18 dxc5 ♗b5 19 ♘d4! bxc5? (19...♗xc4 20 ♕xc4 ♕xc4 21 ♗xc4 ♘e5 gives Black counterplay) 20 ♘xb5 ♕xb5 21 ♕c2 White has the better game (Georgiev-Kozul, Yerevan 1996) – *Game 16.*

Now Black sacrifices a pawn, but sooner or later White's extra pawn falls, and the problem of his other weak c-pawn remains. 18 dxc5 ♘ce5 19 ♘xe5 ♕xe2 20 ♗xe2 ♘xe5 21 ♘d4 e6 22 ♖ab1 ♗f8 and Black equalised (Hübner-Topalov, Dortmund 1997).

> **4.2444212 (1 d4 ♘f6 2 c4 g6 3 g3 ♗g7 4 ♗g2 d5 5 ♘f3 0–0 6 0–0 dxc4 7 ♘a3 c3 8 bxc3 c5 9 e3!? ♘c6 10 ♕e2 ♗f5)**

11 ♗b2　♕a5

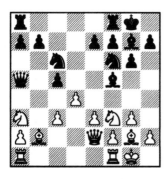

11...♗e4 12 ♖fd1 transposes into the previous section.

12 ♖fc1

After 12 c4!? ♘e4 (12...♗e4!? 13 d5 ♘b4 should be satisfactory for Black) 13 ♖fc1 ♖ad8?! (a dubious idea;

preferable is 13...♘d6! with counterplay) 14 d5 ♗xb2 15 ♕xb2 ♘b4 16 ♘e1! ♘d6 17 f3 ♗c8 18 e4 e6?! (better 18...f6! with the idea of 19...e5) 19 ♗f1 ♖fe8 20 ♘ac2 ♘xc2 21 ♖xc2 White's powerful centre gives him the advantage (Adianto-Wolff, San Francisco 1991). In general 12 c4 requires serious testing, since it looks very logical.

After 12 ♘d2!? (a simple attempt to eliminate the weakness of the e4 square) 12...cxd4 13 cxd4 ♕b4 (preferable is 13...♘b4 14 e4 ♗g4 15 f3 ♗d7 and ...♖fc8) 14 ♘b3 ♖fd8 (very routine; 14...♗e4! is stronger and if 15 f3 ♗d5) 15 e4 ♗g4 16 f3 ♗d7 17 ♖fd1 ♖ac8 (serious measures such as 17...♘e8!? are necessary) 18 ♘c2! ♕b6 19 ♘e3 ♘b4 20 ♘c5 White has the advantage (Rashkovsky-de Boer, Groningen 1991). Again a rather puzzling and logical variation – it is strange that this good alternative has been ignored.

12 ...　♗e4!

The main continuation – it is logical to occupy the light squares. Other moves are clearly weaker:

12...♖ac8 13 d5! ♘b8 (after 13...♘xd5 14 e4 ♘xc3 15 ♗xc3 ♗xc3 16 ♘c4 White has the advantage) 14 ♘d2 ♘a6 15 e4 ♗g4 16 ♕f1 ♕a4 17 h3 ♗d7 18 e5 ♘h5 19 ♕e2 with advantage (Portisch-Adorjan, Hungary 1988).

12...♖fd8 13 ♘d2 ♗g4 14 f3 ♗e6 15 ♘b3 ♗xb3 16 axb3 ♕b6 17 ♕c2 cxd4 18 ♘c4 ♕b5 19 cxd4 ♖ac8 20 f4 and thanks to his strong centre White is better (Atalik-Fogarasi, Budapest 1992).

13 ♘c4　♕a6!

Bad is 13...♕a4? 14 ♘cd2 ♘a5 15 c4 ♖ac8 16 d5 a6 17 ♗h3! ♖cd8 (Adorjan-Kindermann, Altensteig 1989), and here 18 ♘g5! ♗f5 19 ♗xf5 gxf5 20

♗xf6! exf6 21 ♘h3 f4 22 ♘xf4 f5 23 ♖ab1 ♕xa2 24 ♕d3 would have given White the advantage.

14 ♗f1 ♗d5!

Other moves are somewhat weaker:

14...♖ac8 15 ♘fd2 b5 16 ♘e5 c4 17 ♘xe4 ♘xe4 18 ♘xc6 ♕xc6 19 ♗g2 f5 20 a4 and White has a clear advantage (Adorjan-Groszpeter, Hungary 1989).

14...♖fd8 15 ♕d1! ♗d5 16 ♘cd2 ♕b6 17 ♕c2 cxd4 (if 17...e5 18 e4 ♗xe4 19 ♘xe4 ♘xe4 20 ♕xe4 ♕xb2 21 dxe5 ♖e8 22 ♖ab1 ♕a3 23 ♗c4 with the better game, but 17...♖ac8 18 c4 ♗xf3 19 ♘xf3 e6, unclear, requires practical testing) 18 cxd4 ♖ac8 19 ♗c3 e5 20 ♖ab1 ♕c7 21 dxe5 ♘d7 22 e6 and White has the advantage (P.Nikolic-Popovic, Yugoslavia 1990) – *Game 17*.

14...b5 15 ♘cd2 c4 16 ♘xe4 (16 a4 is also good) 16...♘xe4 17 ♗g2 (Ruban-Douven, Sochi 1990), and here Black should have sacrificed a pawn by 17...♖ac8! 18 ♘e5 ♘xe5 19 ♗xe4 ♘d3! in search of equality.

15 ♘fd2 ♖fd8!

Here it is also good to exchange a pair of knights: 15...♘e4! 16 ♘xe4 ♗xe4 17 ♘d2 ♕xe2 18 ♗xe2 ♗f5 19 ♗f3 ♖ac8, again with equality (Bischoff-Grunberg, Hannover 1991).

Now after 16 a4 b6 17 ♘a3 ♕xe2 18 ♗xe2 ♘a5 19 f3 ♗c6 20 ♘ac4 ♗h6 the game is equal (Gulko-Kudrin, Jacksonville 1990).

> **4.244422 (1 d4 ♘f6 2 c4 g6 3 g3 ♗g7 4 ♗g2 d5 5 ♘f3 0–0 6 0–0 dxc4 7 ♘a3 c3 8 bxc3 c5 9 e3!? ♘c6 10 ♕e2)**

10 ... ♕a5
11 ♗b2 ♘d5

It should straight away be mentioned that Black's 10th and 11th moves can be made in either order. Of the alternatives the following are weaker:

11...♘e4 12 ♖fc1 ♖d8 13 ♘e1 ♘d6 14 ♘d3 ♕a6 15 ♕d1 cxd4 16 cxd4 ♗f5 17 ♘c5 with advantage (Adorjan-Dzevlan, Biel 1990).

11...cxd4 12 cxd4 ♕h5 13 ♖ac1 ♗g4 14 e4 (14 ♖c5 is interesting) 14...♘d7 15 ♖fd1 e5 16 d5 ♘d4 17 ♗xd4 exd4 18 h3! ♗xh3 19 ♗xh3 ♕xh3 20 ♘g5 ♕h6 21 f4! again with advantage (Adianto-Adamek, Liechtenstein 1992).

12 ♖fc1

This rook, since sometimes the bishop needs the f1 square to control c4.

Weaker is **12 ♖ac1 ♗g4** (not 12...b6? 13 ♘d2 e6 14 ♘b3 ♕a6 15 c4 ♘db4 16

♘b5 ♕a4 17 a3! and Black resigned!, Gelfand-Ivanchuk, Linares 1991) 13 h3 ♗xf3 14 ♗xf3 ♘b6 15 ♕b5 ♕xb5 16 ♘xb5 ♘c4 17 ♖c2 ♖ac8 18 dxc5? (better 18 ♗e2, playing for equality) 18...♘6e5 19 ♗e2 ♖xc5 with advantage (Shabalov-Krasenkov, Gausdal 1992).

12 ♘c4 is also unpromising: 12...♕a6 13 ♖fe1 ♗e6 14 ♘cd2 ♕xe2 15 ♖xe2 ♘b6 16 ♘b3 cxd4 17 cxd4 ♗d5 18 ♘c5 ♖ab8 19 e4 ♗c4 20 ♖d2 e6 with a reasonable ending for Black (D'Amore-Manca, Montecatini 1997).

12 ... ♗g4

Black should prevent the manoeuvre of the knight from f3 to b3, and this is possible only by giving up his important bishop. After **12...♘b6** 13 ♘d2 ♘a4 14 ♘b3:

(a) 14...♕d8 15 ♘xc5 (or 15 ♖ab1 e5 16 d5 ♘e7 17 ♖d1 ♗f5 18 ♖bc1 ♘xb2 19 ♕xb2 e4 20 ♕e2 ♖c8 21 g4!, Gerber-Pelletier, Biel 1996) 15...♘xc5 16 dxc5 ♕a5 17 ♘b5 ♗g4?! (17...♗d7 is stronger, but here too White is better after 18 c4) 18 ♕xg4 ♕xb5 19 ♖ab1 ♕xc5 20 ♕a4 with advantage (P.Nikolic-Damljanovic, Belgrade 1991);

(b) 14...♕b6! 15 ♖ab1 cxd4 16 cxd4 ♗f5 17 e4 ♘xb2 18 exf5 ♘xd4 19 ♘xd4 ♕xd4 (Konopka-Lagunov, Germany 1992), and after 20 ♖c2 ♕a4 21 ♖cxb2 ♕xa3 22 ♖xb7 ♖ae8 23 h4 White has the initiative.

13 h3

After 13 ♘c4 ♕a6 14 ♗f1 ♘b6 15 ♘cd2 ♕xe2 16 ♗xe2 ♘a4 17 ♗a3 ♘xc3!? (better is 17...a6 18 ♘e4 cxd4 19 cxd4 ♖fc8 followed by ...b5) 18 ♖xc3 cxd4 19 ♘xd4 ♗xe2 20 ♘xe2 ♖fd8 21 ♘b3 ♗xc3 22 ♘xc3 ♖ac8 23 e4, and as a result of a fierce tactical skirmish White has the better position (Granda-Schulman, Pamplona 1996).

13 ... ♗xf3
14 ♗xf3 ♘b6

White has the two bishops, and Black must play very energetically on the queenside to avoid giving him a quiet life.

Weaker is **14...♖fd8** 15 ♘c4 ♕a4 (if 15...♕a6 16 a4 with advantage) 16 ♘d2! ♖ac8 17 ♘e4! b6 18 c4 ♘xe3?! 19 ♕xe3 ♘xd4 20 ♔g2! and Black faces big problems (Akopian-Kasparov, Ljubljana 1995), or **14...e6** 15 ♘c4 ♕a6 16 ♘d6 ♘xd4 17 cxd4 ♕xd6 18 ♖xc5 and White's two bishops give him the advantage.

15 ♘c4

This is the critical position of the entire variation. Other possibilities:

15 ♖ab1 ♖ac8 16 ♕d1 ♖fd8 17 ♕b3 e5 18 ♘c2 c4 19 ♕a3 ♘a4 with the initiative for Black on the wing (Spasov-Krasenkov, Ostende 1990).

15 ♕b5 ♕xb5 16 ♘xb5 ♘c4 17 ♖ab1 ♖fc8 with an excellent ending.

15 ... ♕a6

The natural continuation, but **15...♘xc4** 16 ♕xc4 ♖ac8 17 ♕b3 is interesting, when Black has a choice:

(a) 17...♖c7 18 a4 (after 18 ♖ab1 ♖fc8 19 ♕a3 b6! 20 dxc5 ♕xc5 21 ♕xc5 bxc5 the position is equal,

P.Nikolic-Anand, Paris 1995) 18...b6 19 ♗xc6 ♖xc6 20 ♕b5! with a slight advantage for White (Bandza-Belov, Karvina 1992);

(b) 17...♕a6 18 ♗a3 (if 18 a4, then the manoeuvre 18...♘a5 19 ♕b5 ♕xb5 20 axb5 ♘c4 21 ♖c2 ♘d6! secures equality, Marin-Konguveel, Linares 1996) 18...b6 19 ♗g2 ♘a5 20 ♕a4 ♕c4 21 ♕d1 ♕e6 22 ♕f1 ♖fd8 and Black is excellently placed (Asanov-Svidler, St Petersburg 1994).

15...♕b5 has also been played: 16 ♘xb6 ♕xe2 17 ♗xe2 axb6 18 a4 ♘a5 19 ♖cb1 ♘b3 20 ♖a3 ♘d2 21 ♖d1 ♘e4 22 ♖da1! ♖fc8 23 ♖b3 ♖c6 (Titenko-Belov, Moscow 1993), and here Belov suggests that 24 ♗c1 intending 25 f3 would have left White with a slight advantage.

Salov-Khalifman (m 1994) now continued 16 ♘d2! ♕xe2 17 ♗xe2, and here 17...♖fc8! 18 ♗a3 cxd4 19 cxd4 e5! was correct, trying to eliminate White's centre, after which an equal position arises.

Game 13
Quinteros-Portisch
Manila 1974

1 d4 ♘f6 2 c4 g6 3 ♘f3 ♗g7 4 g3 0-0 5 ♗g2 d5 6 0-0 ♘c6!? 7 ♘e5

An interesting move order, the point being that Black does not want to play ...dxc4, and he avoids the lines with cxd5 ♘xd5. However, White's active knight move leads to sharp positions, which bear a structural resemblance to one of the variations of the Catalan. At the same time 7 ♘c3 is weak in view of 7...dxc4! 8 d5 ♘b4 9 e4 e6 10 ♗g5 h6 11 ♗e3 ♘d3 12 dxe6 ♗xe6 13 h3 ♕d7 14 ♕d2 ♗xh3 15 ♗xh6 ♖ae8 and Black

has the advantage (Ivanchuk-J.Polgar, Linares 1997).

7...dxc4! 8 ♘xc6 bxc6 9 ♗xc6 ♖b8

This is rather more accurate than 9...♗h3 10 ♖e1 ♖b8 11 ♘a3! ♘d5 12 ♘xc4 ♘b4 13 ♗e4 ♗e6 14 a3 ♗xc4 15 axb4 ♕xd4, when Black equalised (Sveshnikov-A.Mikhalchishin, 49th USSR Ch 1981). In its pawn structure and method of play, this position resembles the English Opening A39 with the sacrifice of a pawn.

10 ♘c3 ♗h3

An active plan, although the positional solution is also good: 10...♗b7!? 11 ♗f3 ♗xf3 12 exf3 ♘d5 13 ♕e2 ♘b4 14 ♕xc4 ♘c2 15 ♖b1 ♖b4 and Black has an excellent game (Hübner-J.Polgar, Dortmund 1996).

11 ♖e1?!

After 11 ♗g2 ♗xg2 12 ♔xg2 ♘d5 White would have maintained equality (but who on the 11th move wants to 'run' for a draw?), whereas now Black acquires play thanks to dynamic factors. This particularly begins to be felt after the next two moves, when White is forced to block in his own bishop at c1.

11...♘g4! 12 e3

After 12 d5 ♕c8! 13 ♗f4 g5! 14 ♗xg5 ♕f5 15 ♗f4 ♖xb2 16 ♖c1 ♗e5

17 f3 ♗xf4! 18 gxf4 ♘e3 it is time for White to resign.

12...e5! 13 ♗f3?!

White should have got rid of the unpleasant bishop by 13 ♗g2 ♗xg2 14 ♔xg2 exd4 15 exd4 ♘h6 16 ♕a4! ♕xd4 17 ♗e3 ♕f6 18 ♖ad1 ♘f5 19 ♗xa7 ♖xb2 20 ♘d5, with chances of equalising.

13...exd4 14 exd4 ♘xf2!

The start of the decisive attack.

15 ♔xf2 ♗xd4+ 16 ♖e3

16 ♗e3 ♖xb2+ 17 ♔g1 ♗xc3 is also bad.

16...♖e8 17 ♘d5 ♗c5 18 b4 cxb3 19 ♗a3!? ♗xe3+

Of course, Black does not fall into the trap 19...♗xa3 20 ♖xe8+ ♕xe8 21 ♘f6+.

20 ♘xe3 b2 21 ♖b1 ♕g5 22 ♕e2 ♕a5!

With this queen manoeuvre Black creates irresistible threats.

23 ♗xb2 ♕xa2 24 ♕c2 ♖xe3!

Drawing the king out into the open and creating a mating attack.

25 ♔xe3 ♗f5 26 ♗e4 ♕b3+!

Not 26...♖e8 27 ♕c3!

27 ♕xb3 ♖xb3+ 28 ♔f4 ♗xe4

28...♖b4 29 ♗f6 ♖xe4+ 30 ♔f3 ♖e3+! would also have won.

29 ♔xe4 a5 30 h4 h5 31 ♔f4

After 31 ♔d4 a4 32 ♔c4 ♖b8 there is no defence against ...a4-a3.

31...a4 32 ♖c1 ♖xb2 33 ♖xc7 a3 34 ♖a7 a2 35 g4

The rook ending is completely hopeless.

35...♖b4+ 36 ♔g5 ♖xg4+ 37 ♔h6 ♔f8 38 ♖xa2 ♖xh4 0–1

Game 14
Karpov-J.Polgar
Wijk aan Zee 1998

---

1 d4 ♘f6 2 ♘f3 g6 3 c4 ♗g7 4 g3 0–0 5 ♗g2 d5 6 0–0 dxc4 7 ♘a3 ♘a6 8 ♘xc4 c5 9 b3 ♗f5 10 ♗b2 ♗e4 11 ♖c1 ♖c8

Dubious is 11...♗h6 12 e3 ♕d5 13 ♘cd2 with advantage to White.

12 ♕d2

A new move by Karpov. In an earlier game Adorjan played 12 ♗h3, but failed to gain any advantage.

12...♕d5

White has a slight advantage after 12...cxd4 13 ♗xd4.

13 ♖fd1 ♕h5

13...♖fd8!? is more logical, but even then after 14 ♕e1 White has a comfortable game.

14 h3! cxd4

Black relieves the tension in the centre. The exchange of blows 14...♗h6 15 ♘e3 ♘d5 16 g4 ♗xe3 17 fxe3 ♕h6 18 g5 ♕h5 19 dxc5 would have led to an advantage for White.

15 ♗xd4 ♖fd8 16 ♘ce5!

White's superiority has become appreciable.

16...♖xc1

The character of the play would have been little changed by 16...♗xf3 17 ♖xc8 ♖xc8 18 ♗xf3.

17 ♕xc1 ♗xf3

The only move.

18 ♗xf3!

White had a broad choice: 18 ♘xf3 with a slight advantage, or 18 exf3!? with the idea after 18...♖xd4? of continuing 19 ♖xd4 ♕xe5 20 ♖d8+ ♗f8 21 ♕c8 with advantage.

18...♕xh3 19 ♗xa7

After 19 ♗xb7 Karpov was afraid that Black might confuse matters by 19...♘g4!? 20 ♘xg4 ♗xd4 21 ♕f4 ♘c5 (21...e5 22 ♘xe5 ♗xf2+ 23 ♔xf2 ♖xd1 24 ♕xf7+, mating), but in fact 22 ♗g2 or 22 ♘h6+ wins comfortably.

19...♖a8 20 ♗d4

After 20 ♕c4 ♕e6! 21 ♕xe6 fxe6 22 ♗d4 ♘b4 23 a4 ♘bd5 Black can still resist.

20...♖c8 21 ♕a3 ♖e8 22 ♗xb7 ♘c7 23 ♗c6 ♖f8 24 ♕xe7 ♘e6 25 ♗c3

Worse is 25 ♗e3? ♕f5 26 ♘c4 ♘g4 when the play becomes double-edged.

25...♕f5 26 ♖d3 h5 27 ♖f3

If 27 ♔g2 White would have to reckon with 27...h4.

27...♕c2 28 ♘xf7 ♕d1+

Things are not changed by 28...♕xe2 29 ♘h6+! ♗xh6 30 ♖xf6, winning.

29 ♔g2 ♕xe2 30 ♖e3 ♕c2 31 ♕xe6 ♖xf7 32 ♗xf6 1–0

Game 15
P.Nikolic-Piket
Wijk aan Zee 1996

1 d4 ♘f6 2 c4 g6 3 g3 ♗g7 4 ♗g2 d5 5 ♘f3 0–0 6 0–0 dxc4 7 ♘a3 ♘c6 8 ♘xc4 ♗e6 9 b3 a5

Undoubtedly Black's most active plan on the queenside, undermining the position of the powerful knight, although the underestimated plan of 9...♕c8 followed by 10...♖d8 and 11...♗h3, exchanging the light-square bishops, is very logical.

10 ♗b2 ♗d5

10...a4 is premature: 11 ♘g5 ♗d5 12 e4 ♗xc4 13 bxc4 h6 14 ♘h3, and White has too strong a centre.

11 ♖c1

The most natural way to 'block' Black's play is by 11 a4 – the weakness of the b4 square is insignificant.

11...a4

The critical move, although 11...♖a6 12 a3 ♘a7 13 e3 ♘b5 14 a4 ♘d6 15 ♕e2 c6 is also possible, with a complicated game (Van der Sterren-Korchnoi, Antwerp 1997).

12 bxa4

Later Nikolic introduced a slight improvement in his game with Ftacnik (Pula 1997): 12 ♘e3 ♗e4 13 bxa4 ♖a6 14 ♘e5 ♗xg2 15 ♘xg2! ♕d5 16 a3, and now 16...♖fa8 17 f3 ♖xa4 18 e4 ♕b5 would have led to an equal game.

12...♖a6

Piket considers that 12...♘e8 is also interesting.

13 ♘fe5

After 13 a3 ♕a8 14 a5 ♖c8! and 15...♖xa5 Black is excellently placed.

13...♗xg2 14 ♔xg2 ♕a8 15 ♘xc6

Here White had the interesting alternative 15 ♔g1 ♖xa4 16 a3 ♘xe5!?

17 dxe5 ♖d8 18 ♕c2 ♘d5 19 e4 b5 20 ♘d2 ♘b6 with a complicated game.

15...bxc6 16 a5?!

Very risky; better was 16 ♔g1 ♖xa4 17 a3 ♘d7 (17...♖b8 18 ♕d2 ♕a6 is also not bad, Karpov) 18 ♘e5 ♘xe5 19 dxe5 ♖b8 with a complicated game (Karpov-Piket, Tilburg 1996).

16...c5+ 17 ♔g1 ♖d8 18 e3 cxd4 19 exd4 ♘e4!

This is stronger than 19...c5 20 ♘b6 ♕b7 21 ♖xc5 ♘e4, although there too Black has strong compensation for the pawn.

20 ♕f3?

White tries to eliminate the unpleasant pressure on the diagonal, but stronger was 20 ♕e2 ♘g5 21 f3 ♘e6, with only a slight advantage to Black.

20...♗xd4 21 ♗xd4 ♖xd4 22 h4

White has to defend against the unpleasant ...♖f6, as is apparent, for example, in the variation 22 ♖fd1 ♖f6 23 ♕e3 ♘xf2! 24 ♖xd4 ♘h3 mate.

22...♖f6 23 ♕e2?

23 ♕b3 was correct, with the idea after 23...♔g7! 24 ♖cd1 of parrying the threat of 24...♕d5 by 25 ♘e3. In addition, this would not have allowed the combination that was overlooked by both players.

23...♕a6

Now White finds himself in an unpleasant pin, but Black misses the chance to decide the game by the elegant rook sacrifice 23...♖xf2! 24 ♖xf2 ♘xg3 25 ♕f3 ♕xf3 26 ♖xf3 ♘e2+ and 27...♘xc1.

24 ♖c2 ♖e6! 25 ♘e3 ♕xa5 26 ♖b1

Black is a pawn up, and White's counterplay is not very serious.

26...h5 27 ♖b8+ ♔g7 28 ♔g2 c6 29 ♖c8 ♘xg3!

Black begins a decisive attack.

30 fxg3

After 30 ♔xg3 ♖g4+ 31 ♔h3 ♖xe3+ 32 ♕xe3 ♕f5 33 ♕c3+ f6 Black has terrible threats.

30...♖de4 31 ♖8xc6 ♖xe3 32 ♖xe6 ♕d5+! 33 ♔h2 ♕xe6 34 ♕b5

If 34 ♕g2 Black has 34...♕g4 followed by ...e7-e5.

34...♕g4 35 ♖g2 e5 36 a4 ♖e1 37 ♖f2 ♕e4 38 ♖g2 ♖a1 39 ♕b6 ♖xa4 40 ♖f2 ♕d5 0–1

Game 16
Kir.Georgiev-Kozul
Yerevan Olympiad 1996

---

1 d4 ♘f6 2 c4 g6 3 g3 ♗g7 4 ♗g2 d5 5 ♘f3 dxc4 6 ♘a3 c3 7 bxc3 0–0 8 0–0 c5 9 e3

One of the predecessors of this, the Adorjan Variation, was the so-called Bulgarian System 9 ♕b3. Here is a recent example: 9...♘c6 10 ♖d1 ♘a5 11 ♕b2 ♗f5 12 ♗d2 ♕b6 13 ♕xb6 axb6 14 ♘e5 ♖fd8 15 ♗e1 cxd4 16 cxd4 ♘g4 17 ♘f3 ♘c6 18 ♘b5 ♗c2 19 ♖d2 ♗a4 20 ♖b1 with a complicated game (Velikov-Miralles, Marseille 1990).

9...♘c6 10 ♕e2

The most accurate move order. If 10 ♗b2 White has to reckon with 10...e5

11 ♘c4 exd4 12 cxd4 ♗e6 13 ♕e2 cxd4 14 ♘xd4 ♘xd4 15 ♗xd4 ♖e8 16 ♖ad1 ♕e7 17 ♘a5 ♕a3 with counterplay (Frolik-Luecke, Germany 1995).

10...♗f5 11 ♖d1 ♗e4 12 ♗b2 ♕b6

Black does not want to clarify the situation in the centre; after 12...cxd4 13 exd4 ♕a5 14 c4 e6 15 ♘b5 ♖fd8 16 a4 ♗xf3 17 ♗xf3 ♖d7 18 d5 exd5 19 cxd5 ♘e7 20 d6 ♘f5 21 ♖ab1! the white d-pawn, supported by the rooks at d1 and b1, is a powerful force.

13 ♘c4 ♕a6 14 ♗f1 ♖fd8

But here he should have fixed the position in the centre: 14...cxd4 15 cxd4 ♖ac8 with a reasonable game.

15 ♘fd2

A manoeuvre typical of the given variation, although two other plans should be considered: 15 a4 or 15 ♘e1 with the idea of f2-f3 and then e3-e4.

15...♗c2 16 ♖dc1 ♗a4 17 ♘b3 b6?!

This looks natural, but better was 17...♘d7 18 dxc5 (18 d5 ♘ce5 19 ♘xe5 ♕xe2 20 ♗xe2 ♗xe5 21 ♖ab1 ♖ac8) 18...♘ce5 and Black has an excellent game.

18 dxc5 ♗b5 19 ♘d4

White also has an alternative: 19 a4 ♗xa4 20 ♘cd2 ♕xe2 21 ♗xe2 ♗xb3 22 ♘xb3 bxc5 23 ♖c2 with advantage,

but after 19...♗xc4 20 ♕xc4 ♕xc4 21 ♗xc4 ♘e5 22 ♗f1 bxc5 23 ♘xc5 ♖ac8 Black has compensation for the pawn.

19...bxc5

A premature capture. Stronger was 19...♗xc4 20 ♕xc4 ♕xc4 21 ♗xc4 ♘e5 22 ♗e2 bxc5 with equality.

20 ♘xb5 ♕xb5 21 ♕c2 ♕b7 22 ♖ab1 ♕c7 23 ♗a3

As usual after the capture on c5, White has unpleasant pressure thanks to his control of the b-file and the weakness of the opponent's light squares.

23...♘d5

Or 23...♘d7 24 ♗g2 ♖ab8 25 ♖b3 with advantage.

24 ♖b5 ♘xc3 25 ♖xc5 ♕d7 26 ♘b2

It does not often happen that one achieves any gains with such a backward move. Weaker was 26 ♗b2 ♘b4 27 ♕b3 ♘cxa2 with complications.

26...♘e5 27 ♖xc3 ♘f3+ 28 ♔g2 ♗xc3 29 ♕xc3 ♖ac8 30 ♘c4 ♕g4

30...♕b7 also loses after 31 e4!

31 ♗xe7 ♕e4 32 ♗xd8

Not fearing a discovery by the knight – here precise calculation was required.

32...♘e1+ 33 ♔g1 ♘f3+ 34 ♔h1 ♘h4+ 35 f3 ♕xf3+ 36 ♔g1 ♖xc4 37 ♕d2 ♖xc1 38 ♕xc1 ♘f5 39 ♗f6 1–0

> **Game 17**
> **P.Nikolic-Popovic**
> *Yugoslavia 1990*

1 d4 ♘f6 2 c4 g6 3 ♘f3 ♗g7 4 g3 0–0 5 ♗g2 d5 6 0–0 dxc4 7 ♘a3 c3 8 bxc3 c5 9 e3 ♘c6 10 ♕e2 ♕a5

In fighting against White's powerful centre, Black must act very energetically and purposefully. He has several other critical plans, for example: 10...♗f5!? 11 ♗b2 (11 ♖d1 transposes to the Georgiev-Kozul game) 11...♗e4 (the untried 11...e5!? is worth considering: 12 ♘xe5 ♘xe5 13 dxe5 ♗d3 14 ♕e1 ♘g4! 15 ♖d1 ♕b6! with a sharp game) 12 ♘c4 ♗d5 13 ♖fd1 ♕c7 14 ♘cd2 cxd4 15 cxd4 ♕b6! 16 ♗a3 ♘e4 17 ♕d3 ♘xd2 18 ♖xd2 ♕a5 with reasonable chances of equalising (Stempin-Schmidt, Poland 1990).

But the strongest is considered to be 10...♘d5 11 ♗b2 ♕a5 12 ♖fc1 ♗g4! with equality – cf. the appropriate section in the analysis.

11 ♗b2 ♗f5 12 ♖fc1

The idea of this move is always to have ♗f1 available (which is especially important with the black bishop at e4), and then ♘d2, fighting for the central light squares. Very logical here is 12 ♘d2!? cxd4 13 cxd4 ♕b4 14 ♘b3 ♖fd8 15 e4 ♗g4 16 f3 ♗d7 17 ♖fd1 ♖ac8 18 ♘c2 ♕b6 19 ♘e3 ♘b4 20 ♘c5 with advantage (Rashkovsky-de Boer, Groningen 1990), but for some reason this plan has not been tried again.

12...♗e4 13 ♘c4 ♕a6 14 ♗f1 ♖fd8

It is better to clarify the situation immediately by 14...♗d5!? 15 ♘fd2 ♘e4! 16 ♘xe4 ♗xe4 17 ♘d2 ♕xe2 18 ♗xe2 ♗f5 19 ♗f3 ♖ac8 with equality (Bischoff-Grunberg, Hannover 1991).

15 ♕d1 ♗d5

15...b5?! 16 ♘cd2 followed by 17 a4 is very risky for Black.

16 ♘cd2 ♕b6 17 ♕c2

After 17 ♗a3 Black frees himself by 17...cxd4 18 cxd4 e5!

17...cxd4

17...e5 was risky: 18 e4 ♗xe4 19 ♘xe4 ♘xe4 20 ♕xe4 ♕xb2 21 dxe5 ♖e8 22 ♖ab1 ♕a3 23 ♗c4 ♘xe5 24 ♘xe5 ♖xe5 25 ♗xf7+! with advantage to White, but 17...♖ac8 18 c4 ♗xf3 19 ♘xf3 e6 was interesting, with an unclear game.

18 cxd4 ♖ac8 19 ♗c3 e5!

Black tries immediately to resolve the problem of the centre – White's threat of e3-e4 was very unpleasant.

20 ♖ab1 ♕c7 21 dxe5 ♘d7

Bad is 21...♘g4 22 ♕a4 ♘gxe5 23 ♗xe5 ♗xe5 24 ♘xe5 ♕xe5 25 ♖xb7 with advantage to White.

22 e6

After 22 e4 ♘cxe5 23 exd5 ♘xf3+ 24 ♘xf3 ♕xc3 25 ♕xc3 ♖xc3 26 ♖xc3 ♗xc3 27 ♖xb7 White has the advantage.

22...♗xe6 23 ♗xg7 ♔xg7 24 ♕b2+ ♘f6 25 ♕xb7

25...♕xb7?

The decisive mistake: after 25...♗xa2 26 ♕xc7 ♖xc7 27 ♖b2 ♗d5 28 ♖bc2 ♖cd7! the position is equal.

26 ♖xb7 ♗xa2 27 ♗h3! ♖b8 28 ♖c7 ♘b4 29 ♖xa7 ♗d5 30 ♘d4 ♖a8 31 ♖ac7 ♖a2?

Black should not have counterattacked, but driven the rook off the seventh rank by 31...♘e8.

32 ♗e6! ♖xd2 33 ♖xf7+ ♔h6 34 ♖xf6 ♘d3 35 ♖f1 ♗e4 36 ♗h3!

White is two pawns up with an easily won position.

36...♘e5 37 ♖e6 ♖d5 38 ♗g2 ♗xg2 39 ♔xg2 ♘d3 40 ♖e7 ♖d6 41 ♘f3 ♖e2 42 h4 1–0

5   Solid Variation with 6 0–0

1	d4	♘f6
2	c4	g6
3	g3	♗g7
4	♗g2	c6

Black strengthens his centre and prepares to defend a slightly passive, but solid position.

5   ♘f3

Sometimes White plays **5 ♘c3** d5 6 cxd5 cxd5:

(a) **7 ♘h3** (aiming to increase the pressure on the d5 pawn by playing the knight to f4):

(a1) this plan was first employed by Botvinnik against Bronstein in game 23 of their 1951 match, which continued 7...♗xh3!? 8 ♗xh3 ♘c6 9 ♗g2 (weaker is 9 0–0 h5! 10 ♗g2 h4 11 ♗f4 e6 12 e3 ♘h5 13 ♕g4 ♘xf4 14 ♕xf4 h3 15 ♗h1 ♕f6 with a sharp game, Najdorf-Bronstein, Buenos Aires 1954) 9...e6 10 e3 0–0 11 ♗d2 ♖c8 12 0–0 ♘d7 13 ♘e2 ♕b6 14 ♗c3 ♖fd8 15 ♘f4 ♘f6 with an equal game;

(a2) 7...0–0 is not worse: 8 ♘f4 e6 9 0–0 ♘c6 10 e3 b6 (10...♗d7 11 ♗d2 ♕e7 12 a3 ♖fc8 13 b4 ♘e8 14 b5 ♘d8

15 ♕b3 ♘d6 16 ♖fc1! and White has a slight advantage, P.Nikolic-Timoshchenko, Moscow 1990) 11 ♗d2 ♗b7 12 ♕a4 ♕d7 13 ♖fc1 ♖fc8 14 ♗e1 ♗f8 15 ♕d1 ♘a5 with an equal game (P.Nikolic-Gulko, Munich 1990).

The other knight route also does not achieve anything: 7 e3 0–0 8 ♘ge2 ♘c6 9 0–0 b6 10 f3 (10 b3 ♗a6 11 ♗a3 ♖e8 12 ♕d2 e5! 13 dxe5 ♘xe5 14 ♖fd1 ♘d3 15 ♕c2 ♘xf2! with a very strong attack, Byrne-Fischer, USA 1963) 10...♘e8 11 ♗d2 e6 12 ♗e1 ♗b7 13 ♗f2 ♕d7 14 ♕b3 ♘d6 15 ♖ad1 ♖fc8 16 e4 ♘a5 17 ♕c2 ♘b5 with an excellent game (P.Nikolic-Kolev, Elenite 1993).

5   ...   d5
6   0–0

6 cxd5 is covered in Chapter 6.

With **6 ♕b3** White can intensify the pressure on d5 before castling, but this move order allows Black an additional possibility (otherwise play transposes into section 5.1) – 6...a5!?, and now:

(a) 7 ♘c3 a4! 8 ♕b4 dxc4 9 ♕xc4 0–0 10 0–0 b5 11 ♕d3 b4 12 ♘e4 ♗a6 13 ♘xf6+ ♗xf6 14 ♕c2 b3 with a good game (Greenfeld-Hellers, Oslo 1992);

(b) 7 c5 ♘e4 8 ♘c3 a4! 9 ♘xa4 ♕a5+ 10 ♘c3 ♘xc5 11 dxc5 d4 12 ♘xd4 ♗xd4 13 0–0 ♕xc5 14 ♗h6 ♕h5 15 ♖ad1 ♗e5 16 ♗e3 0–0 and Black gradually equalised (Dautov-Uhlmann, Dresden 1988);

(c) 7 ♗f4 a4 8 ♕b4 ♘bd7 9 0–0 ♕b6! 10 ♕xb6 ♘xb6 11 c5 ♘c4 and Black has an excellent game (Tukmakov-Uhlmann, Szirak 1985) – *Game 18*;

(d) 7 0–0 a4 8 ♕b4 0–0 9 ♗f4 dxc4 10 ♕xc4 ♕b6 11 ♕c1 ♗g4 12 ♘bd2

♘bd7 13 ♘c4 ♕b5 14 ♖e1 ♘d5 with a good position (Csom-Uhlmann, Ter Apel 1990);

(e) 7 cxd5 a4 8 ♕a3 (after 8 ♕d1 cxd5 9 ♘c3 a3 10 0–0 ♘c6 11 e3 0–0 12 bxa3 ♗g4 13 h3 ♗xf3 14 ♗xf3 e5! 15 dxe5 ♘xe5 Black has an active game, Matlak-Pedzich, Poland 1992) 8...cxd5 9 0–0 ♘c6 10 ♘c3 ♘e4 11 ♗e3 0–0 12 ♖ac1 ♘xc3 13 bxc3 ♗f5 14 c4 ♗e4 with an equal game (C.Hansen-Hellers, Esbjerg 1988).

6 ...   0–0

Now White has several completely different plans: 7 ♕b3 (5.1), 7 ♕a4 (5.2), 7 ♘c3 (5.3), 7 ♘e5 (5.4), 7 ♘a3 (5.5), 7 b3 (5.6) and 7 ♘bd2 (5.7).

The untried 7 ♗f4!? also comes into consideration.

5.1 (1 d4 ♘f6 2 c4 g6 3 g3 ♗g7 4 ♗g2 c6 5 ♘f3 d5 6 0–0 0–0)

---

7 ♕b3

White avoids playing 7 cxd5, so as not to allow Black to activate his queen's knight at c6. In this way he intensifies the pressure on the centre, and sooner or later Black has to concede the centre with ...dxc4 or try to exchange queens. He has the following

possibilities: **7...♕b6 (5.11)**, **7...dxc4 (5.12)**, **7...b6 (5.13)**, **7...e6 (5.14)** and **7...♘e4 (5.15)**.

There is also the interesting **7...a5!?**, transposing into positions similar to the Tukmakov-Uhlmann game (p.159).

5.11 (1 d4 ♘f6 2 c4 g6 3 g3 ♗g7 4 ♗g2 c6 5 ♘f3 d5 6 0–0 0–0 7 ♕b3)

---

7 ...   ♕b6

One of the most critical moves.

8 ♘c3

8 c5 is slightly premature: 8...♕xb3 9 axb3 ♗g4, and now:

(a) 10 b4 ♘bd7 11 e3 ♗xf3 (11... a6?! 12 ♘bd2 e5 13 ♘b3 with a slight advantage to White, Dorfman-Uhlmann, Berlin 1989; after 13 ♘xe5 ♗e2 14 ♖e1 ♗b5 Black stands well) 12 ♗xf3 e5 with a complicated game;

(b) 10 ♘c3 ♘fd7 11 ♖d1 ♘a6 12 ♖a4 ♗xf3 13 ♗xf3 e5! and now 14 ♘xd5?! cxd5 15 ♗xd5 exd4 16 b4 ♖ab8 led to an advantage for Black (Mochalov-Neverov, USSR 1988).

8 ...   ♗f5

Black has several alternatives:

8...♕xb3 9 axb3 ♘a6 (after 9...♖d8 10 ♖d1 ♗e6 11 ♘e5 ♘e8 12 ♗f4 White is better, Dizdarevic-Kozul, Yugoslavia 1991) 10 ♗f4 ♖d8 (less good is 10...h6 11 ♖a4 dxc4 12 bxc4 ♘d7 13 b3 with advantage, Loginov-Starosek, Aika 1992) 11 ♖fc1 (weaker is 11 ♗e5 ♗e6 12 ♘g5 ♗f5 13 cxd5 cxd5 14 ♖a5 e6 with an equal game, Byrne-Geller, USA-USSR 1955) 11... ♗e6 12 c5 ♘e8 13 ♖a4 ♘ac7 14 ♖b4! ♖ab8 15 ♖a1 a6 16 h3 f6 17 g4 ♗f7 18 ♗g3 ♗f8 19 ♖a5 with an unpleasant ending for Black (Romanishin-Ernst, Debrecen 1992).

8...♗e6 9 c5 (after 9 ♘g5 dxc4 10 ♕a4 ♗c8! 11 ♕xc4 h6 12 ♘f3 ♗e6 13 ♕a4 ♘a6 14 ♗d2 c5 15 ♖ac1 ♖ac8 Black has no problems, Csom-Donchev, Prague 1985, or 9 ♘a4 ♕xb3 10 axb3 ♘a6 11 ♘g5 ♗f5 12 ♗f4 ♖fd8 with equality, Petrosian-Stean, Buenos Aires 1978) 9...♕xb3 10 axb3 ♘bd7 11 b4 ♘e4 12 ♗e3 f5 (after 12...a6?! 13 ♘xe4 dxe4 14 ♘g5 White is better) 13 b5! h6 14 bxc6 bxc6 15 ♖a6 ♘b8 16 ♖a4 and White has the better ending, since Black's weaknesses at a7 and c6 will cause him problems for a long time (Davies-Shmuter, Israel 1994).

8...♖d8 9 ♖d1 (less good is 9 ♕xb6 axb6 10 cxd5 ♘xd5 11 ♘xd5 ♖xd5 12 ♖d1, Rogozenko-Donchev, Debrecen 1992, when 12...♗f5 13 ♘e5 ♖d8 gives Black an excellent game) 9... ♕xb3 10 axb3 ♗f5 11 ♘e1 (or 11 cxd5 ♗c2 12 ♖d2 ♗xb3 13 dxc6 ♘xc6 14 ♖a3 ♗e6 15 ♘e5 ♘d5 with active counterplay for Black, Lalic-Hugentobler, Zurich 1989) 11...♘a6 12 ♖a4 h6 13 ♗f4 ♘e4 14 cxd5 cxd5 15 f3 ♘xc3 16 bxc3 g5 17 ♗d2 e5 and Black has to fight for equality in a slightly inferior ending (Portisch-Hort, Tilburg 1979).

8...dxc4 9 ♕xc4 ♗e6, and now:
   (a) 10 ♕d3 ♘a6 (10...♖d8 11 h3 h6 12 e4 ♕a6 13 ♕e3 ♘bd7 14 ♖d1, Lengyel-Golombek, Venice 1966, and 14...♖ac8 15 ♘e2 ♗c4 16 ♗f1 led to an advantage for White) 11 e4 ♖ad8 12 h3 ♘b4 13 ♕e2 ♕a6 14 ♕xa6 ♘xa6 15 ♗e3 and White has some advantage in the ending (Rubinstein-Grünfeld, Mährisch-Ostrau 1923) – Rubinstein did not only play an early e2-e4!;
   (b) 10 ♕a4 ♗d5 (after 10...♘a6 11 e4 ♖fd8 12 h3 ♕b4 13 ♕c2 ♕c4 14 ♖d1 h6 15 ♗e3 White has the advan-

tage, Ionov-Gubanov, St Petersburg 1992) 11 ♖d1 ♘e4 12 ♕c2! f5 13 ♘a4 ♕b4 14 ♘e5! ♗xe5 15 dxe5 ♘d7 16 f3 ♘ec5 17 ♘c3 ♘xe5 18 ♗f4! and White's chances are clearly better (Romanishin-Podobnik, Pula 1994).

8...♘a6 9 ♕xb6 (9 h3 is rather harmless: 9...dxc4 10 ♕xc4 ♗e6 11 ♕a4 ♗d5 12 ♘xd5 cxd5 13 ♘e5 ♕b4! 14 ♕d1 ♘e4 15 ♕d3 ♖fd8 and Black has everything in order, Loginov-Magyar, Budapest 1993) 9...axb6 10 ♘a4! ♘d7 11 cxd5 cxd5 12 ♘c3 ♘f6 13 ♗g5 ♗e6 14 ♖fc1 ♘b4 15 a3 ♘c6 16 ♗xf6! ♗xf6 17 e3 ♖fd8 18 ♘d2 and White has the advantage, since Black's doubled pawns will be a source of trouble (Goldin-Daniliuk, St Petersburg 1993).

Now White's main choices are 9 h3 (5.111) and 9 ♘e5 (5.112).

After 9 ♗f4 dxc4 10 ♕xc4 ♘bd7 (if 10...♕xb2!? 11 ♘g5 White has the initiative after 11...♕b6 12 e4 ♗c8 13 ♖ab1, but after 11...h6!? it is not clear how to continue the attack; therefore he should try 11 ♘e5 with some compensation for the pawn) 11 b3 ♘e4 12 ♖ad1 ♘xc3 13 ♕xc3 ♗e4 the position is equal (Pigusov-Timoshchenko, Moscow 1990).

After **9 ♕xb6** axb6 10 cxd5 ♘xd5 (no weaker is 10...cxd5 11 ♗f4 ♘c6 12 ♖fd1 e6 13 e3 h6 14 ♗c7 ♖fc8! 15 ♗xb6 ♘d7 16 ♗c5 ♘xc5 17 dxc5 ♖a5 with an excellent game, Baudenne-Goloshchapov, Cala Galdana 1996) 11 ♗d2 ♘xc3 (less good is 11...♘d7 12 ♘xd5 cxd5 13 ♗b4 ♖fe8 14 ♖fc1, seizing the file) 12 ♗xc3 ♗e4 13 a4 ♘a6 14 ♘d2 (14 ♖fd1 with the idea of 15 ♘e1 was worth trying) 14...♗xg2 15 ♔xg2 ♖fd8 16 ♘b3 c5! Black opened up the position and equalised (Hübner-Gelfand, Munich 1991).

If **9 cxd5** ♕xb3 10 axb3 ♘xd5 (after 10...cxd5 11 b4 e6 12 b5 ♘e4 13 ♘xe4 ♗xe4 14 ♗e3 ♘d7 15 ♖fc1 ♗xf3! 16 ♗xf3 ♘b6 Black neutralises White's temporary initiative, e.g. 17 ♖c7 ♖fb8 and ...♗f8-d6, Hübner-Khalifman, Germany 1992) 11 ♘e5 (weak is 11 e4 ♘xc3 12 exf5 ♘e2+ 13 ♔h1 ♘xd4 with advantage to Black) 11...♗e6!? (11...♘b4 12 ♖a4 ♘8a6 is worth trying, with a good game for Black) 12 ♘e4 ♘d7 13 ♘xd7 ♗xd7 14 ♘c5 ♗g4! 15 e3 (or 15 ♘xb7? ♗xe2 16 ♖e1 ♗b5 and Black seizes the initiative) 15...b6 16 ♘a6 ♖ac8 with a complicated game (Ornstein-Uhlmann, Stockholm 1989).

5.111 (1 d4 ♘f6 2 c4 g6 3 g3 ♗g7 4 ♗g2 c6 5 ♘f3 d5 6 0–0 0–0 7 ♕b3 ♕b6 8 ♘c3 ♗f5)

9　h3　　♖d8

Weaker is **9...♘bd7** 10 cxd5 ♕xb3 11 axb3 ♘xd5 12 ♗d2 ♘xc3 13 bxc3 ♗e4 14 ♖a4 a6 15 ♘e1! with advantage (Romanishin-Xie, Helsinki 1992).

After **9...dxc4** 10 ♕xc4 ♘a6 11 a3 (11 ♖e1 ♕b4! 12 ♕xb4 ♘xb4 13 e4 ♗e6 14 ♖d1 ♘c2 15 ♖b1 ♘xe4! 16 ♘xe4 ♗xa2 with a complicated game, Ehlvest-Gurevich, New York 1992) 11...♖ad8 12 b4 ♘e4 13 ♘xe4 ♗xe4 14 e3 ♘c7 15 ♗b2 ♕b5 16 ♕xb5 ♘xb5 17 ♖fc1 White has the initiative (Loginov-Ionov, Azov 1991).

If **9...♘a6** White has 10 c5 ♕xb3 11 axb3 ♘c7 12 ♗f4 ♘e6 13 ♗e3 ♗e4 14 ♖a4 ♗xf3 15 ♗xf3 when he stands better (Romanishin-Alterman, Groningen 1993).

10　♗f4

10 g4 is interesting: 10...♗e6 11 ♕c2 dxc4 12 ♘a4 ♕c7 13 ♘c5 ♗c8 14 ♕xc4 b6 15 ♘d3 ♗a6 16 ♕b3 and White is clearly better (Dorfman-Dolmatov, Polanica Zdroj 1993).

Also possible is **10 c5** ♕a6 11 ♖e1 b6 12 ♗f1 ♕b7 13 a4 ♗c8 14 cxb6 axb6 15 ♗f4 ♘bd7 16 g4, again with advantage to White (Romanishin-Dolmatov, Groningen 1993).

10　...　　dxc4
11　♕xc4　　♘d5

11...♕xb2 is too dangerous because of 12 ♘g5 ♖f8 13 e4 and 14 ♖ab1.

Loginov-Ruck (Harkany 1994) now continued 12 ♘g5! ♕xd4 (weak is 12...h6 13 ♘xf7 ♔xf7 14 e4 with advantage to White) 13 ♕b3! ♕b6 14 ♘xd5 ♕xb3 15 ♘xe7+ ♔f8 and here correct was 16 axb3 ♔xe7 17 e4 ♗c8

18 e5 h6 19 ②e4 g5 20 ♗d2 ♗xe5 21 ♗b4+ ♔e8 22 ♖fe1 with an attack.

5.112 (1 d4 ②f6 2 c4 g6 3 g3 ♗g7 4 ♗g2 c6 5 ②f3 d5 6 0–0 0–0 7 ♕b3 ♕b6 8 ②c3 ♗f5)

---

9   ②e5

9   ...   ♗e6

If **9...②g4 10 cxd5** (White retains a minimal advantage after 10 ②xg4 ♗xg4 11 ♗e3 dxc4 12 ♕xc4 ②a6 13 ♖fc1 ♗f5 14 a3 ♖ac8 15 b4 ②c7, Stangl-Ernst, Dortmund 1992) 10...♕xb3 11 axb3 ②xe5 12 dxe5 ♗xe5 13 ②a4! (the untried 13 ♗g5 ♖e8 14 e4 ♗d7 15 ♖fd1 is interesting) 13...♗c7 14 ♗f4 (after 14 ②c5 cxd5 15 ♗xd5 ②c6 16 ②xb7 ②d4, A.Petrosian-Ernst, Dortmund 1992, interesting is 17 ♗h6 with advantage) 14...♗xf4 15 gxf4 a5 (Wojtkiewicz-Schmidt, Katowice 1993), and here 16 ♖fc1 would have consolidated White's advantage, associated with the clearly better placing of his pieces.

After **9...♖d8 10 ♗f4** (or 10 cxd5 ♕xb3 11 axb3 cxd5 12 ♗f4 h6 13 g4 ♗xg4 14 ②xg4 ②xg4 15 ②xd5 ②c6 16 h3 ②f6 17 ②xf6+ ♗xf6 18 e3 e5 with equality, Wojtkiewicz-Pedzich, Poland 1992) 10...②a6 (after 10...♗e6 11 ②a4

♕xb3 12 axb3 ②bd7 13 ♖fc1 ♖ac8 14 ②c3 White has slightly the better ending, Goldin-Schmidt, Belgrade 1988) 11 c5 ♕xb3 12 axb3 ♖dc8 13 ♖a5 ②c7 14 ♖fa1 a6 15 b4 ②h5 16 ♗d2 ♖d8 it is hard for White to breach the opponent's position, although he certainly has some advantage (Akopian-Alterman, Beer Sheva 1992).

9...e6 is a modern move, but it has a serious defect: the retreat of the f5 bishop is cut off: 10 ♗f4 (10 ♗e3 ②bd7 11 h3 h5 12 ♕a3 a5 13 ♖ac1 ♕b4 is equal, Pigusov-Tseitlin, Lyon 1994) 10...②bd7 11 ♕xb6 (in general, White does not especially want to exchange on b6, but here this plan has its good points) 11...axb6 12 f3! (this is the drawback to 9...e6 – e2-e4 is threatened) 12...c5 (after 12...②xe5 13 ♗xe5 g5 14 e4 ♗g6 15 b3 ♖fd8 16 ♖fd1 dxe4 17 fxe4 ②g4 18 ♗xg7 ♔xg7 19 ♗f3 h5 20 ♖d2 ②e5 21 ♗g2 c5 22 d5 ②c6 23 ♖ad1 ②d4 Black equalised in Kramnik-Shirov, m/7 1998, but 15 cxd5 exd5 16 ♖ad1 b5 17 a3 dxe4 18 fxe4 ②d7 19 ♗d6 left White clearly better in Mikhalevski-Vydeslaver, Jerusalem 1996) 13 dxc5 d4 14 ②b5 bxc5 15 ②xd7 ②xd7 16 ♗d6 ♖fc8 (Black also has problems after 16...♖fd8 17 f4) 17 f4! with advantage to White, since his bishops are simply rampant (Kramnik-Gelfand, Dos Hermanas 1996).

10   ♕d1!?

Also interesting is **10 c5 ♕xb3 11 axb3 ②fd7 12 ②f3 ♗g4 13 ♖d1 ②a6 14 h3 ♗xf3 15 ♗xf3** (Portisch-Schmidt, Moscow 1994), and here 15...e6 was correct, with a defensible position.

After **10 ♖d1 dxc4 11 ②xc4 ♕a6 12 d5 cxd5 13 ②xd5 ②xd5 14 ♗xd5 ♗xd5 15 ♖xd5 ♕e6** (or 15...②c6 16 ♗e3 ♖ac8 17 ♖ad1 b6 18 a4 e6 19 ♖5d2, and White is better, Gilding-Beshukov, Elista 1996) 16 ♖d3 again White stands better (Schlosser-Xie, Baden 1992).

10   ...   ♘bd7

After 10...dxc4 11 ♘a4 ♕d8 12 ♘c5 ♕c8 13 ♕c2 White stands better, or 10...♘a6 11 cxd5 ♘xd5 12 ♘a4 ♕c7 13 e4 ♘b6 14 ♗f4, and again Black does not succeed in equalising (Wojtkiewicz-Kaminski, Wisla 1992).

11   cxd5   cxd5

White also has the advantage after 11...♘xd5 12 ♘xd7 ♗xd7 13 ♗xd5 cxd5 14 ♘xd5 ♕d6 15 e4 ♗e6 16 ♗f4 ♕d7 17 ♘c7 ♗g4 18 f3 ♗xd4+ 19 ♔h1.

12   ♘d3!

A fine manoeuvre – in view of the terrible threat of ♘f4, the black queen is forced to embark on a risky journey. Rotstein-Kaminski (Groningen 1992) continued 12...♕xd4 13 ♗e3 ♕c4 14 ♖c1 ♕a6 (or 14...d4 15 b3!, regaining the pawn and obtaining a dominating position) 15 ♘b4 ♕a5 16 ♘bxd5 ♘xd5 17 ♘xd5 ♕xa2 18 ♘xe7+ ♔h8 19 ♗d4 when White stands better, since if 19...♖fe8 there follows 20 ♘d5! ♗xd5 21 ♗xd5, when the b7 pawn and the c7 square are weak – the white rook will invade there.

5.12 (1 d4 ♘f6 2 c4 g6 3 g3 ♗g7 4 ♗g2 c6 5 ♘f3 d5 6 0–0 0–0 7 ♕b3)

7   ...   dxc4
8   ♕xc4

Black has given up the centre, but the white queen will come under attack by the black pieces and be forced to retreat, and Black's lead in development and the activity of his pieces can compensate for the strength of the white centre.

8   ...   ♗e6

Black has several alternatives:

8...♘a6 9 ♘c3 ♗e6 10 ♕a4 (after 10 ♕d3 ♗f5 11 ♕d2 ♘d5 12 ♖e1 ♘xc3 13 bxc3 ♗e4 14 ♕e3 ♗d5 15 ♖b1 ♖b8 Black stands well, Baburin-Kuporosov, Russia 1989) 10...♘d5 (after 10...♕b6!? 11 h3 ♖ad8 12 e4 c5 13 d5 ♗d7 14 ♕b3 e6 15 ♘e5! exd5 16 ♘xd7 ♖xd7 17 exd5 White is slightly better, Korchnoi-Nunn, Skelleftea 1989) 11 ♖d1 ♘b6 (after 11...♕c8 12 ♘g5 ♘b6 13 ♕c2 ♗f5 14 e4 ♗g4 15 f3 ♗d7 16 f4 [16 e5!?] 16...♗g4 17 ♘f3 f5 18 ♕b3+ ♔h8 19 e5 White has the advantage, Romanishin-Lalic, Vrsac 1989) 12 ♕c2 ♘b4 13 ♕b1 a5 14 e4 ♗g4 15 a3 ♘a6 16 h3 ♗xf3 17 ♗xf3 ♕d7 18 ♔g2 ♖fd8 19 ♕a2! with a great advantage, since Black is unable to create any threats against the white centre (Romanishin-Khuzman, Kherson 1989).

8...♕a5 9 ♘c3 ♗e6 10 ♕d3 ♘a6 11 ♘g5! (weaker is 11 e4 b5! with counterplay) 11...♗d7 12 ♗d2 (12 f4!?) 12...♕d8?! (too passive; Black should play 12...♖ac8, with counterplay against the centre, or 12...h6) 13 ♖ad1 h6 14 ♘f3 ♗f5 15 ♕c4! ♘d5 16 ♕b3 ♘db4 (better 16...♘xc3 17 ♗xc3 ♕b6, trying to simplify) 17 ♖c1 with the idea of 18 ♖fd1, and all White's pieces stand better than Black's (Romanishin-Kochiev, Moscow 1989).

8...♘bd7 9 ♘c3 ♘b6 (weak is 9...♕a5 10 e4 ♕h5 11 ♕d3 ♘b6 12 ♘e2 ♖d8 13 a4! ♘bd7 14 b4! with a great advantage, Euwe-Alekhine, m/30 1935) **10 ♕d3 ♗e6** (or 10...♗g4 11 ♖d1 ♕c8 12 e4 ♖d8 13 ♕f1! e5 14 ♗e3 exd4 15 ♖xd4 and White is better, Spasov-Sturua, France 1989) **11 ♖d1 ♗c4** (after 11...♖c8 12 e4 c5 13 d5 ♗g4 14 h3 ♗xf3 15 ♕xf3 ♘fd7 16 ♕e2 White has the advantage, Szmetan-Vescovi, Mar del Plata 1996) **12 ♕c2 ♗a6 13 e4 e6 14 b3** and White has the advantage (Conquest-San Claudio, Oviedo 1993). Black's pieces are uncoordinated and are unable to offer counterplay against White's simple plan of ♗b2, ♖ac1, e4-e5 and ♘e4.

8...♗f5 9 ♘c3 ♘bd7 (after 9...♘a6 10 ♖e1 ♘e4 11 ♗f4 White has the advantage) **10 e3 ♘b6** (after 10...♕c7 11 h3 e5 12 dxe5 ♘xe5 13 ♘xe5 ♕xe5 14 e4 ♗e6 15 ♕e2 ♖fe8 16 ♗e3 ♕a5 17 ♖fd1 ♘d7 18 ♗d4 White has a minimal advantage, Andersson-Lalic, Benasque 1995; the untried 10...♘e4 is also interesting) **11 ♕e2 ♘e4!** (the correct idea – after the exchange of knights the black bishop gains the e4 square) **12 ♖d1** (12 ♗d2!? is stronger) 12...♘xc3 13 bxc3 ♘a4! 14 ♗d2 ♗e4 (bad is 14...♘b2 15 e4 with advantage) 15 ♗e1 ♕c7 16 ♖ac1 h6 17 ♗f1 c5 with an equal game (Wojtkiewicz-Benjamin, USA 1993), since after ...♖ad8 Black has excellent pressure on the centre.

9 ♕a4

After **9 ♕c2** a5 10 ♘c3 ♘a6 11 e4 a4! 12 ♖d1 (bad is 12 ♕xa4? ♘c5 13 ♕c2 ♘b3) 12...♕a5 13 ♗d2 ♘b4 Black equalised (Vidmar-Porreca, Opatija 1953), while after **9 ♕b4 ♕b6 10 ♕xe7**

♘a6 11 ♕a3 ♖fe8 12 ♘c3 ♗c4 13 ♘e5 (after 13 ♖e1 ♘d5 14 ♘xd5 cxd5 15 ♗e3 ♕b5! 16 ♗f1 ♗f8 17 ♕c3 ♗b4 White's compensation for the exchange is dubious) 13...♕xd4 14 ♘xc4 ♕xc4 15 ♗f4 ♖ad8 Black has an excellent game (Zaichik-Kamsky, Pavlodar 1987).

9 ... ♘bd7

9...♘a6 transposes into a line considered earlier.

10 ♘c3

10 ♘g5 is too artificial: 10...♗g4 (10...♘b6 11 ♕d1 ♗c8 is also good, with a reasonable game) 11 ♕d1 (Dorfman-Hulak, Moscow 1977) when 11...h6 12 h3 ♗h5 13 ♘f3 ♗xf3 leads to equality – *Game 19*.

10 ... ♗f5

10...c5? 11 ♖d1 ♕c8 12 ♕a3! ♗c4 13 ♗e3 ♘g4 14 ♗g5 ♖e8 (Tseitlin-Makarychev, USSR 1981) is bad due to 15 h3! h6 16 ♗f4 e5 17 dxe5 ♘gxe5 18 ♖ac1 with advantage to White.

If **10...b5** 11 ♕c2 b4 (11...h6!?) 12 ♘a4 ♗d5 13 b3 ♘e4 14 ♗b2 ♕a5 15 ♘e5 and again White is slightly better (Mednis-Kuijf, Amsterdam 1986).

10...♘b6 11 ♕c2 ♘fd5 12 ♖d1 ♘b4 13 ♕b1 a5 14 h3 ♕c8 15 ♔h2 ♖d8 16 e4 and White has the advantage (Kurajica-Chabanon, Zagreb 1993).

But interesting is 10...♘d5 11 e4 ♘5b6 12 ♕c2 ♗g4 13 ♖d1 e5!? 14 dxe5 ♕e7 15 h3 ♗xf3 16 ♗xf3 ♘xe5 17 ♗g2 ♖ad8 18 ♗f4 ♘ec4 and Black holds on (Romanishin-Glek, Bonn 1994).

11 ♘h4

After 11 ♖d1 a5! 12 ♘h4 ♘b6 13 ♕b3 ♗e6 14 ♕c2 ♘fd5 15 ♘f3 a4 the game is equal (Timoshchenko-Ivanov, Podolsk 1990).

Lombardy-Gligoric (Manila 1973) now continued 11...♘b6 12 ♕d1 ♗g4 13 h3 ♗e6 14 ♘f3 ♗d5 15 ♘xd5 cxd5 with equality.

> **5.13 (1 d4 ♘f6 2 c4 g6 3 g3 ♗g7 4 ♗g2 c6 5 ♘f3 d5 6 0–0 0–0 7 ♕b3)**

7 ... b6

Black does not concede the centre, but builds a Catalan-like position, intending later to attack the centre with ...c6-c5.

8 ♘c3 ♗b7
9 ♗f4

Also possible is 9 ♖d1 e6 10 a4!? ♘bd7 11 cxd5 cxd5 12 ♗f4 ♘e4 13 ♖ac1 ♗a6 14 ♘b5 with the better game (Davies-Hill, Gausdal 1990).

9 ... e6

9...dxc4 10 ♕xc4 ♘d5 11 ♕b3 ♘xf4 12 gxf4 ♘d7 13 ♖fd1 e6 14 ♘e5 leads to an advantage for White (Pavlovic-Ljubinkovic, Yugoslavia 1992).

10 ♖ad1

If 10 ♖ac1 ♘bd7 11 cxd5 exd5 12 ♗d6 ♖e8 13 e3 ♘e4 14 ♘xe4 dxe4 15 ♘d2 c5!, and Black is well placed (Tukmakov-Neverov, Helsinki 1992).

Tukmakov-Neverov (Nikolaev 1993) continued 10...♘bd7 11 e4!? (White's pieces are well placed, so he must open up the game) 11...♘xe4 12 ♘xe4 dxe4 13 ♘g5 c5 14 d5 e5 (after 14...exd5 15 cxd5 ♘f6 16 ♘xe4 ♘xe4 17 ♗xe4 ♕d7 Black is excellently placed) 15 ♗e3 f5 16 ♘e6 ♕e7 17 ♘xf8 ♖xf8 and Black's powerful pawn centre gives him compensation for the exchange.

> **5.14 (1 d4 ♘f6 2 c4 g6 3 g3 ♗g7 4 ♗g2 c6 5 ♘f3 d5 6 0–0 0–0 7 ♕b3)**

7 ... e6

A similar idea in a different interpretation, again somewhat passive.

8 ♘c3 ♘bd7

After 8...b6 9 ♗f4 ♗a6 10 cxd5 exd5 11 ♘e5 ♗b7 12 a4 ♘bd7 13 a5 White has the advantage (Benko-Reshevsky, New York 1960), while if 8...♘a6 9 ♖d1 ♕b6 10 ♗f4 he again stands better.

9 ♗f4

White can try to open the centre by 9 ♖d1 ♖e8 10 e4!? ♘xe4 11 ♘xe4 dxe4 12 ♘g5 ♘f6 (if 12...f5 13 c5 ♕e7 14 ♗f1 ♘f8 15 ♗f4 with the initiative) 13 ♗f4 with the freer position (Velickovic-Basa, Portoroz 1994), or 9 ♖e1 b6 10 ♗g5 h6 11 ♗xf6 ♘xf6 12 ♘e5 ♗b7 13 ♖ad1 ♕e7 14 e4 with advantage (Lesiege-Frias, Bermuda 1995).

9 ... ♘b6

Or **9...Ïe8** 10 Ïfd1 b6 11 cxd5 exd5 12 Ïe5 Ïb7 13 e4! Ïf8 14 exd5 cxd5 15 Ïg5 and White's spatial advantage gives him the better game (Dautov-Vogt, Dresden 1988).

Karpov-Kurajica (Wijk aan Zee 1988) now continued 10 c5 Ïc4 11 Ïc2 Ïh5 12 b3 Ïxf4 13 gxf4 Ïa3 14 Ïd2 b5 15 Ïfe1 Ïb8 16 Ïh1 a5 17 e3 with some advantage to White.

5.15 (1 d4 Ïf6 2 c4 g6 3 g3 Ïg7 4 Ïg2 c6 5 Ïf3 d5 6 0–0 0–0 7 Ïb3)

---

7 ...   Ïe4

With the idea of exchanging knights and intensifying the pressure on d4.

---

8   Ïc3

8 Ïd1 can also be played.

8 ...   dxc4

Weaker is **8...Ïxc3** 9 bxc3! b6 10 cxd5 cxd5 11 Ïe5 e6 12 c4 with advantage (Goldin-Martinovsky, Philadelphia 1992).

9   Ïxc4   Ïf5

10   Ïb3

After 10 Ïh4 Ïe6 11 Ïd3 Ïxc3 12 bxc3 Ïd7 13 a4 Ïb6 Black controls important squares (Khalifman-Ruck, Vienna 1996), while if **10 e3** Ïd7 11 Ïd2 Ïb6 12 Ïb3 (Tukmakov-Bukic, Portoroz 1995) correct is 12...Ïxc3 13 bxc3 e5 with a complicated game.

Now after 10...Ïc8 11 Ïf4 Ïd7 12 Ïac1 Ïxc3 13 bxc3 Ïe4 14 Ïfd1 c5 15 d5 c4 Black has a good game (Mecking-Uhlmann, Hastings 1966/7).

5.2 (1 d4 Ïf6 2 c4 g6 3 g3 Ïg7 4 Ïg2 c6 5 Ïf3 d5 6 0–0 0–0)

---

7   Ïa4

An interesting idea – White does not want to fix the position in the centre immediately and hopes to force Black to concede central control. This continuation has similarities with 7 Ïb3, but it gives Black a few other good possibilities, apart from 7...dxc4, which transposes into 7 ♕b3.

7 ... ♘bd7

Other possibilities are also good:

7...a5!? (this plan of seizing space on the queenside is probably the most unpleasant for White, and new attempts with it can be expected) 8 cxd5 b5 9 ♕d1 cxd5 10 ♘c3 ♗a6 11 ♘e5 e6 12 ♗f4 ♘fd7 with equality (Goldin-Lechtinsky, Trnava 1989).

7...♗g4 8 ♘c3 dxc4 9 ♕xc4 ♘bd7 10 ♖d1 ♕a5 (10...♘b6 11 ♕d3 ♕c8 12 b3 ♖d8 13 ♗a3 ♘bd5 14 ♖ac1 ♘xc3 15 ♕xc3 and White has the advantage, Dorfman-Novopashin, Volgodonsk 1981) 11 ♕b3 ♘b6 12 ♗f4 ♘fd7 13 h3 ♗xf3 14 ♗xf3 e5 with an equal game (Csom-Jakobsen, Esbjerg 1984).

7...b5!? 8 cxb5 cxb5 9 ♕b3 (9 ♕xb5 ♗a6 and 10...♗xe2 is unfavourable for White) 9...a5 10 ♘e5 e6 11 ♗f4 ♕b6 12 ♖d1 ♘c6 (interesting is 12...♗a6 13 ♘c3 ♘bd7 14 ♖ac1 ♖fc8 with a complicated game) 13 ♘xc6 ♕xc6 14 ♘d2 ♕b6 15 ♗e5 ♗b7 16 ♖ac1 ♖ac8 with equality (Csom-Xie, Budapest 1992).

7...♘fd7 and now:

(a) 8 ♘a3 ♘b6 9 ♕c2 ♗f5 10 ♕c3 ♗e4 11 c5 ♘6d7 12 ♗f4 b6 with an excellent game (Grigorian-Sveshnikov, Moscow 1973);

(b) 8 ♕a3!? (more interesting) 8... dxc4 (8...♘b6 9 c5) 9 ♗g5 ♖e8 10 ♘bd2 ♘b6 (or 10...b5 11 b3 cxb3 12 ♘xb3) 11 ♖ac1 ♗e6 12 ♖fd1 ♘8d7 13 e4 with compensation for the pawn.

7...♘e4 8 ♖d1 ♗e6 9 ♕c2 ♗f5 10 ♕b3 ♕b6 11 cxd5 ♕xb3 12 axb3 cxd5 13 ♘h4 ♘c6 14 ♘xf5 gxf5 15 e3 e6 16 f3 ♘d6 17 ♘c3 ♖fc8 with equality (Dorfman-Glek, Tashkent 1984).

8 cxd5 ♘b6

After **8...cxd5** 9 ♘a3 ♘b6 10 ♕a5

♗f5 11 ♗f4 ♘c4 12 ♘xc4 dxc4 (Vaganian-Christiansen, Linares 1985) 13 ♕b4! would have given White the advantage.

9 ♕b3

After **9 ♕a3** correct is 9...♘fxd5! 10 e4 ♘c7 with the idea of 11...♘b5, securing an advantage, although 9...cxd5 is also satisfactory: 10 ♘c3 ♘e4! (10...♘c4 11 ♕b4 with advantage, Portisch-Ivkov, Petropolis 1973; 10...♗f5!? 11 b3 ♘e4 12 ♘d1 a5! led to equality, Oll-Norwood, London 1994) 11 ♗f4 ♘c4 12 ♕b4 ♘xc3 13 bxc3 e6 14 e4 ♕b6 15 ♕b3 ♗d7 16 exd5 exd5 17 ♘d2 ♗c6 with equal chances (Goldin-Epishin, Uzhgorod 1987).

9 ... ♘bxd5

9...♘fxd5 10 ♘c3 ♗e6 11 ♕c2 ♕c8 12 ♗g5 h6 13 ♘xd5 cxd5 14 ♕xc8 ♘xc8 15 ♗f4 g5 16 ♗c7 ♘b6 17 ♗xb6 axb6 18 e3 ♖fc8 is equal (J.Horvath-Neverov, Budapest 1993).

10 ♘bd2

After the more active **10 ♘c3 ♕b6** 11 ♕a4 ♖d8 12 ♖d1 ♗f5 13 ♘e5 ♘xc3 14 bxc3 ♘e4! 15 ♗xe4 ♗xe4 16 ♘d3 ♕b5 the position is equal (Pigusov-Sideif-Zade, Pavlodar 1987).

10...♕b6 11 ♕c2 ♘b4 12 ♕b1 c5 13 dxc5 ♕xc5 14 a3 ♘c6 15 b4 ♕b5 16 e4

(Oll-Dvoiris, Lviv 1990), and here 16...a5!, seizing the initiative on the queenside, would have given Black the advantage.

5.3 (1 d4 ♘f6 2 c4 g6 3 g3 ♗g7 4 ♗g2 c6 5 ♘f3 d5 6 0–0 0–0)

---

      7 ♘c3   dxc4

The critical move. Now a Catalan-type position arises, where White has a strong centre, but Black is a pawn up.

      8 ♘e5

After **8 e4** ♘bd7 9 ♕e2 ♘b6 10 ♖d1 h6 11 ♘e5 ♗e6 12 d5 cxd5 13 exd5 ♗f5 14 ♘xc4 ♘xc4 15 ♕xc4 ♕d7 the position is equal (Colle-Grünfeld, Meran 1924).

8 a4 ♘a6 (8...a5 9 e4 ♘fd7 10 ♕e2 ♘b6 11 ♖d1 ♗g4 12 h3 ♗xf3 13 ♗xf3 ♘a6 14 d5 ♕c7 15 h4 and White has compensation, Udovcic-Filip, Zagreb 1965) 9 e3 (9 ♘e5? ♘e8! 10 ♗e3 ♘d6 11 ♖c1 f6 12 ♘f3 ♘f5 gives Black the advantage, Trabanko-Dias, Kandas 1992) 9...♘d7 10 ♕e2 e5! (Popovic-Gligoric, Yugoslavia 1945), and now 11 ♕xc4 ♘b6 12 ♕e2 ♗e6! 13 ♖e1 ♗c4 14 ♕d1 exd4 would have given Black an excellent game.

      8   ...   ♘g4!

Less good is **8...♗e6** 9 e4 ♘bd7 10 f4 ♕b6 11 ♘f3 (clearly weaker is 11 f5? gxf5 12 exf5 ♗d5 13 ♘xd5 cxd5 14 ♘xd7 ♘xd7 15 ♗xd5 ♖ad8 with a great advantage, Alekhine-Bogoljubow, m/7 1929) 11...♖ad8 12 ♕e2 a5 13 ♔h1 ♕c7 14 a4 ♘b8 15 ♗e3 ♘a6 16 ♘g5 with advantage, Kjeld-Leskiewicz, Szeged 1994) or **8...♘e8** 9 e3 ♘d6 10 f4 ♗e6 11 e4 ♕c8 12 ♗e3 ♗h3 13 ♕e2 with good compensation for the pawn (Sharmse–Muruchak, Calcutta 1994).

      9 f4!

Weak is **9 ♘xg4** ♗xg4 10 d5 cxd5 11 ♕xd5 ♕xd5 12 ♗xd5 ♘c6 13 ♗xc4 ♖ac8 with advantage (Udovcic-O'Kelly, Belgrade 1952), while if **9 ♘f3** Black can repeat moves with 9...♘f6.

      9   ...   ♘xe5
      10 dxe5   ♕xd1

If **10...♕b6+** 11 ♔h1 ♖d8 12 ♕a4 ♗e6 13 e4 with the threat of f4-f5.

Norwood-Babu (Calcutta 1992) now continued 11 ♖xd1 ♘a6 12 ♗e3 ♗e6 13 ♖d2 ♖fc8 14 ♖ad1 h6 15 h3 f6 (if 15...b5 16 ♘xb5! cxb5 17 ♗xa8 ♖xa8 18 ♖d8+ ♖xd8 19 ♖xd8+ ♔h7 20 ♖a8 with advantage) 16 exf6 ♗xf6 17 ♗f2 ♔f7 18 e4 with compensation for the pawn, but not more.

5.4 (1 d4 ♘f6 2 c4 g6 3 g3 ♗g7 4 ♗g2 c6 5 ♘f3 d5 6 0–0 0–0)

---

      7 ♘e5   ♗e6

After **7...dxc4** 8 ♘xc4 ♗e6 9 ♕d3 ♘a6 10 ♖d1 ♕c8 11 e4 White has the advantage (Geller-Simagin, USSR 1958).

If **7...♘fd7** 8 cxd5 ♘xe5 9 dxe5 cxd5 10 f4 e6 11 ♗e3 ♘c6 12 ♗c5 ♖e8 13 ♘d2 ♗f8 (13...b6 14 ♗f2 ♗b7 15 e4 is interesting) 14 ♗xf8 ♖xf8 15 ♔h1 (or 15 e4 with the advantage, Fauland-

J.Horvath, Debrecen 1996) 15...♗d7 16 ♘b3 White is better.

7...♘g4 is an original try: 8 cxd5 cxd5 9 ♕b3 (9 f4!? is interesting) 9...♘c6 10 ♘xc6 bxc6 11 ♖d1 ♗a6 12 ♘c3 ♕b6 13 h3 ♘f6 (Bukal-Ruck, Harkany 1994), and here 14 ♗f4 promises White an advantage.

7...e6, by contrast, is very solid, but passive: 8 ♘c3 ♘fd7 9 ♘xd7?! (9 f4!? ♘xe5 10 dxe5 dxc4 11 ♗e3 also gives White a good game) 9...♘xd7 10 cxd5 exd5 11 ♗e3 ♖e8 12 ♕d2 ♘f6 13 ♗h6 ♗h8 14 f3 b6 15 ♖ad1 c5 16 ♗e3 ♗a6 17 ♖fe1 ♖c8 18 ♗f2 and White has a minimal advantage (Gavrikov-Ivanchuk, Irkutsk 1986).

8   cxd5   ♗xd5

As in all similar positions, the exchange of practically any pieces eases Black's problems. After **8...♘xd5** White gains the advantage by 9 e4 ♘b6 10 f4 ♗c4 11 ♖f3.

9 ♗xd5 cxd5 10 ♘c3 ♘e4 11 ♘xe4 dxe4 12 ♕b3 ♕b6 (12...♕xd4 13 ♕xb7 is dangerous) 13 ♕xb6 axb6 14 ♗e3 ♘c6 15 ♘xc6 bxc6 with equality (Kveinys-Jasnikowski, Polanica Zdroj 1992).

5.5 (1 d4 ♘f6 2 c4 g6 3 g3 ♗g7 4 ♗g2 c6 5 ♘f3 d5 6 0–0 0–0)

---

7   ♘a3!?

Smyslov's old move, which has seen some developments in recent times. Its drawback is that it reduces the pressure on the centre and weakens White's control of e4, although it also denies Black any serious play.

7   ...   ♗f5

After 7...e6 8 ♗f4 b6 9 ♕c1 ♗b7 10 ♗h6 ♘bd7 11 ♗xg7 ♔xg7 12 b3 (12 ♕f4 ♖c8 13 ♖ad1 is interesting)

12...♖c8 13 ♕b2 ♕e7 14 ♖ac1 ♔g8 15 b4! White retained some advantage (Smyslov-Averbakh, USSR 1955).

7...♕b6 8 b3 is possible:

(a) 8...♘e4 9 ♗b2 ♗e6 (9...a5 is interesting) 10 ♖c1 (10 ♘e1! is better) 10...♘a6 11 cxd5 cxd5 12 ♘c2 ♖ac8 with an excellent game (Szilagyi-Schmidt, Polanica Zdroj 1969);

(b) 8...♗f5 9 ♗b2 a5 10 ♘e5 ♖a6 11 ♘c2 ♗e4 12 f3 ♗xc2 13 ♕xc2 c5 with equality (Matlak-Schmidt, Poland 1992).

8   b3

After 8 ♗f4 ♗e4 (or 8...♕b6 9 ♕b3 dxc4 10 ♘xc4 ♕xb3 11 axb3 ♘d5 12 ♗d2 ♗e4 13 e3 ♘d7 and Black should easily equalise, Nogueiras-Pieterse, Tilburg 1992) 9 ♕d2 ♘bd7 10 ♖ac1 ♖e8 11 ♖fd1 ♘b6 12 b3 a5 13 ♕b2 ♘h5 14 ♗e3 e6 the position is equal (P.Nikolic-Hickl, Munich 1990).

8   ...   ♘bd7

After **8...a5** 9 ♗b2 ♘a6 10 ♘c2 ♗e4 11 ♘ce1 dxc4 12 bxc4 b5 13 ♘e5 White has the advantage (Lapienis-Alterman, USSR 1989), while if **8...♗e4** correct is 9 ♗b2 ♘bd7 10 e3 ♖e8 11 ♗h3 with the idea of 12 ♘g5.

9 ♗b2 ♘e4 10 ♘d2 ♘df6 11 ♘xe4 ♘xe4 12 f3 ♘d6 13 c5 ♘e8 14 e4 ♗e6 (P.Nikolic-Kamsky, Tilburg 1990), and

here 15 ♘c2 was correct, with some advantage. In general, it would be interesting to see Smyslov's idea being tested more seriously.

5.6 (1 d4 ♘f6 2 c4 g6 3 g3 ♗g7 4 ♗g2 c6 5 ♘f3 d5 6 0–0 0–0)

---

7   b3

White strengthens his centre and prepares to develop his bishop at b2, where it supports the d4 pawn and counters the bishop at g7. He has two subsequent plans: (a) a2-a3 and b3-b4, developing an initiative on the queenside; (b) e2-e4, gaining an advantage in the centre, although in this case the d4 pawn is weakened. Thematically 7 b3 has much in common with the next variation 7 ♘bd2.

Apart from 7...♗f5, which we cover in section 5.74 under the move order 7 ♘bd2 ♗f5 8 b3, Black's main replies are 7...♘e4 (5.61) and 7...a5 (5.62).

Other possibilities:

7...dxc4 8 bxc4 c5 (radically altering the situation, Black gives White a weakness at c4, but White gains a spatial advantage) 9 ♗b2 ♕b6 (somewhat weaker is 9...cxd4 10 ♘xd4 ♕b6 11 ♘b3 ♖d8 12 ♕c1 ♘c6 13 ♘c3 ♗e6

14 ♘a4 ♕c7 15 ♘ac5 ♗f5, P.Nikolic-Khalifman, Yerevan 1996, when 16 e4 ♗c8 17 ♖e1 with the idea of 18 e5 would have given White some advantage) 10 ♕c1 (after 10 ♕b3 ♘fd7! 11 e3 ♘c6 12 ♖d1 ♘a5 13 ♕xb6 ♘xb6 14 ♗c3 ♘bxc4 15 dxc5 ♗g4 16 ♗xg7 ♔xg7 17 ♘bd2 ♖ac8 Black has an excellent game, Buturin-Yandemirov, Lviv 1995) 10...cxd4 11 ♘xd4 ♘c6! (it is hard for White to strengthen his position, as the pressure on the c4 pawn is very unpleasant) 12 ♘xc6 bxc6 13 ♘d2 ♗e6 14 ♖b1 ♕a6 15 ♗a3 ♖fe8 16 ♖b3 ♘d7 with an equal game (Goldin-Yandemirov, Elista 1995).

7...c5 8 ♘bd2!? (slightly weaker is 8 e3 cxd4 9 exd4 ♘c6 10 ♗b2 ♗f5 11 ♘bd2, A.Maric-Von Allmen, Winterthur 1996, when 11...♖c8 equalises) 8...cxd4 9 ♘xd4 (insufficient is 9 ♗b2 d3 10 exd3 ♘c6 11 d4 ♗f5 12 ♘e5, Polugayevsky-I.Sokolov, Haninge 1989, and here 12...♖c8 would have equalised) 9...e5 10 ♘b5 a6 11 ♘c3 d4 12 ♘d5 ♘c6 13 ♗a3 ♖e8 14 ♗c5! ♘xd5 15 cxd5 ♘e7 (Manor-Brestian, Bern 1990), and here 16 d6 ♘f5 17 ♘c4 would have given White the advantage.

7...♗g4 8 ♗b2 ♘e4 (White has a clear advantage after 8...♗xf3 9 ♗xf3 ♘bd7 10 ♘d2 e6 11 a3 a5 12 ♕c2, Dzindzichashvili-Schmidt, Buenos Aires 1978, as Black has no real counterplay) 9 ♘e5 ♗e6 (Ribli-Smyslov, London 1983), and here White could have gained an advantage with 10 ♘d2 ♘d6 (10...♘xd2 11 ♕xd2 ♗xe5 12 dxe5 dxc4 is risky, as White gains a strong attack by 13 ♕h6 cxb3 14 ♖ad1 ♘d7 15 ♖d4) 11 c5 ♘f5 12 ♕c2 ♘d7 13 ♘ef3! followed by ♖fd1 and e2-e4.

7...b6 8 ♗b2 ♗b7 9 ♘bd2 (also good is 9 ♕c2 ♘bd7 10 ♘c3 e6 11

Rfd1 Qc7 12 Rac1 Rac8 13 Qb1 or 13 e4, in each case with a slight advantage, Darga-Galeb, Leipzig 1960) 9...Nbd7 10 Qb1 (a hypermodern move, but the more classical 10 Re1 or 10 Rc1 is also possible) 10...e6 11 Rc1 (11 Rd1 is also possible) 11...c5 (Larsen recommends 11...Qe7 followed by placing the rooks at d8 and c8, and only then opening the centre) 12 cxd5 Bxd5 13 dxc5 Nxc5 14 Bd4 Qe7 15 Qb2 Rfc8 16 Rc2 and the unpleasant pin on the c-file gives White an advantage (Larsen-Andersson, Buenos Aires 1980).

7...Be6 8 Nbd2 a5 9 e3 (or 9 cxd5 Nxd5 10 Nc4 a4 11 Bd2 Nf6 12 Rc1 axb3 13 axb3 Bd5 with an equal game, Kavalek-Hort, Manila 1976) 9...Nbd7 10 Bb2 a4 11 Bc3 axb3 12 axb3 Qb6 13 Re1 Bf5 14 Bf1 Ne4 15 Nxe4 Bxe4 16 Nd2 Bf5 with equality (P.Nikolic-Dolmatov, Groningen 1993), since White achieves nothing either with 17 c5, or with the plan of preparing e3-e4 by 17 f3.

5.61 (1 d4 Nf6 2 c4 g6 3 g3 Bg7 4 Bg2 c6 5 Nf3 d5 6 0-0 0-0 7 b3)

```
7   ...        Ne4
8   Bb2        Be6
```

After 8...Nd7 9 e3 (also good is 9 Nfd2!? Ndf6 10 Nc3 Nxd2 11 Qxd2 Be6 12 Na4! b6 13 Rac1 Qd7 14 Rfd1 with advantage, Korchnoi-Averbakh, USSR 1955) 9...Ndf6 (less good is 9...Nd6 10 Nbd2 b6 11 Rc1 Bb7 12 Ba3 Rc8 13 Ne1! Rc7 14 Nd3, when White has the better game, Furman-Bannik, USSR 1961) 10 Ne5 Be6 11 Qe2 Rc8 12 Rc1 Rc7 13 f3 Nd6 14 Nd2 Nf5 15 Rc2 c5 Black equalised (Tukmakov-Alterman, Elenite 1995).

If 8...Bf5:
(a) 9 Nc3 Nxc3 (after 9...dxc4 10 bxc4 c5 11 Na4 cxd4 12 Nxd4 Bxd4 13 Bxd4 Nc6 14 Be3 Qxd1 15 Rfxd1 Nd6 16 Rac1 Rfd8 17 h3 White retains the advantage, Ribli-Yermolinsky, Manila 1992) 10 Bxc3 Be4 11 Qd2 Nd7 12 a4 e5!? 13 Nxe5 Bxg2 14 Kxg2 Nxe5 15 dxe5 dxc4 16 Qxd8 Raxd8 17 bxc4 Rfe8 18 f4 f6! with complications (Buturin-Kirichenko, Lviv 1995);
(b) 9 Ne5 Nd7 10 Nd3 dxc4 11 bxc4 Nb6 12 g4 Nxc4 13 gxf5 Nxb2 14 Nxb2 Qxd4 with equality (P.Nikolic-I.Sokolov, Belgrade 1991);
(c) 9 e3 Nd7 10 Qe2 a5 (after 10...Qa5 11 Rc1 Rfe8 12 Nc3 Nxc3 13 Bxc3 Qa6 14 Bf1 dxc4 15 e4! Bg4 16 h3 Bxf3 17 Qxf3 e6 18 a4! White gained the advantage in P.Nikolic-Timman, Moscow 1994 – *Game 20*) 11 Nc3 Nxc3 12 Bxc3 Ndf6 13 Rfc1 Be4 14 Be1 e6 15 Bf1 c5 16 cxd5 cxd4 17 Nxd4 Bxd5 18 Rd1 Qb6 with equality (P.Nikolic-Svidler, Ter Apel 1996);
(d) 9 Qc1 Nd7 10 Rd1 Ndf6 11 Ne5 Qa5 12 Nc3 Nxc3 13 Bxc3 Qd8 14 Qf4 with some advantage to White (Marovic-Filip, Zagreb 1965).
9 Nbd2
After 9 Ne5 f5 10 f3 Nf6 11 Nd2 Nbd7 12 Nd3 Ne8!? 13 Qc2 Rc8 14

e4 White gained the advantage (Dizdar-Hulak, Vinkovci 1993).

9 ♕c1 ♘d7 **10 ♖d1** f5 **11** ♘e1 ♘d6 **12** ♘d2 ♔h8 **13** ♘d3 is a slower alternative, although here too White stands slightly better (Aseev-Glek, Lviv 1985).

9 ... ♘xd2

After 9...f5 10 ♖c1 ♘d7 11 cxd5?! (11 a3 with the idea of 12 ♘e1! looks better) 11...cxd5 12 e3 ♕a5 13 a4? (again 13 a3 is better) 13...♖fc8 14 ♗a3 ♗f6 15 ♖xc8+ ♖xc8 16 b4 ♕a6 17 ♘b1 ♘b6 White has many weaknesses on the c-file (Rechlis-Korchnoi, Jerusalem 1986).

10 ♕xd2

After 10 ♘xd2 c5 11 cxd5 ♗xd5 12 e4 ♗c6 13 ♘f3 ♗xe4 14 ♕e2 ♗xf3 15 ♗xf3 (Bönsch-Lechtinsky, Berlin 1982) 15...♘c6 16 dxc5 ♗xb2 17 ♕xb2 ♕a5 18 ♖ac1 ♖ad8 would have led to equality.

10 ... ♘a6

After 10...dxc4? 11 ♘g5! ♗g4 (11...cxb3 12 ♘xe6 fxe6 13 axb3 ♕d7 14 ♖fc1 e5 15 d5 e6 16 e4 cxd5 17 exd5 ♘c6! 18 ♗h3 ♖fd8! led to equality in Doda-Trifunovic, Halle 1963, although it looks dangerous for Black) 12 bxc4 h6 13 ♘f3 ♘d7 14 ♖fd1 White has an obvious advantage in the centre (Schmidt-Gauglitz, Dresden 1985), while **10...h6** 11 ♖ac1 ♘d7 12 ♖fd1 ♕b6 13 c5 ♕c7 14 ♕e3 b6 15 ♘e5! bxc5 16 ♘xg6 also gave White a clear advantage in Van Scheltinga-Stahlberg (Beverwijk 1963).

Now after 11 ♖ac1 ♕d6 12 ♘e5 ♖fd8 13 ♖fd1 ♖ac8 14 ♕a5! dxc4 15 ♘xc4 ♕c7 16 ♕e1! ♕b8 17 e4 White has an obvious advantage in the centre, although Black has a fairly solid position (Tal-Botvinnik, m/11 1960).

5.62 (1 d4 ♘f6 2 c4 g6 3 g3 ♗g7 4 ♗g2 c6 5 ♘f3 d5 6 0–0 0–0 7 b3)

7 ... a5
8 ♘c3

After 8 ♗b2 a4! 9 bxa4 dxc4?! 10 ♘a3 ♘bd7 11 ♘xc4 ♘b6 12 ♘xb6 ♕xb6 13 ♗c3 White is slightly better (Vasiliev-Ebralidze, USSR 1949), but 9...♕a5 is stronger, when Black has counterplay.

8 ... ♘e4
9 ♗b2

Now Black's main options are 9...♗f5 (5.621) and 9...♘xc3 (5.622).

9...a4?! is risky: 10 ♘xa4 dxc4 11 ♘e5 cxb3 12 axb3 ♗xe5 13 dxe5 ♘d2 14 ♖e1 ♗e6 15 ♘c5 ♖xa1 16 ♕xa1 ♘xb3 17 ♘xe6 fxe6 18 ♕a3 with advantage (Dautov-Belotti, Reggio Emilia 1996).

5.621 (1 d4 ♘f6 2 c4 g6 3 g3 ♗g7 4 ♗g2 c6 5 ♘f3 d5 6 0–0 0–0 7 b3 a5 8 ♘c3 ♘e4 9 ♗b2)

9 ... ♗f5

Now White has a number of possibilities:

10 ♘h4 ♘xc3 (play such as 10...♘a6!? 11 ♘xf5 gxf5 deserves to be tested) 11 ♗xc3 ♗e6 12 ♕d3 (12 c5 with the idea of ♕d2 is very interesting) 12...♘a6 13 e4!? (13 e3 is also good, but White wants to play more actively) 13...♘b4 14 ♕d2 (14 ♗xb4 axb4 15 ♖fd1 ♕a5 does not promise White anything, in view of the weaknesses at a2 and d4) 14...dxc4 15 bxc4 ♗xc4 16 ♖fd1 with compensation for the pawn (Tal-Dory, Berlin 1986).

10 ♘e5!? ♘xc3 **11 ♗xc3** ♘a6 (11...dxc4 12 bxc4 ♘d7 looks stronger) 12 cxd5 (12 ♕c1 with the idea of 13 ♖d1 is interesting) 12...cxd5 13 ♕d2! ♘b8 (13...b6 would weaken the critical c6 square) 14 a4 ♘c6 15 ♘xc6 bxc6 16 b4 axb4 17 ♗xb4 ♖e8 18 ♖fc1 with advantage to White in view of the weakness at c6 (Osnos-Lepyoshkin, USSR 1965).

10 ♖c1 ♘d7 **11** ♘h4 ♘xc3 **12** ♗xc3 ♗e6 (or 12...♘f6 13 ♘xf5 gxf5 14 ♕d3 ♘e4 15 ♗b2 ♕d7, A.Maric-Peng, Tilburg 1994, and here 16 f3 would have given White an advantage) 13 e4! dxe4 (bad is 13...dxc4 14 d5! with the better game) 14 ♗xe4 ♘f6 15 ♗g2 a4 16 ♕d2 axb3 17 axb3 ♕b6 18 ♕b2 ♖a6 19 d5! and White has the initiative, since in the centre he has a serious advantage (P.Nikolic-Gelfand, Sarajevo 1991).

10 e3 ♘d7 (after 10...♘xc3 11 ♗xc3 ♗e4 12 ♕e2 ♕c8 13 ♖fc1 a4 14 b4 dxc4 15 ♕xc4 ♘a6 16 ♕e2 White retains the advantage, Hulak-J.Horvath, Hungary 1993) 11 ♕e2 ♘xc3 12 ♗xc3 a4 13 cxd5 cxd5 14 ♕b5 axb3 15 axb3 ♕b6 16 ♕xb6 ♘xb6 17 ♗a5 ♖a6 18 ♗b4!, with the better game, since Black has to concede the important rook's file or to allow the creation of a weak a6 pawn after 18...♗f6 19 ♖xa6 bxa6 (P.Nikolic-Ftacnik, Manila 1992).

5.622 (1 d4 ♘f6 2 c4 g6 3 g3 ♗g7 4 ♗g2 c6 5 ♘f3 d5 6 0–0 0–0 7 b3 a5 8 ♘c3 ♘e4 9 ♗b2)

9	...	♘xc3
10	♗xc3	♗f5

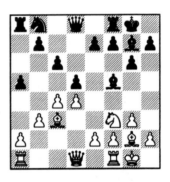

Alternatives:

10...a4 11 ♕d2 (a similar plan is 11 e3 ♗f5 12 ♕e2 ♘d7 13 ♖fc1 ♘f6 14 cxd5 cxd5 15 ♕b5 with advantage, Tseitlin-Zifroni, Israel 1996) 11...♘d7 12 cxd5 cxd5 13 ♗b4 ♖e8 (Pirc-Najdorf, Amsterdam 1950) and 14 ♖fc1 would have given an advantage.

10...♘d7 11 e3 (or 11 ♖c1 ♘f6 12 ♘e5 ♗e6 13 ♗a1 a4 14 b4 ♘d7, Matveeva-Xie, Moscow 1994, 15 cxd5 cxd5 16 ♕d3 with advantage) 11...♘f6 12 ♘e5 ♕b6 (P.Nikolic-Gelfand, Zurich 1994), and correct here was 13 ♖c1 ♗f5 14 f3 ♘d7 15 g4 ♗e6 16 c5 ♕a6 17 ♘d3 with the better game.

10...b5!? 11 ♖c1 ♘d7 12 cxd5 cxd5 13 ♗d2 ♗b7 14 ♗f4 ♕b6 15 ♖c7 ♗c6! 16 ♕c2 ♖fc8 and Black equalised (Tukmakov-Glek, Biel 1996).

11 ♘e5

Also interesting is **11 e3** ♗e4 12 ♕e2 ♘d7 13 ♖fc1 e6 14 ♗f1 ♗xf3 15 ♕xf3 f5 16 cxd5 exd5 17 b4 axb4 18 ♗xb4 ♖f7 19 a4 with the better game (Marin-

Hebert, Yerevan 1996); this is a model plan for White in this type of position.

Goldin-Svidler (Novosibirsk 1995) now continued 11...♘d7 12 cxd5 cxd5 13 ♖c1 (if 13 ♗xd5 ♘xe5 14 dxe5 ♕c7! 15 ♖c1 ♖fd8 with equal chances) 13...♗e4 14 ♗h3 ♘xe5 15 dxe5 ♖a6 16 ♕d2 a4 17 ♗d4 with a great advantage to White – the change in the structure after f2-f3 is unfavourable for Black, and in addition White has the plan with b3-b4 on the other side of the board.

5.7 (1 d4 ♘f6 2 c4 g6 3 g3 ♗g7 4 ♗g2 c6 5 ♘f3 d5 6 0–0 0–0)

7 ♘bd2

The ideas behind this move are similar to the previous variation. White avoids variations with the exchange on c4, and also he is ready to play e2-e4, without developing his bishop at b2.

Black can reply 7...♘e4 (5.71), 7...♘bd7 (5.72), 7...a5 (5.73) or 7...♗f5 (5.74).

5.71 (1 d4 ♘f6 2 c4 g6 3 g3 ♗g7 4 ♗g2 c6 5 ♘f3 d5 6 0–0 0–0 7 ♘bd2)

7 ...   ♘e4!?

---

8 b3

If **8 ♕b3** ♘xd2 (weaker is 8...♕b6 9 e3 ♘d7 10 cxd5 ♕xb3 11 axb3 cxd5 12 ♘xe4 dxe4 13 ♘g5, when Black has difficulties, Stein-Krogius, USSR 1962) 9 ♗xd2 dxc4 10 ♕xc4 ♗g4 11 ♕b4 ♕d7 12 ♘e5?! ♗xe5 13 dxe5 ♘a6 and Black stands well (Portisch-Chiburdanidze, Linares 1988).

8 e3 is not very active: 8...♘xd2 (also quite strong is 8...♗f5 9 cxd5 cxd5 10 ♕b3 ♕d7 11 ♘xe4 ♗xe4 12 ♗d2 ♘c6 13 ♖fc1 ♖fc8 with equality, Drasko-Schaefer, Budapest 1991) 9 ♘xd2 ♗e6 10 ♕b3 ♕d7 11 cxd5 ♗xd5 12 ♗xd5 cxd5 13 ♘f3 ♘c6 and the position is equal (Sandler-Handoko, Malaysia 1995).

8 ...   c5?!

8...♗f5 looks stronger, transposing into variation 5.74, whereas weaker is 8...f5 9 ♗b2 e6 10 ♘e5 ♘d7 11 ♘df3 ♕b6 12 c5 ♕c7 13 ♘d3 with the better game (Stern-Vokler, Germany 1992), or 8...♘c3 9 ♕e1 ♘e4 10 ♗b2 f5 11 e3 ♘d7 12 cxd5 cxd5 13 ♕e2 and White has a serious advantage (Livner-Olsson, Sweden 1995).

9 ♗b2

After **9 e3** ♘c6 10 ♗b2 ♘xd2 (not 10...e6? 11 ♖b1 ♕a5 12 ♘xe4 dxe4 13 ♘e5 ♘xe5 14 dxe5, and White's advantage is appreciable) 11 ♕xd2 dxc4 12 bxc4 cxd4 13 exd4 ♕b6 White has a hanging centre, which is rather dangerous for him.

P.Nikolic-Svidler (Yerevan 1996) now continued 9...♘xd2 10 ♕xd2 dxc4 11 bxc4 cxd4 12 ♘xd4 ♘c6 13 ♖fd1 ♘xd4 14 ♗xd4 ♕xd4 (interesting is 14...♗xd4 15 ♕xd4 ♕a5 16 c5 ♖b8 17 ♖ab1 ♕c7! when Black threatens to free himself by ...♗e6, but not 15...♕c7 16 ♖ab1 when White has the advantage) 15

♕xd4 ♗xd4 16 ♖xd4 ♖b8 17 c5! ♗e6 18 ♖a4 a6 19 c6! bxc6 20 ♖xa6 c5 21 a4 with a clear advantage to White in the ending.

5.72 (1 d4 ♘f6 2 c4 g6 3 g3 ♗g7 4 ♗g2 c6 5 ♘f3 d5 6 0–0 0–0 7 ♘bd2)

---

7 ... ♘bd7

Less good is **7...dxc4 8** ♘xc4 ♗e6 9 b3 ♘e4 10 ♗b2 ♘d7 11 ♕c2 ♘d6 12 e4 with a big spatial advantage (Csom-Hradeczky, Hungary 1972).

8 b3

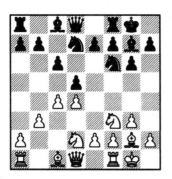

If **8 ♕c2** the correct move is not 8...♘b6? 9 c5 ♘bd7 10 b3 ♘e4 11 ♘xe4 dxe4 12 ♕xe4 ♘xc5 13 ♕h4 ♘e6 14 ♖d1 with a big advantage (Speelman-Szabo, Hastings 1981), but 8...dxc4 9 ♘xc4 ♘b6 10 ♘a5 ♗f5 11 ♕b3 ♕c8 12 ♗g5 ♖d8 13 ♕a3 h6 14 ♗xf6 ♗xf6 15 ♖ac1 ♗e4 16 e3 ♖d5 with a complicated game (Vaganian-Kupreichik, USSR 1983).

8 ... a5!?

Weaker is **8...♘e4 9** ♘xe4 dxe4 10 ♘g5 ♘f6 11 e3 ♗f5 12 ♕c2 c5 13 ♗b2 with a big advantage (Foldi-Gempe, Budapest 1996), or **8...e5 9** dxe5 ♘g4 10 ♗b2 (10 cxd5 cxd5 11 ♗b2 ♘dxe5

12 ♕c2 ♘xf3+ 13 ♗xf3 and White is slightly better, Kashdan-Sideman, USA 1940) 10...♘dxe5 11 ♘xe5 ♘xe5 12 cxd5 cxd5 13 ♗d4 ♗g4 14 ♘f3 ♗xf3 15 exf3 with the better game (Michalet-Delebarre, Paris 1991).

9 a4

9 ♗b2 or **9 a3!?** is worth trying.

9 ... b6
10 ♗b2 ♗b7
11 e3

11 ♕b1 c5 12 ♖d1, maintaining the centre, is interesting.

Now 11...e6 12 ♕e2 ♕e7 13 ♖fd1 c5 14 ♘e5 ♖fd8 15 ♖ac1 ♖ac8 leads to a symmetric position, where it is hard for White to make use of his two extra tempi (Georgiev-Andersson, Wijk aan Zee 1988).

5.73 (1 d4 ♘f6 2 c4 g6 3 g3 ♗g7 4 ♗g2 c6 5 ♘f3 d5 6 0–0 0–0 7 ♘bd2)

---

7 ... a5
8 b3

Other moves are weaker:

8 ♘e5 ♘bd7 (8...♘g4! may be even stronger, when White has nothing better than 9 ♘ef3 ♘f6, repeating the position) 9 ♘xd7 (if 9 ♘df3 ♘xe5 10 dxe5 ♘e4 11 cxd5 cxd5 12 ♗e3 ♗e6 13 ♖c1 ♕d7 14 ♕d4, Olafsson-Uhlmann, Havana 1966, 14...♖fc8 with equality) 9...♗xd7 10 a4 ♗e6 11 c5 ♘d7 12 e3 b6 with an excellent game for Black (Wichmann-Kaminski, Dresden 1996).

8 e3 ♗f5 9 ♕e2 ♘bd7 (weaker is 9...♖e8 10 ♘e5 ♕c8 11 b3 ♘bd7 12 ♗b2 a4 13 f3! with a great advantage, Kurajica-Tkachiev, Manila 1992) 10 b3 ♕b8 with the idea of ...b7-b5 and good counterplay.

Now Black has a number of different possibilities:

8...♗f5 9 ♗b2 ♘a6 (or 9...a4!? 10 ♘h4 ♗e6 11 ♕c2 a3!? 12 ♗c3 c5! 13 ♖ad1 cxd4 14 ♗xd4 ♘c6 with a sharp game, Adorjan-Horvath, Hungary 1992) 10 ♘e5 ♘g4 (or 10...♘d7 11 ♘xd7 ♕xd7 12 ♖c1 ♗h3, equalising) 11 ♘xg4 ♗xg4 12 cxd5 cxd5 13 ♘f3 ♗f5 14 ♕d2 ♗e4 15 ♖fc1 ♕b6 with equality (Butnorius-Kasparov, Daugavpils 1978).

8...a4, and now:

(a) 9 ♗b2 axb3 (after 9...a3 10 ♗c3 ♘e4 11 ♘xe4 dxe4 12 ♘g5 White is slightly better) 10 axb3 ♖xa1 11 ♕xa1 ♘a6 12 ♘e5 ♘g4 with equality (A.Petrosian-Faibisovich, Daugavpils 1978);

(b) 9 ♗a3 ♖e8 10 e3 ♗g4 11 h3 ♗xf3 12 ♘xf3 ♘bd7 13 ♕c2 e6 14 ♖fb1 with somewhat the better chances for White (Smejkal-Schmidt, Dubai 1986);

(c) 9 b4!? avoiding the opening of the rook's file) 9...b5 (less good is 9...♘bd7 10 b5! cxb5 11 cxb5 ♕a5 12 ♗a3 with advantage to White, but 9...♘e4 might be worth trying) 10 cxb5 cxb5 11 ♘e5 ♘g4 12 ♗b2 ♘xe5 13 dxe5 ♗b7 (after 13...♘c6 14 ♖c1!

♘xe5 15 ♖c5 e6 16 ♕a1 White has the initiative) 14 a3 ♘d7 15 f4 ♖c8 16 ♘f3 ♘b6 17 ♗d4 ♘c4 with a complicated game (Todorcevic-Fernandez, Leon 1991), although in view of the passivity of the black bishops after 18 ♕d3 ♕d7 19 h4, White nevertheless has the initiative.

8...♘e4 9 ♗b2 a4 (9...♗f5 leads to variations examined earlier) 10 bxa4 (after 10 ♘xe4 dxe4 11 ♘e1 f5 12 ♘c2 the game is equal, Ribli-Glek, Germany 1996) 10...♘c5! (weaker is 10...♕a5 11 cxd5 ♘xd2 12 ♘xd2 cxd5 13 ♘b3 ♕d8 14 a5 ♘c6 15 ♗c3 with advantage to White, Kaplan-Keene, Hastings 1967/8) 11 a5 (otherwise Black is threatening even to obtain the better game against the weak a-pawn, although 11 ♖c1 ♘xa4 12 ♗a1 with the idea of 13 e4 is worth trying) 11...♖xa5 (after 11...♕xa5 12 ♘b3 ♕b4 13 ♘xc5 ♕xb2 14 cxd5 cxd5 15 a4 ♗f5 16 e3 b6 17 ♘d3 ♕c3, Kavalek-Kupper, Thessaloniki 1984, 18 ♘fe5! would have given White some advantage) 12 ♘b3 ♘xb3 13 axb3 ♗f5 14 ♘h4 ♗e6 15 ♕c2 ♖xa1 16 ♖xa1 ♘a6 17 e3 ♕d7 18 ♗f1 ♖a8 and Black gradually equalised (Ribli-Stefansson, Altensteig 1992).

8...♗e6 9 ♗b2 a4! (the correct plan of creating counterplay on the flank) 10 bxa4 (this looks natural, but the following line deserves a more serious testing: 10 ♖e1 axb3 11 axb3 ♖xa1 12 ♕xa1 ♘a6 13 ♗c3 ♖e8 14 e4 ♘xe4 15 ♘xe4 dxe4 16 ♖xe4 ♕c8 17 ♘e5 and White has a slight advantage, Pigusov-Hauchard, Paris 1992) 10...♕a5 11 cxd5 cxd5 12 ♘e5 ♘bd7 13 ♘xd7 ♗xd7 14 ♘b3 ♕xa4 15 ♘c5 ♕xd1 16 ♖fxd1 ½-½ (Polugayevsky-Kasparov, Reggio Emilia 1992). White's a-pawn is too weak.

> **5.74 (1 d4 ♘f6 2 c4 g6 3 g3 ♗g7 4 ♗g2 c6 5 ♘f3 d5 6 0–0 0–0 7 ♘bd2)**

7 ...   ♗f5
8 b3

If **8 e3** ♘bd7 9 ♕e2 ♕a5 (or 9...♘e4 10 ♘h4 ♘xd2 11 ♗xd2 ♗e6 12 cxd5 cxd5 13 ♗b4 ♗f6 14 ♖fc1 ♕b6 with equality, Stempin-Bany, Poznan 1987) 10 a3 ♕a6 11 ♖e1 c5! 12 ♘h4 (Kurajica-A.Mikhalchishin, Sarajevo 1985) Black would have had an excellent game after 12...♗e6 13 cxd5 ♕xe2 14 ♖xe2 ♗xd5 15 e4 ♗c6!

8 ...   ♘e4

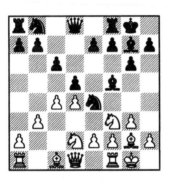

Less good is **8...♗e4** 9 ♗b2 e6 (Speelman-Bukic, Banja Luka 1983) 10 ♘xe4 ♘xe4 11 ♕c2 with advantage, or **8...♘bd7** 9 ♗b2 a5 (9...♗e4 10 ♘xe4 ♘xe4 11 ♘e5 e6 12 ♕c2 f5 13 ♘d3 and Black has many weaknesses, Marovic-Gligoric, Zagreb 1970) 10 h3!? ♘e4 11 g4 ♘xd2 12 ♘xd2 ♗e6 13 e4 dxc4 14 ♘xc4 and White is better (Piskov-Ftacnik, Germany 1993), or **8...♕a5** 9 ♘h4!? ♕c3 10 ♗a3 ♘e4 11 ♘xf5 gxf5 12 ♘xe4 fxe4 13 ♗xe7 ♖e8 14 ♗g5 dxc4 (Drasko-Pribyl, Tallinn 1985), and here 15 e3 cxb3 16 axb3 was correct, with a great advantage.

But the typical plan with the advance of the rook's pawn comes into consideration: **8...a5!?** 9 ♗b2 a4 10 ♘h4 ♗e6 11 ♕c2 a3! 12 ♗c3 c5! 13 ♖ad1 cxd4 14 ♗xd4 ♘c6 15 ♗xf6 ♗xf6, completely equalising (Polugayevsky-Gelfand, Reggio Emilia 1987).

9 ♗b2
Here Black has the following possibilities: **9...♘xd2 (5.741)**, **9...♕a5 (5.742)**, **9...♘d7 (5.743)** and **9...a5 (5.744)**.

> **5.741 (1 d4 ♘f6 2 c4 g6 3 g3 ♗g7 4 ♗g2 c6 5 ♘f3 d5 6 0–0 0–0 7 ♘bd2 ♗f5 8 b3 ♘e4 9 ♗b2)**

9 ...   ♘xd2
10 ♕xd2

After **10 ♘xd2** ♕d7 11 ♖c1 ♘a6 12 cxd5 cxd5 the game is equal (Lengyel-Dely, Kecskemet 1968).

10 ...   ♗e4
Weaker is **10...a5** 11 ♖fc1! ♗e4 12 e3 e6 13 ♕e2! with the better game.

Particular note should be made of this set-up, which is typical for White. After 13...a4 14 ♗f1 ♗xf3 15 ♕xf3 ♘d7 16 ♕e2 ♕e7 17 ♕c2 ♖fe8 18 ♗c3 he has the advantage (Ribli-Najdorf, Nice 1974).

If **10...♘a6** 11 ♘h4 ♗e6 12 ♖ac1 ♗f6 13 ♖fe1 ♕d7 14 ♘f3 ♖fd8 15 e4, and again White has the advantage in the centre (Osnos-Sakharov, USSR 1969).

Izeta-de la Villa (Leon 1996) now continued 11 ♖ac1 e6 12 ♖fd1 ♘d7 13 ♗f1 ♗xf3 14 exf3 a6 15 h4 ♘f6 16 a4 ♕d7 17 ♔g2 ♖fb8 18 ♗a3 with advantage to White.

5.742 (1 d4 ♘f6 2 c4 g6 3 g3 ♗g7 4 ♗g2 c6 5 ♘f3 d5 6 0–0 0–0 7 ♘bd2 ♗f5 8 b3 ♘e4 9 ♗b2)

---

9   ...   ♕a5

Introduced by Gligoric, this was for a long time considered the main move, but recent games have shaken its reliability – it does after all provoke White into seizing space on the queenside, without any real counterplay for Black.

10   a3

Nothing is achieved by other continuations:

10 ♘xe4 ♗xe4 11 e3 ♘d7 12 ♕e2 (12 cxd5?! ♕xd5 13 ♘e1 ♗xg2 14 ♘xg2 ♖fd8 15 ♕e2 e5 16 e4 ♕e6 and Black's chances are slightly better, Pachman-Gligoric, Havana 1966)

12...♘f6 13 ♖fc1 e6 14 ♗f1 ♗xf3 15 ♕xf3 ♘e4 16 ♕e2 ♖fe8 17 ♖c2 ♖ad8 with equal chances (Andersson-Gligoric, Hastings 1971/2).

10 ♕e1 ♘xd2 11 ♕xd2 ♕xd2 12 ♘xd2 ♖d8 13 ♖fd1 ♘a6 14 ♖ac1 ♖ac8 15 a3 ♘c7 16 cxd5 cxd5 17 ♘f1 ♗d7 and the game is equal (Portisch-Gligoric, Skopje 1968).

10 ♕c1 ♗h6 (10...♘d7 11 ♖d1 ♗h6 12 e3 ♖ac8 13 ♘xe4 ♗xe4 14 ♕d2 ♕xd2 15 ♘xd2 ♗xg2 with an equal game, Averkin-Gufeld, Moscow 1969) 11 e3 ♘d7 12 ♘xe4 ♗xe4 13 ♗c3 ♕d8 14 ♖d1 (Smyslov-Scholl, Amsterdam 1971), and now 14...e6! 15 ♕b2 ♕f6 would have given an equal game (Keres).

10   ...   ♘d7
11   b4   ♕d8

After **11...♕a6** 12 ♖c1 ♗h6 13 e3 ♘xd2 14 ♘xd2 ♗d3 15 ♕b3! ♗xf1 16 ♗xf1 ♕b6 17 cxd5 cxd5 18 ♕xd5 ♘f6 19 ♕b3 ♖ac8 20 ♖c5 White has a strong initiative for the exchange (Georgiev-Ftacnik, Varna 1987).

12   ♕b3

Better than 12 ♖c1 b5! 13 cxd5 cxd5 14 a4 bxa4 15 ♕xa4 ♘b6 16 ♕a6 ♕d7, when the chances are equal (Tseshkovsky-Dvoretsky, USSR 1974).

12   ...   ♘b6

After **12...♘df6** 13 a4 ♖e8 14 ♖fd1 ♘g4 15 ♘xe4 ♗xe4 16 c5 White's position is preferable (Ribli-Andersson, Wijk aan Zee 1973).

Ribli-Timman (Novi Sad 1990) continued 13 c5 ♘d7 14 a4 ♖e8 15 ♖fd1! e5 16 dxe5 ♘xd2 (after 16...♘xe5 17 ♘xe4 ♗xe4 18 ♘xe5 ♗xe5 19 ♗xe4 ♗xb2 White gains the advantage by 20 ♗xd5!, Ribli) 17 ♘xd2 ♗xe5 18 ♗xe5 ♖xe5 19 e3 ♕f6 20 ♕c3! with advantage to White.

> **5.743 (1 d4 ♘f6 2 c4 g6 3 g3 ♗g7
> 4 ♗g2 c6 5 ♘f3 d5 6 0–0 0–0 7
> ♘bd2 ♗f5 8 b3 ♘e4 9 ♗b2)**

> **9 ...   ♘d7**
> **10 ♘h4**

The logical continuation. Weaker is
10 ♘xe4 ♗xe4 11 ♕d2 a5 12 cxd5
cxd5 13 ♖fe1 ♘f6 14 ♕f4 ♕d6 15 ♕h4
h6 with an excellent game for Black
(Krivonosov-Kutsyn, Minsk 1996).

> **10 ...   ♘xd2**
> **11 ♕xd2   ♗e6**

After 11...♘f6 12 ♘xf5 gxf5 (Hort-
Kavalek, Tilburg 1980) 13 ♕f4 gives
White the advantage.

> **12 e4   dxe4**
> **13 ♗xe4   ♗h3**
> **14 ♖fe1**

Slightly weaker is 14 ♖fd1 ♕c7 15
♗g2 ♗xg2 16 ♘xg2 ♖ad8 17 ♕e2
♖fe8 18 ♘e3 ♘f6 19 ♖ac1 ♕a5 20 ♗c3
♕h5 with equality (Razuvaev-Vogt,
Leipzig 1983).

> **14 ...   ♖e8**

After 14...e6 15 ♗h1 ♗f6 16 ♘f3
♗g4 17 ♖ad1 ♕c7 18 ♖e4! ♗xf3 19
♗xf3 ♖fd8 20 ♕e2 ♘f8 21 h4 White
has the advantage (Portisch-Pachman,
Moscow 1967).

> **15 f4!?**

Nothing is achieved by 15 ♗h1 ♕c7
16 d5 ♗xb2 17 ♕xb2 cxd5 18 ♗xd5
♘f6 19 ♗h1 ♗d7 (Vukic-Pietzsch,
Sarajevo 1967).

> **15 ...   ♕b6**
> **16 ♘f3**

White has a slight advantage
(A.Mikhalchishin-Lutz, Dortmund 1991).

> **5.744 (1 d4 ♘f6 2 c4 g6 3 g3 ♗g7
> 4 ♗g2 c6 5 ♘f3 d5 6 0–0 0–0 7
> ♘bd2 ♗f5 8 b3 ♘e4 9 ♗b2)**

> **9 ...   a5**

The most logical continuation. The
plan of creating counterplay on the
queenside demands of White an active
response in the centre.

> **10 ♘h4**

After 10 ♖c1 a4 11 b4 ♘a6 (11...a3!?
12 ♗a1 ♘d7 is worth trying, with
adequate counterplay) 12 a3 ♘c7 13
cxd5 cxd5 14 ♘e5 White has the advantage (Todorcevic-Averbakh, Palma
de Mallorca 1989).

Or 10 e3 a4 11 ♘xe4 ♗xe4 12 cxd5
cxd5 13 bxa4 ♘c6 14 ♗c3 ♖a7 15 ♘e5
♘xe5 16 dxe5 ♗xg2 17 ♔xg2 e6 and
Black equalised (Pelts-Westerinen,
Thessaloniki 1984).

> **10 ...   ♘xd2**

11 ♕xd2   ♗e6

After 11...♗c8 12 e4 dxe4 13 ♗xe4 ♗h3 14 ♖fe1 ♘d7 15 ♗h1 (15 ♖ad1!?) 15...♘f6 16 ♘f3 h6 (Spassky-Najdorf, Santa Monica 1966), 17 ♖ad1 ♗g4 18 ♕f4 gives White the advantage.

12 f4!?

After 12 e4 correct is 12...dxc4! 13 d5 ♗xb2 14 ♕xb2 cxd5 15 exd5 ♗xd5 16 ♖fd1 c3 17 ♕xc3 e6 and Black has no problems (Najdorf).

Now after 12...f5 13 ♖fc1 ♘d7 14 ♕e3 ♗f7 15 cxd5 cxd5 16 ♗a3 ♖e8 17 ♘f3 ♘f6 (Ljubojevic-Uhlmann, Manila 1976), 18 ♘e5 would have maintained the pressure.

Game 18
Tukmakov-Uhlmann
Szirak 1985

---

1 d4 ♘f6 2 c4 g6 3 g3 c6 4 ♘f3 ♗g7 5 ♗g2 d5 6 ♕b3 a5!?

Black tries to develop a pawn offensive on the queenside, and it has to be said that there are weighty arguments in favour of this interesting plan. Bad now is 7 ♘c3 a4! 8 ♘xa4 dxc4, and in general the threat of ...a5-a4 is very unpleasant.

7 ♗f4 a4 8 ♕b4 ♘bd7 9 0–0

9 ♘c3 looks slightly better, but even after this move Black has no problems.

9...♕b6!

Very strong: the ending is very good for Black in view of his queenside superiority.

10 ♕xb6 ♘xb6 11 c5

After 11 cxd5 ♘fxd5! 12 ♗d2 f5 Black has an excellent game.

11...♘c4 12 ♘e5

White sacrifices a pawn. After 12 ♘a3 ♘xa3! (12...♘xb2!? 13 ♖ab1 ♘c4 14 ♘xc4 dxc4 15 ♘e5 ♘d5 16 ♘xc4

♘xf4 17 gxf4 ♗e6 gives Black a slight edge) 13 bxa3 ♘e4 with the threat of ...♘c3-b5 Black has the advantage.

12...♘xb2 13 ♘a3 ♘d7 14 ♖ab1 ♗xe5! 15 ♗xe5

If 15 dxe5, then 15...♘c4 16 ♘xc4 dxc4 and Black has a serious advantage.

15...♘xe5 16 dxe5 ♘c4 17 ♘xc4 dxc4 18 ♖fc1

White appears to have a lead in development and the open b-file, but in fact after the next move it becomes clear that Black has the advantage – the white bishop at g2 is completely out of play.

18...♔d8! 19 ♖xc4 ♔c7 20 ♗e4

This attempt to reanimate the bishop does not help much.

20...♖d8 21 ♗d3 ♗e6 22 ♖c2

If 22 ♖cb4 there follows 22...♖a7 with a big advantage.

22...a3!

The fixing of the a2 pawn signifies that White faces a gruelling defence.

23 f4 h5 24 h4 ♖d4 25 ♔f2 ♖aa4! 26 ♖c3 ♔b8

Clearly not 26...♗xa2? 27 ♖a1 ♗e6 28 ♖axa3 with equality.

27 ♔e3 ♗d5 28 ♖xa3?

White wants to extricate himself by tactical means, but 28 ♔f2 was better.

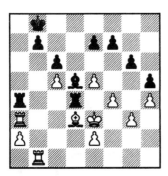

28...⊒xf4! 29 ⊒ab3 ⊒fe4+!!
Black too finds some tactics.
30 ⌾f2
If 30 ⌾xe4 ⊒xe4+ 31 ⌾d3 ⌾xb3 32 ⌾xe4 (32 axb3 ⊒xe5 33 b4 is like the game) 32...⌾c2+ with a concluding fork.
30...⌾xb3 31 axb3 ⊒ab4 32 ⌾xe4 ⊒xe4 33 ⌾f3 ⊒xe5 34 b4
This rook ending, where Black is a pawn up and the opponent has numerous weaknesses, is easily won.
34...⊒d5 35 ⌾e3 ⌾c7 36 ⊒a1 e5!
Creating an outpost for the rook.
37 ⊒a8 ⊒d8!
Depriving the opponent of counterplay is one of the main principles of endgame play.
38 ⊒a3 ⊒d4 39 ⊒b3 ⌾d7 40 ⌾f3
After 40 b5 ⊒c4 White loses a second pawn.
40...⌾e6 41 e4 f5 42 exf5+ ⌾xf5
White resigned, since if 43 b5 Black wins most simply by 43...⊒d3+!, going into a pawn ending.

Game 19
Dorfman-Hulak
Moscow 1977

---

1 d4 ⌽f6 2 c4 g6 3 g3 ⌾g7 4 ⌾g2 c6 5 ⌽f3 0–0 6 0–0 d5 7 ⌾a4 dxc4

Black decides to concede the centre immediately and to gain several tempi for the development of his pieces by attacking the queen, but two other continuations look more logical:
(a) 7...⌽bd7 8 cxd5 ⌽b6 9 ⌾a3 cxd5 10 ⌽c3 ⌾f5 11 b3 ⌽e4 12 ⌽d1 a5! with an excellent game (Oll-Norwood, London 1994);
(b) 7...b5!? 8 cxb5 cxb5 9 ⌾b3 a5 10 ⌽e5 e6 11 ⌾f4 ⌾b6 and Black again has no problems (Csom-Xie, Budapest 1992).
In fact the most interesting continuation is 7...a5!?, leading to an initiative for Black on the queenside.
From these variations one can draw the simple conclusion that, if White really wants to move his queen, then 7 ⌾b3 is more logical.
8 ⌾xc4 ⌾e6
The critical move, although another idea is also not bad: 8...⌾f5 9 ⌽c3 ⌽e4 10 ⌽h4 ⌾e6 11 ⌾d3 ⌽xc3 12 bxc3 ⌽d7 13 a4 (13 e4 b5!) 13...⌽b6 14 a5 ⌾c4 15 ⌾c2 ⌽d7 with a complicated game (Khalifman-Ruck, Vienna 1996).
At the same time, 8...⌽a6 is weaker: 9 ⌽e5 ⌾a5 10 e4 ⌾e6 11 ⌾e2 ⊒ad8 12 ⊒d1 and White occupies the centre (Csom-Schwarz, Budapest 1994).
9 ⌾a4
Weaker is 9 ⌾b4 ⌾b6!? 10 ⌾xe7 ⌽a6 11 ⌾a3 ⊒fe8 12 ⌽c3 ⌾c4 13 ⌽e5 ⌾xd4 14 ⌽xc4 ⌾xc4 15 ⌾f4 ⊒ad8 16 ⌾b3 ⌾b4 with excellent counterplay (Zaichik-Kamsky, Pavlodar 1987).
9...⌽bd7 10 ⌽g5
After 10 ⌽c3 ⌾f5 11 ⊒d1 a5! 12 ⌽h4 ⌽b6 13 ⌾b3 ⌾e6 14 ⌾c2 ⌽fd5 15 ⌽f3 a4 16 h3 h6 17 e4 ⌽b4 18 ⌾b1 ⌾c8 19 ⌾h2 ⊒a5! Black has good piece pressure on the centre (Timoshchenko-Ivanov, Podolsk 1990).

10...♗g4

10...♘b6 11 ♕d1 ♗c8 is also possible, although more passive.

11 ♕d1 ♘b6

Black is reluctant to make such a move, although the white queen is forced to retreat, but his bishop also has to find a new post. It would have been stronger to exchange the light-square bishop by 11...h6! 12 h3 ♗h5! 13 ♘f3 ♗xf3, which leads to equality.

12 h3 ♗c8 13 ♘c3 h6 14 ♘f3 ♗f5

As always in cramped positions, it was worth exchanging a piece by 14...♘bd5 or else gaining space by 14...a5 and 15...a4.

15 ♘h4 ♗e6 16 e4 ♕d7 17 ♔h2 ♖ad8 18 ♘f3 ♘h7

Somewhat decentralising – better was 18...♕c8 with the idea of ...♗c4 and ...c6-c5, attacking the centre.

19 ♕c2 ♕c8 20 b3 ♖fe8

If 20...f5 White has the strong reply 21 ♘h4!

21 ♗e3 ♘g5 22 ♘xg5 hxg5 23 ♖ad1 g4 24 hxg4

It also looks good to block the file by 24 h4, but White himself is intending to use it.

24...♗xg4 25 f3 ♗e6 26 ♘e2 ♔h7

26...♘d7 is unpleasantly met by 27 ♘f4.

27 ♖h1 ♖h8 28 ♔g1+ ♔g8 29 ♖xh8+ ♗xh8 30 ♘f4 ♗d7 31 ♔f2 ♗g7

(see diagram next column)

32 ♕c5!

Threatening to switch the queen to the h-file by ♕g5-h4.

32...♖e8 33 ♖h1 e5

33...e6 looks a tougher defence.

34 ♘d3 f6

The exchange 34...exd4 35 ♗xd4 also does not bring any relief.

35 dxe5 fxe5 36 ♕d6 ♖e6 37 ♕a3 ♕b8 38 ♘c5 ♗f8 39 ♕c1 ♖e8 40 ♗f1 ♗c8 41 a4 a5

This weakens Black's pawns, but he has no adequate defence against the gradual improvement of White's position.

42 ♕d2 ♕c7 43 ♕xa5 ♘d5 44 ♕xc7 ♘xc7 45 ♗c4+ ♘e6 46 ♖d1 ♗xc5 47 ♗xc5 ♔f7 48 ♖h1 ♔f6 49 ♗b6 ♔g7 50 ♔e3 ♖f8 51 f4 ♔f6

After 51...exf4+ 52 gxf4 ♘xf4 White wins by 53 ♗d4+.

52 ♖h7 ♖e8 53 b4 ♖f8 54 ♗a7 1–0

Game 20
P.Nikolic-Timman
Moscow Olympiad 1994

1 d4 ♘f6 2 c4 g6 3 ♘f3 ♗g7 4 g3 0–0 5 ♗g2 c6 6 0–0 d5 7 b3 ♘e4

With this active move Black tries to exchange a pair of knights and thereby reduce his slight lack of space. The other moves 7...♗f5, 7...♗e6 and 7...a5 are also logical in their own way.

8 ♗b2 ♗f5 9 e3

Somewhat weaker is 9 ♘e5 ♘d7 10 ♘d3 dxc4 11 bxc4 ♘b6 12 g4 ♘xc4 13 gxf5 ♘xb2 14 ♘xb2 ♕xd4 15 ♕xd4 ♗xd4 16 ♗xe4 ♗xb2 with full equality (P.Nikolic-I.Sokolov, Belgrade 1991).

9...♘d7 10 ♕e2 ♕a5 11 ♖c1 ♖fe8 12 ♘c3

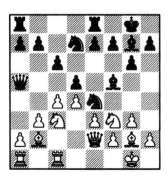

12...♘xc3

Initially Black was planning the central break 12...e5, but after lengthy reflection he decided against it, although nothing terrible for him is apparent:

(a) 13 cxd5 exd4 14 ♘xd4 ♗xd4 15 exd4 ♘xg3 16 ♕d1 ♘e4 17 dxc6 bxc6 18 d5 with a slight advantage for White;

(b) 13 dxe5 ♘xe5 14 ♘d4 ♗g4 15 f3 and now there is the sharp possibility 15...♘xf3+!?. However, all these variations are very hard to calculate, so Timman decided to play logically and quietly against the weakness at c4, but he ran into an unexpected pawn sacrifice.

13 ♗xc3 ♕a6 14 ♗f1 dxc4 15 e4!

Weaker is 15 bxc4 e5! with an excellent game.

15...♗g4 16 h3 ♗xf3 17 ♕xf3 e6 18 a4!

An excellent prophylactic move, not only denying Black play on the queenside, but also seizing the initiative there. After 18 ♗xc4 b5 19 ♗f1 ♕b6 Black has an excellent position.

18...♕b6 19 a5 ♕d8

After 19...♕xb3? 20 ♖cb1 ♕c2 21 ♖b2 the queen is lost.

20 ♗xc4 b5 21 axb6 axb6 22 e5!

This increases White's spatial advantage and opens the way to Black's main weakness – his c6 pawn.

22...♖xa1 23 ♗xa1!

The pressure on the c6 pawn is much more important than the occupation of the a-file. Now 23...c5 is bad because of 24 ♗b5.

23...♗h6 24 ♖c2 ♕a8 25 ♗b2 ♖c8 26 ♔g2

The immediate 26 ♗d3 was more accurate, with the idea of avoiding the counterplay that Black obtains in the game.

26...b5 27 ♗d3 ♘b6 28 ♗e4 ♘d5 29 h4!

Black has improved somewhat his position on the queenside and in the centre, so White begins play on the opposite side.

29...♘b4 30 ♖e2 ♕a7 31 h5 c5?!

It would have been better to move the queen closer to the king.

32 hxg6 hxg6 33 ♕g4 c4

If 33...♕b6 there follows 34 dxc5 ♕xc5 35 ♖e1! when White has a strong attack.

34 ♗xg6! c3 35 ♗e4+ ♔f8 36 ♕h4 ♔g7 37 ♗xc3! 1–0

6 Solid Variation with 6 cxd5

1	d4	♘f6
2	c4	g6
3	g3	♗g7
4	♗g2	c6
5	♘f3	d5
6	cxd5	cxd5

The exchange on d5 always leads to symmetric positions with a slight advantage to White, since he has the possibility of being the first to begin an attack. Black does best to depart from the symmetry as soon as possible.

White has three main options: 7 ♘e5 (6.1) , 7 0–0 (6.2) and 7 ♘c3 (6.3).

6.1 (1 d4 ♘f6 2 c4 g6 3 g3 ♗g7 4 ♗g2 c6 5 ♘f3 d5 6 cxd5 cxd5)

7	♘e5	♘c6

Or 7...♘fd7 8 ♘xd7 (after 8 ♗xd5 ♘xe5 9 dxe5 e6 10 ♗g2 ♕xd1+ 11 ♔xd1 ♗xe5 12 ♘c3 ♘a6 13 ♗e3 White has a slight plus, King-I.Sokolov, Dortmund 1989) 8...♕xd7 9 ♘c3 ♘c6 (if 9...0–0 there follows 10 ♘xd5 e6 11 ♘c3 ♕xd4 12 0–0 ♘c6 13 ♗g5 e5 14 ♖c1 ♗e6 15 ♗xc6! bxc6 16 e4 c5 17

♕c2 with some advantage to White (Dorfman-Chiburdanidze, Tashkent 1980) 10 ♘xd5 ♘xd4 11 ♗d2 ♘c6 12 ♕b3 0–0 13 ♗c3 e6 14 ♗xg7 ♔xg7 15 ♘b4! ♘d4 16 ♕c4 ♖d8 17 e3 and White has the advantage (Romanishin-Sveshnikov, Sochi 1984).

8	♘c3	♗d7!?

8...e6 or 8...0–0 transposes into the main positions, examined below.

Andersson-Glek (Biel 1996) now continued 9 0–0 e6 10 ♗g5 (10 ♗f4 or 10 e4!? is also possible) 10...h6 11 ♗xf6 ♗xf6 12 ♘xd7 ♕xd7 13 e4!? dxe4 14 d5!? exd5 15 ♘xd5 ♗g7 (rather dangerous is 15...♗xb2 16 ♖b1 0–0–0 17 ♗xe4 ♖he8 18 ♗g2, when the black king comes under attack) 16 ♗xe4 ♖d8 (also good is 16...♕d6!? 17 ♕b3 ♖b8 18 ♖ad1 0–0 with an equal game, Glek) 17 ♕a4 0–0 18 ♖ad1 ♕g4 (or 18...♕d6!? with a complicated game, Glek) 19 ♘e3 ♕c8 20 b3 ♖fe8!? and Black gradually equalised.

6.2 (1 d4 ♘f6 2 c4 g6 3 g3 ♗g7 4 ♗g2 c6 5 ♘f3 d5 6 cxd5 cxd5)

7	0–0	0–0
8	♘e5	

Now Black has 8...♘c6 (6.21) or 8...♘g4 (6.22).

8...e6 9 ♘c3 transposes into variation 6.321.

6.21 (1 d4 ♘f6 2 c4 g6 3 g3 ♗g7 4 ♗g2 c6 5 ♘f3 d5 6 cxd5 cxd5 7 0–0 0–0 8 ♘e5)

8	...	♘c6

9 ♘c3

Here Black's main options are **9...♘xe5 (6.211)** and **9...♗f5 (6.212)**.

Less good is **9...♗e6** 10 ♗f4 ♖c8 11 ♖c1 ♕a5 12 ♕d2 ♖fd8 13 ♖fd1 ♘xe5 14 ♗xe5 ♘e8 15 ♗xg7 ♔xg7 16 ♕e3 ♘f6 17 h3 with advantage to White (Hug-Balster, Gelsenkirchen 1991), or **9...♘d7** 10 ♘xd5 (10 f4 ♘dxe5 11 fxe5 is also possible) 10...♘dxe5 (bad is 10...♘xd4? 11 ♕xd4 ♘xe5 12 ♕c5 e6 13 ♘e7+ ♔h8 14 ♗f4 ♕b6 15 ♖ac1 with clearly the better game, Mager-ramov-Malaniuk, Daugavpils 1978) 11 dxe5 ♗xe5 12 ♗h6 ♖e8 13 ♕d2 with some advantage (Filip-Hort, Czechoslo-vakia 1968).

The unexpected **9...♗d7** 10 ♗g5 ♗e8 11 ♗xf6? (better 11 ♕d2! with advantage) 11...♗xf6 12 ♘xd5 ♗g7 13 e3 ♘xe5 14 dxe5 ♗xe5 15 ♕b3 e6 enabled Black to equalise in Korchnoi-Ljubojevic (Brussels 1986).

> **6.211 (1 d4 ♘f6 2 c4 g6 3 g3 ♗g7 4 ♗g2 c6 5 ♘f3 d5 6 cxd5 cxd5 7 0–0 0–0 8 ♘e5 ♘c6 9 ♘c3)**

9 ...   ♘xe5

This exchange is clearly premature, as the white pieces occupy the centre.

10 dxe5   ♘g4
11 ♕xd5!

This is what the experts on this variation play, although *ECO* considers **11 ♘xd5 ♘xe5** (less good is 11...e6? 12 ♘f6+ ♘xf6 13 ♕xd8 ♖xd8 14 ♗g5 and wins, Taleb-Campos, Halle 1995, or 11...♗xe5 12 ♕b3 ♖b8 13 ♗g5 ♖e8 14 ♖ad1 with a great advantage), and now:

(a) 12 ♗g5 ♘c6 13 ♕d2 (or 13 ♕a4 h6 14 ♗e3 ♗d7 15 ♖ad1 e6 16 ♘c3 ♕c8 17 ♕b3 b6 18 ♘e4 with the better chances, Stohl-Uhlmann, Germany 1994) 13...f6 14 ♗e3 e6 15 ♘b4 ♕xd2 16 ♗xd2 and White stands better;

(b) 12 ♕b3 ♘c6 (if 12...e6 13 ♘c3 ♕a5 14 ♖d1 ♖b8 15 ♗d2 ♗d7 16 a4 ♕b6 17 ♕xb6 axb6 18 b3 with the better game, Schmidt-Uhlmann, Poland 1974) 13 ♖d1 (possibly no worse is 13 ♗e3 e6 14 ♘c3 ♘d4 15 ♗xd4 ♕xd4 16 ♖fd1 ♕e5 17 ♖d3 with advantage, Sämisch-Grünfeld, Carlsbad 1923) 13...e6 14 ♘c3 ♕a5 15 ♗e3 e5 16 ♕b5 and White is better, since Black is weak on the dark squares (Petrosian-Uhlmann, Havana 1966).

11 ...   ♘xe5
12 ♕c5!

After **12 ♗g5 ♘c6** 13 ♖fd1 (or 13 ♕c5 ♕b6! 14 ♕xb6 axb6 15 ♖fd1 h6

16 ♗e3 b5! and Black stands well, Lisitsyn-Zurakhov, USSR 1956) 13...♕b6 14 ♕b3 ♕xb3 15 axb3 h6 16 ♗e3 ♗e6 17 b4 a6 Black equalised in Conquest-Hauchard (Clichy 1993).

12 ... ♕d6

After 12...♘c6 13 ♖d1 ♕b6 14 ♕a3 ♗e6 15 ♗e3 ♕a5 16 ♕xa5 ♘xa5 17 ♘d5 ♗xb2 18 ♘xe7+ ♔g7 19 ♖ab1 ♗e5 20 ♘d5 White has an obvious advantage (Romanishin-Martin, Barcelona 1984).

Romanishin-Kuzmin (Kiev 1978) now continued 13 ♕xd6 exd6 14 ♗g5 ♘c4 15 ♖ac1 ♗e6 (after 15...♘xb2 16 ♘b5 White has many threats) 16 ♘d5 ♘xb2 17 ♘c7 ♖ac8 18 ♗xb7 with advantage.

6.212 (1 d4 ♘f6 2 c4 g6 3 g3 ♗g7 4 ♗g2 c6 5 ♘f3 d5 6 cxd5 cxd5 7 0–0 0–0 8 ♘e5 ♘c6 9 ♘c3)

---

9 ... ♗f5
10 ♘xc6

If 10 ♗f4 ♘e4 11 ♖c1 ♖c8 12 ♕a4 (12 ♘xe4 dxe4 13 ♘xc6 ♖xc6 14 ♖xc6 bxc6 15 e3 ♕a5, Lehmann-Gheorghiu, Las Palmas 1972, and here 16 g4 ♗d7 17 ♗xe4 ♕xa2 18 ♕a1 would have retained the advantage) 12...♘xc3 13 bxc3 e6 14 ♖fd1 g5 with a complicated game.

10 ♗g5!? is more interesting: 10...♘xe5 11 dxe5 ♘e4 12 ♘xe4 dxe4 13 ♕a4 h6 14 ♗f4 g5 15 ♗e3 ♕d5 16 ♖ad1 ♕xe5 17 ♗d4 ♕e6 18 ♗xg7 ♔xg7 19 ♖d4 e3 20 f4 with a very complicated game (Shirov-Anand, Moscow 1989).

10 ... bxc6
11 ♗f4

A different move order looks fairly logical: 11 ♘a4 ♘d7 12 b3 e5 (this

advance leads to the creation of an isolated pawn pair, therefore it is better to aim for ...c6-c5 – 12...♖c8 13 ♗b2 ♕a5 14 ♕e1 ♕b5 15 ♕d2 e6 16 ♖fc1 c5 17 dxc5 ♗xb2 18 ♕xb2 ♘xc5 and Black equalised, Salov-Kamsky, Biel 1993) 13 dxe5 ♗xe5 14 ♗h6 ♖e8 15 ♖c1 ♖c8 16 ♕d2 with a minimal advantage to White (Botvinnik-Smyslov, m/11 1957).

11 ... ♘d7

Or 11...♕b6 12 ♘a4 ♕b5 13 b3 ♖ac8 14 ♖c1 ♘e4 15 f3 ♘d6 16 ♕d2 ♖fe8 (A.Ledger-Hill, Oakham 1990), and here 17 ♖c5 would have consolidated White's advantage.

12 ♘a4 ♕a5
13 b3 ♘b6

After 13...c5 14 ♗xd5 ♖ad8 15 ♗d2 ♕a6 16 ♗c4 ♕b7 Black has threats; 13...♖ac8 is also interesting, with the idea after 14...♖fd8 of playing ...c6-c5 at a convenient moment.

14 ♗d2

14 ♘c5 e5 15 ♗e3 ♖fe8 16 ♗f3!? deserves a practical testing.

Vaganian-Hjartarson (Debrecen 1992) now continued 14...♕b5 15 ♘c3 ♕a6 16 ♗e3 ♖ad8 17 ♕d2 c5 (17...e5 18 ♖fd1) 18 ♖fd1 c4! 19 b4 ♕a3 20 b5 a6 with a complicated game.

6.22 (1 d4 ♘f6 2 c4 g6 3 g3 ♗g7 4 ♗g2 c6 5 ♘f3 d5 6 cxd5 cxd5 7 0–0 0–0 8 ♘e5)

8 ... ♘g4

Black wants to evict the unpleasant knight from e5. White has **9 f4 (6.221)** or **9 ♘xg4 (6.222)**.

6.221 (1 d4 ♘f6 2 c4 g6 3 g3 ♗g7 4 ♗g2 c6 5 ♘f3 d5 6 cxd5 cxd5 7 0–0 0–0 8 ♘e5 ♘g4)

9 f4 ♘xe5
10 fxe5!?

Also possible is **10 dxe5** e6 11 ♘c3 ♘c6 12 b3 ♕a5 13 ♗b2 ♗d7 14 ♔h1 ♖fd8 15 a3 ♗e8 16 ♖c1 ♗f8 17 b4 ♕b6 with a complicated game (P.Nikolic-Watson, Bor 1986).

10 ... ♘c6
11 ♘c3 e6
12 e4!

More passive is **12 ♗e3** f6 13 exf6 ♖xf6 14 ♕d2 ♗d7 15 ♔h1 ♖xf1+ 16 ♖xf1 ♕e7 17 ♗g1 ♖d8 18 a3 ♔h8 and Black has no difficulties (Ribli-Nunn, Dortmund 1987), or **12 ♖f2** f6 13 exf6 ♗xf6 14 ♗e3 ♗d7 15 ♕d2 ♗g7 16 ♖af1 ♖xf2 17 ♗xf2 ♕e7 18 e4 dxe4 19 ♘xe4 ♖f8 and again Black should be

able to beat off the attack (Vaganian-Smejkal, Baden 1980).

12 ... dxe4
13 ♗e3 f5
14 exf6 ♖xf6
15 ♘xe4

Less good is **15 ♖xf6 ♗xf6 16 ♘e2 ♘b4 17 ♗xe4 ♘d5** with equal chances (Sveshnikov-A.Mikhalchishin, Lviv 1983).

15 ... ♖xf1+
16 ♕xf1 ♗xd4!

Bad is **16...♘xd4** 17 ♖d1 e5 18 ♘g5 with a decisive attack (Kasparov-Nunn, Brussels 1986).

Now 17 ♗xd4 ♘xd4 18 ♖e1 e5! 19 ♕f6 ♕b6! 20 ♕xb6 axb6 21 ♘f6+ ♔g7 leads to an equal game (analysis by Gutman).

6.222 (1 d4 ♘f6 2 c4 g6 3 g3 ♗g7 4 ♗g2 c6 5 ♘f3 d5 6 cxd5 cxd5 7 0–0 0–0 8 ♘e5 ♘g4)

9 ♘xg4 ♗xg4
10 ♘c3 ♘c6
11 h3

After **11 ♗e3** e5! 12 ♘xd5 (if 12 dxe5 d4 13 ♗xc6 dxc3 14 ♗xb7 ♖b8 Black's chances are better) 12...exd4 13 ♗c1 ♖e8 14 ♖e1 ♖c8 Black has an excellent game, while **11 ♗xd5 ♘xd4 12 ♗xb7 ♘xe2+** (12...♖b8 13 ♗a6) **13 ♘xe2 ♛xd1 14 ♖xd1 ♗xe2 15 ♗xa8 ♗xd1 16 ♗g5 ♖xa8 17 ♖xd1 ♗xb2** led to a draw in Velickovic-Henley (Tbilisi 1983).

11 ... ♗d7

After 11...♗e6 **12 e4!** (more modest is 12 e3 ♖c8 13 ♗d2 ♛d7 14 ♔h2 f6 15 ♛a4 ♗f7, Smyslov-Korchnoi, Riga 1975 – *Game 21*, and here 16 ♖fd1, hindering ...e7-e5, was correct) 12...♘xd4 13 exd5 ♗f5 (after 13...♗d7 14 ♗g5 ♘f5 15 g4! h6 16 gxf5 hxg5 17 fxg6 fxg6 18 ♘e4! White has the advantage, Sturua-Plachetka, Trnava 1980) 14 ♗g5 White has some advantage (A.Mikhalchishin-Heinig, Leipzig 1979).

12 e3

The alternatives 12 e4 and 12 ♘xd5 also cannot bring White any advantage.

12 ... e6

And now:

13 ♘a4 b6 14 ♗d2 ♛e7 15 ♘c3 ♖ac8 16 ♘e2 ♖fd8 17 ♘f4 ♗e8 with equal chances (Kochiev-Kuzmin, Lviv 1978).

13 b3 ♛a5 14 ♗d2 ♛c7 15 ♖c1 ♖ac8 with an equal game (Polugayevsky-Kasparov, Moscow 1981).

6.3 (1 d4 ♘f6 2 c4 g6 3 g3 ♗g7 4 ♗g2 c6 5 ♘f3 d5 6 cxd5 cxd5)

7 ♘c3

Here we consider 7...♘e4 **(6.31)**, 7...0-0 **(6.32)** and the symmetric 7...♘c6 **(6.33)**.

6.31 (1 d4 ♘f6 2 c4 g6 3 g3 ♗g7 4 ♗g2 c6 5 ♘f3 d5 6 cxd5 cxd5 7 ♘c3)

7 ... ♘e4
8 0-0

Alternatives:

8 ♘xe4 dxe4 9 ♘e5 ♗xe5! (if 9...♘d7 10 0-0 ♘xe5 11 dxe5 ♗f5 12 ♛b3!, Preisler-Berezin, Pardubice 1996, White has the better ending after 12...♛b6 13 ♛a4+ ♛c6 14 ♛xc6+ bxc6 15 ♗f4) **10 dxe5 ♛xd1+ 11 ♔xd1 ♗f5 12 g4** (this looks good, but 12 ♗f4!? ♘c6 13 ♔d2 is worth trying: 13...0-0-0+ 14 ♔e3 ♘b4 15 ♖hc1+ and White is better, or 13...g5 14 ♗xg5 ♘xe5 15 ♖ac1 and Black has problems) 12...♗xg4 13 ♗xe4 ♘c6 14 ♗xc6+ (somewhat premature – 14 f4 0-0-0+ 15 ♔e1 with the idea of 16 ♗e3, or 14 f3 0-0-0+ 15 ♔e1 ♗e6 16 ♗e3 is worth trying) 14...bxc6 15 f3 0-0-0+ 16

♔c2 ♗e6 17 ♗g5 ♖d5 with equality (Hjartarson-Watson, Hastings 1985/6.

8 ♕b3!? (a new idea of Karpov, with the idea after the knight exchange and e2-e3 of gaining a central advantage by c3-c4) 8...♘xc3 9 bxc3 ♘c6 (9...0–0 is quite good) 10 ♘d2 e6 (the sharp 10...e5!? 11 ♗xd5 0–0 12 ♗a3 ♘a5! should have been considered) 11 ♗a3 f5 (11...♗f8 12 e4! is unpleasant for Black) 12 e3 ♘a5 13 ♕b2 b6 14 ♗b4 ♘c6?! (14...♗a6!? looks stronger) 15 c4 with some advantage (Karpov-Gelfand, Sanghi Nagar 1995), since Black's position looks rather weakened.

8 ... 0–0

Here White has **9 ♘xe4 (6.311)**, **9 ♕b3 (6.312)** or **9 ♘e5 (6.313)**.

A quite unexpected idea was tried by Ivanchuk in his game with Kasparov (Linares 1998) – **9 ♘d2**, but after 9...f5 (if 9...♗xd4 10 ♘dxe4 dxe4 11 ♗h6 ♖e8 12 ♗xe4 with the freer game; if 9...♘f6 10 ♘b3 ♘c6 11 ♗g5 e6 12 ♕d2 ♕b6 13 ♖fd1 a5 14 ♖ac1 ♕b4 15 ♘a1! a4 16 ♘c2 ♕a5 17 f3 and White is ready for play in the centre, Fominykh-Glek, Elista 1995, or 10...b6 11 ♗g5 ♗b7 12 ♕d2 ♖e8 13 f3! ♘bd7 14 e4 and again White is better, Fominykh-Yandemirov, Alushta 1993) 10 ♘dxe4 dxe4 11 ♕b3+ ♔h8 12 ♖d1 ♘c6 13 ♗e3 ♗d7 14 ♖ac1 ♖c8 15 ♕a3 ♕a5! Black had a good game.

6.311 (1 d4 ♘f6 2 c4 g6 3 g3 ♗g7 4 ♗g2 c6 5 ♘f3 d5 6 cxd5 cxd5 7 ♘c3 ♘e4 8 0–0 0–0)

---

9 ♘xe4 dxe4
10 ♘e5 ♕d5

Black's other possibilities:

10...♘d7 11 ♗f4 (after 11 ♗xe4 ♘xe5 12 dxe5 ♗h3 13 ♖e1 ♗xe5 Black

has no problems, while if 11 ♘xd7 ♗xd7 12 ♗xe4 ♗h3 13 ♗xb7 ♖b8 14 ♗g2 ♗xg2 15 ♔xg2 ♗xd4 16 ♗h6 ♕d5+ with an excellent game, Ornstein-Moberg, Borlange 1995) 11...♘f6 12 ♕d2 ♗e6 (if 12...♕b6 13 ♘c4 ♕a6 14 b3 with advantage) 13 ♖fc1 ♕b6 14 ♖c5!? (after 14 ♘c4 ♕a6 15 ♘e3 ♖fd8 16 ♗e5 ♖d7 Black stands well, Alterman-Glek, Haifa 1996) 14...♖fd8 15 ♖ac1. White has control of the c-file and some advantage.

10...♕b6 11 ♗xe4 (after 11 e3 f6 12 ♘c4 ♕a6 13 b3 f5 14 ♗b2 ♖d8 15 f3 exf3 16 ♕xf3 ♘c6 17 g4! White has the advantage, Ilincic-Dragojlovic, Yugoslavia 1995) 11...♖d8 12 ♕c2 (12 ♘f3!? is interesting) 12...♕xd4 13 ♗f4 ♗xe5 14 ♖fd1 ♕b6 15 ♖xd8+ ♕xd8 16 ♗xe5. White has the advantage in view of his two bishops and lead in development (Andersson-Wahls, Biel 1990).

10...f6 11 ♕b3+ e6 12 ♘c4 ♘c6 13 e3 (after 13 ♗e3 Black equalises by 13...f5 14 ♖ad1 ♕d5 15 f3 ♗d7 16 fxe4 fxe4 17 a4 ♖fc8, while 13 ♗xe4 ♘xd4 14 ♕d1 f5 15 ♗g2 ♕c7 16 ♘a3 ♖d8 gives Black the advantage, Espig-Kaminski, East Germany 1989) 13...f5 14 ♗d2 ♖b8 15 a4 (after 15 ♖ac1 ♗d7 16 ♖fd1 b5 17 ♘e5 ♘xe5 18 dxe5 b4! Black holds the position with difficulty, Yusupov-Dolmatov, m 1991) 15...♖f7 (after 15...♗d7 16 ♕a3 ♖e8 17 a5 ♗f8 18 ♕a2 ♕e7 19 ♖fc1 ♖ec8 20 ♗f1 ♕d8 21 ♖ab1 ♗e8 22 b4 White retains the initiative, Ribli-Andersson, Clermont Ferrand 1989) 16 ♖ac1 b6 17 f3! (White must open up his bishop to gain effective control of d5) 17...exf3 18 ♗xf3 ♗b7 19 ♗xc6! ♗xc6 20 ♘e5 with advantage to White (Yusupov-Timman, m 1992).

11 ♗e3

The other development of the bishop may be stronger: **11 b3 ♘c6 12 ♗b2 ♗e6 13 e3 ♖fd8 14 ♘d3 f5 15 ♘f4 ♕d7 16 g4 ♗f7 17 gxf5 ♕xf5 18 ♘e2 e5 19 ♘g3** (Salov-Gelfand, Linares 1991) and White has some advantage in view of 19...♕c8 20 d5! ♗xd5 21 ♕e2 followed by 22 ♗xe4, when Black has a bad pawn structure.

| **11** | **...** | **♘d7** |

If **11...♘c6** White gains the advantage by 12 ♘xc6 bxc6 13 ♕c2 ♗f5 14 ♖fd1 ♖fd8 15 b3 (Adianto-Liang, Bejing 1992).

After **11...f6** 12 ♘d3 f5 13 ♘b4 ♕d6 14 ♕b3+ ♔h8 15 ♖fd1 ♘a6 16 ♘c2 e6 17 f3 he also stands better (Burmakin-Ivacic, Portoroz 1994).

Ilincic-Simic (Novi Sad 1995) now continued 12 ♘d3 (if 12 ♕c2 ♘xe5 13 ♗xe4 ♕c4 14 dxe5 ♕xc2 15 ♗xc2 ♗xe5 16 ♗e4 ♗f5 with an equal game) 12...♘f6 13 h3 ♕b5 14 a4 ♕b6 15 a5 ♕b5 16 ♘c5 ♕xb2 17 ♕a4 ♘d5 18 ♖a2 ♕b4 with a complicated game.

6.312 (1 d4 ♘f6 2 c4 g6 3 g3 ♗g7 4 ♗g2 c6 5 ♘f3 d5 6 cxd5 cxd5 7 ♘c3 ♘e4 8 0–0 0–0)

| **9** | **♕b3** | **♘c6** |

In Rabinovich-Botvinnik (Moscow 1935) Black played **9...♘xc3** 10 bxc3 ♘c6 11 ♘d2 e6 12 ♗a3 ♖e8 13 e4 ♘a5 14 ♕c2 b6 and equalised.

| **10** | **♖d1** |

After **10 ♗e3 ♘a5 11 ♕b5 ♘xc3 12 bxc3 ♘c4 13 ♗f4 e6 14 e4 ♘d6 15 ♗xd6 ♕xd6 16 ♘e5 ♗xe5 17 dxe5 ♕xe5 18 exd5 exd5 19 ♗xd5 ♕xc3 20 ♖ac1 ♕f6 21 ♖c7 ♗e6!** the game is equal.

| **10** | **...** | **e6** |

After **10...♘a5 11 ♕b4 ♘xc3 12 ♕xc3 ♗f5** (if 12...b6 13 ♗f4 ♗a6 14 ♕e1! and White has the advantage, Inkiov-Lukov, Bulgaria 1986) 13 ♗f4 ♖c8 14 ♕a3! (after 14 ♕e1? ♕b6 15 b3 ♘c6 16 ♕d2 ♗e4! Black seized the initiative, Donner-Botvinnik, Palma de Mallorca 1967 – *Game 22*) 14...a6 15 b3 followed by 16 ♖ac1 and 17 ♗e5 White has the freer position.

Karpov-Epishin (Las Palmas 1994) continued 11 ♗f4 ♘xc3 12 ♕xc3 ♗d7 13 ♗d6 ♖e8 14 ♕d2! (a correct prophylactic move – White should combine threats on the c-file and on the kingside) 14...♖c8 15 h4 ♘e7 16 ♖ac1 ♘f5 17 ♗b4 ♕b6 18 ♗c5 ♕a6 19 ♗f1 with unpleasant threats and the more active position for White.

6.313 (1 d4 ♘f6 2 c4 g6 3 g3 ♗g7
4 ♗g2 c6 5 ♘f3 d5 6 cxd5 cxd5 7
♘c3 ♘e4 8 0–0 0–0)

9 ♘e5

Black can choose 9...♘xc3 (6.3131)
or 9...♗f5!? (6.3132).

6.3131 (1 d4 ♘f6 2 c4 g6 3 g3 ♗g7
4 ♗g2 c6 5 ♘f3 d5 6 cxd5 cxd5 7
♘c3 ♘e4 8 0–0 0–0 9 ♘e5)

9 ... ♘xc3
10 bxc3 ♘c6

10...♘d7 is more passive, but quite
playable: 11 ♘xd7 ♕xd7 12 ♕b3 ♖d8
13 a4 (after 13 e4 dxe4 14 ♗xe4 e5 15
♗g5 ♖e8 16 ♖fe1!? exd4 17 ♗d5
White has rather strong threats) 13...b6!
14 a5 ♗a6 15 axb6 axb6 16 ♗f4 ♕c6
17 ♖fb1 ♗c4 18 ♖xa8 ♖xa8 19 ♕xb6
♕xb6 20 ♖xb6 e5! with an equal game
(Gutman-Andersson, Biel 1985).

After the eccentric **10...♕a5** 11
♗d2?! (11 ♕b3, attacking the d5 pawn,
is more active) 11...♘c6 12 ♘d3 (12
c4!? is interesting) 12...♕d8 13 ♗g5 h6
14 ♗f4 e6 15 e4 b6 16 ♖e1 dxe4 17
♗xe4 ♗b7 18 h4 ♘a5 Black has no
problems (Rashkovsky-Petrushin, Baku
1977).

11 ♘xc6 bxc6
12 ♕a4

In a symmetric position it is usually
important to be the first to attack, and so
this is the most obvious and correct
continuation. There are other possibilities, but they are weaker:

12 e4 ♗e6 13 ♗a3 (White can try 13
e5!? ♕a5 14 ♗d2 ♕a6 15 g4 f5 16 exf6
exf6 17 ♗f4 ♖fe8 18 h3 ♗f7, but here
too he has nothing, Geveke-Derikum,
Germany 1993) 13...dxe4 (the weak
13...♖e8?! 14 e5 ♗f5 15 g4 ♗e6 16 f4
♕d7 17 h3 leads to a great advantage
for White, Averkin-Kupreichik, USSR
1969) 14 ♗xe4 ♗d5 and Black holds
on.

12 ♗a3 ♗a6 (also possible is
12...♖e8 13 e4 ♗a6 14 ♖e1 e5! 15 exd5
exd4 16 ♖xe8+ ♕xe8 17 cxd4 cxd5 18
♗c5 ♗c4 with equality, but not 18
♗xd5? ♖d8 19 ♕b3 ♗xd4 20 ♖d1
♕e2!, Neat) 13 ♖e1 ♖e8 14 e4 e6 15 h4
h5 16 e5 ♗f8 17 ♗xf8 ♔xf8 18 ♗f3
♕e7 with an equal game (Vadasz-
Schmidt, Wijk aan Zee 1975).

12 ... ♕b6

Weaker is **12...♗e6** 13 ♖b1 ♕d7 14
♕a6 ♖fc8 15 ♗f4 with advantage to
White (Jasnikowski-Pedzich, Poland
1990), while if **12...♗d7** 13 ♕a3 ♗f5
14 ♗f4 ♖c8 15 ♖fd1 ♕b6 16 ♖ac1 a5!
and Black successfully equalises
(Larsen-Xie, Vienna 1993).

13 ♗a3

After 13 e4 ♗a6 14 ♖e1 e6 15 ♗f4
♗d3 the game is equal (Schmidt-
Averbakh, Polanica Zdroj 1975).

Now after 13...♕a6 14 ♕xa6 ♗xa6
15 ♖fb1 (or 15 ♖fe1 ♖fe8 16 ♗f1 ♗f8,
Schmidt-Timman, Wijk aan Zee 1975)
15...♗xe2 16 ♗xe7 ♖fb8 (Smejkal-
Mariotti, Milan 1975) the position is
equal.

6.3132 (1 d4 ♘f6 2 c4 g6 3 g3 ♗g7 4 ♗g2 c6 5 ♘f3 d5 6 cxd5 cxd5 7 ♘c3 ♘e4 8 0–0 0–0 9 ♘e5)

9	...	♗f5!?
10	♗f4	

10 ♗e3 is more passive: 10...♘xc3 11 bxc3 ♘c6 12 ♘xc6 bxc6 13 ♕a4 ♕b6 14 ♖ac1 ♖ab8 (Geller-Fischer, Palma de Mallorca 1970) with equality after 15 ♖fd1.

If **10 ♕b3** there follows 10...♘c6! 11 ♖d1 ♘xc3 12 bxc3 ♕c7 13 ♗xd5 ♘xe5 14 dxe5 ♕xe5 15 ♗f4 ♕xc3 16 ♕xb7 ♕a3 with an equal game (Flesch-Hübner, Sombor 1970).

10 ♘xe4 is not very good: 10...♗xe4 11 ♗xe4 dxe4 12 ♕b3 ♘c6 13 ♘xc6 bxc6 14 e3 ♖b8 15 ♕c2 ♕d5 16 ♖d1 ♖fc8 17 ♖d2 h5 18 b3 c5 with advantage (Sunye-Illescas, Linares 1994).

10	...	f6!

Clearly stronger than 10...♘c6 11 ♘xc6 bxc6 12 ♘a4 ♕a5 13 ♖c1 ♖ac8 (13...♕b5 14 e3 ♖ac8 15 f3 ♘d6, Petrosian-Korchnoi, Moscow 1979, and here 16 g4! ♗e6 17 ♖f2 would have given an advantage, Korchnoi) 14 ♖e1 ♖fd8 15 f3 ♘d6 16 ♗d2 ♕c7 17 e3 h5 18 b3 and White maintains pressure (Portisch-Reshevsky, Palma de Mallor-

ca 1970). In general, such positions with a backward c6 pawn are old-fashioned, and nowadays everyone avoids them – modern players seek active play.

If **10...e6** 11 ♘xe4 dxe4 12 f3 White has the advantage (Chiburdanidze).

10...♘xc3 11 bxc3 ♘c6 12 ♕b3 ♘xe5 13 ♗xe5 ♗xe5 14 dxe5 ♕c7 (14...e6 would have given White the advantage, Korchnoi) 15 ♕xd5 ♕xc3 16 ♖fc1 ♕b2 17 ♕xb7 ♕xe5 18 ♕c7 ♕xc7 19 ♖xc7 ♖fc8 20 ♖xe7 ♔f8 and Black is a pawn down but has some drawing chances (Kirov-Andersson, Rome 1986).

| 11 | ♘d3 | |

Weaker is **11 ♘f3** ♘xc3 12 bxc3 ♘c6 13 ♘d2 ♕d7 14 e4 dxe4 15 ♘xe4 b6 16 ♖e1 ♖ac8 17 ♘d2, and now not 17...e5? (Fedorowicz-A.Mikhalchishin, Hastings 1985/6), as after 18 dxe5 ♘xe5 19 ♗xe5! fxe5 20 ♘e4 White has slightly the better ending, but 17...♖fd8 or 17...♘a5 with an excellent game.

11	...	♘c6
12	♘c5	♘xc3
13	bxc3	b6

Also good is **13...♘a5** 14 e4 dxe4 15 ♘xe4 ♖c8 with an excellent game (analysis).

| 14 | c4 | |

After **14 e4** dxe4 15 ♘xe4 ♖c8 (15...♕d7!? is also good) 16 ♖e1 ♕d7 17 ♕e2 ♖fe8 Black stands well (Browne-Hübner, Chicago 1982).

Har-Zvi–Kaminski (Duisburg 1992) now continued 14...e6 15 ♘b7 ♕d7 16 ♘d6 ♘e7 17 ♘xf5 gxf5 (17...♘xf5 is also good) 18 ♖c1 ♖ac8 19 cxd5 ♘xd5 when Black was excellently placed in the centre.

> **6.32 (1 d4 ♘f6 2 c4 g6 3 g3 ♗g7 4 ♗g2 c6 5 ♘f3 d5 6 cxd5 cxd5 7 ♘c3)**

　　　7 ...　　　0-0
　　　8 ♘e5　　　e6

Black avoids the symmetry, supports his d5 pawn, and prepares to combat the knight at e5. Now White has **9 0-0** (6.321) or **9 ♗g5** (6.322).

> **6.321 (1 d4 ♘f6 2 c4 g6 3 g3 ♗g7 4 ♗g2 c6 5 ♘f3 d5 6 cxd5 cxd5 7 ♘c3 0-0 8 ♘e5 e6)**

　　　9　0-0

Black in turn has a choice: **9...♘c6** (6.3211) or **9...♘fd7** (6.3212).

9...♗d7 looks rather unnatural: 10 b3 ♕b6 11 ♗g5 ♗c6 12 ♕d2 ♘fd7 13 ♘f3 a5 14 ♖ab1 ♘a6 15 ♖fc1 and White has the freer game (Hulak-Lein, Palma de Mallorca 1989).

9...♘bd7 is more logical: 10 ♗f4 (White is also better after 10 ♘d3 ♕b6 11 e3 ♘b8 12 b4 ♗d7 13 a4 ♖c8 14 ♕b3 ♘c6 15 a5, Tukmakov-Kuzmin, USSR 1978, or 10 f4 a6 11 ♗e3 ♘e8 12 ♗f2 f5 13 ♗f3 ♘ef6 14 e3 ♘e4 15 g4 ♘xe5 16 dxe5 ♘xc3 17 bxc3 b5 18 gxf5 gxf5 19 ♔h1, Izeta-Sanabria, 1996) 10...♘h5 11 ♘xd7 ♕xd7 12 ♗g5 h6 13 ♗e3 b6 14 a4, although here too White has the initiative (Romanishin-Hort, Dortmund 1982).

> **6.3211 (1 d4 ♘f6 2 c4 g6 3 g3 ♗g7 4 ♗g2 c6 5 ♘f3 d5 6 cxd5 cxd5 7 ♘c3 0-0 8 ♘e5 e6 9 0-0)**

　　　9 ...　　　♘c6

A fairly logical continuation: Black is ready temporarily to accept a weak pawn at c6, and then play ...c6-c5.

White's main possibilities are **10 ♘xc6** (6.32111) and **10 ♗g5** (6.32112). Others:

10 ♗f4, and now:

(a) 10...♘xe5 11 ♗xe5 ♗d7 12 ♕d2 (after 12 ♕b3 ♗c6 13 e3 ♘d7 14 ♗xg7 ♔xg7 15 ♖fe1 ♕b6 the position is equal, Smyslov-Najdorf, Moscow 1957, or 12 ♕d3 ♕b6 13 ♖fc1 ♖fc8 14 ♖c2 ♘e8 15 ♗xg7 ♔xg7 16 ♖ac1 ♘d6 and Black is not worse, Azmaiparashvili-Malaniuk, Tbilisi 1986) 12...♖c8 13 ♖fc1 ♗c6 14 ♖c2 ♘e8 15 ♗xg7 ♔xg7 16 ♖ac1 ♘d6 17 ♕f4 ♕d7 with equality (Sturua-Ernst, Debrecen 1992);

(b) 10...♗d7 11 ♕d2 ♗e8 12 ♖fd1 ♘h5 13 ♗h6 f5 14 ♗xg7 ♔xg7 15 ♖ac1 ♘f6 16 ♕e3 ♖c8 17 a3 ♕d6 and White achieves nothing in particular (Pigusov-Bareev, Sochi 1987).

10 f4 is a logical continuation, supporting the knight in the centre, but Black has adequate counterplay:

(a) 10...♘d7 11 e3 (interesting is 11 ♗e3 or 11 ♘xc6 bxc6 12 ♗e3 – cf. Gauglitz-Malisauskas, Eger 1987, p.179) 11...f6 12 ♘d3 ♕e7 13 ♗d2 f5 14 ♘e5 ♘f6 with a solid position (Yudasin-Smirin, Las Palmas 1993);

(b) 10...♗d7 11 ♗e3 (less good is 11 e3 ♘e8 12 ♘xd7 ♕xd7 with an excellent game) 11...♘e7 (after 11...♕e7 12 ♖c1 ♖ac8 13 ♕d3 ♘e8 14 ♗f2 ♘d6 15 ♖fd1 ♖fd8 16 b3 ♗e8 Black has a solid enough position, Rustemov-Baby, Vladivostok 1994) 12 g4 ♘c8 13 g5 ♘e8 14 ♕b3 ♘ed6 15 ♗f2 ♘b6 and Black has a good game thanks to his control of c4 (Teske-Glek, Hamburg 1995).

6.32111 (1 d4 ♘f6 2 c4 g6 3 g3 ♗g7 4 ♗g2 c6 5 ♘f3 d5 6 cxd5 cxd5 7 ♘c3 0–0 8 ♘e5 e6 9 0–0 ♘c6)

---

10 ♘xc6 bxc6
11 ♘a4

Or 11 ♗f4:

(a) 11...♘h5 12 ♗e3 f5 13 ♕d2 ♖b8 (or 13...♕d6 14 f4 ♕b4 15 ♖fd1 ♖b8 16 b3 c5 17 ♖ac1 with the better game, Ilivitsky-Moiseev, USSR 1964) 14 ♖fd1 and White has the advantage;

(b) 11...♘d7 12 ♕d2 ♕b6 (12...a5 13 ♖fd1 ♗a6 14 ♖ac1 ♖e8 also fails to equalise, Petrosian-Korchnoi, Moscow 1957, because of 15 b3) 13 ♖fd1 c5 14 dxc5 ♕xc5 15 ♖ac1 ♕b6 16 ♗e3 ♕a6 17 ♗d4 ♘f6 18 e4! and the game opens up to White's advantage (Abramovic-P.Nikolic, Belgrade 1992).

11 ... ♘d7
12 ♗f4

After the modest **12 b3** c5 13 ♗a3 ♗xd4 (sharper is 13...cxd4 14 ♗xf8 ♕xf8 with compensation) 14 ♖c1 ♗a6 15 ♕d2 ♕f6 16 ♘xc5 ♘xc5 17 ♗xc5 ♗xc5 18 ♖xc5 ♖ac8 the chances are equal, but stronger is 13 ♗b2 ♗b7 14 ♖c1 ♖c8 15 ♕d2 cxd4 16 ♖xc8 ♕xc8 17 ♖c1 ♕b8 18 ♗xd4 e5! 19 ♘c5! ♘xc5 20 ♗xc5 ♖d8 21 ♕a5 with the better game for White (Ilincic-Sibarevic, Yugoslavia 1992).

12 ... ♕a5

Black's c6 pawn and c5 square are weak, but after forcing b2-b4 he will try then to create counterplay by ...a7-a5.

12...e5 is an attempt to open the centre immediately, but after 13 dxe5 ♘xe5 14 ♖c1 it should not bring Black any particular success:

(a) 14...♗d7 15 b3 (15 e4 is also good) 15...♖c8 16 ♕d2 ♖e8 17 ♗g5 f6 18 ♗e3 and White has a big advantage (Jurek-Browne, Germany 1996);

(b) 14...♖e8 15 b3 ♗a6 16 ♖e1 ♖c8 17 ♘c5 ♕a5 18 ♗d2 ♕a3 19 ♗h3! with advantage (Sanchez-Lopez, Alicante 1992);

(c) 14...♕a5 15 b3 (the tactical 15 ♗xe5 ♗xe5 16 ♖xc6 ♗d7 17 ♖c5! ♕xa4 18 ♖xd5 is also possible, Neat) 15...♗d7 16 ♕d2 ♕xd2 17 ♗xd2 ♖fe8

18 ♖fe1 h5 19 h3 with some endgame advantage to White in view of the weakness of the c6 and d5 pawns (Jurek-Seeling, Germany 1996).

12...♗a6 is somewhat better:

(a) 13 ♗d6 ♖e8 14 ♘c5 ♘xc5 15 ♗xc5 e5 16 dxe5 ♖xe5 17 ♖e1 ♖e8 and with no knights on the board it is hard for White to exploit the c6 weakness (Forintos-Lukacs, Hungary 1972);

(b) 13 ♖e1 ♕a5 14 ♗d6 ♖fc8 15 b4 ♕d8 16 ♘c5 ♗c4, again holding the position, Dzindzichashvili-Benjamin, USA 1984;

(c) 13 ♖c1 ♕a5 (13...♗b5!? 14 ♘c3 ♗a6, threatening ...c6-c5, is a good alternative) 14 ♖e1 (after 14 b3 ♖fc8 15 ♗d6 ♗b5! 16 ♘c3 ♕b6! 17 ♗c5 ♘xc5 18 dxc5 ♕xc5 19 ♘xd5 ♕a3 Black has an excellent game, Smyslov-Korchnoi, Leningrad 1960) 14...♗b5 15 ♘c3 ♖fc8 16 ♗d6 ♕b6 17 e3 a5 with an equal game (Ubilava-Foisor, Linares 1994);

(d) 13 ♕d2 ♗b5 (less good is 13...♖e8 14 ♖ac1 ♗b5 15 ♘c3 ♗a6 16 ♖fd1 ♖c8 17 ♗h6 ♗f6 18 h4! when White is better, Larsen-Krogius, Le Havre 1966, or 13...♕e7 14 ♖ac1 ♖fc8 15 ♖fe1 ♗b5 16 ♘c5 ♘xc5 17 ♖xc5 e5 18 ♗g5 ♕d6 19 ♖ec1, and here too the weak c6/d5 structure gives White has the advantage, Boleslavsky) 14 ♘c3 ♕b6 15 ♖fd1 ♖ac8 16 e4 ♖fd8 17 ♖ac1 ♗f8 18 h4 and White has some advantage (Podgaets-Butnorius, USSR 1970).

13 a3

According to analysis by Chiburdanidze, 13 ♗d6 ♖e8 14 b4 ♕d8 15 e4 ♗a6 16 ♖e1 dxe4 leads to an equal game, while 13 b3 ♗a6 14 ♖c1 ♖fc8 15 ♗d6 ♗b5 16 ♘c3 ♕b6 17 ♗c5 ♘xc5 18 dxc5 ♕xc5 19 ♘xd5 ♕a3 led to an advantage for Black in Donner-Gipslis (Amsterdam 1976).

But **13 ♖c1** is interesting: 13...♗a6 14 ♗d6 ♖fc8 15 ♖e1 ♗f8 16 ♗xf8 ♔xf8 17 b3 ♕b4 18 e3 with some advantage to White (Baburin-Schwarz-Ubeda 1996).

| 13 | ... | ♗a6 |
| 14 | b4 | ♕d8 |

Also interesting is **14...♕b5!?** 15 ♖e1 e5! 16 dxe5 ♘xe5 with a complicated game (Chiburdanidze).

Now after 15 ♖e1 ♗c4 16 ♘c5 ♖e8 17 ♖c1 ♘xc5 18 bxc5 ♕a5 the game is equal (Akhmilovskaya-Chiburdanidze, Sofia 1986).

> **6.32112** (1 d4 ♘f6 2 c4 g6 3 g3 ♗g7 4 ♗g2 c6 5 ♘f3 d5 6 cxd5 cxd5 7 ♘c3 0–0 8 ♘e5 e6 9 0–0 ♘c6)

10 ♗g5 h6

The pin is rather unpleasant, although 10...♘e7!? is also interesting: 11 ♕d2 ♘e8 12 ♗h6 b6 13 ♗xg7 ♔xg7 (Schmidt-Tseshkovsky, Trnava 1986) 14 h4 with slightly the better game.

11 ♗f4

After 11 ♘xc6 bxc6 12 ♗f4 (illogical is 12 ♗xf6 ♗xf6 13 ♕d2 ♗g7 14 ♖ac1 ♕a5 15 ♖fd1 ♖d8 16 a3 ♖b8 when Black has no problems, I.Ivanov-

Shamkovich, New York 1983) 12...♘d7 (weaker is 12...♘h5 13 ♗e3 f5 14 f4 with the better game, Ree-Rogulj, Smederevska Palanka 1980) 13 ♕d2 g5! (bad is 13...♔h7 14 ♗d6 ♖e8 15 ♖fd1 ♘b6 16 ♗c5 e5 17 dxe5 ♗xe5 18 ♗d4 when the weakness on c6 gives White the advantage, Petrosian-Gheorghiu, Palma de Mallorca 1968) 14 ♗e3 (if 14 ♗d6 ♖e8 15 e4 ♘b6 16 ♗c5 ♘d7 with equality, Portisch-Gligoric, Ljubljana/Portoroz 1973) 14...e5 15 f4! gxf4 16 gxf4 exd4 17 ♗xd4 ♗xd4+ 18 ♕xd4 ♕f6 19 ♖ad1 White has a minimal advantage (Schmidt-Doda, Polanica Zdroj 1976).

11 ... ♗d7

After 11...♘xe5 12 ♗xe5 ♗d7 13 ♕d3 ♖c8 14 ♖fd1 ♕a5 15 ♕f3 ♘e8 White has no advantage, but 11...♘h5 12 ♘xc6 bxc6 13 ♗e3 ♘f6 leads to a better version for White of positions already considered.

12 ♕d2 ♘xe5!
13 ♗xe5

After 13 dxe5 ♘g4 Black has no problems.

Now after 13...♗c6 14 ♖ac1 ♕e7 15 ♖c2 ♖fd8 Black again does not experience any problems (Lengyel-Gligoric, Wijk aan Zee 1971).

6.3212 (1 d4 ♘f6 2 c4 g6 3 g3 ♗g7 4 ♗g2 c6 5 ♘f3 d5 6 cxd5 cxd5 7 ♘c3 0–0 8 ♘e5 e6 9 0–0)

10 ... ♘fd7

Now White has 10 ♘f3 (6.32121) or 10 f4 (6.32122).

The game is completely equal after 10 ♘xd7 ♗xd7 (10...♕xd7 11 b3 ♘c6 12 ♗a3 ♖e8 13 e3 b6 14 ♕d3 ♗b7 15 ♖fc1 ♖ac8 also equalises, Hjartarson-Csom, Esbjerg 1985) 11 ♗f4 (dubious is 11 e4!? dxe4 12 ♘xe4 ♗b5 13 ♖e1 ♕xd4 14 ♕xd4 ♗xd4 15 ♗h6 ♗g7 16 ♘f6+ ♗xf6 17 ♗xf8 ♔xf8 18 ♗xb7 ♗c6 when Black is better, Webb-Bednarski, Hamburg 1977) 11...♘c6 12 e3 ♘a5 (Jansa-Ftacnik, Prague 1985).

6.32121 (1 d4 ♘f6 2 c4 g6 3 g3 ♗g7 4 ♗g2 c6 5 ♘f3 d5 6 cxd5 cxd5 7 ♘c3 0–0 8 ♘e5 e6 9 0–0 ♘fd7)

10 ♘f3

On the one hand this is a retreat, but the knight at d7 will also have to move, and so the move has some point. The disadvantage is that, if Black is satisfied with a draw, he can revert to the previous position by 10...♘f6.

10 ... ♘c6
11 ♗f4

Other possibilities:

11 b3 b5!? (or 11...♘f6 with a good game) 12 ♘xb5 ♕b6 13 ♘c3 ♘xd4 14 ♘a4 ♘xf3+ 15 ♗xf3 ♕b5 16 ♗a3 ♗xa1 17 ♗xf8 ♗f6 18 ♗d6 ♗a6 with a good game for Black (Izsak-Shushpanov, Budapest 1994).

11 ♗e3 ♘f6 (if 11...♘b6 12 b3 ♗d7 13 ♖c1 ♘c8 14 ♗g5 ♘6e7 15 ♘e5 ♗e8 16 ♗f4 ♘d6 17 h4 f6 with a complicated game) 12 ♘e5 (12 ♕d3 b6 13 a3 ♗b7 14 b4 ♘e8 15 ♗g5 ♕d7 16 b5 ♘a5 17 ♘e5 ♕c7 18 ♗f4 g5!? leads to an unclear position, Osnos-Karasev, Leningrad 1987) 12...♗d7 13 h3 ♘e8 14 f4 ♘d6 15 ♗f2 f6 16 ♘d3 b6 17 ♖c1 ♖c8 with equality (Hort-Ivanchuk, Biel 1989).

11 ♗g5 ♕b6 12 ♘a4 ♕a6 13 ♖c1 b5 14 ♘c3 b4 15 ♘a4 ♕b5 16 b3 ♗a6 17 ♕d2 ♖ac8 18 ♖fe1 ♖fe8 19 ♗f1 ♗b7 with equality (Yusupov-Dolmatov, m 1991).

11 a3?! ♘b6 12 ♗g5 f6 13 ♗e3 g5 14 h3 h6 15 ♗c1 f5 with the initiative for Black (Bronstein-Stein, Moscow 1964).

11 h4 ♘f6 12 ♗f4 ♘h5 13 ♗g5 f6 14 ♗e3 f5 15 ♕d2 ♕d6 16 ♘b5 ♕b8 17 ♗f4 ♘xf4 18 gxf4 ♗d7 19 ♖fd1 ♕d8 with a complicated game (Romanishin-Gulko, Biel 1988).

11 ... ♘f6

11...♕b6 is the alternative: 12 ♘a4 ♕a6!? (or 12...♕a5 13 ♖c1 b5 14 ♘c5 ♘xc5 15 ♖xc5 ♗d7 16 a3 ♕a4 17 e3 ♕xd1 18 ♖xd1 ♖fc8 equalising, Akhmilovskaya-Chiburdanidze, Borzhomi 1986; less good is 12...♕b5?! 13 ♖b1 a5 14 ♖e1 ♕a6 15 ♘c3 b5 16 e4 dxe4 17 ♖xe4 with advantage to White, V.Sokolov-Bogdanovic, Yugoslavia

1965) 13 ♖c1 b5 14 ♘c3 ♗b7 15 ♕d3 (sharper is 15 e4!? ♘b6 16 exd5 with the freer game for White) 15...b4 16 ♘b5 e5 with equality (Kir.Georgiev-Uhlmann, Bulgaria 1986).

12 ♘e5!

Shrewd play again – now there is no point in Black playing **12...♘d7** because of 13 ♘xc6.

After **12 ♖c1** ♘e4! 13 ♘e5 ♘xc3 14 bxc3 ♘xe5 15 dxe5 ♗d7 16 e4 dxe4 17 ♗xe4 ♕c7 18 ♕f3 ♗xe5 19 ♗xe5 ♕xe5 20 ♗xb7 ♖ab8 21 c4 ♕c5 Black has an excellent game (Romanishin-Andersson, Indonesia 1983).

This manoeuvre can be prevented by **12 ♕d3**, but after 12...b6 13 ♖ac1 ♗b7 14 ♘e5 ♘xe5 15 ♗xe5 ♖c8 16 ♖c2 ♘e8 17 ♖fc1 ♗h6 18 ♗f4 ♗xf4 19 gxf4 ♘d6 White has no advantage (Gutman-Hulak, Wijk aan Zee 1987).

12 ... ♗d7
13 ♕d2

The game is equal after **13 ♘xc6** ♗xc6 14 ♗e5 ♘d7 (Adorjan-Csom, Budapest 1992), or **13 ♗g5** h6 14 ♗xf6 ♗xf6 15 ♘xc6 ♗xc6 16 ♕d2 ♔g7 17 e3 ♕b6 (Sunye-Martinovic, Amsterdam 1985).

Karpov-Kasparov (m/3 1986) now continued 13...♘xe5 14 ♗xe5 (less

good is 14 dxe5 ♘g4 15 e4 d4! 16 ♕xd4 ♗c6 17 ♕d6 ♕b6 with advantage to Black, Dlugy) 14...♗c6 15 ♖fd1 ♘d7 16 ♗xg7 ♔xg7 17 ♖ac1 ♘f6 18 ♕f4 ♕b8! With accurate exchanges Black reduces the activity of the white pieces, and White's spatial advantage is not significant – the game is equal.

6.32122 (1 d4 ♘f6 2 c4 g6 3 g3 ♗g7 4 ♗g2 c6 5 ♘f3 d5 6 cxd5 cxd5 7 ♘c3 0–0 8 ♘e5 e6 9 0–0 ♘fd7)

---

10 f4

White logically seizes space and supports his strong knight in the centre. Black must take serious counter-measures. We consider **10...f6** (6.321221) and **10...♘c6** (6.321222).

The exchange **10...♘xe5 11 fxe5** is considered in a previous variation (cf. p.166).

6.321221 (1 d4 ♘f6 2 c4 g6 3 g3 ♗g7 4 ♗g2 c6 5 ♘f3 d5 6 cxd5 cxd5 7 ♘c3 0–0 8 ♘e5 e6 9 0–0 ♘fd7 10 f4)

---

10 ...   f6

White in turn has a choice: **11 ♘f3** (6.3212211) or **11 ♘d3** (6.3212212).

6.3212211 (1 d4 ♘f6 2 c4 g6 3 g3 ♗g7 4 ♗g2 c6 5 ♘f3 d5 6 cxd5 cxd5 7 ♘c3 0–0 8 ♘e5 e6 9 0–0 ♘fd7 10 f4 f6)

---

11 ♘f3   ♘c6

If **11...f5 12 ♗e3** (weaker is 12 b3 ♕a5 13 ♕d3? ♘c5! 14 ♕d2 ♘xb3 with advantage to Black, Mochalov-Yande-mirov, Minsk 1996) 12...♘f6 13 ♘e5 ♗d7 14 ♖c1 ♘c6 15 ♘a4 ♘e4 16

♗xe4! fxe4 17 ♘c5 and White has the advantage   (Kharitonov-Yandemirov, Elista 1995).

12 ♗e3

After **12 e4 dxe4 13 ♘xe4 ♘b6 14 ♗e3 ♘d5 15 ♗f2 b6 16 ♖e1 ♖e8 17 ♘c3 ♗b7 18 ♘xd5 exd5 19 ♖xe8+ ♕xe8 20 f5** White has the initiative (Sideif-Sade–Bitman, Berlin 1992).

Gutman's idea **12 b3!?** is also interesting: 12...f5 (worse is 12...♘b6 13 ♗a3 ♖e8 14 ♕d2 f5 15 ♖ac1 with a big advantage) 13 ♗a3 ♖e8 14 e3 and White retains the advantage.

12 ...   ♘b6
13 ♗f2   f5

13...♗d7 is unfavourable: 14 e4 dxe4 15 ♘xe4 ♘d5 16 ♖e1 b6 17 ♘c3 ♘ce7 18 ♕b3 a5 19 a3 a4 20 ♕d1 ♘c7 21 ♖c1 ♘ed5 22 ♘d2! with the better game (Karpov-Gelfand, Sanghi Nagar 1995).

But **13...♘c4** is interesting, e.g. 14 e4!? ♘xb2 15 ♕b3 ♘c4 16 exd5 exd5 17 ♘g5 ♘6a5 18 ♗xd5+ ♔h8 19 ♕b4 fxg5 20 ♗xc4 ♘xc4 21 ♕xc4 gxf4 with active play, so White must play 14 ♕c2 or 14 b3 ♘d6 15 ♖c1, which in principle favours Black.

14 ♘e5   ♗d7
15 ♕d2   ♘c8

After **15...♕e7** 16 b3 ♖fc8 17 ♖ac1 White has the advantage.

16 ♕e3 ♔h8
17 ♖fc1!

17 ♖fd1 ♘d6 18 b3 ♖c8 19 ♖ac1 ♗e8 20 ♗e1 ♗f6 21 ♘a4 b6 22 ♘b2 ♘e4 23 ♘bd3 g5! led to a sharp game in Karpov-Kasparov (m/13 1986).

Now after 17...♘d6 18 b3 ♖c8 19 ♗e1 with the idea of ♘a4-b2-d3, ♘xc6 and ♘e5, White has chances of an advantage (Kasparov).

> **6.3212212 (1 d4 ♘f6 2 c4 g6 3 g3 ♗g7 4 ♗g2 c6 5 ♘f3 d5 6 cxd5 cxd5 7 ♘c3 0–0 8 ♘e5 e6 9 0–0 ♘fd7 10 f4 f6)**

11 ♘d3 ♘c6
12 e3!

Or 12 ♗e3 ♘b6 and now:

(a) 13 b3 ♗d7 14 ♗f2 (14 ♘c5 ♖b8 15 ♕d2 f5 16 ♖fc1 ♘c8 17 ♗f2 ♘d6 18 e3 ♖c8 19 ♗f1 ♕e7 20 a4 ♗e8 and Black held on, P.Nikolic-Nunn, Linares 1988) 14...♕e7 15 ♖c1 ♖ad8 16 ♖c2 ♗e8 17 ♖d2 ♘c8 18 e3 ♘d6 19 g4 ♔h8 20 ♕e2 f5 21 g5 ♘e4 and again Black holds the position (Karpov-Timman, m/12 1993);

(b) 13 ♗f2 f5 14 ♘e5 ♗d7 15 a4 (15 ♖c1 ♕e7 16 ♕d3 ♘c8 leads to equality; 15 ♕d2!? is better, intending 16 ♖fc1, preparing play on the queenside) 15...a5 16 ♕b3 ♘b4 17 ♖fc1 ♕e7 18 ♘b5 ♖fc8 19 ♖c5 ♗f8 and White has no advantage (Ilincic-Leko, Belgrade 1996).

12 ... f5

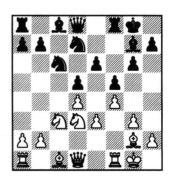

Weaker is **12...♘b6** 13 b3 ♗d7 14 ♗a3! (here the bishop is much more active than at f2) 14...♖e8 15 ♕d2 ♘e7 16 ♘c5 ♖b8 17 ♖fe1! f5 18 ♗f1 ♘ec8 19 ♖ac1 ♗c6 20 ♘d3 ♘d6 21 ♘e5 ♗f8 22 ♕b2! with advantage to White (Andersson-Nunn, Brussels 1988).

13 ♘e5

After **13 b3** ♖f7 14 ♗d2 b6 15 b4 ♗f8 16 a3 ♗b7 17 ♕b3 ♘f6 18 ♖fc1 ♖c7 19 ♘e5 White has the initiative (Maiwald-Kaposztas, Budapest 1993).

Also good is **13 ♗d2** ♘f6 14 ♖c1 ♗d7 15 ♘e5 ♖e8 16 h3 ♘xe5?! 17 dxe5 ♘e4 18 ♘xe4 dxe4 19 ♕b3 with the better game (Hulak-Olafsson, Wijk aan Zee 1987).

13 ... ♘dxe5

Here is a crucial difference with the previous variation – Black cannot tolerate for long such a powerful knight at e5. After **13...♘e7** 14 b3 ♘f6 15 ♗a3 ♗d7 16 ♖c1 ♖e8 17 ♖f2 ♘e4 18 ♖c2 ♘c6 19 ♗f1 a6 20 ♘xe4 fxe4 21 ♗d6

White has the advantage (Dzindzi-chashvili-Mestel, Reykjavik 1990).

14 dxe5 ♗d7

An alternative plan is interesting: 14...♖f7 15 ♕e2 b6 16 ♖d1 ♘b4 17 a3 ♗a6 18 ♘b5 ♕e8 19 ♗f1 ♘c2! and Black has everything in order (Hulak-Watson, Palma de Mallorca 1989), but 15 a3 (intending 16 b4) is clearly stronger, and if 15...a5 16 ♕e2 b6 17 ♖d1 with slightly the better game for White.

15 b3 ♖c8

After 15...♖e8 16 ♔h1 ♕a5 17 ♗b2 ♖ec8 (17...♖ac8 18 a3 with the better game) 18 e4 d4 19 ♘e2 ♖d8 20 exf5 gxf5 (Jasnikowski-Pedzich, Poland 1992) correct was 21 a3 with the better position.

Here 16 ♗b2 followed by 17 ♖c1 gives White some advantage.

> **6.321222 (1 d4 ♘f6 2 c4 g6 3 g3 ♗g7 4 ♗g2 c6 5 ♘f3 d5 6 cxd5 cxd5 7 ♘c3 0-0 8 ♘e5 e6 9 0-0 ♘fd7 10 f4)**

10 ... ♘c6

11 ♗e3

11 e4?! is incorrect: 11...dxe4 12 ♘xc6 bxc6 13 ♗xe4 ♘b6 with a good game, but the following plan is also possible: 11 ♘xc6 bxc6 12 ♗e3 ♗a6 13 ♕d2 ♕a5 14 ♖fc1 ♖fc8 15 ♖ab1 ♖ab8, and now not 16 b3 ♗f8 17 ♗f2 c5 when Black equalised (Gauglitz-Malisauskas, Eger 1987), but 16 b4! (Neat), since if 16...♖xb4 17 ♘xd5.

11 ... ♘b6

After **11...f6** White can transpose into previous variations by retreating his knight, but he also has the plan of play against the weak c6 pawn: 12 ♘xc6 bxc6 13 ♖c1 ♕b6 14 ♕d2 ♗a6 15 ♖c2 ♖fc8 16 ♖fc1 ♗f8 17 ♗f2 f5 (Georgadze-Kuzmin, Uzhgorod 1987) and now 18 ♘a4 ♕b4 19 ♕e3 with advantage.

If **11...♘cxe5** 12 dxe5 ♘b6 13 ♗c5 ♖e8 14 e4 dxe4 15 ♘xe4 ♘d5 (Supatashvili-Janakiev, Brno 1994) 16 ♕d4 with advantage.

If **11...♘dxe5**, then 12 fxe5 transposes into variations already considered, but 12 dxe5 is possible: 12...f6 (after 12...d4 13 ♗xc6 dxe3 14 ♗f3 f6 15 ♕xd8 ♖xd8 16 ♖ad1 White has the advantage in the ending) 12...f6 13 exf6 ♗xf6 14 ♗f2 ♕a5 15 ♕d3 ♖d8 16 a3 ♘e7 17 b4 ♕a6 18 ♕xa6 bxa6 19 ♖ac1 with the better game (Kharitonov-Godes, Smolensk 1992).

After **11...♘e7** 12 **♗f2** ♘b6 13 a4 f6 14 ♘d3 ♘c4 15 b3 ♘d6 16 ♖c1 ♘c6 17 e3 f5 18 ♗e1 White is a little better (Portisch-Xie, Prague 1995).

12   ♗f2

Possible is **12 b3** ♗d7 13 ♕d2 ♘e7 14 ♗f2 ♗c6 15 a4 f5 16 ♖fc1 ♘bc8 17 ♕e3 ♗d7 18 ♘d1 ♘d6 19 ♘b2 ♘e4 20 ♘bd3 with advantage (Foisor-Kaminski, Ibercaja 1996).

12   ...   ♘e7

Other moves are weaker:

12...♗d7 13 e4 ♘e7 (no better is 13...♗e8 14 exd5 exd5 15 ♖c1 ♕d6 16 ♕f3 ♖d8 17 ♖fe1 ♘e7 18 g4 with a serious spatial advantage, Ribli-Hort, Germany 1993), and now:

(a) 14 ♘xd7 ♕xd7 15 e5 ♖fc8! (weaker is 15...♖ac8 16 ♖c1 a6 17 b3 ♖c7 18 ♕d2 ♖fc8 19 g4 with advantage to White, Karpov-Kamsky, Moscow 1992 – *Game 23*) 16 ♖c1 (16 ♖e1! is an improvement: 16...♘c4 17 ♕e2 ♖c7 [17...b5?! is risky in view of 18 b3 ♘a3 19 ♖ac1 ♖c7 20 ♕b2 b4 21 ♘a4, when the knight establishes itself at c5] 18 ♖ad1 ♖ac8 19 ♖d3 ♘b6 20 g4 ♘a4 21 ♕d2! with the initiative, Illescas-Topalov, Madrid 1991) 16...♗f8! 17 ♗f3 ♖c7! and Black equalised (Karpov-Kasparov, m/1 1987);

(b) 14 a4! dxe4 15 a5 ♘bd5 16 ♘xe4 ♖b8 17 ♕b3 ♗e8 (17...♗c6 18 ♘c5! ♘c7 19 ♗xc6! leads to an advantage for White) 18 ♖fc1 ♘c6 19 ♕a3 ♘cb4 20 ♘c3! and White has the better chances (P.Nikolic-Hulak, Zagreb 1987);

12...f6 13 ♘xc6 bxc6 14 ♖c1 ♖b8 15 b3 ♗d7 16 e4 ♔h8 17 ♕d2 ♗e8 18 e5 and Black is very cramped (Granda-Oll, Groningen 1993).

13   ♖c1

13 ♕b3 is interesting: 13...♗d7 14 ♖fd1 ♗c6 15 ♖ac1 ♖b8 (15...♘bc8!?)

16 ♕a3 (Azmaiparashvili-Alterman, Struga 1995) 16...♘bc8 with a complicated game.

If **13 a4** a5 14 e4!? (14 ♕b3?! ♗d7 15 ♖fc1 ♗c6 16 ♘b5 ♘bc8 17 e3 ♘d6 18 ♘xd6 ♕xd6 19 ♗e1 ♖fb8! led to equality, Karpov-Kasparov, m/3 1987) 14...dxe4 15 ♗xe4 ♘bd5 16 ♕b3 f6 17 ♘c4 ♔h8 18 ♖fe1 ♘b4 19 ♖ad1 and White is better (Greenfeld-Birnboim, Tel Aviv 1988).

Gutman's suggestion **13 ♕d3** ♗d7 14 g4!? ♗c6 15 ♗h4 has not yet been tried.

Belyavsky-Smirin (Novosibirsk 1995) now continued 13...♗d7 14 g4!? (the correct plan; it is true that there is also 14 ♕b3, switching play to the queenside, but on the kingside White has more chances of success) 14...♖c8 15 e3 f6 16 ♘d3 ♘c4 17 e4! dxe4 18 ♘xe4 ♘d5 19 ♕e2 b6 20 f5! ♔h8, and here 21 b3 ♘a5 22 ♘d6 ♖xc1 23 ♖xc1 ♕e7 24 ♗g3 would have given White a serious advantage.

6.322 (1 d4 ♘f6 2 c4 g6 3 g3 ♗g7 4 ♗g2 c6 5 ♘f3 d5 6 cxd5 cxd5 7 ♘c3 0–0 8 ♘e5 e6)

---

9   ♗g5!?

A reasonable plan, with the idea of temporarily preventing ...♘fd7 and at the same time supporting the d4 pawn.

9 ... ♕b6

After **9...h6** there can follow:

(a) 10 ♗f4 ♘fd7 11 ♕d2 g5! 12 ♘xd7 ♗xd7 13 ♗e3 b5 14 h4 b4 15 ♘d1 ♕b6 16 hxg5 hxg5 17 ♗xg5 ♕xd4 18 ♕c2 (it is dangerous to accept the pawn sacrifice: 18 ♕xd4 ♗xd4 19 ♗e7 ♖c8 20 ♗xb4 ♘c6 21 ♗c3 ♗xc3 21 ♘xc3 ♖ab8, and Black has strong play) 18...f5 19 ♖h4 ♕b6 20 ♗h6 ♘c6 21 ♕d2 (Kharitonov-Glek, USSR 1988), and the black king is too weakened, e.g. 21... ♗f6 22 ♗xf8 ♗xh4 23 ♗h6 ♗f6 loses to 24 ♗xd5!;

(b) 10 ♗e3! ♕b6 (10...♘bd7 11 0–0 ♘e8 12 ♕d2 ♔h7 13 ♖ac1 ♘d6 14 b3 ♘f5 15 f4 ♘xe5 16 fxe5 ♘xe3 17 ♕xe3 ♗d7 18 h4 f5 19 exf6 ♖xf6 20 ♕d3 with advantage to White, Gutman-Wahls, Berlin 1988) 11 ♕d2 ♔h7 12 0–0 ♘c6 13 ♖fc1! ♗d7 14 ♘a4 ♕c7 15 ♘c5 ♖ad8 16 b4 and White has the better chances (Gutman-Zuse, Biel 1988).

10 ♕d2

Black's main options are **10...♘c6 (6.3221)** and **10...♘fd7 (6.3222)**.

After **10...♘bd7** 11 ♗f4 (weaker is 11 ♗e3 ♘e8! 12 f4 ♘d6 13 b3 f6 14 ♘d3 f5 15 ♘e5 ♘f6 with equality, P.Nikolic-Nunn, Amsterdam 1988, but 11 h3!? h6 12 ♗e3 is interesting, retaining some advantage, Gutman) 11...♘e8 (if 11...♘xe5 12 ♗xe5 ♗d7 13 0–0 with the better game) 12 ♖c1 ♘xe5 13 dxe5 ♗d7 (also inadequate is 13...f6 14 exf6 ♗xf6 15 0–0 ♗d7, Yrjola-Krnic, Helsinki 1990, when 16 e4! would have consolidated White's advantage) 14 ♗e3 ♕a5 15 f4 ♗c6 16 0–0 ♖d8 17 ♕d4 White has the advantage, since he has the option of b2-b4 and a2-a4 with a queenside offensive, or else g3-g4 and f4-f5, creating threats on the other side (Vaganian-Nunn, Reykjavik 1990).

6.3221 (1 d4 ♘f6 2 c4 g6 3 g3 ♗g7 4 ♗g2 c6 5 ♘f3 d5 6 cxd5 cxd5 7 ♘c3 0–0 8 ♘e5 e6 9 ♗g5 ♕b6 10 ♕d2)

---

10 ... ♘c6
11 ♘xc6 bxc6

After **11...♕xc6** 12 0–0 ♕d7 (if 12...b6 13 ♗xf6 ♗xf6 14 e4 with advantage) 13 ♗xf6 ♗xf6 14 e4 dxe4 15 ♖fd1 ♖d8 16 ♘xe4 White is clearly better (Gutman).

12 0–0 ♘d7
13 ♗e3!?

After **13 ♖fd1 ♖b8** 14 b3 f6 (if
14...e5 15 dxe5 ♘xe5 16 ♗e3 and ♗d4
with advantage to White) 15 ♗h6 (15
♗e3!? is also good) 15...♗xh6 16 ♕xh6
c5 17 ♘a4 White has an excellent game
(Kharitonov-Ivanchuk, USSR 1988).

13   ...   ♗a6

After **13...♕b4?** 14 ♘xd5 ♕xd2 15
♘e7+ ♔h8 16 ♗xd2 ♗xd4 17 ♗xc6
White wins (Yrjola-Tsevremes, Katerini
1992).

If **13...♖b8** 14 b3 ♗a6 (after
14...♕b4 15 ♖ac1 c5 16 ♖fd1 cxd4 17
♗xd4 ♗xd4 18 ♕xd4 ♕xd4 19 ♖xd4
♘e5 20 f4 White has the advantage,
Janjgava-Odeev, Yurmala 1989, but
19...♘b6 20 ♖d2 ♗b7 21 e4 dxe4 22
♘xe4 ♔g7 is better, when Black has
chances of holding on, as sooner or later
he will establish a piece at d5,
Vaganian-Epishin, Tel Aviv 1992) 15
♖ac1 ♕b4 16 ♖fd1 ♖fc8 17 ♗f4 ♖b7
18 e4 ♕f8 19 ♗e3 White has a stable
advantage (Makarov-Neverov, USSR
1991).

13...a5 is better, transposing into the
next variation.

Now after 14 ♖ac1 ♖ac8 15 ♖fd1
♖fe8 16 ♖c2 ♕b4 17 ♗h6 ♗h8 18 e4
♘b6 19 b3 White has a minimal advantage, but Black, with his pressure on d4,
can face the future with confidence
(Cvitan-Ernst, Debrecen 1992).

**6.3222 (1 d4 ♘f6 2 c4 g6 3 g3 ♗g7
4 ♗g2 c6 5 ♘f3 d5 6 cxd5 cxd5 7
♘c3 0–0 8 ♘e5 e6 9 ♗g5 ♕b6 10
♕d2)**

---

10   ...   ♘fd7
11   ♗e3

If **11 ♘f3 ♘c6** 12 ♖d1 (Averbakh-
Gufeld, USSR 1966) 12...♕b4! 13 0–0
♘b6 14 b3 ♗d7 with equality, while

after **11 ♘a4 ♕b5** 12 ♘xd7 ♘xd7 13
♘c3 ♕b4 14 ♖d1 ♘b6 15 b3 ♗d7 16
♘b1 a5 Black has a good game (King–
Sideif-Zade, Baku 1986).

11   ...   ♘c6

After **11...♘xe5** 12 dxe5 ♕a5 (if
12...♕a6 13 ♗h6 ♗xh6 14 ♕xh6 d4 15
♘e4 ♕a5+ 16 b4! ♕xe5 17 f4 ♕g7
with an unclear position, Savchenko-
Janjgava, Simferopol 1988) 13 f4 ♘c6
14 0–0 ♖d8 15 ♗f2 ♗d7 (P.Nikolic-
Nunn, Brussels 1988) correct was 16
♖fd1 with advantage.

After **11...♕d8** 12 ♘xd7 (12 f4 looks
stronger) 12...♗xd7 13 ♗h6 ♗xh6 14
♕xh6 ♘c6 15 e3 ♖c8 16 0–0 (16 h4!?
♕f6 17 h5 is interesting) 16...♕e7 17
♖fd1 f5 Black has a reasonable game.

12   ♘xc6

Here nothing is achieved by **12 f4**
♘dxe5 13 fxe5 f6 with an unclear game
(Korchnoi).

12   ...   bxc6

Weak is **12...♕xc6?!** 13 ♗h6 ♗xh6
14 ♕xh6 ♕d6 15 f4 with the initiative
(Shpilker-Kuzmin, USSR 1986).

13   0–0

13 ♖c1 leads to the same positions.
13 h4 is sharper:

(a) **13...a5** 14 h5 ♗a6 15 ♖d1? (15
hxg6 hxg6 16 ♖h4! was correct, with

chances for both sides) 15...♖fb8 16 hxg6 hxg6 17 b3 ♕b4 and Black gained the advantage (P.Nikolic-Korchnoi, Amsterdam 1988);

(b) 13...♖b8 14 ♖b1 (14 b3? c5 15 dxc5 ♕b4) 14...c5!? 15 ♘a4 (if 15 dxc5 ♕b4 16 a3? ♕xc3! and wins, but 16 ♘d1! keeps the extra pawn, Neat) 15...♕b5 16 ♘xc5 ♘xc5 17 dxc5 d4! with advantage to Black (Korchnoi).

Now after 13...a5 14 b3 ♗a6 15 ♖ac1 ♖fc8 (if 15...♖fe8 16 ♖fd1 with advantage to White) 16 ♖fd1 ♕b4 17 ♘a4 ♗b5 the game is equal (Kharitonov-Karasev, Moscow 1992).

6.33 (1 d4 ♘f6 2 c4 g6 3 g3 ♗g7 4 ♗g2 c6 5 ♘f3 d5 6 cxd5 cxd5 7 ♘c3)

7 ... ♘c6
8 0–0 0–0

The classic symmetric position, which offers Black the least chances.

9 ♘e5

The natural move.

Donner's favourite continuation 9 ♕b3 does not give any advantage after 9...e6 (9...♘e4 is also good, transposing into other variations, as well as 9...♕b6 10 ♖d1 ♕xb3 11 axb3 ♗f5 12 ♘e5 e6

13 ♘xc6 bxc6 14 ♗f4 ♗c2 15 ♖dc1 ♗xb3 16 ♖a3 ♗c4 17 b3 ♗b5 18 ♘xb5 cxb5 19 e3 and White merely has compensation for the pawn, but not more, Alekhine-Carls, Baden Baden 1925) 10 e3 b6 11 ♗d2 ♗b7 12 ♖fc1 ♕e7 13 ♘b5 ♘e4 with equality (Donner-Gligoric, Havana 1968).

9 ♗f4 is also harmless: 9...a6 (9...♘e4 10 ♖c1 ♗e6 is also satisfactory for Black) 10 e3 ♗g4 11 h3 ♗xf3 12 ♗xf3 e6 13 ♖c1 ♖c8 with a good game.

9 ... ♗f5

The other main continuation 9...e6 transposes into variation 6.3211.

9...♘xe5 10 dxe5 ♘g4 11 ♕xd5 transposes into variation 6.211.

Other possibilities:

9...♗d7 (a rare continuation, where Black considers his main problem to be the avoidance of a weak c6 pawn after ♘xc6) 10 ♗g5 (after 10 ♘xc6 ♗xc6 11 ♗f4 e6 12 ♗e5 ♕b6 Black has no problems, Hort-Hartoch, Amsterdam 1970) 10...♗e8 11 ♕d3 (if 11 ♗xf6 ♗xf6 12 ♘xd5 ♗g7! Black regains his pawn after 13 e3 ♘xe5 14 dxe5 ♗xe5 15 ♕b3 e6 16 ♘c3 ♕e7 with equality, Korchnoi-Ljubojevic, Brussels 1986) 11...e6 12 ♘g4 h5 13 ♘xf6+ ♗xf6 14 ♗xf6 ♕xf6 15 ♖fd1 (Gutman-Kapetanovic, New York 1987) and here 15...♖d8, preventing e2-e4, would have led to equality.

9...♘d7?! (Black tackles the e5 knight, but blocks in his queen's bishop) 10 ♘xd5 (after 10 ♘xd7 ♗xd7 11 ♗e3 e6 12 ♕d2 ♖c8 13 ♖fd1 ♘a5 14 b3 ♘c6 there is complete peace, Hort-Stein, Hastings 1967/8, while 10 f4 leads to other variations) 10...♘dxe5 (after 10...♘xd4? 11 ♕xd4 ♘xe5 12 ♕c5 e6 13 ♘e7+ ♔h8 14 ♗f4 ♕b6 15

Hac1 Black has serious problems, Magerramov-Malaniuk, Daugavpils 1978, and things are also not easy for him after 10...♘cxe5 11 dxe5 e6? 12 ♘f6+ ♘xf6 13 ♕xd8 Hxd8 14 ♗g5, Kotov-Bannik, Riga 1958) 11 dxe5 ♗xe5 (worse is 11...♘xe5 12 ♗g5) 12 ♗h6 He8 13 ♕d2 followed by Hfd1 and Hac1 with powerful centralisation (Filip-Hort, Czechoslovakia 1968).

9...♗e6 (this too is rather passive – the bishop defends d5, but blocks the e-pawn) 10 ♘xc6 (after 10 f4 ♘e4! 11 ♘xe4 dxe4 12 ♘xc6 bxc6 13 e3 f5 14 ♕c2 ♕b6 15 ♗d2 c5! Black frees himself, Gomez-S.Arkell, Seville 1993, while after 10 ♗f4 Hc8 11 Hc1 ♕a5 12 ♕d2 Hfd8 13 Hfd1 ♘xe5 14 ♗xe5 ♘e8 15 ♗xg7 ♚xg7 16 ♕e3 ♘f6 the position is equal, Hug-Balster, Gelsenkirchen 1991) 10...bxc6 11 ♗f4 (also possible is 11 ♘a4 ♘d7 12 ♗e3 ♕a5 13 Hc1 Hfc8 14 b3 with some advantage) 11...Hc8 12 ♘a4 ♘d7 13 Hc1 ♕a5 14 b3 c5 15 ♗d2 ♕b5 16 ♘c3 ♕b7 17 e4 dxe4 18 ♗xe4 ♕a6 19 d5 ♗h3 20 He1 with the better game for White, as his pieces are better centralised (Groenn-Santos, Manila 1992).

9 ...   ♗f5
10 ♘xc6

A logical move – White creates a weakness at c6 and should be able to exploit the strongpoint at c5.

10 ♗f4 is also good: 10...♘e4 11 Hc1 (again 11 ♘xc6 bxc6 12 ♘a4 ♕a5 13 a3 is possible with typical play) 11...Hc8 12 ♕a4 (after 12 ♘xe4 dxe4 13 ♘xc6 Hxc6 14 Hxc6 bxc6 15 e3 ♕a5, Lehmann-Gheorghiu, Las Palmas 1972, 16 g4 ♗d7 17 ♗xe4 ♕xa2 18 ♕a1 would have given an advantage) 12...♘xc3 13 bxc3 e6 14 Hfd1 g5 15 ♗e3 a6 16 c4 ♘xe5 17 dxe5 Hxc4 18

♕xc4! dxc4 19 Hxd8 Hxd8 20 ♗xb7 with advantage (Sergeev-Bezman, USSR 1985).

10 ...   bxc6
11 ♘a4

This move is best made immediately. After 11 ♗f4 ♕b6 (11...♘d7 12 ♘a4 leads to positions examined below) 12 ♘a4 ♕b5 13 Hc1 ♘d7 14 h3 Hac8 with the idea of ...c6-c5 Black equalises (Varga-Csom, Budapest 1996).

11 ...   ♘d7

After 11...♕c8 12 ♗f4 ♗h3 13 Hc1 ♕e6 14 ♕c2 ♗xg2 15 ♚xg2 ♘h5 16 ♗e3 Hac8 17 ♘c5 White has a clear advantage (Mikhalchishin-Shul, Lviv 1972).

Now after 12 b3 Hc8 (or 12...c5 13 ♗b2, Klaman-Nikitinikh, USSR 1963, 13...cxd4 14 ♗xd4 e6 15 Hc1 with slightly the better game, or 12...e5 13 dxe5 ♗xe5 14 ♗h6 He8 15 Hc1 Hc8 16 ♕d2 and in view of the weakness of the c6/d5 pawn pair, White stands better, Botvinnik-Smyslov, m/11 1957) 13 ♗b2 ♕a5 14 ♕e1 ♕b5 15 ♕d2 e6 16 Hfc1 c5! 17 dxc5 ♗xb2 18 ♕xb2 ♘xc5 19 ♘xc5 Hxc5 20 Hxc5 ♕xc5 21 Hc1 ♕d6 22 ♕d2 ♕a3! Black was able to hold the position (Salov-Kamsky, Biel 1993).

Game 21
Smyslov-Korchnoi
Riga 1975

1 d4 ♘f6 2 ♘f3 g6 3 c4 ♗g7 4 g3 0–0 5 ♗g2 c6 6 0–0 d5 7 cxd5 cxd5 8 ♘e5

In this way White avoids the variation 8 ♘c3 ♘e4, but allows Black an interesting possibility.

8...♘g4

This 'sideways' knight leap has the aim of combating the powerful central knight at e5. Clearly weaker is 8...♘bd7 9 ♘c3! ♘xe5 10 dxe5 ♘g4 11 ♕xd5 ♘xe5 12 ♕c5! ♕d6 13 ♕xd6 exd6 14 ♗g5 ♘c4 15 ♖ac1 ♗e6 16 ♘d5! ♘xb2 17 ♘c7 ♖ac8 18 ♗xb7 ♖b8 19 ♗a6 with a serious advantage for White in the ending (Romanishin-Kuzmin, Kiev 1978).

9 ♘xg4

9 f4 looks quite logical.

9...♗xg4 10 ♘c3 ♘c6 11 h3 ♗e6

Risky, in Korchnoi's style, but the modest 11...♗d7 was correct, after which neither 12 e4 nor 12 ♘xd5 gives White any advantage.

12 e3

Smyslov decides against initiating a very sharp battle by 12 e4 ♘xd4 13 exd5 ♗d7 14 ♗g5 ♘f5 15 g4! h6 16 gxf5 hxg5 17 fxg6 fxg6 18 ♘e4! with a great advantage (Sturua-Plachetka, Trnava 1980). However, although this solution was more correct, it was not in Smyslov's style.

12...♖c8 13 ♗d2

Smyslov considers that the bishop at e6 is badly placed, and that sooner or later it will have to make way for the e-pawn.

13...♕d7 14 ♔h2 f6 15 ♕a4 ♗f7 16 b4?!

Logical, but premature – it was correct to counter Black's freeing attempt by 16 ♖fd1! e5 17 dxe5 fxe5 18 ♘xd5! ♗xd5 19 ♗e1! with advantage. Now, however, a forcing variation gives Black serious play for the pawn.

16...e5! 17 b5 ♘e7 18 ♕xa7 ♖a8 19 ♕c5 ♖fc8 20 ♕b4 ♖c4 21 ♕b2 exd4 22 exd4 ♖xd4 23 ♘e2 ♖da4 24 ♗c3!

White must try to block the d5 pawn and not allow the bishop at g7 to be activated.

24...d4 25 ♗xd4 ♖xa2 26 ♖fe1!

By tactical means White escapes from the unpleasant pressure.

26...f5?!

Bad was 26...♖xb2 27 ♖xa8+ and ♗xb2 with advantage to White. Now Black is threatening this, but 26...♘f5 was better.

27 ♖xa2 ♖xa2 28 ♕c3 ♗f8?

A passive plan. It was better to go into a slightly inferior ending after 28...♗xd4 29 ♕xd4 ♕xd4 30 ♘xd4. Less good was 28...♖xe2 29 ♖xe2 ♗xd4 30 ♕d3 f4 31 ♖d2 fxg3+ 32 fxg3 ♘f5 33 ♗e4! with the better game for White.

29 ♕e3!

This was overlooked by Korchnoi – now the unpleasant 30 ♕e5 is threatened.

29...♗d5 30 ♘c3 ♗xg2 31 ♔xg2

White should not be diverted by 31 ♘xa2 f4! He simply has domination of the dark squares.

31...♖a8 32 ♕e5! ♔f7 33 ♕h8 ♕d6

Not 33...h5 34 ♕h7+ and 35 ♕xg6+.

34 ♕xh7+ ♔e8 35 ♗e5 ♕e6 36 ♖e3 ♕f7 37 ♕h4 ♖d8 38 ♗f6 ♖d6 39 ♗xe7

The simplest solution – a pawn up, White can also attack.

39...♗xe7 40 ♕h8+ ♕f8

After 40...♔d7 White has the decisive 41 ♕b8!

41 ♕e5! ♔f7 42 ♘d5 ♗d8 43 h4 ♔g8 44 h5! 1–0

If 44...gxh5 White wins by 45 ♖f3.

Game 22
Donner-Botvinnik
Palma de Mallorca 1967

---

1 d4 ♘f6 2 c4 g6 3 g3 c6 4 ♗g2 d5 5 cxd5 cxd5 6 ♘f3 ♗g7 7 0–0

Botvinnik himself preferred to defer castling, in order to create piece pressure in the centre, which in symmetric positions is very important: 7 ♘c3 0–0 8 ♘e5 ♘c6 9 0–0 ♗f5 10 ♘xc6 bxc6 11 ♘a4 ♘d7 12 b3 (according to Botvinnik, 12 ♗f4 or 12 ♗g5 is interesting) 12...e5 (less good is 12...c5 13 ♗b2

cxd4 14 ♗xd4 e6 15 ♖c1 with advantage) 13 dxe5 ♗xe5 14 ♗h6 ♖e8 (14... ♗xa1 15 ♕xa1 ♕f6 16 ♕xf6 ♘xf6 17 ♗xf8 ♔xf8 18 ♖c1 with advantage) 15 ♖c1 ♖c8 16 ♕d2 ♕e7 17 ♖fe1 ♗d6 18 ♕d4, with advantage to White (Botvinnik-Smyslov, m/11, 1957).

7...0–0 8 ♘c3 ♘c6

8...♘e4 is a reasonable alternative, when Black is the first to occupy an active central square.

9 ♕b3?!

This seems logical and unpleasant for Black, but 9 ♘e5 is correct or at least 9 ♗f4. After Black's reply White is unable to capture on d5 with either piece.

9...♘e4! 10 ♖d1 ♘a5! 11 ♕b4 ♘xc3!

At the time this was a new idea – Donner had already reached this position several times. Barcza played 11...b6 against him and Filip 11...♘c6, but Botvinnik's move is stronger.

12 ♕xc3

After 12 bxc3 Black has complete control of c4.

12...♗f5 13 ♗f4 ♖c8 14 ♕e1

Too passive – White should have considered 14 ♕a3, when although the queen is on the edge of the board, from there it can create some threats.

14...♕b6 15 b3 ♘c6 16 ♕d2 ♗e4!

Improving the bishop's position and threatening ...♗xf3.

17 ♗e3 ♕b4!

The c-file can be seized only by the exchange of queens. Besides, White's queenside is already slightly weakened, and there are targets that can be threatened.

18 ♘e1 ♕xd2 19 ♖xd2

19...e5!

Black is not afraid of an 'isolani' – with his pieces better placed it is important to create new threats and activate his forces.

20 dxe5 ♗xe5 21 ♖c1 ♘b4

After 21...♗xg2 22 ♔xg2 d4 23 ♗h6 ♘b4 24 ♖xc8 ♖xc8 25 ♘f3 Black too has a weakness at d4. But now, in seizing the c-file Black concedes the d-file.

22 ♖xc8 ♖xc8 23 ♗xe4 dxe4 24 ♖d7 ♖c7 25 ♖xc7 ♗xc7 26 a3

After 26 ♗xa7? b6 White would have had problems with his bishop.

26...♘c6 27 ♘c2 ♗e5 28 f3 f5!

Black has a spatial advantage and the better king position, but the win is by no means easy.

29 ♔f2 ♔f7 30 ♗d2 ♔e6 31 a4 ♗d4+ 32 ♔g2 a6 33 fxe4 fxe4 34 g4 ♗e5 35 h3 ♘e7! 36 ♔f2 ♘d5

The win is a long way off, but White overlooks a rather simple tactical stroke.

37 ♘b4? e3+! 0–1

Game 23
Karpov-Kamsky
Moscow 1992

---

1 d4 ♘f6 2 c4 g6 3 ♘f3 ♗g7 4 g3 c6 5 ♗g2 d5 6 cxd5 cxd5 7 ♘c3 0–0 8 ♘e5 e6 9 0–0 ♘fd7 10 f4 ♘c6 11 ♗e3 ♘b6

Black must decide what to do about the knight at e5. He can ignore it, as happens in the game, or he can drive it away by 11...f6 12 ♘f3 (in games with Kasparov and Timman, Karpov played 12 ♘d3, which after 12...f5 reduces White's possibilities, as the d4 pawn is attacked) 12...♘b6 13 ♗f2 ♗d7 14 e4 dxe4 15 ♘xe4 ♘d5 16 ♖e1 b6 17 ♘c3 ♘ce7 18 ♕b3 and White maintains pressure, despite Black's blockade (Karpov-Gelfand, Sanghi Nagar 1995).

12 ♗f2 ♗d7 13 e4!

Earlier Karpov tried several times to exploit Black's bad bishops, but then he realised that it was essential to open the position, and that Black must at any cost maintain his d5 pawn.

13...♘e7 14 ♘xd7 ♕xd7 15 e5 ♖ac8

In Karpov-Kasparov (m/1 1987) Black played the more logical 15...♖fc8. It is obvious that his only play is to occupy the c-file.

16 ♖c1 a6 17 b3 ♖c7 18 ♕d2 ♖fc8 19 g4 ♗f8 20 ♕e3!

Essential prophylaxis – White wanted to play 20 ♗h4, but after 20...♘c6 there is the unpleasant threat of ...♘xd4.

20...♘c6 21 f5! ♗a3

It was very dangerous to accept the pawn sacrifice – after 21...exf5 22 gxf5 ♕xf5 23 ♘e2 there are all sorts of threats, including ♗h3 and ♘g3.

22 ♖cd1 ♘b4

The subtle point of Karpov's play is that after 22...♘xd4 23 ♕xd4 ♗c5 24 ♕f4 ♗xf2+ 25 ♕xf2 the knight at b6 is attacked.

23 ♕h6!

Very precise play – after 23 ♘b1 ♘c2! 24 ♕h6 ♗f8 Black would have freed his bishop.

23...♕e8 24 ♘b1 ♗b2 25 ♕d2!

Unusual play – White invites the black pieces into his position and then begins pursuing them.

25...♘c2

After 25...a5 26 a3! (26 ♕xb2? ♖c2) 26...♖c2 27 ♕e1! ♕b5 28 axb4 ♖e2 29 ♕xe2 ♕xe2 30 bxa5 ♘d7 31 ♖d2 White has the advantage.

26 ♔h1

The other regrouping 26 ♕e2 and 27 ♖d2 was also good.

26...♕e7 27 ♗g1 ♘d7 28 ♖f3 ♕b4

White was planning ♖h3 and ♕h6 with mating threats.

29 ♕h6

Less good was 29 ♕f4 ♗xd4! 30 ♗xd4 ♘xd4 31 ♖xd4 ♖c1+ 32 ♖f1 ♖xf1+ 33 ♗xf1 ♕e1 34 ♘d2 ♘xe5 with an unclear game.

29...♕f8 30 ♕g5 ♕g7 31 ♕d2!

Again the queen is on its best square, whereas its black colleague is out of play.

31...b6 32 ♖df1

Karpov also considered another good possibility: 32 ♗f1 a5 33 ♗a6 ♖d8 34 ♕g5 with advantage to White.

32...a5 33 h4 ♘b4 34 a3 ♖c2 35 ♕f4 ♘c6 36 ♗h3 ♘d8 37 ♗e3!

Prophylaxis to the end – the black bishop must not be allowed onto the c1-h6 diagonal.

37...b5

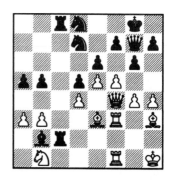

38 ♖3f2!

Black has reinforced his kingside, but what is he to do with his bishop at b2? Karpov has a phenomenal mastery of this method of alternating play.

38...b4 39 axb4 axb4 40 ♖xc2 ♖xc2 41 ♖f2 ♖xf2 42 ♕xf2 ♗a3

After 42...♗c3 43 f6 ♕f8 44 ♕c2 Black immediately loses a pawn.

43 ♕c2 ♘xe5

This is a bluff, but after 43...♘b8 44 f6 followed by ♘f3 and ♗f1 Black is helpless.

44 dxe5 ♕xe5 45 ♕c8 ♕e4+ 46 ♗g2 ♕xb1+ 47 ♔h2 ♗b2 48 ♕xd8+ ♔g7 49 f6+ ♗xf6 50 ♗h6+ ♔xh6 51 ♕xf6 ♕c2 52 g5+ ♔h5 53 ♔g3 ♕c7+ 54 ♔h3 1-0

Index of Variations

2.2131   8...cxd4 9 ♘xd4 ♘xc3
    10 bxc3 *40*
     2.21311   10...♘c6 *41*
     2.21312   10...♕a5 *41*
   2.2132   8...♘xc3 9 bxc3 ♘c6 *44*
    2.21321   10 dxc5 *44*
    2.21322   10 e3 *45*
     2.213221   10...♗e6 *46*
     2.213222   10...♕a5 *46*
2.22   7...♘c6 *47*
2.23   7...♘b6 8 ♘c3 *48*
  2.231   8...♘a6 *49*
  2.232   8...♘c6 *50*
  2.2321   9 ♗f4 *50*
  2.2322   9 d5 *51*
   2.23221   9...♘b8 *51*
   2.23222   9...♘a5 10 e4 c6 *52*

2.232221   11 ♖e1 *53*
2.232222   11 ♗f4 *55*
2.232223   11 ♗g5 *56*
  2.2322231   11...cxd5 *56*
  2.2322232   11...♘ac4 *57*
  2.2322233   11...h6 12 ♗f4 *58*
   2.23222331   12...♗g4 *58*
   2.23222332   12...♘ac4 *59*
   2.23222333   12...cxd5 13 exd5
     ♘ac4 14 ♕e2 *60*
    2.232223331   14...♗g4 *62*
    2.232223332   14...e5 *62*
    2.232223333   14...g5
     15 ♗c1 *63*
     2.2322233331   15...♗g4 *63*
     2.2322233332   15...e5 *64*

3   1 d4 ♘f6 2 c4 g6 3 g3 ♗g7 4 ♗g2 d5 5 cxd5 ♘xd5 6 ♘f3 ♘b6 7 0-0 ♘c6 *74*

3.1   8 ♘c3 *74*
3.2   8 e3 *75*
  3.21   8...e5 9 ♘c3 *75*
   3.211   9...exd4 *75*
   3.212   9...♗g4 *76*
  3.22   8...0-0 9 ♘c3 *77*
   3.221   9...a5 *77*
    3.2211   10 b3 *77*
    3.2212   10 ♕e2 *78*
    3.2213   10 d5 *78*
   3.222   9...♖e8 *79*
    3.2221   10 ♘e1 *80*

3.2222   10 ♖e1 *81*
3.2223   10 d5 ♘a5 11 ♘d4 ♗d7 *81*
  3.22231   12 e4 *82*
   3.222311   12...c6 *83*
   3.222312   12...c5 *84*
  3.22232   12 a4 *84*
3.223   9...e5 10 d5 *85*
  3.2231   10...e4 *85*
  3.2232   10...♘e7 11 e4 ♗g4 *87*
   3.22321   12 h3 *87*
   3.22322   12 a4 c6 13 a5 ♘c4 *88*
    3.223221   14 ♕b3 *89*
    3.223222   14 a6 *89*
   3.22323   12 ♕b3 *90*
  3.2233   10...♘a5 11 e4 c6 12 ♗g5 f6
   13 ♗e3 cxd5 *91*
   3.22331   14 ♗xb6 ♕xb6 15 ♘xd5
    ♕d8 16 ♖c1 ♘c6 *93*
    3.223311   17 b4 *93*
    3.223312   17 ♕b3 *94*
   3.22332   14 exd5 *95*
    3.223321   14...♗g4 *95*
    3.223322   14...♘ac4 *96*
    3.223323   14...♖f7 *97*

5.6　7 b3 *149*
　5.61　7...♘e4 *150*
　5.62　7...a5 8 ♘c3 ♘e4 9 ♗b2 *151*
　　5.621　9...♗f5 *151*
　　5.622　9...♘xc3 *152*
5.7　7 ♘bd2 *153*
　5.71　7...♘e4 *153*

5.72　7...♘bd7 *154*
5.73　7...a5 *154*
5.74　7...♗f5 8 b3 ♘e4 9 ♗b2 *156*
　5.741　9...♘xd2 *156*
　5.742　9...♕a5 *157*
　5.743　9...♘d7 *158*
　5.744　9...a5 *158*

6　　1 d4 ♘f6 2 c4 g6 3 g3 ♗g7 4 ♗g2 c6 5 ♘f3 d5 6 cxd5 cxd5 *163*

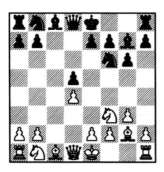

6.1　7 ♘e5 *163*
6.2　7 0-0 0-0 8 ♘e5 *163*
　6.21　8...♘c6 9 ♘c3 *163*
　　6.211　9...♘xe5 *164*
　　6.212　9...♗f5 *165*
　6.22　8...♘g4 *166*
　　6.221　9 f4 *166*
　　6.222　9 ♘xg4 *166*
6.3　7 ♘c3 *167*
　6.31　7...♘e4 *167*

6.311　9 ♘xe4 *168*
6.312　9 ♕b3 *169*
6.313　9 ♘e5 *170*
　6.3131　9...♘xc3 *170*
　6.3132　9...♗f5 *171*
6.32　7...0-0 8 ♘e5 e6 *172*
　6.321　9 0-0 *172*
　　6.3211　9...♘c6 *172*
　　　6.32111　10 ♘xc6 *173*
　　　6.32112　10 ♗g5 *174*
　　6.3212　9...♘fd7 *175*
　　　6.32121　10 ♘f3 *175*
　　　6.32122　10 f4 *177*
　　　　6.321221　10...f6 *177*
　　　　　6.3212211　11 ♘f3 *177*
　　　　　6.3212212　11 ♘d3 *178*
　　　　6.321222　10...♘c6 *179*
　6.322　9 ♗g5 ♕b6 10 ♕d2 *180*
　　6.3221　10...♘c6 *181*
　　6.3222　10...♘fd7 *182*
6.33　7...♘c6 *183*

List of Illustrative Games